FOURTH EDITION REVISED

Real Estate
Fundamentals

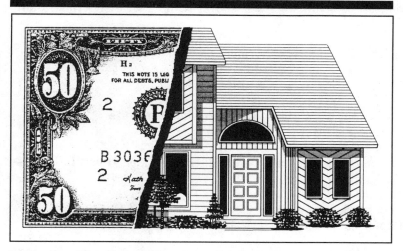

Wade E. Gaddy, Jr. & Robert E. Hart

**Real Estate
Education Company**
a division of Dearborn Financial Publishing, Inc.

This publication is designed to provide accurate and authoritative information in regard to the subject matter covered. It is sold with the understanding that the publisher is not engaged in rendering legal, accounting, or other professional service. If legal advice or other expert assistance is required, the services of a competent professional person should be sought.

Publisher: Carol L. Luitjens
Acquisitions Editor: Margaret M. Maloney
Senior Real Estate Writer: Evan M. Butterfield, JD
Project Editor: Debra M. Hall
Cover Designer: Salvatore Concialdi

Published by Real Estate Education Company®,
a division of Dearborn Financial Publishing, Inc.®
155 North Wacker Drive, Chicago, IL 60606-1719

Printed in the United States of America.

96 97 98 10 9 8 7 6 5 4 3 2 1

Library of Congress Cataloging-in-Publication Data

Gaddy, Wade E.
    Real estate fundamentals / Wade E. Gaddy, Jr. & Robert E. Hart.—
4th ed., revised.
        p.   cm.
    Includes index.
    1. Real estate business.   I. Hart, Robert E.   II. Title.
HD1375.G335   1995   95-39704
333.33—dc20   CIP

Contents

Preface

The real estate industry has changed dramatically in recent years. Today the profession demands specialized knowledge of its intricate and highly diversified facets. It also requires its licensees to know the ethical and business practices necessary for success in the field. Many states have developed licensing examination programs to ensure that real estate professionals are competent at their work. The goal of *Real Estate Fundamentals* is to provide both prospective and practicing real estate salespeople with the information they need to meet state requirements and to perform their jobs well.

While the establishment of educational and examination requirements for real estate licensees has been the responsibility of the individual states, such national organizations as the Association of Real Estate License Law Officials (ARELLO) have worked to elevate professional standards through more stringent educational requirements for earning a license and for continuing education.

One result of this national interest in real estate educational standards has been the development of multistate licensing examinations. These national exams require prospective licensees to demonstrate their understanding of five broad topic areas: law, public control, valuation, finance, and special fields. *Real Estate Fundamentals* is specifically designed to prepare prospective licensees for these examinations, whether they are created by the PSI Licensing Examination Service, Assessment Systems, Incorporated (ASI), or a state licensing authority. The book's thorough coverage also makes it appropriate for principles courses. Its value as a reference tool will make it of continuing use to students of such courses.

Real Estate Fundamentals breaks the five major topic areas mentioned above into their essential components and devotes a separate chapter to each. For example, law encompasses chapters on the nature and description of real estate, rights and interests in land, acquisition and transfer of title, different kinds of ownership, title records, contracts, landlord and tenant, and real estate brokerage. The organization of lessons enables the instructor to take a flexible approach in teaching the fundamentals of real estate. Since each chapter is a self-contained entity, the lessons may be taught in any sequence. The material is completely generic.

The text presents challenging concepts in a clear, concise manner that makes the most difficult information easy to understand and absorb. Key terms are listed at the beginning of each chapter; their boldfacing and definition in the text reinforce students' learning. To increase its usefulness as a source book, *Real Estate Fundamentals* contains a comprehensive index. Questions are included at the end of each chapter to test students' comprehension. Correct answers are provided in an answer key for self-evaluation. The book's charts and illustrations illuminate and expand upon verbal explanations and are especially essential in the chapters on financing.

Included in this edition is a chapter covering real estate mathematics, designed to familiarize math-shy students with basic real estate computations. Property management, appraisal, and insurance are now covered in Real Estate Brokerage. Real Estate Taxation includes a discussion of tax benefits for homeowners and investors. A glossary is included to assist students in studying and referencing real estate terms.

The authors wish to thank the following people for their contributions to the original text: Patricia Anderson, Gregory J. Dunn, William Harrington, Lorna Horton, Robert Marshall, and George Williams.

The authors also wish to thank the following people for their assistance in revising *Real Estate Fundamentals:* Kathleen M. Witalisz, Richard S. Thomas REALTORS®, Massachusetts; Paul Harris, National Real Estate School, Arkansas; John F. Rodgers III, Catonsville Community College, Maryland; Nancy Daggett White, Mississippi County Community College, Arkansas; James C. Clinkscales, American Institute of Real Estate, Inc., Georgia; Mary Coveny, CareerMatch Consultants, Inc., Illinois; John Ballou, Moraine Valley Community College, Palos Hills, Illinois; David A. Floyd, Tennessee Real Estate Education Systems, Inc., Chattanooga, Tennessee; Kenneth R. Greenwood, Southern Oaks School of Real Estate, Decatur, Alabama; Dr. Jack N. Porter, The Spencer Group: School of Real Estate, Newton Highlands, Massachusetts; and Don W. Williams, Alabama Courses in Real Estate, Birmingham, Alabama. Special thanks are extended to James A. Gorzelany for development of the manuscript.

The authors wish to thank Terrence M. Zajac, DREI, of Terry Zajac Seminars, Scottsdale, Arizona, who was instrumental in developing the fourth edition of this text.

For contributions to the fourth edition of this text, the authors wish to thank Joseph M. Brice, JMB Real Estate Academy, Lowell, Massachusetts; David Floyd, Tennessee Real Estate Education Systems, Inc., Chattanooga, Tennessee; D.D. Nordstrom, PRO/ED, Sioux Falls, South Dakota; Mary Wezeman, Coldwell Banker School of Real Estate, Oakbrook, Illinois. Rose Mary Chambers, Dean, First Institute of Real Estate, Birmingham, Alabama; and Judith Gesell, Mykut Real Estate School, Edmunds, Washington assisted in the preparation of the revised fourth edition.

Wade E. Gaddy, Jr.
Robert E. Hart

1: Nature and Description of Land

KEY TERMS

air rights
bundle of legal rights
chattel
fixture
improvement
land
legal description
littoral rights
metes and bounds

plat of survey
prior appropriation
real estate
real property
rectangular survey system
riparian rights
situs
subsurface rights
trade fixture

The real estate business centers around the ownership, possession, and transfer of land. However, as you will learn in this chapter and in following chapters, land is more than just the earth we walk upon. The ownership and possession of land brings into play a body of highly complex laws that define the various rights and interests of property owners, third parties, and the general public. Land is further affected by local, state, and federal laws and court decisions that regulate the orderly transfer of real estate.

PROPERTY RIGHTS

The word *property* refers not so much to the article owned, but more importantly to the rights or interests involved in its ownership. Ownership of property in general, and real estate in particular, has often been described as a **bundle of legal rights.** In other words, when a person purchases a parcel of real estate, he or she is actually buying ownership

Figure 1.1 Bundle of Legal Rights

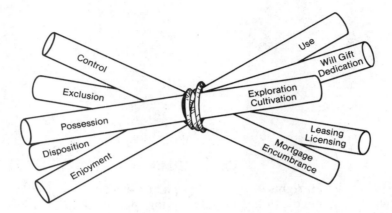

rights previously held by the seller (see Figure 1.1). These rights of ownership include the rights of

1. possession;

2. control within the framework of the law;

3. enjoyment in any legal manner;

4. exclusion (to keep others from entering or occupying the property); and

5. disposition (to be able to sell or otherwise convey the property).

Within these ownership rights are included further rights to sell, will, devise, mortgage, encumber, cultivate, explore, lease, license, dedicate, give away, share, trade, or exchange. However, one's ownership is subject to any rights that others may have in the property. The various rights and interests in property ownership will be discussed in detail in Chapter 2.

Property may be classified as *real property*—that which is immovable, and *personal property*—that which is movable. The early English courts, through a legal system known as *common law,* distinguished between a lawsuit in which a landowner, if wrongfully ousted, could recover the land itself, the "real thing," and those lawsuits in which the owner could recover money damages only. In the first category, by bringing a "real" action, the owner received the return of the land. This ownership interest came to be known as real property or *realty.* In the second category, a suit for money damages was called a "personal" action; therefore, an owner's limited interest in the land came to be known as personal property, *personalty,* or a *chattel.*

REAL PROPERTY

You may have heard the terms land, real estate, and real property used interchangeably. Though they may seem to be describing the same thing, there are important subtle differences in their meanings.

Land

The *land* is commonly thought of as the ground or soil, but from a legal standpoint, land ownership also includes possession and control of the minerals and substances below the earth's surface together with the airspace above the land up to infinity. Thus, **land** is defined as *the earth's surface extending downward to the center of the earth and upward to infinity, including those things permanently attached by nature,* such as trees and water (see Figure 1.2).

Figure 1.2   Land, Real Estate and Real Property

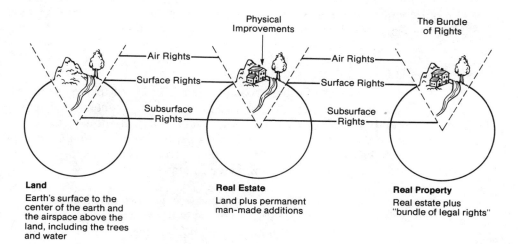

Land
Earth's surface to the center of the earth and the airspace above the land, including the trees and water

Real Estate
Land plus permanent man-made additions

Real Property
Real estate plus "bundle of legal rights"

Real Estate

The term *real estate* is somewhat broader than the term *land* and includes not only the physical components of the land as provided by nature, but also anything that is permanently affixed to the land by either natural or artificial attachment.

Items attached to the land by a root system are considered *natural attachments*. *Fructus naturales* (real property) are products of the earth that are naturally grown and require no annual labor or cultivation, such as trees and bushes. *Fructus industriales* (personal property) are products of the earth that require annual planting or cultivation, such as unharvested wheat or vegetables.

Artificial attachments, called **improvements,** are normally those things that have been placed on the land by people. Improvements may be embedded in the land, such as walls, footings, in-ground swimming pools, and water or gas lines; placed or resting upon the land, such as building slabs, driveways, streets, and patios; erected on the land, such as buildings and towers or any other man-made additions to property. Land that has been "improved" has not necessarily been made "better"—it has only been changed in some way by human activity.

Real estate, therefore, is defined as *the earth's surface extending downward to the center of the earth and upward into space, including all things permanently attached to it by nature or by people* (see Figure 1.2).

In practice, the term *real estate* is most often used to describe that commodity with which real estate as a business and the real estate broker and salesperson are concerned. It is sometimes referred to as *realty.*

Real Property

The term *real property* further broadens the definition of real estate to include the bundle of legal rights involved in real estate ownership. Thus, **real property** is defined as *the earth's surface extending downward to the center of the earth and upward into space, including all things permanently attached to it by nature or man, as well as the interests, benefits, and rights inherent in its ownership* (see Figure 1.2).

As you can see, the concept of real property ownership involves more than just the rights to use the surface of the earth; it also includes the rights to those things *appurtenant* to the land. An appurtenance is defined as anything that, by right, is used by the land for its benefit. Such rights include **subsurface** (mineral) **rights, air rights,** easements appurtenant, and water rights.

Subsurface (mineral) rights. Ownership of real property includes rights of ownership in all minerals and other substances located below the surface of the land. For example, a landowner may sell an oil company his or her rights to any oil and gas found in the land. Later the same landowner can sell the property to a purchaser and in the sale reserve the rights to all coal that may be found in the land. After these sales, three parties have ownership interests in this real property: (1) the oil company, which owns all oil and gas; (2) the seller, who owns all coal; and (3) the purchaser, who owns the rights to all the rest of the real property. In the absence of an agreement to the contrary, any individual acquiring the rights to minerals in the subsurface also acquires what is known as an *implied easement,* which allows the holder of the subsurface rights to come back onto the surface of the land for the purpose of removing the minerals. Easements will be discussed in Chapter 2.

Air rights. As with subsurface rights, the rights to use the air above the land may be sold independently of the land itself. Air rights are an increasingly important part of real property, particularly in large cities. Huge office buildings like the Pan-Am Building in New York City and the Amoco building in Chicago have been built over railroad tracks. For the construction of such a building, the developer must purchase not only the air rights above the tracks but also numerous small portions of the surface of the land in order to construct the building's foundation supports (called caissons). The caisson locations are regularly spaced between the tracks and are usually planned to rise about 30 feet above the tracks so that the finished foundation supports do not interfere with the operation of trains on the railroad's remaining land ownership.

Until the development of airplanes, a property owner's air rights were considered to be unlimited. Today, however, the courts permit reasonable interference with these rights, such as is necessary for aircraft, as long as the owner's right to use and occupy the property is not lessened. Governments and airport authorities often purchase air rights adjacent to an airport to provide glide patterns for air traffic.

Water rights. One of the interests that may attach to the ownership of real property is the right to use bodies of water. In the United States, the ownership of water and the adjacent land is determined by the doctrines of *riparian rights, littoral rights,* or *prior appropriation.* Navigable waters are considered public highways on which the public has an easement or right to travel. Thus, the land is generally owned to the water's edge, with the state holding title to the submerged land.

Many states subscribe to the common law doctrine of **riparian rights.** *Rivers Streams* These rights are granted to owners of land located along the course of flowing water such as a river or stream and to owners who have water located within the subsurface of their land. Such subsurface water is known as *percolating water.* The level at which such water is located beneath the surface of the earth is called the water table.

Riparian owners have the right to make use of the water for irrigation, swimming, boating, fishing, or in any legal way that does not interfere with the same rights of owners downstream. In addition, an owner of land that borders a nonnavigable waterway owns the land to its exact center. The laws governing riparian rights differ from state to state.

Closely related to riparian rights are the **littoral rights** of owners whose *Lakes* land borders on large, navigable but nonflowing lakes and oceans. These owners may make reasonable use of the available waters but only own the land adjacent to the water down to the mean high-water mark.

In states where water is scarce, the ownership and use of water is often determined by the doctrine of **prior appropriation.** Under prior appropriation, the right to use water for any purpose other than limited domestic use is controlled by the state rather than by the adjacent landowner. However, ownership of the land bordering bodies of water is generally determined by the rules for riparian and littoral ownership.

Property purchasers are also interested in potable water—water safe and agreeable for drinking that is available on the property.

Fixtures (Real Property)

Real property is by definition immovable, so personal property that has been affixed to the land or to a building so that it becomes immovable, is by definition real property. The law construes this addition to be a part of the real property known as a **fixture.** Courts apply five tests to determine whether an article is a fixture or personal property: (1) method of attachment; (2) agreement between the parties; (3) relationship of the parties; (4) intention of the parties and (5) adaptation of the article to the real property. To help you remember the tests, the first letters of the five tests spell the name *MARIA.*

1. *Method.* The permanence of the manner of annexation or attachment often provides a basis for court decisions relating to fixtures. For instance, a furnace, although it is removable, is usually attached in such a way that it cannot be taken out without causing extensive damage to the property. Moreover, the furnace is considered an essential part of the complete property and, as such, a fixture.

2. *Agreement.* The existence of an agreement between the parties involved as to the nature of the property affixed to the land is normally the first test to be applied by the court. *If the existence of an agreement can be established, all other tests are generally disregarded.* For instance, if an agreement clearly stated that the tenant could remove any articles he or she attached during the lease term, the court would infer that this agreement should be followed because the parties had displayed sufficient foresight to anticipate the problem.

3. *Relationship.* The relationship between the person who adds the article and the person with whom a dispute arises is another test applied by the court. The relationship is typically between a landlord and a tenant or between a seller and a purchaser.

4. *Intention.* The intention of the parties at the time an article was attached is a very important factor in deciding whether or not an article is a fixture. For instance, a tenant who opens a jewelry store may bolt her display cases to the floor and later remove them. Since these items are an integral part of her business property and it was never her intent to make them a permanent part of the structure, they would be considered personal property essential to conducting a business, or trade fixtures. It should be noted that tenants must remove all trade fixtures before the expiration of the lease. After the expiration of the lease, the tenant has no right to come back onto the landlord's property to remove trade fixtures.

5. *Adaptation.* The adaptation of the article to use in a particular building is another test of the nature of the article. For instance, air conditioners installed by a tenant into wall slots specifically constructed for that purpose would be considered fixtures even though they could be removed. Likewise, storm windows custom-made for a particular house would be considered fixtures even though they could be readily removed. In addition, all the integral parts necessary for the operation of a fixture are considered real estate. Examples are house keys, garage door openers, and the remote control of a built-in TV.

It is clear from these tests that it is possible to convert an item of personal property into real property. It is also possible to convert real property into personal property. For example, a growing tree is real property, but if the owner cuts down the tree, severing it from the land, the tree becomes personal property. Likewise, clay existing in the subsurface of the land is real property; but if the owner mines the clay and mills it into bricks, the bricks are considered personal property.

The final question to be asked is this: Once the tree has been severed and milled into lumber and the clay has been milled into bricks, becoming personal property, can either once again become real property? The answer is yes. If the lumber and bricks are used in the construction of a house, they become real property again.

PERSONAL PROPERTY

Personal property, also called a **chattel,** is considered to be all property that does not fit the definition of real property. Personal property has the unique characteristic of being movable and includes such items as furniture, clothing, money, stocks and bonds, notes, mortgages, leases, trade fixtures, annual flowers and plants, and growing crops (emblements).

Trade Fixtures

An article attached to a rented space or building by a tenant for use in conducting a business is known as a **trade fixture.** While fixtures are legally construed to be real estate, trade fixtures are considered personal property. Examples of trade fixtures are bowling alleys, store shelves, restaurant equipment, and agricultural fixtures such as chicken coops and tool sheds. Trade fixtures must be removed on or before the last day the business property is rented, or they become the real property of the landlord.

Emblements

Growing crops that are produced annually as a result of someone's labor are called *emblements* (fructus industriales, as discussed earlier). Emblements are regarded as personal property even prior to harvest. Thus, a tenant farmer has the right to take the annual crop resulting from his or her labor, even if the harvest occurs after the lease has expired. A landlord cannot terminate a tenant farmer's lease and not give the tenant the right to re-enter the land to harvest his or her crops.

Figure 1.3   Characteristics of Real Estate

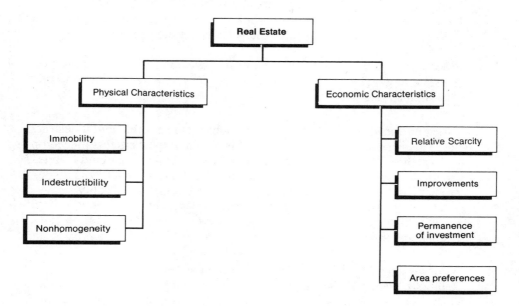

CHARACTERISTICS OF REAL ESTATE

Unlike many commodities sold on the open market, real estate possesses certain unique characteristics that affect its use both directly and indirectly. These characteristics fall into two broad categories—physical characteristics and economic characteristics (see Figure 1.3).

Physical Characteristics

The basic physical characteristics of land are: (1) immobility, (2) indestructibility, and (3) nonhomogeneity.

Immobility.   Land, which is the earth's surface, is immobile. It is true that some of the substances of land are removable and topography can be changed, but still that portion of the earth's surface always remains. The geographic location of any given parcel of land can never be changed. It is rigid and fixed.

Because land is immobile, the rights to use land are more easily regulated than other forms of property. For example, local governments are supported largely by property taxes on real estate. The fixed amount of land in a given area enables the local government to rely on a certain amount of annual revenue from property taxes, which, in turn, allows the government to make long-range plans based on the projected income.

Since land is immobile, the rights to use it are controlled by the laws of the state in which it is located. Likewise, real estate markets tend to be local in character.

Indestructibility.   Just as land is immobile, it is durable and indestructible. This permanence, which also holds for the improvements placed on it, has tended to *stabilize investments in land*. The fact that land is indestructible does not, of course, change the fact that improvements do depreciate and can become obsolete, thereby reducing, or possibly destroying, values. This gradual depreciation should not be confused with the fact that the economic desirability, or *situs,* of a given location can change and thus create a "ghost town."

Nonhomogeneity.   No two parcels of land are ever exactly the same. Although there may be substantial similarity, *all parcels differ geographically,* as each parcel has its own location. Because of land's nonhomogeneity, the courts have long held that a person cannot be required to accept a substitute for a specific parcel of land. The law grants the right to either a buyer or a seller to sue for *specific performance*. This means that the seller must convey, or the buyer must buy, the specific parcel for which he or she has contracted. The subject of specific performance will be discussed later in the text.

Economic Characteristics

The basic economic characteristics of land are: (1) relative scarcity, (2) improvements, (3) permanence of investment, and (4) area preferences.

Relative scarcity.   Although the total supply of land is fixed, land as such is not scarce in this country. Despite the considerable amount of land not in use, available land in a given location or of a particular quality may be limited.

Improvements.   The improvement of one parcel of land has an effect on the value and utilization of other neighboring tracts, and often a direct bearing on whole communities. For example, constructing a steel plant or building an atomic reactor can directly influence a large area. Such land improvements can influence other parcels and communities favorably or unfavorably and may affect not only the land use itself, but also the value and price of land.

Permanence of investment.   Once land has been improved, capital and labor expenditures represent a fixed investment. Although older buildings can be razed to make way for new buildings or other land uses, improvements such as drainage, electricity, water, and sewerage remain fixed investments because they generally cannot be dismantled or removed economically. The income return on such investments is long-term and relatively stable, and usually extends over what is referred to as the economic life of the improvement. However, this permanence may make improved real estate unsuitable for short, rapid-turnover investing.

Area preferences.   This very important economic characteristic, often referred to as situs, does not refer to a geographical location per se, but rather to people's choices and preferences for a given area. It is the unique quality of people's preferences that results in different valuations being attributed to similar units. This nonhomogeneity, as previously discussed, means that no two parcels are exactly the same, partly because of the variable likes and dislikes people possess.

Preferences are not static; they are constantly changing. For example, social influences caused the rapid movement of people to suburban areas. However, some are now returning to urban areas, preferring the environments and amenities offered by city living to those offered by suburbia.

The effect of situs on land value can be seen in the approach of salespeople selling homes in a new development who try to influence prospects into preferring the location of the new development over other locations. This is an illustration of the saying, "People make value."

Land Characteristics Define Land Use

The various characteristics of a parcel of real estate affect its desirability for a specific use. Physical and economic factors that affect land use include: (1) contour and elevation of the parcel, (2) prevailing winds, (3) transportation, (4) public improvements, and (5) availability of natural resources, such as water. For example, hilly, heavily wooded land would need considerable work before it could be used for industrial purposes, but would be ideally suited for residential use. Likewise, flat land located along a major highway network would be undesirable for residential use, but would be well located for industry.

LEGAL DESCRIPTIONS

In conveying title to real property or preparing an instrument for recording, a legally sufficient description of the real property is required. A **legal description** is one that describes no other property but the one in question and that characterizes the property in such a manner that a competent surveyor could locate it, as it appears on the surface of the earth, using nothing more than the description. Descriptions of real property are classified as being informal or formal.

Informal descriptions, while considered "adequate" to locate and identify a parcel of real estate, are not accepted as legal descriptions by the courts; and title companies will not insure the title to real property described in this manner. Informal descriptions may be in the form of street number (6065 Roswell Road, Atlanta, Georgia), name (the Pan-Am Building in New York City), or blanket ("all the real property of John Adams").

Formal descriptions, or legal descriptions, constitute three basic types used throughout the United States: metes and bounds, rectangular survey, and subdivision lot and block (plat).

Metes and Bounds

A **metes** (distance and direction) **and bounds** (landmarks, monuments) description makes use of the boundaries and measurements of the land in question. These descriptions start at a specifically designated point called the *point of beginning* (POB) and proceed around the boundaries of the tract by reference to linear measurements and directions (see Figure 1.4). Often, a metes and bounds description will use compass directions and measurements to the one one-hundredth of a foot.

Metes and bounds descriptions tend to be lengthy, especially when naming the owners of adjoining parcels. Descriptions that vary from those used in previous conveyances tend to cause gaps and overlaps. Because of the possibility of discrepancies and disputes concerning property by metes and bounds, it is particularly important to have the land surveyed by an authorized surveyor in order to clearly establish the boundaries of the tract.

In a metes and bounds description, the actual distance between monuments takes precedence over linear measurements set forth in the description, if the two measurements differ. *Monuments* are fixed objects used to establish real estate boundaries. Monuments may be either *natural* or *artificial.* Artificial monuments include roads, fences, canals, and iron pins

Figure 1.4   Metes and Bounds Description

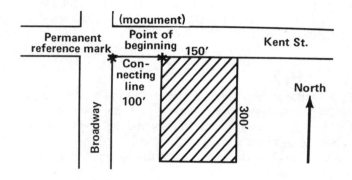

Beginning at a point on the southerly side of Kent St., 100 ft. east from the corner formed by the intersection of the southerly side of Kent St. and the easterly side of Broadway, thence east 150 ft., thence south 300 ft., thence west 150 ft., thence north 300 ft. to the point of beginning.

or posts placed by surveyors as markers. Natural monuments include rocks, trees, lakes, and streams.

One rule in a metes and bounds description is that the boundary *must return to the point of beginning* so that the tract being described is fully enclosed (this is known as *closure*). Metes and bounds descriptions are highly complicated and should be handled with extreme care. When they include compass directions of the various lines (always "called" from a true north-south heading) and concave and convex curved lines, metes and bounds can be difficult to understand. In such cases, the advice of a surveyor should be sought. Another obvious problem arises when the monuments change or disappear: a fence may be moved, the "big oak tree" may die, or a stream may change its course.

Bench marks.   As mentioned earlier, one vital element of a metes and bounds description is the establishment of a definite point of beginning. This is normally done by referencing the point of beginning as being located a certain distance from a bench mark. While standard bench marks have been established throughout the country by the U.S. Geological Survey, local surveyors normally use street intersections as bench marks.

For example, in preparing a metes and bounds description of a particular parcel a surveyor might reference a bench mark as follows: *"Beginning* at a point on the south side of Hammond Drive 325 feet east of the corner formed by the intersection of the south side of Hammond with the east side of Roswell Road . . . ."

Rectangular Survey

The rectangular survey system, sometimes called the government survey method, was established by Congress in 1785, soon after the federal government was organized. The system was developed as a standard method of describing all lands conveyed to or acquired by the federal government, including the extensive area of the Northwest Territory.

The **rectangular survey system** is based on two sets of intersecting lines: principal meridians and base lines. Principal meridians are north and south lines and base lines run east and west. Both can be located exactly by reference to degrees of longitude and latitude. Each principal meridian has a name or a number and is crossed by its own base line. Each principal meridian and base line is used to survey a specific area of land.

Ranges.   The land on either side of a principal meridian is divided into six-mile-wide strips by lines that run north and south, parallel to the meridian. These north-south strips of land are called *ranges* (see Figure 1.5). They are designated by consecutive numbers east or west of the principal meridian. For example, Range 3 East would be a strip of land between 12 and 18 miles east of its principal meridian.

Townships.   Lines running east and west of the base line six miles apart are referred to as township lines and form strips of land (or *tiers*) called *townships* (see Figure 1.5). These tiers of townships are designated by consecutive numbers north or south of the base line. For example, the strip of land between 6 and 12 miles north of a base line is Township 2 North.

The township squares formed by the intersecting township and range lines are the basic units of the rectangular survey system. Theoretically, townships are six miles square and contain 36 square miles.

Sections.   Each township contains 36 sections. Sections are numbered consecutively, 1 through 36, as illustrated in Figure 1.6, with section 1 being in the upper right-hand corner of the township. By law, each section number 16 has been set aside for school purposes and is referred to

Figure 1.5 Townships in the Rectangular Survey System

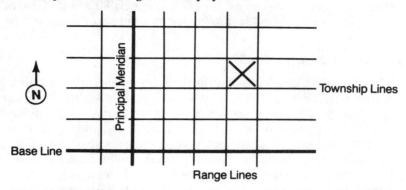

as a school section. The sale or rental proceeds from this land were originally available for township school use.

Each section contains 1 square mile, or 640 acres of land, and is commonly divided into half sections (containing 320 acres), quarter sections (160 acres), and further divisions of halves and quarters for reference purposes.

Land descriptions are made by referring to a particular portion of a section in a township that is either north or south of a specified base line and either east or west of a certain meridian. The following is a sample of a rectangular survey description:

"The E½ of the NW¼ of Section 17, Township 14 North, Range 4 West of the 6th. Principal Meridian."

Figure 1.6 Sections

		N			
6	5	4	3	2	1
7	8	9	10	11	12
18	17	(16)	15	14	13
19	20	21	22	23	24
30	29	28	27	26	25
31	32	33	34	35	36

W   E

S

16=School Section

In the above example, the land described would have an area of 80 acres (the NW¼ equals 160 acres; ½ of this ¼ equals 80 acres). Generally, the smaller a parcel of land is, the *longer* its legal description will be.

Subdivision Lot and Block

The third method of land description is by lot and block number in a subdivision plat. When land is subdivided by its owner, the first step is the preparation of a **plat of survey** by a licensed surveyor or engineer. On this plat, the land is divided into blocks and lots, and streets or access roads for public use are indicated. Reference is usually made to the official legal description of the larger property divided either by metes and bounds or rectangular survey method. The blocks and lots are assigned numbers or letters. Lot sizes and street details must be completely indicated and must comply with all local ordinances and requirements. When properly signed and approved, the subdivision plat may be recorded in the county in which the land is located, thereby becoming part of the legal description. In describing a lot from a recorded subdivision plat, the lot and block number, name or number of the subdivision plat, plat book number and page number, and name of the county and state are used. Some states have passed *plat acts,* which limit the minimum size tract that may be conveyed without a subdivision plat being prepared, approved, and recorded. For example, in some states the minimum size is five acres.

Measuring Elevations

Air lots.   The owner of a parcel of land may subdivide the air above his or her land into air lots. *Air lots* consist of airspace within specific boundaries located over a parcel of land. This type of description is found in titles to tall buildings that are located on air rights, generally over railroad tracks. Similarly, a surveyor, in preparing a subdivision plat for condominium use, describes each condominium unit in reference to the elevation of the floors and ceilings on a vertical plane above the city datum.

Datum.   A *datum* is a point, line, or surface from which elevations are measured or indicated. For the purpose of the U.S. Geological Survey, datum is defined as the *mean sea level at New York Harbor.* While most cities throughout the country have established a local datum in relation to the U.S. Geological Survey, the most common datum used for a particular property is simply the *surface* of the land. Therefore the location of a particular unit in a high-rise condominium could be referenced as being "Air Lot _____, located _____ feet above the surface of the land." A datum is also used to describe the area of the subsurface subject to an oil lease, to establish the grade of streets, and so on.

SUMMARY

Although most people think of *land* as the surface of the earth, the definition of this word not only applies to the earth's surface but also includes everything below the surface to the center of the earth and the air above the surface. *Real estate,* on the other hand, refers to the earth's surface, everything below and above it, *plus* all things permanently attached to it. The term *real property* further expands this definition to include all natural and artificial improvements attached to the land and those rights owned by the land and used by the land for its own benefit.

All property that does not fit the definition of real property is classified as *personal property,* or *chattels.* When articles of personal property are permanently affixed to the land they become *fixtures* and, as such, are considered a part of the real property. However, personal property attached to real property by a tenant for the purpose of his or her business is classified as a *trade* (or *chattel*) *fixture.* Trade fixtures must be removed by the tenant before the end of the lease period.

The unique nature of land is apparent in both its economic and physical characteristics. The economic characteristics are *relative scarcity, improvements, permanence of investment,* and *area preferences.* The physical characteristics are *immobility, nonhomogeneity,* and *indestructibility.* All of these characteristics affect the investment potential of and competition for a specific parcel of land.

Documents affecting or conveying interests in real estate must contain a *legal description* that will accurately identify the property involved. Three methods of description are used in the United States: (1) *metes and bounds,* (2) *rectangular survey,* and (3) *subdivision plat.* A legal description is a precise method of identifying a parcel of land as it exists on the surface of the earth. Air lots, condominium descriptions, and other measurements of vertical elevations may be computed from the U.S. Geographical Survey *datum,* which is the mean sea level at New York Harbor. Most large cities have established local survey datums for surveying within the area. The elevations from these datums are further supplemented by reference points, called *bench marks,* placed at fixed intervals from the datum.

QUESTIONS

Please complete all of the questions before turning to the Answer Key.

1. Real property includes all of the following EXCEPT

    a. the land.
    b. fixtures.
    c. the rights of the bundle.
    d. trade fixtures.

2. A metes and bounds legal description must include a(n)

    a. datum.
    b. acreage for the parcel.
    c. point of beginning.
    d. partial enclosure.

3. Personal property is distinguished from real property by its

    a. cost.
    b. mobility.
    c. scarcity.
    d. size.

4. The method of legal description based upon lots and blocks is

    a. the rectangular survey.
    b. the subdivision plat.
    c. metes and bounds.
    d. the government survey.

5. Items that are attached to the land are considered to be

    a. real property.
    b. emblements.
    c. trade fixtures.
    d. chattel.

6. The economic characteristic that is referred to as *situs* is

    a. scarcity.
    b. permanence of investment.
    c. area preference.
    d. improvements.

7. All of the following are included in the concept of water rights EXCEPT

    a. riparian rights.
    b. subsurface rights.
    c. littoral rights.
    d. prior appropriation.

8. Evergreen trees and lilac bushes on a property that were planted by the current owner are examples of

    a. real estate.   c. chattels.
    b. personal property.   d. trade fixtures.

9. All of the following are physical characteristics of property EXCEPT

    a. immobility.   c. indestructibility.
    b. scarcity.   d. nonhomogeneity.

10. Trade fixtures are considered to be

    a. real property.   c. personal property.
    b. emblements.   d. real estate.

11. All of the following would be used to determine whether an article is real property or personal property EXCEPT

    a. adaptation.   c. method.
    b. intention.   d. cost.

12. The land includes all of the following EXCEPT the

    a. structures.   c. subsurface.
    b. surface.   d. air above the surface.

13. All of the following can be used in formal legal descriptions EXCEPT

    a. monuments.   c. bench marks.
    b. points of beginning.   d. chattels.

14. A parcel of ground containing 640 acres is a

    a. township.   c. range.
    b. section.   d. plat.

15. Township 4 North, Range 3 East would be how far east of the principal meridian?

    a. Between 6 and 12 miles
    b. Between 12 and 18 miles
    c. Between 18 and 24 miles
    d. Between 24 and 30 miles

1. d.
2. c
3. b
4. b
5. a
6. c
7. b.
8. a.
9. b.
10. c
11. d.
12. a.
13. d.
14. b.
15. b.

2:   Rights and Interests in Land

KEY TERMS

ad valorem	fee simple
allodial system	feudal system
community property	freehold estate
curtesy	homestead
deed restriction	judgment
determinable fee	leasehold estate
dower	lien
easement	life estate
encumbrance	mechanic's lien

As discussed in Chapter 1, when a person holds title to a parcel of real estate, he or she owns not only the land itself but also certain rights to the property—possession, control, enjoyment, exclusion, and disposition.

These rights, however, are not absolute; certain rights are always retained by the government. In addition, ownership rights may be restricted, depending on the type of interest held, or be subject to the rights of third parties who may have some legal interest in the real estate.

HISTORICAL BACKGROUND OF REAL ESTATE OWNERSHIP

According to English common law, the government or king held title to all lands under what was known as the **feudal system** of ownership. Under this system, the individual was merely a tenant whose rights to use and occupy real property were held at the sufferance of an overlord.

Through a series of social reforms in the seventeenth century, the feudal system evolved into what was referred to as the **allodial system** of ownership. Under the allodial system, the individual was entitled to property rights without being subject to control by the crown.

Land in the United States is held under the allodial system. The Bill of Rights of the U.S. Constitution firmly establishes the private ownership of land free from any of the overtones, obligations, or burdens of the feudal system.

GOVERNMENT POWERS   P.E.E.T.

The individual has maximum rights in the land he or she owns, but these rights are subject to certain powers, or rights, held by federal, state, and local governments. Government limitations on ownership of real property are for the general welfare of the community and include the following:

1. *Taxation.* Taxation is a charge on real property to raise funds to meet the operating costs of a government.

2. *Police power.* This is the power vested in a state to establish legislation to preserve order, protect the public health and safety, and promote the general welfare. The use and enjoyment of property is subject to restrictions imposed by such legislation, which includes zoning and building ordinances that regulate the use, occupancy, size, location, construction, and rents of real property as well as environmental protection laws.

3. *Eminent domain.* Through a *condemnation suit,* a government may exercise this right to acquire privately owned real estate for the use and benefit of the general public. Two conditions must be met: (1) the proposed use must be declared by the court to be a public use and (2) just compensation, determined by the court, must be paid to the owner. The right of eminent domain is generally granted by state laws to quasi-public bodies, such as land clearance commissions and public housing or redevelopment authorities, as well as to railroads and public utility companies.

4. *Escheat.* While escheat is not actually a limitation on ownership, state laws provide for ownership of real estate to revert, or escheat, to either the state or the county when an owner dies and leaves neither heirs nor will disposing of his or her estate. Escheat occurs only when a property becomes ownerless. Government powers will be discussed in more detail in Chapter 9.

ESTATES IN LAND

An estate in land is the character and extent of ownership interest that a person has in real property. Estates in land are divided into two major classifications: (1) *freehold estates* and (2) *less-than-freehold estates* (also known as leasehold estates or nonfreehold estates).

Freehold Estates

These are estates for an indefinite time, existing for a lifetime or longer. **Freehold estates** include: (1) *fee simple,* (2) *determinable fee* and (3) *life estates* (see Figure 2.1). The first two of these estates continue for an indefinite period and are inheritable by the heirs of the owner; the third terminates upon the death of the person on whose life the estate is based.

Fee simple.   An estate in fee simple is the most complete type of interest in real estate recognized by law. A **fee simple** estate is one in which the holder is entitled to all rights of property ownership. There is no time limit on its existence—it is said to run forever, or until the property is sold or otherwise transferred. Because this estate is of unlimited duration, upon the death of its owner it passes to his or her heirs or as provided in the owner's will. The terms *fee, fee simple,* and *fee simple absolute* are basically the same. The holder of a fee simple estate is, of course, subject to governmental powers.

Determinable fee.   A **determinable fee** estate, sometimes referred to as a *qualified fee, conditional fee,* or *base fee,* is an estate that may be inherited. However, this estate will be extinguished, or determined (come to an end), upon the occurrence of a designated event, the time of its happening being uncertain. Such an estate may also be based on an uncertain condition or event.

For example, when the deed of conveyance for a parcel of real estate specifically states that the land is granted as long as it is used for a certain purpose (for example, as a schoolhouse or a church), the estate conveyed is a determinable fee. The phrase "as long as" is the key to the creation of this estate. If the specified purpose ceases, title will revert (go back) to either the original grantor or his or her heirs or to some specified third party (or that person's heirs). This future interest is called a *possibility of reverter.*

Fee simple subject to condition subsequent.   A *fee simple subject to condition subsequent* is similar to a determinable fee in that a grantor conveys a parcel of real estate subject to a condition of ownership, but

Figure 2.1 Freehold Estates

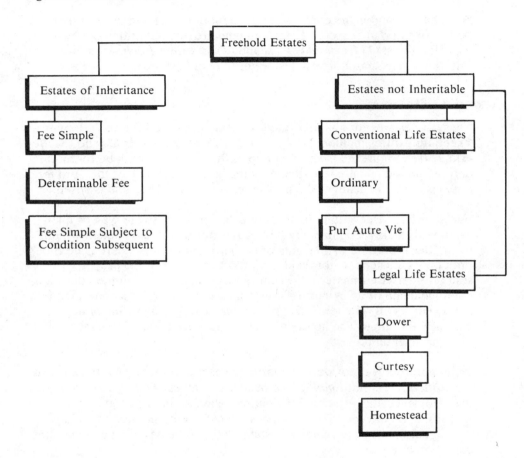

differs in the way the estate will terminate upon violation of this condition. In a determinable fee, title to the subject property reverts to the original owner (or his or her heirs) upon violation of the specified condition. However, with a fee simple subject to condition subsequent, the original owner (or his or her heirs) must go to court to assert this right. The original grantor's interest in this case is called a *right of re-entry*.

Fee tail.   Some states recognize a **fee tail** estate, in which property is limited to the recipient and his or her biological children, usually referred to as the recipient's "issue of the body."

Conventional life estates (with remainder or reversion).   A conventional **life estate** is an estate in land that is limited in duration to the life

Figure 2.2   Ordinary Life Estate

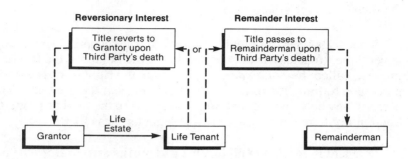

of the owner or to the life of some other designated person (or persons). It is not an estate of inheritance—that is, the rights cannot be passed on to the owner's heirs—because the estate terminates at the death of the owner or designated person.

There are two types of conventional life estates—ordinary and pur autre vie. When the owner of a fee simple estate grants an *ordinary life estate* to someone, it is limited to the lifetime of the owner of the life estate, the life tenant (see Figure 2.2). However, a life estate can also be created based on the life of a third party. For example, Smith, who owns a fee simple estate, can convey a life estate in the land to Jones, for as long as Washington is alive. This is known as an estate *pur autre vie,* meaning "for the life of another." In this type of life estate, Jones is the life tenant.

When the original fee simple owner creates a life estate, he or she must also consider the future ownership of the property after the life tenant's death. The future interest may take one of two forms:

1. *Remainder interest.* When the deed or will creating the life estate names a third party or parties to whom title will pass upon the death of the life estate owner, then this third party is said to own the remainder interest, or estate.

2. *Reversionary interest.* When the creator of a life estate (the original fee simple owner) does not convey the remainder interest to a third party or parties, then upon the death of the life estate owner, full ownership reverts to the original fee simple owner; if the original owner is deceased, it reverts to the heirs or devisees set forth in his or her will. This interest or estate is called a *reversion.*

Thus, upon the death of the life estate owner or other designated person, the holder of the future interest, whether remainder or reversion, will be the owner of a fee simple estate.

A life tenant's interest in real property is a true ownership interest. In general the life tenant is not answerable to the holder of the future interest, called the *remainderman,* to whom the right of possession will pass upon termination of the life estate. However, the life tenant cannot perform any acts that would permanently injure the land or property. Such injury to real estate is known in legal terms as *waste.*

A life tenant is entitled to all income and profits arising from the property during the term of ownership and is also responsible for paying the real estate taxes. A life interest may be sold, leased, or mortgaged, but finding an interested party can be difficult. The life tenant may only lease, mortgage, or sell the interest he or she has. The interest of any buyer, tenant, or lender will terminate at the end of the measuring life.

Legal life estates.   Curtesy, dower, homestead, and community property are legal life estates; that is, they are created by state law.

Curtesy is a husband's life estate in the real estate of his deceased wife. **Dower** is the life estate that a wife has in the real estate of her deceased husband. In most states, a dower or curtesy interest means that upon the death of the owning spouse, the surviving spouse has a right to either a one-half or a one-third interest in the real property for the rest of his or her life. Generally, the right of dower or curtesy becomes effective only upon the death of a spouse. During the lifetime of the parties, the right is merely the possibility of an interest. It is *inchoate,* or incomplete, until the death of the spouse who owns the property. Upon the death of the owning spouse, the dower or curtesy right becomes *consummate* (complete). Curtesy and dower have been abolished in most states and replaced by the Uniform Probate Code.

A **homestead** is a tract of land that is owned and occupied as the family home. In those states that have homestead exemption laws, a portion of the value is protected from judgment debts. In some states it is necessary to file a declaration of homestead. This is not to say that the homestead cannot be sold—it can. The homestead exemption simply sets aside a portion of the court-ordered sale proceeds to go to the property owner before any disbursement is made to the judgment creditor. In most cases, the homestead exemption is only operative against unsecured judgment creditors and has no effect on the claim of a mortgage lender whose loan is secured by the property, the government's claim for unpaid property taxes, or a mechanic's lien against the property for labor and materials supplied in improving the real estate.

Community property consists of all property, real and personal, acquired by either spouse during the marriage. Any conveyance of or encumbrance on community property requires the signature of both spouses. Upon the death of one spouse, the survivor automatically owns one-half of the community property. The other half is distributed according to the deceased's will. If the deceased died without a will, the other half is inherited by the survivor or by the deceased's other heirs, depending upon state law. The concept of community property originated in Spanish law, not English common law, and has been adopted by many of the western and southwestern states. The only property not subject to the community property statutes in these states is *separate property,* that which is acquired and owned by either spouse prior to marriage or acquired by either spouse during marriage through gift, devise, or descent.

Leasehold Estates

Through an agreement called a *lease,* an owner of real estate transfers to a tenant the right to exclusive possession and use of the owner's property for a specific period of time. When a landowner leases real estate to a tenant, the tenant's right to occupy the land for the duration of the lease is called a **leasehold estate.** Since the leasehold estate is not an estate of ownership, the ownership interest in the property remains with the landlord in what is known as an *estate in reversion.* This means that the landlord has the right to retake possession of the property after the lease term has expired. All leasehold estates are classified as being either *definite* or *indefinite.* The four most important are (1) *estate for years,* (2) *estate from period to period,* (3) *estate at will,* and (4) *estate at sufferance.*

The legal specifics of the relationship between landlord and tenant will be discussed in detail in Chapter 7.

ENCUMBRANCES

An owner's rights in real estate may be subject to the rights of others. Among such other interests are those of mortgage lenders, judgment creditors, mechanic's lien claimants, and state and local governments with regard to taxation. These rights are termed encumbrances. An **encumbrance** is defined as a charge or burden on a property that may diminish its value or obstruct the use of the property, but does not necessarily prevent a transfer of title. Encumbrances may be divided into

Figure 2.3   Encumbrances

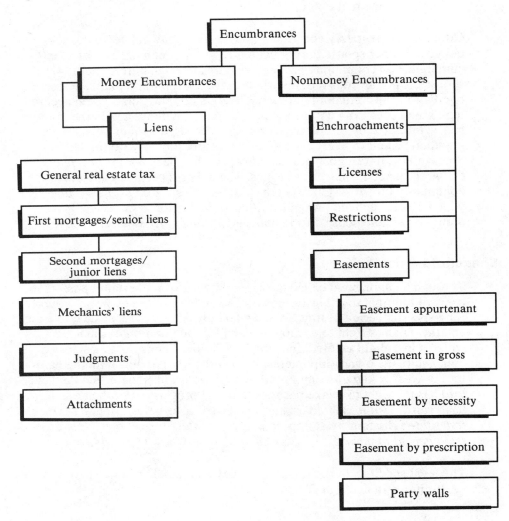

two general classifications: (1) *money encumbrances,* or *liens,* which affect the title, and (2) *nonmoney encumbrances,* which affect the physical
condition and use of the property (see Figure 2.3).

Liens

A **lien** is a claim or charge imposed upon a property by which it is made security for the performance of some act, usually the payment of a monetary debt. A lien allows a creditor to force the sale of property given as security by a debtor to settle his or her debt in case of default. Liens may be *voluntary* or *involuntary*. They are classified into two categories, *specific* and *general*.

Voluntary liens.   These arise in situations where the owner of the property agrees to use the title to real estate as security for a debt. Perhaps the best example of a voluntary lien is the financial security device known as a *mortgage*. A mortgage is a written contract through which the borrower's real estate is *hypothecated* (used as security for a loan without giving up possession of the property) to the lender in order to secure a loan.

Involuntary liens.   These arise in situations where a lien is placed on the title to real estate by statute or by court order, against the express will of the property owner. Examples of involuntary liens are real estate tax liens and court-ordered judgment liens.

Specific liens.   These are usually secured by one or more specific parcels of real estate, and include mortgages, taxes, special assessments, liens for public utilities, mechanics' liens, vendees' liens, vendors' liens, surety bail bond liens, attachment liens, and execution liens.

General liens.   These usually affect all the nonexempt property of the debtor. Included are real and personal property, judgment liens, debts of a deceased person, state inheritance taxes, federal estate taxes on a decedent's estate, and franchise taxes levied against corporations.

A typical real estate owner's fee simple estate may be reduced in value by the lien and encumbrance rights of others. The fee simple title to encumbered property can be conveyed to another party by the owner, but the existence of one or more liens against the property threatens the buyer with possible loss of the real estate if creditors take court action to enforce payment.

Real estate tax liens.   Real estate ownership is subject to certain government powers, among them the right of state and local governments to levy taxes for the support of their governmental functions. Because the location of real estate is permanently fixed, the government can levy taxes with a rather high degree of certainty that the taxes will be collected. The annual taxes levied on real estate usually have *priority over* *previously recorded liens.* This means that if the property is subjected to a court-ordered sale to satisfy unpaid debts, outstanding real estate taxes will be paid from the proceeds *first.*

Real estate taxes can be divided into two types: (1) *general real estate tax,* or *ad valorem tax,* and (2) *special assessments* or *improvements tax.* Both of these taxes are levied against specific parcels of property and automatically become liens on those properties. Real estate tax liens are specific, involuntary liens.

General real estate taxes are levied for the general support or operation of the governmental agency authorized to impose the levy, such as the state, county, municipality and/or local school district. These taxes are known as **ad valorem** taxes (from the Latin phrase meaning "to the value"), because the amount of the tax varies in accordance with the *value* of the property being taxed. To be enforceable, real estate taxes must be valid, which means they must be (1) properly levied, (2) for a legal purpose, and (3) applied equitably to all affected property. Real estate taxes that have remained delinquent for the period of time specified by state law can be collected through either tax foreclosure or tax sale. While there are substantial differences in the methods and details of the various states' tax-sale procedures, the results are the same.

Special assessments are special taxes levied on real estate that require property owners to pay for municipal improvements that benefit the real estate they own. Such taxes often are levied to pay for streets, street lighting, curbs, public sewers, and similar items. They are enforced in the same manner as general real estate taxes.

Both general and special assessment real estate taxes will be covered in detail in Chapter 9.

Mechanics' liens.   A **mechanic's lien** is a right granted by statute to give security to those who perform labor or furnish materials in the improvement of real property. In general, the mechanic's lien right is based on the *enhancement of value* theory. Because of the labor performed and material furnished, the real estate has been enhanced in value. Therefore, the parties who performed the work or supplied the materials are given the right of lien on the real estate on which they worked as security for the payment of their proper charges. A mechanic's lien is a specific, involuntary lien.

In order for a person to be entitled to file for a mechanic's lien, the work completed *must have been done by contract with the owner or the owner's representative.* Such a lien is relied on to cover situations in which the owner has not fully paid for work, or when the general contractor has been paid but has not paid the subcontractors or suppliers of materials. Generally, a person claiming a mechanic's lien must record a notice of lien within a limited time after the work is completed.

The point in time at which a mechanic's lien attaches to the real estate varies according to state law. For example, priority may be established as of the date: (1) the construction began or materials were first furnished (the beginning of what is called the *scheme of improvements*); (2) the work was completed; (3) the individual subcontractor's work was either commenced or completed; (4) the contract was signed or work ordered; or (5) a notice of lien was recorded.

Inasmuch as the rights of a mechanic's lien claimant are statutory, they are controlled by the requirements of the laws of the state in which the real estate is located. These laws usually provide that a claimant must take steps to enforce his or her lien within a certain time, usually one or two years after the filing of the lien claim, or the lien will expire. Enforcement usually requires a court action to foreclose the lien through the sale of the subject real estate in order to obtain the money to satisfy the lien.

Judgment liens. A **judgment** is a final order or decree of a court at the end of a court suit. When the decree provides for the awarding of money and sets forth the amount owed to the creditor, the judgment is referred to as a *money judgment.* The details of the judge's or jury's final determination are put in writing into an *abstract of judgment.* Until the abstract of judgment is recorded, it has no direct effect upon the debtor's property. In fact, until the abstract of judgment is recorded the judgment constitutes a potential *cloud on the title.* Once recorded, it becomes an involuntary, general lien on all nonexempt real and personal property in that county possessed by the debtor or subsequently acquired, as long as the judgment is effective.

If a money judgment is awarded by the court and the debtor fails to pay, the creditor may force payment through sale of the property. This is done by having the court issue a *writ of execution,* which authorizes the sheriff or some other officer of the court to seize and sell the debtor's property in order to satisfy the judgment. From the time the writ of execution is issued by the court until the debtor's property is actually sold to satisfy the debt, the writ constitutes another type of involuntary lien awarded by the court, known as an *execution lien.*

Since a judgment or other decree affecting real estate is rendered at the conclusion of a lawsuit, generally there is a considerable time lag between the filing of a lawsuit and the rendering of a judgment. When any suit is filed that affects title to a specific parcel of real estate, a notice known as *lis pendens* is recorded. A lis pendens filed in the public records gives constructive notice to all interested parties of the creditor's possible claim against the real estate, and constitutes a cloud on the title.

Attachments.   To prevent a debtor from conveying title to his or her unsecured real estate (realty that is not mortgaged or encumbered) while a court suit is being decided, a creditor may seek a *writ of attachment,* or an attachment lien. By this writ, the court retains custody of the property until the suit is concluded. In order to obtain an attachment, a creditor must first post with the court a surety bond or deposit sufficient to cover any possible loss or damage the debtor may sustain during the period the court has custody of the property, in case the judgment is not awarded to the creditor. The writ of attachment and subsequent attachment lien are placed against the debtor's property *before* the court suit is decided.

Although a judgment lien is said to affect *all* property of a debtor, the courts hold that certain property is exempt from attachment or execution. When a written *declaration of homestead* is filed for record prior to the recording of an abstract of judgment, it protects the debtor's equity up to the amount of the exemption. A *joint tenant's interest* is another example of exempt property. A lien or a joint tenant's interest is extinguished if the joint tenant dies prior to the court-ordered sale of the property.

Nonmoney Encumbrances

Although all liens are encumbrances, not all encumbrances are liens. Nonmoney encumbrances are those that affect the physical condition or limit the use of real estate. Nonmoney encumbrances are normally classified as *easements, deed restrictions, licenses,* or *encroachments.*

Easements.   An **easement** is a right acquired by one party to use the land of another party for a special purpose. Note, however, that it is also possible to have an easement right in the air above a parcel of real estate or land. Because an easement is a right to use land, it is classified as an interest in real estate, but it is not an estate in land. The holder of an easement merely has a *right.* He or she does not have an estate or ownership interest in the land over which the easement exists. An easement is sometimes referred to as an *incorporeal right* in land (a nonpossessory interest). An easement may be either appurtenant or it may be in gross (see Figure 2.4).

Figure 2.4 Easements

The owner of Lot A has an *appurtenant easement* across Lot B to gain access to his property from the paved road. Lot A is domi- nant, and Lot B is servient. The owner of Lot B has an *appur- tenant easement* across Lot A to gain access to the beach. In this situation Lot B is dominant and Lot A is servient. The utility company has an *ease- ment in gross* across both parcels of land for its power lines.

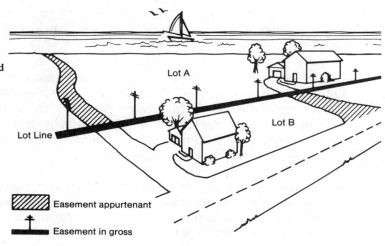

An *easement appurtenant* is an easement that is annexed to the owner- ship and used for the benefit of another party's parcel of land. For an easement appurtenant to exist, there must be *two tracts of land owned by different parties.* The tract over which the easement runs is known as the *servient estate (tenement);* the tract that is to benefit from the easement is the *dominant estate (tenement).* An easement appurtenant is considered part of the dominant estate. If the dominant tenement is conveyed to an- other party, the easement will pass with the title. In legal terms, it is said that the easement "runs with the land." However, title to the actual land over which an easement runs is retained by the owner of the servient estate.

An *easement in gross* is a mere personal interest in or right to use the land of another and is not appurtenant to any ownership estate in the land. Commercial easements in gross include the easement right a rail- road or utility company has for its tracks, pipeline, or high tension power lines. It may assigned, conveyed, or inherited.

A personal easement in gross is granted to an individual for his or her life- time. It permits access to the property for some use. This type of ease- ment is usually not assignable and will terminate upon the death of the easement holder.

An *easement by necessity* is an appurtenant easement that arises when an owner sells part of his or her land that has *no access* to a street or public way except over the seller's remaining land. An easement by necessity arises because all owners have rights of ingress to and egress from their land—they cannot be landlocked.

An *easement by prescription* is acquired when the claimant has used another's land for a certain period of time as defined by state law. This *prescriptive period* is usually from five to 20 years. The claimant's use must have been continuous, exclusive with the claim of right, and without the owner's approval. Additionally, the use must be visible, open, and notorious, so that the owner could readily learn of it.

A *party wall* is an exterior wall of a building that straddles the boundary line between two owners' lots, with half of the wall on each lot. Each lot owner owns the side of the wall on his or her lot, and each has an easement right in the other side for support of his or her building. A written party-wall agreement should be used to create these easement rights. Each owner must pay half the cost of building and maintaining the wall.

Easements may be created by

1. *mutual agreement expressed by the parties*—generally in writing through a grant or by reservation in a deed of conveyance;

2. *necessity*—for ingress to and egress from an otherwise landlocked property, often by a court order;

3. *prescription*—through visible, open, and notorious use of another person's property;

4. *condemnation*—such as when a public utility installs new towers or pipelines across a property; and

5. *implication*—when the situation or the parties' actions imply the intention to create an easement.

To create an easement there must be two separate parties, one of whom owns the land over which the easement runs. It is impossible for the owner of a parcel of property to hold an easement running over his or her own land. Thus, where a valid easement exists and the dominant tenement is acquired by the owner of the servient tenement, the easement becomes dormant. The user's express or implied intention is required to terminate the easement.

Easements may be *terminated* when

1. the purpose for which the easement was created no longer exists;

2. the owner of either the dominant or servient tenement becomes the owner of both in a process called merger;

3. the owner of the dominant tenement releases the right of easement;

4. the easement is abandoned (again, the intention of the parties controls);

5. the easement is taken by eminent domain or is lost through adverse possession; and

6. the person acquiring the easement uses it for an improper or illegal purpose.

Deed restrictions.   Private agreements that affect the use of land are called **deed restrictions** and covenants. A real estate owner can create a deed restriction by including it in the deed when the property is conveyed.

There is a distinction between restrictions on the owner's right to *sell* and restrictions on his or her right to *use*. In general, provisions in a deed conveying a fee simple estate that bar the grantee from selling, mortgaging, or conveying it are considered void. Such restrictions attempt to limit the basic principle of the *free alienation (transfer) of property,* and the courts usually consider them against public policy and therefore unenforceable. There are exceptions to this, of course, but they are technical.

A subdivider may establish restrictions on the right to use land through a covenant in a deed or by a separate recorded declaration. These use restrictions are usually considered valid if they are reasonable restraints and are for the benefit of all property owners in the subdivision. If such restrictions are too broad in their terms, however, they may prevent the free transfer of property. If they are "repugnant" to the estate granted, such restrictions will probably not be enforceable. If any restrictive covenant or condition is considered void by a court, it will not affect the validity of the deed or divest the grantee of his or her estate. The estate will then stand free from the invalid covenants or conditions.

Plats of new subdivisions will frequently set forth restrictive covenants concerning the use of the land. When a lot in that subdivision is conveyed by an owner's deed, the deed will refer to the plat or declaration of restrictions and will incorporate these restrictions as limitations on the title conveyed by the deed. In this manner, the restrictive covenants are included in the deed by reference and become binding on all grantees. Covenants or restrictions usually relate to: (1) type of building; (2) use to which the land may be put; and (3) type of construction, height, setbacks, and square footage.

Most restrictions have a *time limitation,* for example, "effective for a period of 25 years from this date." After that time, the restrictions become inoperative unless they are extended by majority agreement of the owners of the property at that time. Frequently, it is also provided that the effective term of the restrictions may be extended with the consent of a majority, or two-thirds, of owners in a subdivision. Generally, a deed restriction may be removed only by unanimous consent of all lot owners.

In most states, *deed restrictions take precedence over zoning ordinances.* Deed restrictions may be more restrictive of an owner's use, so if there is a conflict between a zoning ordinance and the restrictions in a deed or plat of subdivision, the latter will prevail.

Subdividers usually place restrictions on the use of all lots in a subdivision as a general plan for the benefit of all lot owners. Such restrictions give each lot owner the right to apply to the court for an *injunction* to stop a neighboring lot owner from violating the recorded restrictions. If granted, the court injunction will direct the violator to stop the violation upon penalty of being in contempt of court. The court retains the power to punish the violator for failure to obey the court order. Adjoining lot owners who stand by idly while a violation is being committed can lose the right to the court's injunction by their inaction; the court might claim *laches,* that is, loss of a right through undue delay or failure to assert it.

Conditions in a deed are different from restrictions or covenants. A grantor's deed of conveyance of land can be subject to certain stated conditions whereby the buyer's title may *revert* to the seller. For example, Bill Potter conveys a lot to Jane Knish by a deed that includes a condition forbidding the sale, manufacture, or giving away of intoxicating liquor on the lot and provides that in case of violation, the title (ownership) reverts to Potter. If Knish operates a tavern on the lot, Potter can file suit and obtain title to the property. In this case, a condition in the title is enforced by a reverter, or reversion, as discussed earlier in the chapter.

License.   A license is *a privilege to enter the land of another party for a specific purpose.* It is *not* an estate in land; it is a personal right of the person to whom it is given. A license differs from an easement in gross in that *it can be terminated or canceled by the licensor* (the person who granted the license) and is usually not transferable. Examples of licenses are permission to park in a neighbor's driveway or permission to attend the theater or a sporting event granted by the purchase of a ticket.

Encroachments.   An encroachment arises when a portion of a building, a fence, or driveway illegally *extends beyond its owner's land* and covers some land of an adjoining owner or a street or alley. Encroachments are usually disclosed by either a physical inspection of the property or a spot survey. A *spot survey* shows the location of all improvements located on a property and reveals whether any improvements extend over the lot lines. Encroachments are not disclosed by the usual title evidence provided in a real estate sale unless a survey is submitted at the time the examination is made. If the building on a lot encroaches on neighboring land, the neighbor may be able to either recover damages or secure removal of the portion of the building that encroaches. Encroachments of long standing (for the prescriptive period) may give rise to easements by prescription.

SUMMARY

Under the *allodial system,* an individual in the United States may acquire the ownership rights of *possession, use/enjoyment, control,* and *disposition* in real property, but may not acquire absolute ownership of real property because certain rights—such as *escheat, eminent domain,* and *police power*—are always retained by the government.

An *estate* in real property is the degree, quantity, nature, and extent of interest that a person has in that property. If the estate is of *indeterminable* length, it is known as a *freehold* estate and may be a *fee simple, determinable fee,* or *life estate,* with either an estate in *reversion* or a *remainder* estate. If the estate exists less than a lifetime, it is known as a *leasehold* estate and may be an *estate for years, estate from period to period, estate at will,* or *estate at sufferance.*

Although generally an owner of real estate controls the various rights to his or her real estate, an owner's rights in real estate may be subject to the rights of others. These rights are known as encumbrances and include *money encumbrances,* where the right is acquired due to some monetary debt or obligation, and *nonmoney encumbrances,* where the right affects the physical condition and use of the property.

Liens (money encumbrances) may be *voluntary* or *involuntary,* and are classified as *general* or *specific.* They include *mortgage liens, attachment liens, judgment liens, execution liens,* and *tax liens.*

Easements and *restrictions* are nonmoney encumbrances. Easements may be either *appurtenant* or *in gross,* while restrictions are largely of two kinds, *private* or *public.*

QUESTIONS

Please complete all of the questions before turning to the Answer Key.

1. All of the following are government powers that limit the ownership of real estate EXCEPT

    a.   taxation.
    b.   police power.

    c.   easement.
    d.   escheat.

2. The term *freehold estate* encompasses

    a.   an ownership interest.
    b.   a lease for one year or less.
    c.   tenancy at will.
    d.   tenancy at sufferance.

3. A widow is willed property from her deceased husband for the rest of her life, and upon her death, the title passes to her children. This type of ownership is best described as a

    a.   determinable fee estate.
    b.   legal life estate.
    c.   life estate with a reversionary interest.
    d.   life estate with a remainder interest.

4. A mechanic's lien

    a.   attaches to the owner's personal property.
    b.   protects the contractor and the subcontractor.
    c.   cannot affect future purchasers of the property.
    d.   cannot affect future lenders on the property.

5. An easement is granted to an electric company to erect high-tension power lines. This type of easement is called a(n)

    a.   easement appurtenant.
    b.   commercial easement in gross.
    c.   license.
    d.   encroachment.

6. Money encumbrances that affect the title to property are called

    a. restrictions.   c. encroachments.
    b. easements.   d. liens.

7. An encumbrance granted by statute that gives security to those who
    perform labor or provide materials in the improvement of real property is
    a(n)

    a. mortgage lien.   c. mechanic's lien.
    b. judgment lien.   d. attachment.

8. If *V* has an easement appurtenant to cross over *K*'s property, *V* is
    considered to have a(n)

    a. dominant tenement.   c. encroachment.
    b. servient tenement.   d. license.

9. A homestead exemption will protect against which of the following?

    a. An unpaid mortgage   c. A mechanic's lien
    b. An unsecured loan   d. Unpaid property taxes

10. All of the following statements concerning encroachments are true
    EXCEPT

    a. they are an unauthorized use of another's property.
    b. a spot survey will reveal any encroachments.
    c. title to the encroached property may be marketable.
    d. encroachments represent liens on the encroached property.

11. When property is granted for as long as it is used for a particular purpose,
    the interest granted is a

    a. fee simple.   c. leasehold estate.
    b. determinable fee.   d. life estate.

12. Which of the following real property interests is inheritable?

    a. Ordinary life estate   c. Homestead
    b. Pur autre vie life estate   d. Determinable fee

13. Charges levied against real estate for municipal improvements that benefit the real estate, such as street paving and street lighting, are called

    a. ad valorem taxes.
    b. general real estate taxes.
    c. special assessments.
    d. judgment liens.

14. *H* has given property to *T* for *T*'s lifetime, and at *T*'s death, the property is to be transferred to *F*. In this situation, what is F's interest?

    a. Reversionary
    b. Remainder
    c. Fee simple
    d. Determinable

15. Which of the following is a voluntary lien?

    a. Real estate tax lien
    b. Mechanic's lien
    c. Judgment lien
    d. Mortgage lien

16. The interest of a husband in the real estate of his deceased wife is the

    a. dower right.
    b. curtesy right.
    c. homestead exemption.
    d. determinable fee estate.

17. When a lawsuit is filed that affects the title to a parcel of real property, which of the following documents is recorded to give public notice of the action?

    a. Attachment
    b. Execution
    c. Judgment lien
    d. Lis pendens

18. The most complete type of interest in real estate is the

    a. fee simple.
    b. determinable fee.
    c. leasehold estate.
    d. conventional life estate.

19. An easement may be terminated when any of the following occur EXCEPT when

    a. the purpose for which the easement was created no longer exists.
    b. the owner of the servient tenement decides that he or she no longer needs the easement.
    c. the easement is taken by eminent domain or is lost through adverse possession.
    d. the person who acquired the easement uses it for some improper or illegal purpose.

20. Deed restrictions usually address or regulate all of the following EXCEPT

    a. the types of buildings or other improvements.
    b. the types of construction acceptable in the area.
    c. the legal uses to which the land can be put.
    d. the occupants of the various types of property.

3: Acquisition and Transfer of Title

KEY TERMS

accession	grantee
accretion	granting clause
acknowledgment	grantor
adverse possession	habendum clause
attorney-in-fact	intestate
avulsion	power of attorney
bargain and sale deed	probate
descent	quitclaim deed
devise	testate
erosion	testator
escheat	title
executor	warranty deed
grant deed	will

Title to real estate gives the ownership right to the land and represents evidence of ownership. The laws of each state govern real estate transactions for land located within state boundaries. Each state has adopted legislative acts that affect the methods of transferring title or other interests in real estate. A parcel of land may be transferred from one owner to another in a number of different ways: through voluntary alienation (by sale or gift); through involuntary alienation (by operation of law); or by will or descent (after an owner's death).

VOLUNTARY ALIENATION

Voluntary alienation (transfer) of title may be made by either gift, will, or sale. To transfer title by voluntary alienation during his or her lifetime, an owner must normally use some form of deed of conveyance. Examples of voluntary alienation involving a *gift* would include *patent,* a public grant in which the state or federal government conveys title to public land to an individual; and *dedication,* which generally results from the intention of the owner to dedicate (give) his or her private property to the government for a public use. Dedication is normally accomplished by use of a deed. The best example of voluntary alienation involving a sale would be a typical real estate sale transaction, in which a property owner negotiates with a purchaser concerning the price and terms, with the understanding that at the closing the property owner will convey title to the purchaser through use of a deed.

A *deed* is a written instrument by which an owner of real property intentionally conveys to a purchaser his or her right, title, or interest in a parcel of real property. All deeds must be in writing in accordance with the requirements of each state's statute of frauds. The owner (who sells the land) is known as the **grantor,** and the purchaser (who acquires the land) is known as the **grantee.** A deed is *executed* (signed) by the grantor. (If the grantor is incapable of signing his or her name, a *mark* can be used.)

Requirements for a Valid Conveyance

Although the formal requirements for a valid deed are not uniform in all states, certain requirements are basic. As illustrated in Figure 3.1, these are:

1. a *grantor* having legal capacity to execute (sign) the deed;

2. a *grantee* named with reasonable certainty, so that he or she can be identified;

3. a recital of *consideration;*

4. a *granting clause* (words of conveyance);

5. a *habendum clause* (specifies type of estate to be conveyed and any recorded encumbrances);

6. designation of any *limitations* on the conveyance of a full fee simple estate;

7. a *legal description* of the property conveyed;

8. *exceptions* and *reservations* affecting the title ("subject to" clause);

9. the *grantor's signature,* sometimes with a seal; and

10. *delivery* of the deed and *acceptance* to pass title.

Figure 3.1   Requirements for a Valid Deed

```
                    DEED

          1.  Grantor
          2.  Grantee
          3.  Consideration
          4.  Granting clause
          5.  Habendum clause
          6.  Limitations
          7.  Legal description
          8.  Exceptions and reservations
          9.  Grantor's signature
         10.  Delivery and acceptance
```

Grantor.   A grantor must have a legal existence, be of lawful age, and be legally competent in order to convey title to real estate. The laws of the state in which the real estate is located will control the precise legal requirements to convey title. To determine if a grantor is competent to convey title to real property, rules governing contracts usually apply.

A grantor must be of sound mind and of lawful age, usually at least 18 years old. A grantor is generally held to have sufficient mental capacity to execute a deed if he or she is capable of understanding the action.

It is important that a grantor's name be spelled correctly and that there be no variation in its spelling throughout the deed. If for any reason a grantor's name has been changed from that by which title was originally acquired, he or she must show both names. It is customary for such a grantor to be described as, for example, "John Smith, now known as John White." A grantor should first state the name under which the title was acquired and then indicate his or her current name. When title to property has been acquired under a woman's maiden name and she subsequently marries, if she takes her husband's name the conveyance must show both her maiden name and her married name. In addition, in many states her spouse, if living, must join in the deed to release marital rights. When the husband is the grantor, the wife must also join in the deed.

Grantee.   To be valid, a deed must name a grantee in such a manner that he or she is readily identifiable. A deed naming as the grantee a wholly fictitious person, a company that does not legally exist, or a society or club that is not properly incorporated is considered void, and as such has no legal effect.

Consideration.   In order to be valid, all deeds must contain a clause acknowledging the grantor's receipt of a consideration—something given by the grantee in exchange for the property. In most states, the amount of consideration must be stated in dollars. When a deed conveys real estate as a gift to a relative, "love and affection" is usually sufficient consideration. In deeds conveying property as a gift to a nonrelative, it is customary in most states to specify a nominal consideration, such as "ten dollars and other good and valuable consideration." The full dollar amount of such other consideration is seldom set forth in the deed except when the instrument is executed by a corporation or trustee, or pursuant to court order.

Granting clause.   A deed of conveyance transfers a present interest in real estate. Therefore, it must contain words of grant, or conveyance, that state the grantor's intention to convey the property at this time; an expression of intent to convey at some future time is inadequate. Such words of grant are contained in the **granting clause.** Depending on the type of deed and the obligations agreed to by the grantor, the wording is generally either "convey and warrant," "grant," "grant, bargain, and sell," or "remise, release, and quitclaim" (these will be explained under the discussions of the individual types of deeds that follow).

If more than one grantee is involved, the granting clause should cover the creation of their specific rights in the property and state, for example, that the grantees will take title as joint tenants or tenants in common. The wording is especially important in states where specific wording is necessary to create a joint tenancy. (Joint tenancy and tenancy in common will be discussed in Chapter 4.)

Habendum clause.   This clause follows the granting clause when it is necessary to define or explain the extent of ownership to be enjoyed by the grantee, such as a fee simple, life estate, or easement. The **habendum clause** begins with the words "to have and to hold." The provisions of the clause must agree with those set down in the granting clause. If there is a discrepancy between the two, the provisions of the granting clause are usually followed.

Limitations.   The granting clause should also specify what interest in the property is being conveyed by the grantor. Deeds that convey the entire fee simple interest of the grantor usually contain a phrase such as "to Jacqueline Smith and to her heirs and assigns forever." If the grantor is conveying less than his or her complete interest—for instance, a life estate to property—the wording must indicate this limitation on the grantee's interest. For example, a deed creating a life estate would convey property "to Jacqueline Smith for the duration of her natural life."

Legal description.   For a deed to be valid, it must contain an adequate description of the real estate conveyed. Land is considered adequately described if a competent surveyor can locate the property from the description. (As discussed in Chapter 1, a street address alone is not an adequate legal description of real estate.)

Exceptions and reservations ("subject to" clause).   A deed should specifically note any encumbrances, reservations, or limitations that affect the title being conveyed. Exceptions to a clear title include mortgage liens, taxes, restrictions, and easements that run with the land. For example, a deed may convey title to a grantee "subject to an existing first mortgage loan, which the grantee assumes and agrees to pay."

In addition to existing encumbrances, a grantor may reserve some right in the land for his or her own use (an easement, for example). A grantor may also place certain restrictions on the grantee's use of the property. For example, a developer may restrict the number of houses that may be built on a one-acre lot. Restrictions must be clearly stated in the deed or contained in a previously recorded document that is expressly cited in the deed.

Grantor's signature.   To be valid, a deed must be signed by *all grantors* named in the document. Most states permit a grantor who is unable to write to sign his or her name *by mark*. Generally, with this type of signature, two persons must witness the grantor's execution of the deed and sign as witnesses.

Most states permit a grantor's signature to be signed by an attorney-in-fact acting under a power of attorney. An **attorney-in-fact** is any person who has been given power of attorney (specific written authority) to execute and sign legal instruments for a grantor. It is usually necessary for an authorizing document known as a **power of attorney** to be recorded in the county where the property is located. Since the power of attorney terminates upon the death of the person granting such authority, adequate evidence must be submitted that the grantor was alive when the attorney-in-fact signed the deed.

An **acknowledgment** is a form of declaration made voluntarily by a person who is signing a formal, written document before a notary public or authorized public officer. This acknowledgment usually states that the person signing the deed or other document is known to the officer or has produced sufficient identification, and is signing freely and voluntarily. The acknowledgment provides evidence that the signature is genuine.

Although it is customary to acknowledge the execution of a deed to real property, it is not essential to the validity of the deed. In some states, however, an unacknowledged instrument is not admissible as evidence in court without proof that the signature is genuine, and an unacknowledged deed cannot be recorded. Although an unrecorded deed is valid between grantor and grantee, it is often not a valid conveyance against subsequent innocent purchasers. To help ensure that he or she receives good title, a grantee should always require acknowledgment of the grantor's signature on a deed.

Delivery and acceptance.   Before a transfer of title by conveyance can take effect, there must be an actual delivery of the deed by the grantor and either actual or implied acceptance by the grantee. Delivery may be made by the grantor to the grantee personally or to the grantee's attorney. The transfer is done "inter vivos"; title passes from a living grantor to a living grantee and must happen during the lifetime of each to be valid. Arrangements may also be made for delivery and for acceptance requirements to be fulfilled by a third party, commonly known as an *escrow agent* or *escrowee,* for ultimate delivery to the grantee upon the completion of certain requirements. *Title is said to pass when a deed is delivered.* The effective date of the transfer of title is the date the deed itself is delivered. When a deed is delivered in escrow, the date of delivery of the conveyance is generally the date that it was deposited with the escrow agent. However, when property is registered under the Torrens system (see Chapter 5), title does not pass until the deed has been examined and accepted for registration.

Execution of Corporate Deeds

Under the law, a corporation is considered to be a legal entity. The laws affecting corporations' rights to convey real property vary widely from state to state, but there are some basic rules that must be followed:

1. A corporation can convey real property only upon the proper *resolution* passed by its board of directors. If all or a substantial portion of the corporation's real property is being

Figure 3.2 Sample Deeds

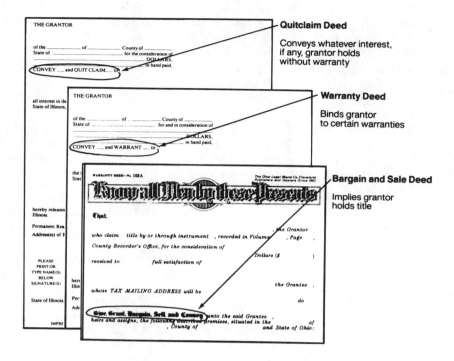

conveyed, a resolution authorizing the conveyance usually must be secured from the stockholders as well.

2. Deeds to real property can be signed only by *authorized officers.* The authority of the officer who signs must be granted by a resolution properly passed by the board of directors.

3. The corporate *seal* must be affixed to the conveyance.

Types of Deeds

The forms of deeds used in any given state are regulated and authorized by the laws of the state in which the land is located. The most common forms are (1) *warranty deed,* (2) *grant deed,* (3) *bargain and sale deed,* (4) *quitclaim deed,* (5) *deed in trust,* (6) *trustee's deed,* and (7) *deed executed pursuant to a court order.*

Warranty deeds.   **Warranty deeds** are normally divided into two types, general warranty deeds and special (or limited) warranty deeds.

For a purchaser of real estate, a *general warranty deed* provides the greatest protection of any deed (see Figure 3.2). It is referred to as a general warranty deed because the grantor is legally bound by certain *covenants* or *warranties*. In many states, these warranties are usually implied by the use of certain words, such as "convey and warrant," "warrant generally," and, in some states, "grant, bargain, sell, and convey." Other states require that such warranties be expressly written into the deed itself. The basic warranties are:

1. *Covenant of seisin.* The grantor warrants that he or she is the owner of the property and has the right to convey title to it. The grantee may recover damages up to the full purchase price if this covenant is broken.

2. *Covenant against encumbrances.* The grantor warrants that the property is free from any liens and encumbrances except those specifically stated in the deed. Encumbrances generally include such items as mortgages, mechanics' liens, and easements. If this covenant is breached, the grantee may sue for expenses to remove the encumbrance.

3. *Covenant of quiet enjoyment.* The grantor guarantees that the grantee's title is good against third parties who might bring court actions to establish superior title to the property. In such cases, if the grantee's title is found to be inferior, the grantor is liable for damages.

4. *Covenant of further assurance.* The grantor also promises to obtain and deliver any instrument needed in order to make the title good. For example, if the grantor's spouse has failed to sign away dower rights, the grantor must deliver a quitclaim deed executed by the spouse to clear the title.

5. *Covenant of warranty forever.* The grantor guarantees that if at any time in the future the title fails, he or she will compensate the grantee for the loss sustained.

Note that these covenants in a general warranty deed are not limited to matters that occurred during the time the grantor owned the property, but extend back through the chain of title to its origins.

A *special warranty deed* is a conveyance that carries only one covenant by the grantor. That is, the grantor warrants only that the property was not encumbered during the time he or she held title, except as noted in the deed. Special warranty deeds carry additional warranties only when they are specifically stated in the deed. Some states may refer to this as a *statutory warranty deed.*

A special warranty deed is usually used by fiduciaries—those entrusted to handle the monies of others. Fiduciaries include trustees, executors, and corporations. In addition, special warranty deeds are sometimes used by grantors who have acquired title at tax sales. Such deeds are based on the theory that a fiduciary or corporation has no authority to warrant against acts of its predecessors in title.

Grant deeds. In certain areas of the country, the **grant deed** has replaced the warranty deed as the most popular form of conveyance. A grant deed carries two implied warranties: (1) that the owner has the right to convey the property as stated in the deed and (2) that the owner has not encumbered the property except as noted in the deed. In addition, the grant deed conveys to the grantee any future, or *after-acquired,* title to the property that the owner may later acquire. For example, if at the time of conveyance the grantor had an interest in the property that was less than he or she thought or was defective, and the grantor acquired title or perfected the title after the conveyance, this after-acquired title would automatically pass to the grantee. These warranties are not stated in the deed but are implied by the use of the word "grant" in the deed's words of conveyance. Clearly, a grant deed contains fewer warranties than a general warranty deed; specifically, it does not warrant against the acts of any previous owners. Therefore, the grant deed is commonly used in many western states only in conjunction with a title insurance policy that protects the new owner against prior liens and claims against the property.

Bargain and sale deeds. A **bargain and sale deed** contains no real warranties against encumbrances; it only implies that the grantor holds title and possession of the property (see Figure 3.2). Because the warranty is not specifically stated, the grantee has little legal recourse if defects later appear in the title. In some areas, a covenant against encumbrances initiated by the grantor may be added to a standard bargain and sale deed to create a bargain and sale deed with covenant against the grantor's acts, which is roughly equivalent to a special warranty deed.

Quitclaim deeds. A **quitclaim deed** provides the grantee with the *least* protection of any deed. It carries no covenant or warranties whatsoever; and, in most states, it conveys only whatever interest the grantor may have when the deed is delivered (see Figure 3.2). By a quitclaim deed, the grantor "remises, releases, and quitclaims" his or her interest in the property to the grantee. In some states, a quitclaim deed does not actually convey property; rather, it conveys only the grantor's right, title, and interest, whatever that may be. Thus, if the grantor has no interest in the property, the grantee will acquire nothing by virtue of the quitclaim deed, nor will he or she acquire any right of warranty claim against the grantor.

A quitclaim deed can convey title as effectively as a warranty deed if the grantor has good title when he or she delivers the deed, but it provides none of the guarantees that a warranty deed does.

A quitclaim deed is frequently used to cure a technical defect in the chain of title (a "cloud on the title"). For example, if the warranty deed misspells the name of the grantee, a quitclaim deed with the correct spelling may be executed to the grantee in order to perfect the title. When a quitclaim deed is used for the special purpose of clearing a cloud on the title or releasing an interest in property of which the grantor never had possession, the wording should read "releases and quitclaims all interest, if any." In this way, the quitclaim deed will pass, without warranty, any title the grantor may have.

Deeds in trust.   A deed in trust is used to convey real estate to a trustee, usually in order to establish a *land trust* or *living trust*. Under the terms of such an instrument, full powers to sell, contract to sell, mortgage, subdivide, and the like are granted to the trustee. The trustee's use of these powers, however, is controlled by the beneficiary under the provisions of the trust agreement.

Trustee's deeds.   A trustee's deed is a deed of conveyance normally used when a trustee named in a will, agreement, or deed in trust sells or conveys title to real estate out of the trust. The instrument states that the trustee is acting in accordance with the powers and authority granted to him or her by the trust instrument or the deed in trust.

Deeds executed pursuant to court order.   This classification includes such deed forms as *executors' deeds, masters' deeds, administrators' deeds, sheriffs' deeds,* and many others. These statutory deed forms are used to convey title to property that is transferred by court order or by will. The forms of such deeds must conform to the laws of the state where the property is located.

As mentioned earlier in the chapter, one characteristic of such instruments is that the deed states the full amount of consideration. Since the deed is executed pursuant to court order, which has authorized the sale of the property for a given amount, verification of this amount must be included in the document.

INVOLUNTARY ALIENATION

Title to property can be transferred involuntarily—without the owner's consent. This is known as *involuntary alienation*. Such transfers are usually carried out by: (1) operations of law; (2) court order; and (3) natural forces. (These methods are illustrated in Figure 3.3.)

Operations of Law

When a person dies leaving no heirs capable of inheriting, the title to his or her property passes to the state (or county, in some states) by operation of law based on the principle of **escheat.** Likewise, federal, state, and local governments, school boards, some government agencies, and certain public and quasi-public corporations and utility companies have the power of *eminent domain*. Under this power, these entities may take private property through a *condemnation action* if two conditions are fulfilled: (1) the use for which the property is being taken must benefit the public, and (2) an equitable amount of compensation must be paid to the property owner for the taking.

Adverse possession is another means of involuntary transfer by operation of law. An owner who does not use his or her land or does not inspect it for a number of years may lose title to another person who takes possession of the land and, most importantly, uses it. The person claiming title by adverse possession may substantiate his or her claim through an action to *quiet title*. Usually the claimant's possession must be *open, exclusive, notorious, hostile,* and *uninterrupted* for the number of years set by state law. While states generally require that possession be uninterrupted, several states recognize the concept of tacking on. This means that if several claimants possess the property at different but continuous times, they can add to, or tack on, each successive time of occupation in order to reach the statutory number of years needed for the adverse possession claim of title. For example, suppose the statutory period for an adverse possession claim is 10 years. Claimant A occupies the property under claim for 3 years, then claimant B takes possession for 5 years, and finally claimant C takes A's 3 years and B's 5 years toward the statutory requirement of 10 years.

Court Order

Title to real property may also be transferred without the owner's consent under the dictates of a court order, such as a court-ordered sale in order to satisfy debts contracted by the owner. The debt is foreclosed, the property is sold, and the proceeds of the sale are applied to pay off the debt. Debts

Figure 3.3 Involuntary Alienation

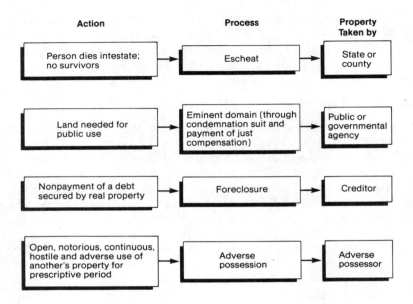

that could be foreclosed and result in a court-ordered sale include real estate taxes, mortgage loans, mechanics' liens, and judgment liens against the property owner. Other examples of court-ordered sales and transfers of title to real property include *partition actions* (normally to satisfy creditors from the assets of an estate or to terminate a joint tenancy) and bankruptcy (to satisfy creditors by selling assets).

Natural Forces

Owners of land bordering on rivers, lakes, oceans, and other bodies of water may acquire or lose additional land through natural forces. Additional land may be acquired through **accretion,** which is the slow increase in land mass caused by *alluvion,* the accumulation of soil, rock, and other matter deposited by the movement of water. Additional land can also be acquired through a process called *reliction,* the gradual withdrawal of water from along a shore, uncovering more land.

An owner may also lose land through natural forces. For example, the opposite of accretion can take place through **erosion,** the gradual wearing away of land by the action of water and wind, or **avulsion,** the sudden tearing away of land generally caused by a change in the course of a river or other body of water.

Whenever additional land is acquired through natural causes, title to the new land is acquired by the owner through a process called **accession.** Accession generally relates to acquiring title to real property by having land added to the land mass of an owner.

TRANSFER OF A DECEASED PERSON'S PROPERTY

Every state has a law known as the *statute of descent and distribution.* When a person dies **intestate** (without leaving a will), the decedent's real estate and personal property pass to his or her heirs according to this statute. In effect, the state makes a will for such decedents. In contrast, people who die **testate** are those who have prepared their own will indicating the way their property should be disposed of after death.

Legally, when a person dies, title to his or her real estate immediately passes either to heirs by descent, to persons named in the will, or to the state under the laws concerning *escheat.* Before the heirs can take possession of the property, however, the estate must be probated, and all claims against it must be satisfied.

Probate

Probate is a legal process by which a court determines who will inherit the property of a deceased person and what the assets of the estate are. In the case of a person who has died testate, the court also rules on the validity of the will. If the will is upheld, the property is distributed according to its provisions. If a person has died intestate, the court determines who will inherit by reviewing a proof of heirship. This document, usually prepared by an attorney, gives personal information regarding the decedent's spouse, children, and relatives. From this document, the court decides which parties will receive what portion of the estate.

To initiate probate proceedings, the custodian of the will, an heir, or another interested party must petition the court. The court will then hold a hearing to determine the validity of the will or the order of descent if no will exists. If for any reason a will is declared invalid by the court, any property owned by the decedent will pass by the laws of descent. Once the heirs are established, the court will approve an **executor,** who was usually named in the will, or appoint an *administrator* to oversee the administration and distribution of the estate. Probate proceedings vary from state to state; local procedures must be followed.

The court gives the administrator or executor the authority to have the assets of the estate appraised and satisfy all debts that were owed by the decedent. He or she is also responsible for paying federal estate taxes and, in most states, state inheritance taxes. Once all these liens against the property have been satisfied, the executor/administrator distributes the remaining assets of the estate according to the provisions of the will or the state law of descent.

Transfer of Title by Will

A *last will and testament* is an instrument made by an owner to voluntarily convey title to his or her property after death. A will takes effect only after the death of the decedent. Until that time, any property covered by the will can be conveyed by the owner, the executor named in the will can be changed, and any other provisions of the will itself can be changed. This is because until the death of the decedent the will is *ambulatory* (changeable). Amendments to the will are known as *codicils*.

A person who has died and left a will is said to have died testate. A party who makes a will is known as a **testator.** A gift of real property by will is known as a **devise.** A person who receives a gift of real property by will is known as a *devisee,* and the decedent who has willed the property is a *devisor.* A gift of personal property by will is known as a *bequest,* and a person who receives a gift of personal property by will is known as the *legatee.*

The privilege of disposing of property by will is statutory. To be effective, a will must conform to all the statutory requirements of the state in which the real estate is located. Generally a person must be of legal age and sound mind in order to be able to execute a valid will. The drawing of the will must also be a voluntary act, free of any undue influence by other people. In addition, a will cannot supersede state laws of dower and curtesy that were enacted to protect the inheritance rights of the surviving spouse. In a case in which a will does not provide the minimum inheritance allowed by law, the surviving spouse has the option of informing the court that he or she will take the minimum statutory share rather than the lesser share provided in the will. This practice, called *renouncing the will,* is a right reserved only to a surviving spouse. In states with community property laws, a surviving spouse automatically owns one-half of the couple's community property acquired during the marriage. No statutory inheritance rights are necessary to protect the surviving spouse's interest in the community property.

Three types of **wills** are recognized: (1) *formal* or *witnessed will,* (2) *holographic will,* and (3) *nuncupative will.*

Formal or witnessed will.   This kind of will is typically prepared by an attorney. Generally it is typed or a preprinted form is filled out, then the testator signs it before two or more witnesses, who also must sign the will. Usually the witnesses cannot be people named in the will as devisees or legatees.

Holographic will.   This is a handwritten will. Normally it is prepared, dated, and signed in the testator's own handwriting.

Nuncupative will.   This is an oral will, normally a declaration made by someone in immediate fear of dying. The oral declaration must be committed to writing within 30 days, and it can bequeath personal property of only $1,000 or less in value.

Many states do not permit the use of holographic or nuncupative wills.

Transfer of Title by Descent (Succession)

By law, the title to real estate and personal property of a person who dies intestate passes to his or her heirs. Under the **descent** statutes, the primary heirs of the deceased are the spouse and blood relatives, such as children, parents, brothers, sisters, aunts, uncles, and first and second cousins. The closeness of the relationship to the decedent determines the specific rights of the heirs, although the relative's right to inherit must be established by proof of heirship during the probate process.

The right to inherit under descent laws (also called *laws of intestate succession*) varies from state to state. When a husband dies leaving a wife and one child, the wife and child usually take the entire estate between them, some states dividing it equally and some allowing one-third to the surviving spouse. If, however, a wife and two or more children survive, it is customary for the wife to take one-third and the children to divide the remaining two-thirds equally among them. If a wife, but no children or descendants of children, exists, some state laws give the wife one-half of the estate and divide the other half equally among collateral heirs, such as parents and siblings of the decedent. In other states, the wife receives the entire estate. As discussed earlier, if no heirs are found, the deceased person's real estate will escheat to the state (or county) in which the land is located.

SUMMARY

Title to real estate may be transferred in four ways. The first two take effect during the owner's lifetime, and the other two after the death of the owner.

The voluntary transfer of an owner's title *(voluntary alienation)* is made by a *deed,* executed (signed) by the owner as *grantor* to the purchaser, or donee, as *grantee.* The form and execution of a deed must comply with the statutory requirements of the state in which the land is located. The obligation of a grantor is determined by the form of the deed; that is, whether it is a *general warranty* deed, *grant* deed, *special warranty* deed, *bargain and sale* deed, or *quitclaim* deed. The words of conveyance in the granting clause are important in determining the form of the deed.

In order to create a valid conveyance, a deed must meet the appropriate state requirements. Among the most common of these are: a grantor with legal capacity to contract, a readily identifiable grantee, a granting clause, a legal description of the property, a recital of consideration, exceptions and reservations on the title ("subject to" clause), and the signature of the grantor, properly witnessed if necessary. In addition, the deed should be acknowledged before a notary public or other officer in order to provide evidence that the signature is genuine and to allow recording. If required by state law, deeds are subject to state transfer taxes when they are recorded. Title to the property passes when the grantor delivers a deed to the grantee and it is accepted. The deed may also be accepted on the buyer's behalf by an agent, such as the buyer's attorney.

An owner's title may be transferred without his or her permission *(involuntary alienation)* by a court action, such as a *foreclosure* or judgment sale, a tax sale, *condemnation* under the right of eminent domain, *adverse possession,* or *escheat.* Land may also be transferred by the natural forces of water and wind that either increase property by *accretion* or decrease it through *erosion.*

The real estate of an owner who makes a valid *will* (who dies testate) passes to the devisees through the probating of the will. Generally, an heir or a devisee will not receive a deed, as title passes by the law or the will. The title of an owner who dies without a will (intestate) passes according to the provisions of the *law of descent* of the state in which the real estate is located.

QUESTIONS

Please complete all of the questions before turning to the Answer Key.

1. A will that is drawn in its maker's own handwriting and then signed by that person is known as a

    a.   formal will.   c.   nuncupative will.
    b.   witnessed will.   d.   holographic will.

2. The conveyance of land from the government to an individual uses a document called a

    a.   patent.   c.   devise.
    b.   dedication.   d.   bequest.

3. The type of deed that offers the greatest measure of protection to the grantee is the

    a.   general warranty deed.   c.   bargain and sale deed.
    b.   special warranty deed.   d.   quitclaim deed.

4. To be valid, a deed must contain a(n)

    a.   grantee's signature.   c.   acknowledgment.
    b.   grantor's signature.   d.   date.

5. A person who signs a deed on the grantor's behalf under a power of attorney is known as a(n)

    a.   agent.   c.   attorney at law.
    b.   successor.   d.   attorney-in-fact.

6. When a person dies testate, all of the following could be involved EXCEPT a(n)

    a.   devisee.   c.   executor.
    b.   legatee.   d.   administrator.

7. When the title to additional land is created by the natural forces of accretion and reliction, it is acquired by

    a.   alluvion.   c.   accession.
    b.   erosion.   d.   avulsion.

8. Property can be transferred from an individual to the government by any of the following methods EXCEPT by

    a. escheat.
    b. eminent domain.
    c. dedication.
    d. patent.

9. The covenant in a deed in which the grantor guarantees the title against third parties who might bring a court action to establish superior title is the

    a. covenant of further assurance.
    b. covenant of quiet enjoyment.
    c. covenant of seisin.
    d. covenant against encumbrances.

10. All of the following are court-ordered transfers of real property EXCEPT

    a. foreclosure.
    b. partition.
    c. dedication.
    d. probate.

11. The deed providing the weakest claim of ownership would be the

    a. general warranty deed.
    b. special warranty deed.
    c. bargain and sale deed.
    d. quitclaim deed.

12. For a legitimate claim of adverse possession, the claimant must be able to prove that his or her possession was all of the following EXCEPT

    a. notorious.
    b. involuntary.
    c. hostile.
    d. uninterrupted.

13. Title to real property transfers when the

    a. grantor executes the deed.
    b. consideration is stated.
    c. deed is delivered and accepted.
    d. property is surveyed.

14. The type of deed that warrants only that the owner of the property did not encumber the property during his or her term of ownership, except as noted in the deed, is the

    a. general warranty deed.
    b. special warranty deed.
    c. bargain and sale deed.
    d. quitclaim deed.

4: How Ownership Is Held

KEY TERMS

beneficiary

community property

condominium

cooperative

co-ownership

fiduciary

general partnership

joint tenancy

limited partnership

separate property

severalty

syndicate

tenancy by the entirety

tenancy in common

trust

trustee

trustor

A fee simple estate in land may be owned by one owner or by two or more co-owners under one of several forms of co-ownership. The choice of ownership form determines such matters as an owner's legal right to sell the real estate without the consent of others, to choose who will own the property after his or her death, and the future rights of creditors. The choice, in many cases, also has tax implications, in terms of both a possible gift tax resulting from a present transfer and future income and death taxes.

The form by which property is owned is important to the real estate broker and salesperson for two reasons: (1) the form of ownership existing at the time a property is sold determines who must sign the various documents involved (listing contract, acceptance of offer to purchase, or sales contract and deed); and (2) the purchaser must determine in what form he or she wishes to take title. For example, if one purchaser is taking title alone, the form of ownership is tenancy in severalty. If there are two or more purchasers, they may take title as tenants in common or as joint tenants. What's more, married purchasers' choices are governed by state laws. Some states provide for married persons to own real estate as tenants by the entireties or under community-property laws. Most states allow the couple to choose the form of ownership they prefer.

The forms of ownership available are controlled by the laws of the state in which the land is located. When questions of this type are raised by the parties to a transaction, a real estate licensee should recommend that the parties seek legal advice.

In most states, real estate may be owned in three basic forms: (1) in **severalty** title is held by one owner; (2) in **co-ownership** title is held by two or more persons; or (3) in **trust** title is held by a third person for the benefit of another or others.

OWNERSHIP IN SEVERALTY

When title to real estate is *vested in* (currently owned by) one person or one organization, that person or organization is said to own the property in *severalty*. This person is also referred to as the sole owner. All states have special laws that affect title held in severalty by either a husband or a wife. In most states, when either the husband or wife owns property in severalty (alone), the spouse must join in signing documents: (1) to release *dower* or *curtesy* in states that have such rights; (2) to release *homestead rights* in states that provide a homestead exemption; or (3) when the other spouse is a minor. In a few states, only the owner's signature is needed.

CO-OWNERSHIP

When title to a parcel of real estate is vested in two or more parties such persons or organizations are said to be *co-owners,* or *concurrent owners,* of the property. Each concurrent owner shares in the rights of ownership, possession, and so forth. Several forms of co-ownership exist, each with unique legal characteristics. The forms of co-ownership most commonly recognized by the various states are (1) *tenancy in common;* (2) *joint tenancy;* (3) *tenancy by the entirety;* (4) *community property;* and (5) *partnership property.* Each of these forms will be discussed separately.

Tenancy in Common

When a parcel of real estate is owned by two or more people as *tenants in common,* each of the owners holds an undivided interest in severalty; that is, *each owner's fractional interest is held just as though he or she*

Figure 4.1 Tenancy in Common

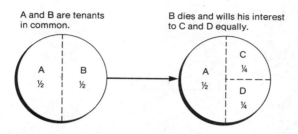

were a sole owner. There are two important characteristics of a **tenancy in common.**

First the ownership interest of a tenant in common is an *undivided interest.* This means that although a tenant in common may hold a one-half or one-third interest in a property, it is impossible to distinguish physically which specific half or third of the property he or she owns. The deed creating a tenancy in common can state the fractional interest held by each co-owner; but if no fractions are stated and two people hold title to the property as co-owners, each has an undivided one-half interest. Likewise, if five people hold title, each would own an undivided one-fifth interest.

Second, each owner holds his or her undivided interest in severalty and can sell, convey, mortgage, or transfer that interest without consent of the other co-owners. Upon the death of a co-owner, his or her undivided interest passes to heirs or devisees according to the deceased's will (see Figure 4.1). The interest of a deceased tenant in common does not pass to another tenant in common unless the surviving co-owner is an heir, devisee, or purchaser. In many states, the spouse of a married tenant in common is generally required to sign a deed to a purchaser in order to release the spouse's dower or homestead rights.

When two or more people acquire title to a parcel of real estate and the deed of conveyance does not identify the form of tenancy created, then by operation of law, the grantees usually acquire title as tenants in common. However, if the conveyance is made to a husband and wife with no further explanation, this presumption may not apply. In some states, a conveyance made to a husband and wife creates tenancy by the entireties; in others, community property; and in at least one state, a joint tenancy. Therefore, it is important to know the legal interpretation of such a situation under your particular state's law.

Figure 4.2   Joint Tenancy with Right of Survivorship

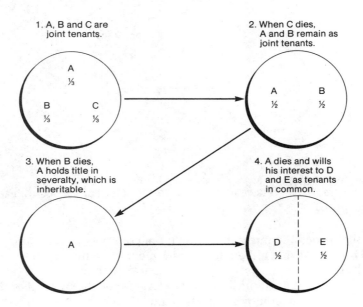

Joint Tenancy

A **joint tenancy** is an estate, or unit of interest, in land owned by two or more persons, and is based on unity of ownership. *Only one title exists,* and it is vested in a unit made up of two or more persons. The death of one of the joint tenants does not destroy the unit. It only reduces by one the number of persons who make up the owning unit. The remaining joint tenants receive the interest of the deceased tenant by *right of survivorship* (see Figure 4.2).

This right of survivorship is one of the distinguishing characteristics of joint tenancy. As each successive joint tenant dies, the surviving joint tenants acquire the interest of the deceased joint tenant. The last survivor takes title in severalty, and upon such person's death, the property goes to his or her heirs or devisees. Some form of joint tenancy is recognized by most states.

How joint tenancies are created.   A joint tenancy can be created only by grant or purchase (through a deed of conveyance) or by devise (giving the property by will). It cannot be implied or created by operation of law. The conveyance must specifically state the intention to create a joint tenancy, and the grantees or devisees must be explicitly identified as joint tenants. For example, typical wording in a conveyance creating a joint tenancy would be "to *A* and *B* as joint tenants and not as tenants in common." A number of states, however, have abolished automatic right of survivorship as a distinguishing characteristic of joint tenancy. In these states, the conveyance to two or more parties as joint tenants must explicitly indicate the intention to create the right of survivorship in order for that right to exist. In such cases, appropriate wording might be "to *A* and *B* and to the survivor of them, his or her heirs and assigns, as joint tenants."

Four unities are required to create a valid joint tenancy:

1. Unity of *time*—all joint tenants acquire their interest at the same time.

2. Unity of *title*—all joint tenants acquire their interest by the same instrument of conveyance.

3. Unity of *interest*—all joint tenants hold equal ownership interests.

4. Unity of *possession*—all joint tenants hold an undivided interest in the property.

These four unities are present when title is acquired by one deed, executed and delivered at one time, and conveys equal interests to all the grantees who hold undivided possession of the property as joint tenants.

In many states, if real estate is owned in severalty by a person who wishes to create a joint tenancy between himself or herself and others, the owner will have to convey the property to an intermediary (usually called a nominee or straw man), and the nominee must convey it back to them naming all the parties as joint tenants in the conveyance.

Some states have eliminated this "legal fiction" by allowing an owner in severalty to execute a deed to himself or herself and others "as joint tenants and not as tenants in common," thereby creating a valid joint tenancy without the actual presence of the four unities. However, in a few states that have tried to accomplish this same result, the courts have held that such a conveyance creates a wholly new estate, usually referred to as an *estate of survivorship*.

How joint tenancies are terminated. A joint tenancy is destroyed when any of the previously mentioned essential unities has been destroyed. Thus, while a joint tenant has the legal right to convey his or her

Figure 4.3   Combination of Tenancies

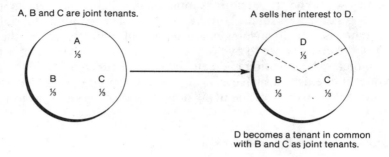

A, B and C are joint tenants.

A sells her interest to D.

D becomes a tenant in common
with B and C as joint tenants.

interest in the joint property, such a conveyance destroys the unity of interest and, consequently, voids the joint tenancy insofar as the interest conveyed is concerned. For example, if Lee, Sims, and Tobey hold title as joint tenants and Lee conveys her interest to Wilbur, then Wilbur will own an undivided one-third interest as a sole owner while Sims and Tobey will continue to own the undivided two-thirds interest as joint tenants. Wilbur will be a *tenant in common* with joint tenants Sims and Tobey (see Figure 4.3).

Joint tenancies may also be terminated by operation of law, such as in bankruptcy or foreclosure sale proceedings. In addition, in states in which a mortgage is a conveyance of land subject to reconveyance upon payment of the debt, a joint tenant who mortgages his or her interest without the other joint tenants joining in the mortgage will destroy the existing joint tenancy (by removing that interest from the joint tenancy).

Most state laws hold that there is no dower in joint tenancy. Thus, business associates can hold title to a parcel of real estate as joint tenants, and their spouses, if any, are not required to join in a conveyance in order to waive dower rights.

Termination of co-ownership by partition suit.   Tenants in common or joint tenants who wish to terminate their co-ownership of real estate may file in court a suit to *partition* the land. The right of partition is a legal way to dissolve a co-ownership when the parties do not voluntarily agree to its termination. If the court determines that the land cannot actually be divided into parts, it will order the real estate sold and divide the proceeds of the sale among the co-owners in accordance with their fractional interests.

Tenancy by the Entirety

A **tenancy by the entirety** is a *special joint tenancy between husband and wife.* The distinguishing characteristics of this tenancy are (1) the owners must be husband and wife; (2) the owners have rights of survivorship; (3) during the owners' lives, title can be conveyed only by a deed *signed by both parties* (one party cannot convey a one-half interest); and (4) there is generally no right to partition. Under early common law, a husband and wife were held to be one legal person—the wife's legal personality was merged with that of her husband. As a result, real estate owned by a husband and wife as tenants by the entireties is considered as being held by one indivisible legal unit.

Like a joint tenancy, a tenancy by the entirety *cannot be created by operation of law;* it must be created by grant, purchase, or devise. Most states now require that the intention to create a tenancy by the entirety be specifically stated in the original document, or a tenancy in common usually results.

A number of states recognize tenancy by the entirety in some form. If you live in a state that recognizes this form of tenancy, you should thoroughly research the legal aspects of this form of ownership.

Community Property Rights

The concept of community property originated in Spanish law rather than English common law and has been adopted by eight western and southern states. (Arizona, California, Idaho, Louisiana, Nevada, New Mexico, Texas, and Washington; Wisconsin recognizes "marital property" that is similar to community property.) There are many variations among the community property laws of these states. Community property laws are based on the concept that a husband and wife, rather than merging into one entity, are equal partners. Thus, any property acquired during a marriage is considered to be obtained by mutual effort. Community property states recognize two kinds of property.

Separate property is that which is owned solely by either spouse before the marriage or is acquired by a gift or inheritance after the marriage. Such separate, or exempted, property also includes any property purchased with separate funds after the marriage. Any income earned from a person's separate property generally remains part of his or her separate property. Property classified as sole and separate can be mortgaged or conveyed by the owning spouse without the signature of the nonowning spouse.

Community property consists of all other property, real and personal, acquired by either spouse during the marriage. Any conveyance or encumbrance of community property requires the signature of both spouses. Upon the death of one spouse, the survivor automatically owns one-half of the community property. The other half is distributed according to the deceased's will. If the deceased died without a will, the other half is inherited by the survivor or by the deceased's other heirs, depending upon state law.

Examples of Types of Co-Ownership

To clarify the concepts of co-ownership further, note the following four examples of co-ownership arrangements.

1. A deed conveys title to *A* and *B*. The intention of the parties is not stated, so generally ownership as tenants in common is created. If *A* dies, her one-half interest will pass to her heirs or according to her will.

2. A deed conveying title one-third to *C* and two-thirds to *D* creates a tenancy in common, with each owner having the fractional interest specified.

3. A deed to *H* and *W* as husband and wife may create a tenancy by the entirety, community property, or other interests between the husband and wife as provided by state law.

4. A conveyance of real estate to two persons (not husband and wife) by such wording as "to *Y* and *Z*, as joint tenants and not as tenants in common" may create a joint tenancy ownership. Upon the death of *Y*, the title to the property will usually pass to *Z* by right of survivorship. However, in those states that do not recognize the right of survivorship, additional provisions are required, such as "and to the survivor and his or her heirs and assigns."

A combination of interests can exist in one parcel of real estate. For example, while *M* and spouse may hold title to an undivided one-half as joint tenants, the relation between the owners of the two half interests is that of tenants in common.

TRUSTS

In most states, title to real estate can be held in a trust. To create a trust, the **trustor**, or person originating the trust, must convey title to the real es-

Figure 4.4   Trust Ownership

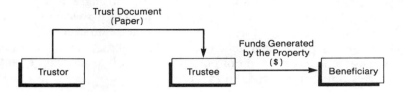

tate involved to a **trustee,** who will own the property for one or more persons or legal entities, called **beneficiaries.** The trustee is a **fiduciary,** or one who acts in confidence or trust, and has a special, legal relationship with the beneficiary or beneficiaries. The trustee can be either an individual or a corporation, such as a trust company. The trustee has only as much power and authority as is given by the instrument that creates the trust. Such an instrument may be a trust document, will, trust deed, or deed in trust (see Figure 4.4). Trusts may be classified as (1) living and testamentary trusts, (2) land trusts, or (3) business trusts.

Living and Testamentary Trusts

Property owners may provide for their own financial care and/or that of their families by establishing a trust. Trusts may be created by agreement during a property owner's lifetime (living) or established by will after his or her death (testamentary). The individual makes an agreement with a trustee (usually a corporate trustee) by which the trustor conveys his or her assets (real and/or personal), or a certain portion of them, to the trustee with the understanding that the trustee will assume certain duties. These duties include the care and investment of the trust assets to produce an income. After payment of operating expenses and trustee's fees, this income is paid to or used for the benefit of the beneficiaries. Trusts may continue for the lifetime of the beneficiaries, or the assets can be distributed when the children reach certain predetermined ages.

Land Trusts

A few states permit the establishment of land trusts in which real estate is the only asset. As in all trusts, legal title to the property is conveyed to a trustee, and the beneficial interest is in the beneficiary, who in case of land trusts is usually the trustor.

One of the distinguishing characteristics of a land trust is that the public records do not indicate the beneficiary's identity. A land trust agreement is executed by the trustor and trustee. Under this agreement, the trustee deals with the property only upon the beneficiary's written direction. While the beneficial interest in the trust real estate is considered to be *personal property,* the beneficiary retains management and control of the property and has the right of possession as well as the right to any income from it or proceeds from its sale.

Usually only individuals create land trusts, but corporations as well as individuals can be beneficiaries. A land trust generally continues for a definite term, such as 20 years. At the expiration of the term, if the beneficiaries do not extend the trust term, the trustee is usually obligated to sell the real estate and distribute the net proceeds to the beneficiaries.

Business Trust

This form of trust, when used in a real estate syndicate operation, is usually designated a real estate investment trust (REIT). Much like mutual fund operations, real estate investment trusts pool an assortment of large-scale income-producing properties (apartment buildings, shopping centers, and so forth) and sell shares to investors. The distinguishing benefit of a REIT is that the trust is exempt from corporate taxation of profits as long as it distributes at least 95 percent of its income to the investors. In order to meet the requirements to form a REIT, a group of 100 or more members must hold shares in the trust.

BUSINESS ENTITY OWNERSHIP OF REAL ESTATE

A business entity is an organization like a corporation that exists independently of the people who are its members. Ownership by a business organization makes it possible for many people to hold an interest in the same parcel of real estate. There are various ways in which investors may be organized to finance a real estate project. Some provide for the real estate to be owned by the entity itself; others provide for direct ownership of the real estate by the investors. Business organizations may be categorized as (1) partnerships, (2) corporations, or (3) syndicates. The purchase or sale of real estate by any business organization involves complex legal questions, and legal counsel is usually required.

Partnerships

A partnership is an association of *two or more persons who carry on a business as co-owners* and share the profits and losses of the business. There are two kinds of partnerships, general and limited. In a **general partnership,** all partners participate to some extent in the operation and management of the business and may be held personally liable for business losses and obligations. A **limited partnership** includes general partners as well as limited, or silent, partners. The business is run by the general partner or partners. The limited partners do not participate, and each can be held liable for the business's losses only to the extent of his or her investment. The limited partnership is a popular method of organizing investors in a real estate project.

Generally, a partnership is not a legal entity, and technically, under common law, a partnership cannot own real estate. Title must be vested in the names of the partners as individuals in a tenancy in common or joint tenancy, and not in the name of the firm. Most states, however, have adopted the Uniform Partnership Act, under which realty may be held in the partnership name, and the Uniform Limited Partnership Act, which establishes the legality of the limited partnership form and also provides that realty may be held in the partnership name.

General partnerships are dissolved and must be reorganized if one partner dies, withdraws, or goes bankrupt. In a limited partnership, the agreement creating the partnership may provide for the continuation of the organization upon the death or withdrawal of one of the partners.

Corporations

A corporation is an artificial person, or legal entity, created under the authority of the laws of the state from which it receives its charter. Because the corporation is a legal entity, real estate ownership by a corporation is an *ownership in severalty.* A corporation is managed and operated by its board of directors. A corporation's charter sets forth the powers of the corporation, including its right to buy and sell real estate after passage of a *resolution to that effect by its board of directors.* Some charters permit a corporation to purchase real estate for any purpose; others limit such purchases to land that is needed to fulfill its corporate purpose.

As a legal entity, a corporation may exist in perpetuity. The death of one of the officers or directors does not affect title to property that is owned by the corporation.

Individuals participate, or invest, in a corporation by purchasing stock certificates. Since stock is *personal property,* stockholders do not have a direct ownership interest in real estate owned by a corporation. Each stockholder's liability for the corporation's losses is usually limited to the amount of his or her investment.

One of the main disadvantages to corporate ownership of income property is that the *profits are subject to double taxation.* As a legal entity, a corporation must file an income tax return and pay tax on its profits. In addition, portions of the remaining profits distributed to stockholders as dividends are taxed again as part of the stockholders' individual incomes.

A *subchapter S corporation,* also known as a *tax-option corporation,* combines the features of corporate and partnership ownership. Under this arrangement, the Internal Revenue Service permits stockholders to enjoy the limited liability of a corporation while avoiding double taxation of profits.

Participation in a subchapter S corporation is usually limited to a maximum of 35 stockholders. The corporation's profits are not taxed at the corporation level, but are taxed at the shareholder's level. On an individual income tax return, each stockholder declares his or her share of the profits as personal income, and can also deduct a proportional share of corporate losses.

Limited Liability Companies

The *limited liability company* (LLC) is a new form of business entity that combines features of limited partnerships and corporations. The members of an LLC enjoy the limited liability offered by a corporation, the tax advantages of partnership, and flexible management without the complicated requirements of S corporations or limited partnerships. The structure and establishment of an LLC varies from state to state. LLCs may be attractive for small groups of owners to hold real property.

Syndicates

Generally speaking, a **syndicate** is a *joining together of two or more persons or firms* in order to make and operate a single real estate investment. A syndicate, also known as a *joint venture,* is not in itself a legal entity; however, it may be organized into a number of ownership forms, including co-ownership (tenancy in common, joint tenancy), partnership, trust, or corporation. A syndicate differs from a real estate investment trust in that a syndicate is formed to purchase one particular property; a REIT is formed to pool a number of different properties. Furthermore, joint ventures differ from partnerships in that syndicates are characterized by a time limitation resulting from the fact that the investors do not intend to establish a permanent relationship.

Real estate licensees are required by state law to possess a separate securities license to be able to sell ownership shares in an investment syndicate.

OCCUPANT OWNERSHIP OF APARTMENT BUILDINGS

During the first half of this century, the country's population grew rapidly and was concentrated in the large urban areas. This population concentration led to multiple-unit housing—highrise apartment buildings in the center city and low-rise apartment complexes in adjoining suburbs. Initially, these buildings were occupied by tenants under the traditional rental system. However, the traditional urge to "own a part of the land," together with certain tax advantages that accrue to such ownership, gave rise at first to **cooperative** ownership and, more recently, to the **condominium** form of ownership of multiple-unit buildings.

Cooperative Ownership

Under the usual cooperative arrangement, title to the land and the building is held by a corporation (or land trust). The building management sets a price for each apartment in the building. Each purchaser of an apartment in the building receives stock in the corporation when he or she pays the agreed-upon price for the apartment. The purchaser then becomes a stockholder of the corporation and, by virtue of that stock ownership, receives a *proprietary lease* to his or her apartment for the life of the corporation. Real estate taxes are assessed against the corporation as owner. The mortgage is signed by the corporation, creating one lien on the entire parcel of real estate. Taxes, mortgage interest and principal, and operating and maintenance expenses on the property are shared by the tenant-shareholders in the form of monthly assessments similar to rent. Thus, while the tenant-owners do not actually own an interest in real estate (they own stock, which is personal property), for all practical purposes they control the property through their stock ownership and their voice in the management of the corporation.

Under the cooperative form of ownership, an apartment occupant is not subject to annual rent increases or to the possibility of losing possession through the landlord's refusal to renew the annual lease. In an effort to maintain a congenial group of occupants in the building, the bylaws of the corporation generally provide that each prospective purchaser of a proprietary lease must be approved by an administrative board.

One disadvantage of cooperative ownership became particularly evident during the depression years and must still be considered. This is the possibility that if enough owner-occupants become financially unable to make prompt payment of their monthly assessments, the corporation may be forced to allow mortgage and tax payments to go unpaid. Through such defaults, the entire property could be ordered sold by court order in a foreclosure suit. Such a sale would usually destroy all occupant-shareholders' interests. Another disadvantage is that some cooperatives provide that a tenant-owner can only sell his or her interest back to the cooperative at the original purchase price, so that the cooperative gains any profits made on the resale. These limitations have diminished the attraction of this form of ownership and resulted in greater popularity for the condominium form of ownership.

Condominium Ownership

The condominium form of occupant ownership of apartment buildings has gained increasing popularity in recent years. Condominium laws, often called horizontal property acts, have been enacted in every state. Under these laws, the occupant-owner of each unit holds a *fee simple title* to his or her apartment, as well as a specified share of the indivisible parts of the building and land, known as the *common elements*. The individual unit owners in a condominium own these common elements together as *tenants in common*. State law usually limits this relationship among unit owners in that there is *no right to partition*.

The condominium form of ownership is usually used for apartment buildings. These may range from freestanding highrise buildings to townhouse arrangements. The common elements include such items as the land, walls, hallways, elevators, stairways, and roof. In some instances, particularly with townhouse developments, lawns and such recreational facilities as swimming pools, clubhouses, tennis courts, and golf courses may also be considered common elements. In addition, the condominium form of ownership is used for other types of properties, such as office buildings or large buildings that contain offices and shops as well as residential units.

To create a condominium, a condominium declaration and a plat of subdivision are recorded in the county in which the real estate is located. The condominium declaration sets out the rights and obligations of each unit owner. The plat subdivides the land and building into apartment units, describes each apartment by unit number, and assigns a fractional share of the common elements to each unit. The apartments are described by the airspace that each actually occupies (the boundary planes extending through the floor, walls, and ceiling). The total of all units and their respective shares of common elements represents the entire parcel of real estate.

Once the property is established as a condominium, each unit becomes a separate parcel of real estate. A condominium unit may be owned in fee simple and be held by one or more people in any type of ownership or tenancy recognized by state law.

Real estate taxes are collected on each unit as an individual property. Default in the payment of taxes or a mortgage loan by a unit owner may result in a foreclosure sale of that owner's unit, but will not affect the interests of the other unit owners.

The condominium property is generally administered by an association of unit owners, established by the condominium declaration. The association is responsible for the maintenance, repair, cleaning, sanitation, and insurance of the common elements and structural portions of the property. These expenses are paid for by the unit owners in the form of monthly assessments collected by the owners' association.

Timeshare ownership.   Through a specialized classification of condominium ownership, called *timesharing,* multiple purchasers can own undivided interests in real estate (usually a building or condominium unit located in a resort or vacation area) with a right to use the facility for a fixed or variable time period, generally one or two weeks each year. This timeshared ownership may take one of two forms:

1. *Fee simple ownership*—unlimited ownership in the property for a specified time period each year. This ownership may be sold, leased, or otherwise treated as any other real property owned in fee.

2. *Right-to-use*—ownership limited to a specific length of time, usually anywhere from 15 to 50 years. This ownership may likewise be sold, leased, or otherwise treated like other real property owned in fee, but only for the specified right-to-use period.

The purchaser's initial cost will depend upon the time of year desired, the location and popularity of the resort, and the form of ownership, with right to use generally being somewhat less expensive. Annual maintenance fees are also charged and include the general management and staffing of the project, hazard and liability insurance premiums, record-keeping, maid service, structural maintenance, and pool and golf club services—plus fees for the replacement of furniture, linens, and glassware.

Developers of multiple properties may provide an exchange service for a fee. Resort exchange companies have also become popular in order to permit owners to trade their time and location for alternative spots at other resorts, literally around the world, depending on the value of what they own.

SUMMARY

Sole ownership, or *ownership in severalty,* indicates that title is held by one person or entity. Title to real estate can be held concurrently by more than one person, a situation called *co-ownership.*

Under a *tenancy in common,* each party holds an undivided interest in severalty. An individual owner may sell his or her interest. Upon death, an owner's interest passes to his or her heirs or according to the will. There are no special requirements for creating this interest. When two or more parties acquire title to real estate, they will hold title as tenants in common unless there is an expressed intention otherwise. *Joint tenancy* indicates two or more owners with the right of survivorship. The intention of the parties to establish a joint tenancy with right of survivorship must be clearly stated. In some states, the four unities of *time, title, interest,* and *possession* must be present; other states have eliminated this legal requirement by statute.

Tenancy by the entirety, in those states where it is recognized, is actually a joint tenancy between husband and wife. It gives the husband and wife the right of survivorship in all lands acquired by them *jointly* during marriage. Both must sign the deed for any title to pass to a purchaser. *Community property* rights exist only in certain states and pertain only to land owned by husband and wife. Usually the property acquired by joint efforts during the marriage is community property, and one-half is owned by each spouse. Properties acquired by a spouse before the marriage and through bequests, death, or gifts after the marriage are termed *separate property.* Community property is a statutory right and, as a result, each state that has established the rights of community property has also defined those specific rights.

Real estate ownership may also be held *in trust.* In creating a trust, title to the property involved is conveyed to a *trustee* under a living or testamentary trust, a land trust, or a business trust.

Various types of business organizations may own real estate. A *corporation* is a legal entity and holds title to real estate in severalty. While a *partnership* is technically not a legal entity, the Uniform Partnership Act and the Uniform Limited Partnership Act, adopted by most states, enable a partnership to own property in the partnership's name. A *syndicate* is an association of two or more persons or firms to make a single investment in real estate. Many syndicates are joint ventures and are organized for only a single project. A syndicate may be organized as a co-ownership, trust, corporation, or partnership.

Cooperative ownership of apartment buildings indicates title in one entity (corporation or trust), which must pay taxes, mortgage interest and principal, and all operating expenses. Reimbursement comes from shareholders or beneficiaries through monthly assessments. Shareholders have proprietary, long-term leases entitling them to occupy their apartments. Under *condominium ownership,* each occupant-owner holds fee simple title to his or her apartment unit plus a share of the common elements. Each owner receives an individual tax bill and may mortgage his or her unit as desired. Expenses to operate the building are collected by an association of unit owners through monthly assessments.

QUESTIONS

Please complete all of the questions before turning to the Answer Key.

1. Real estate owned by a corporation to provide housing for its stockholders is called a(n)

    a.   condominium.   c.   timeshare.
    b.   cooperative.   d.   investment trust.

2. Under the cooperative form of ownership, which of the following would a purchaser receive?

    a.   A proprietary lease   c.   A real estate tax bill
    b.   A warranty deed   d.   A title insurance policy

3. All of the following are forms of concurrent ownership EXCEPT

    a.   tenancy in common.   c.   tenancy by the entirety.
    b.   joint tenancy.   d.   severalty.

4. All of the following would be included in a condominium form of ownership EXCEPT

    a.   a stockholder's agreement.
    b.   an association of unit owners.
    c.   fee simple title to the individual units.
    d.   concurrent ownership of the common elements.

5. Which of the following is an ownership arrangement in which property is held by one party for the benefit of another?

    a.   Trust   c.   Joint tenancy
    b.   Condominium   d.   Tenancy by the entirety

6. All of the following are unities of joint tenancy EXCEPT

    a.   time.   c.   interest.
    b.   title.   d.   survivorship.

7. The person for whom a trust is created is called the

    a.   trustor.   c.   beneficiary.
    b.   trustee.   d.   fiduciary.

8. Under the terms of a trust, the trustee is the person who will

    a. create the trust.
    b. benefit from the trust.
    c. own the property for another.
    d. act in a nonfiduciary capacity.

9. Under a joint tenancy, a joint tenant may perform all of the following acts EXCEPT

    a. devise the interest.   c. encumber the interest.
    b. sell the interest.   d. file a partition suit.

10. Tenancy in common provides for all of the following EXCEPT

    a. unequal interests among the owners.
    b. the right to freely convey any interest.
    c. an individual deed for each of the property owners.
    d. the right of one owner to encumber the entire property.

11. A married couple could own real property in all of the following manners EXCEPT

    a. in severalty.   c. in community property.
    b. as joint tenants.   d. as tenants by the entirety.

12. Regarding tenancy by the entirety, all of the following statements are true EXCEPT

    a. the owners must be married to each other.
    b. the owners have rights of survivorship.
    c. both owners must sign a deed conveying the property.
    d. either owner may file a suit to partition.

13. Individual ownership of a single unit with common ownership of the common areas would be found in a

    a. partnership.   c. cooperative.
    b. corporation.   d. condominium.

14. One of the principal disadvantages of corporate ownership of income property is

    a. personal liability for its profits and losses.
    b. inability to transfer its stock.
    c. double taxation of all of its profits.
    d. control by the general partner.

15. A large group of investors wishing to invest in real estate will usually use which of the following entities?

    a. General partnership   c. Corporation
    b. Limited partnership   d. Joint venture

16. All of the following can be created by operation of law EXCEPT

    a. severalty ownership.   c. tenancy in common.
    b. joint tenancy.   d. community property.

17. Which of the following statements is characteristic of joint tenancy?

    a. There are multiple deeds, one for each joint tenant.
    b. There is a distinct right of survivorship.
    c. The last remaining owner continues as a joint tenant.
    d. Only married couples can hold title as joint tenants.

18. If tenants in common cannot agree on a voluntary method of terminating their co-ownership, an action may be filed in court to legally dissolve the co-ownership. This action is known as a

    a. foreclosure suit.   c. partition suit.
    b. quiet title action.   d. separation action.

19. All of the following types of ownership are available to corporations EXCEPT

    a. severalty ownership.   c. tenancy in common.
    b. joint tenancy.   d. trust ownership.

20. Under which of the following types of ownership can the interests of the owners be unequal?

    a. Tenancy by the entirety   c. Tenancy in common
    b. Community property   d. Joint tenancy

5:   Title Records

KEY TERMS

abstract of title	recording
actual notice	security agreement
certificate of title	subrogation
chain of title	suit to quiet title
constructive notice	title insurance
evidence of title	Torrens system
marketable title	Uniform Commercial Code
priority	

Before purchasing a parcel of real estate, a buyer should always ascertain that the seller is able to convey a marketable title by making a thorough search of the public records regarding the property. Generally, a **marketable title** is one that is free from significant defects such as undisclosed liens and encumbrances. A buyer of a marketable title can generally be assured against having to defend the title after purchasing the property. An unmarketable title does not mean that the property cannot be transferred under any circumstances; rather, it means that certain defects in the title may limit or restrict ownership of the property.

For the protection of real estate purchasers, owners, taxing bodies, and creditors, public records are maintained by designated officials as required by state laws. Such records help to officially establish real estate ownership, give notice of encumbrances, and establish the priority of liens. Records involving taxes, special assessments, ordinances, and zoning and building codes also fall into this category. These records are administered by local officials, such as the recorder of deeds, county clerk, county treasurer, city clerk, and clerks of various courts of record.

Questions of marketable title must be raised by the buyer prior to accepting a deed to the property. The present owner of the real estate undoubtedly purchased his or her interest from a previous owner, so the same questions regarding the kind and condition of title have been inquired into many times in the past. All states have enacted a Statute of Frauds, which requires that instruments affecting interests in real estate must be in writing in order to be enforceable. In addition, state laws require owners or parties with interests in real estate to file in public records all documents affecting their interest in order to give legal, public, and constructive notice to the world of their interest. Thus, the public records should reveal the condition of a title and a purchaser should be able to rely on a search of such public records.

PUBLIC RECORDS AND RECORDING

The placing of documents in the public record is known as **recording.** Under each state's *recording acts,* all written instruments affecting any estate, right, title, or interest in real estate must be recorded in the county where the property is located. Recording acts give notice of the various interests of all parties in title to a parcel of real estate. From a practical point of view, the recording acts give legal priority to the interests that are recorded first.

To be eligible for recording, an instrument must be drawn and executed in accordance with local recording statutes. The prerequisites for recording are not uniform. For example, many states require that the names be typed below the signatures on a document and that the instrument be acknowledged before a notary public or other authorized officer. In a few states, the instrument must also be witnessed. Many states require that the name and address of the attorney or other authorized person who prepared the document appear on it as well.

Notice

Through the common law doctrine of *caveat emptor* ("let the buyer beware"), the courts charge a prospective real estate buyer or mortgagee (lender) with the responsibility of inspecting the property and searching the public records to learn of the possible interests of other parties. **Constructive notice** is a presumption of law that makes the buyer responsible for learning this information. The information is available for buyers or lenders to learn, so they are responsible for learning it (see Figure 5.1). Failure to do so is no defense for not knowing of a right or interest, because the recording of that interest in the public records or possession of the real estate gives notice to the world, or constructive notice, of various rights in the property.

Figure 5.1 Notice

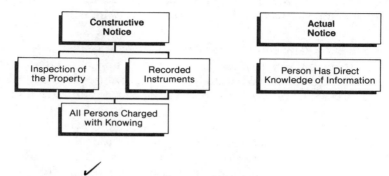

Constructive notice, or what a buyer is charged with knowing, is distinguished from **actual notice,** or what the person actually knows (see Figure 5.1). Once an individual has searched the public records and inspected the property, he or she has actual notice, or direct knowledge, of the information. If an individual has actual knowledge of information concerning a parcel of real estate and this knowledge can be proven, he or she cannot rely on a lack of constructive notice, such as an unrecorded deed or an owner who is not in possession. For example, Bill Wilson mortgages his land to Jane Fry, and she fails to record the mortgage. Wilson later mortgages the same land to Edgar Morse, who knows of the earlier mortgage. In this case, Morse is charged with actual knowledge of the existing mortgage, so his mortgage becomes secondary to Fry's mortgage, which has a prior claim on the property.

Real estate taxes and special assessments are direct liens on specific parcels of real estate and *need not be recorded* in the recorder's office, as they are already considered to be matters of public record. Real estate taxes and special assessments are direct liens on specific parcels of real estate. They are considered matters of public record already and, thus, will not be found in the recorder's office. Real estate taxes are collected by and filed at the county tax collector's office. Special assessments may be found at the municipal clerk's or city clerk's office.

Other liens, such as inheritance taxes and franchise taxes, are placed by statutory authority against all real estate owned either by a decedent at the time of death or by a corporation at the time the franchise tax became a lien; these are not recorded.

Foreign language documents.   Deeds or mortgages written in a foreign language, although valid between the parties to a transaction, usually do not impart constructive notice when recorded. Recorded documents must be in the English language. An official translation by a consulate of the country in which the language is used, when attached to a foreign language document, may meet state recording requirements.

Priorities.   Many complicated situations can arise that affect the **priority** of rights in a parcel of real estate. For example, a purchaser may receive a deed and take possession, but not record the deed. By taking possession of the property, the purchaser gives constructive notice that he or she has an interest in the land. Such a purchaser's rights would be considered superior to those of a subsequent purchaser who acquired a deed from the original owner at a later date and recorded the deed but did not inspect the property to determine who was in possession. How the courts will rule in any situation depends, of course, on the specific facts of the case. A real estate licensee must recognize that these are strictly legal questions that the parties should refer to their lawyers.

Chain of Title

State statutes generally require that recorded instruments must be within what is known as the chain of title so that a search of the grantor-grantee indexes will reveal the document and the interest. The **chain of title** shows the record of ownership of the property over a period of time, depending on the length of the title search. Thus, if a mortgage executed by a purchaser were recorded prior to the recording of the deed of conveyance to the purchaser (who would become the mortgagor), there would be no notice to the world because the mortgage is not within the chain of title. The mortgage could become constructive notice if the deed to the mortgagor were dated *on or before* the date of the mortgage. When recorded, the mortgage would be properly indexed by date to show that the purchaser obtained title on or before the date on which he or she executed the mortgage.

In the United States, chains of title in colonial states frequently date back to a grant from the king of England. In those states admitted to the union after the formation of the United States, the deeds of conveyance in the chain of title generally stem from the *patent* issued by the U.S. government. In a few states, such as Louisiana and Texas, chains of title date back to a point prior to the acquisition and annexation, respectively, of the states by the federal government.

Through the chain of title, it should be possible to trace the ownership of the property from its origin to its present owner. If this cannot be done, there is a gap in the chain. In such cases, it is usually necessary to establish ownership by a court action called a **suit to quiet title.**

EVIDENCE OF TITLE

When dealing with an owner of real estate, a purchaser or lender requires satisfactory proof that the seller is the owner and has good title to the property. The owner is generally required to produce documentary proof called **evidence of title.** There are four forms of title evidence: (1) abstract of title and lawyer's opinion; (2) title insurance policy; (3) Torrens certificate; and (4) certificate of title.

Sometimes the question is raised as to whether a recorded warranty deed or other conveyance is evidence of title. A deed conveys the interest of the grantor, but even though it is a warranty deed, it contains no proof of the kind or condition of the grantor's title. The only effective proof is one of the evidences of title based upon an adequate search of the public records to determine the ownership interests and condition of the title.

Abstract of Title and Lawyer's Opinion

An **abstract of title** is a brief history of the instruments appearing in the county record that affect the title to the parcel in question. The legal description of the property is in the caption of the abstract. Abstracts usually commence with the government's ownership of the land. They usually consist of several sections, or continuations, each of which covers a specific period of time. It is therefore necessary for each succeeding section of the abstract to begin with a search of the public record from a *date immediately following* the date of the previous section to eliminate the possibility of a gap in the abstract.

When an abstract is first prepared or is continued, the abstractor lists and summarizes each instrument in chronological order along with information relative to taxes, judgments, special assessments, and the like. The abstractor concludes with a certificate indicating which records were examined and when, and then signs the abstract. An abstractor must exercise due care, since he or she can be liable for negligence for any failure to include or accurately record all pertinent data. However, an abstractor does *not* pass judgment on or guarantee the condition of the title.

In a sale of land, the seller's attorney usually orders the abstract continued to cover the current date. When the abstract has been completed, it is submitted to the purchaser's attorney, who examines the entire abstract from the origin of that title. Following his or her detailed examination, the purchaser's attorney evaluates all the facts and material in order to prepare a written report, called an *attorney's opinion of title,* on the condition of the ownership.

As transfers of title have accumulated through the years, abstracts of title have become voluminous; and the time needed by an attorney to examine an abstract has therefore increased. Because of the need to examine the record carefully and the number of potential errors, many attorneys have filed court suits to protect their clients' claims to title. These quiet suits are filed to secure court decrees to clear up actual or potential defects in the abstracts.

In many ways, the title evidence system of abstract examination and opinion and the certification of title by attorneys (to be explained later) were imperfect and open to objection. For example, it is difficult to detect forged deeds or other documents or false statements, including incorrect marital information and transfers involving incompetent parties or minors. Also, an honest mistake could be made against which the owner of real estate had no recourse. To provide a purchaser with protection against this type of error and to give insurance along with defense of the title, title insurance became available.

Title Insurance

A **title insurance** policy is a contract by which a title insurance company agrees, subject to the terms of its policy, to indemnify (compensate or reimburse) the insured (the owner, mortgagee, or other interest holder) against loss sustained as a result of defects in the title other than those exceptions listed in the policy. The title company agrees to defend, at its own expense, any lawsuit attacking the title if the lawsuit is based on a defect in title the policy insures against.

A seller seeking to obtain a title insurance policy as evidence of his or her ownership makes application to the title insurance company. The person agrees to pay a certain fee, and the title company makes an examination of the title records and agrees to insure against certain undiscovered defects. Which defects the title company will insure against depends upon the type of policy it issues (see Table 5.1). A *standard coverage* policy usually insures against defects found in the public records plus such matters as forged documents, documents of incompetent grantors, incorrect marital statements, and improperly delivered deeds. An *extended coverage* policy generally includes all the protection of a standard policy plus additional protection to cover risks that may be discovered only through inspection of the property, inquiries of persons in actual possession of the

Table 5.1   Owner's Title Insurance Policy

Standard Coverage	Extended Coverage	Not Covered by Either Policy
1. Defects found in public records	Standard coverage plus defects discoverable through:	1. Defects and liens listed in policy
2. Forged documents	1. Property inspection, including unrecorded rights of persons in possession	2. Defects known to buyer
3. Incompetent grantors		3. Changes in land use brought about by zoning ordinances
4. Incorrect marital statements	2. Examination of survey	
5. Improperly delivered deeds	3. Unrecorded liens not known of by policyholder	

land, or examination of a correct survey. The company does not agree to insure against defects in or liens against the title that are found by the title examination and listed in the policy.

Upon completion of the examination, the title company usually issues a report of title, or a commitment to issue a title policy. This describes the policy that will be issued and includes the following: (1) the name of the insured party; (2) the legal description of the real estate; (3) the estate, or interest, covered; (4) a schedule of all exceptions, consisting of encumbrances and defects found in the public records; and (5) conditions and stipulations under which the policy is issued. An *owner's policy usually excludes coverage* against the following exceptions: unrecorded documents, unrecorded defects of which the policyholder has knowledge, rights of parties in possession, and questions of survey. Under the contract, the title insurance company provides for the defense of the title at its own expense as well as for the payment of any claims against the property if the title proves to be defective. This is subject, of course, to the conditions and stipulations of the policy itself.

Like any other contract of insurance, a title insurance policy contains the names of the insured parties and the consideration (the premium, which in the case of title insurance is paid once for the life of the policy). The maximum loss for which the company may be liable cannot exceed the face amount of the policy. When a title company makes a payment to settle a claim covered by a policy, the company acquires, by right of **subrogation,** all the remedies and rights of the insured party against anyone responsible for the settled claim.

Title companies issue various forms of title insurance policies, the most common of which are the *owner's, mortgage, leasehold,* and *certificate of sale* title insurance policies. As the names indicate, each of these policies is issued to insure specific interests. For example, a mortgage title insurance policy insures a mortgage company or lender that it has a valid first lien against the property. A leasehold title insurance policy insures a lessee that he or she has a valid lease. A certificate of sale policy is issued to a purchaser in a court sale and insures the purchaser's interest in any property sold under a court order.

In some jurisdictions, statewide groups of attorneys have formed corporations or business trusts with funds to guarantee the titles covered by opinions rendered by member attorneys. These guaranteed titles offer protection from hidden defects that may be present in the public records.

ALTA.   The American Land Title Association (ALTA) is an association of approximately 2,000 land title companies throughout the nation, organized to maintain professional standards and ethics within the industry. Some ALTA members provide abstracts only; others issue title insurance; still others act as agents for title insurance underwriting companies. Many members are both abstractors and title insurance agents. ALTA members use uniform ALTA title insurance forms, designed by the association to achieve a satisfactory measure of standardization within the industry.

The Torrens System

Under the **Torrens system** of land registration, all records regarding a parcel of real estate are filed with a public official generally called the *registrar of titles.* Developed in 1857 by an Australian, Sir Robert Torrens, the land registration system bearing his name is currently used in ten of the 50 states. In the states that have adopted the Torrens system of land title registration, the established recording system is also still in use. Registration of land titles is not compulsory. The owner of real estate may continue under the standard recording system or may register title under the Torrens system.

Although the provisions of the Torrens system are not uniform, the procedures to be followed in registering land titles in the various states are substantially the same. A written application to register a title to real estate is made with the county court of the county in which the real estate is located. The application lists all facts regarding the title and liens against the real estate. A court hearing is held, and all persons known to have an interest in the real estate are given notice. Any interested person may appear to present a claim. If the applicant proves that he or she is the owner, the court enters an order for the registration of the real estate, and the registrar of titles is directed to register the title.

Transferring title under the Torrens system.   Once real estate is registered under the Torrens system, a **certificate of title** is prepared by the registrar, who keeps the original and issues a duplicate to the owner of the property. At the same time, the owner signs a signature card for protection against forgery.

When a title to registered property is conveyed, mortgaged, or encumbered in any way, the owner delivers the deed, mortgage, or other instrument to the grantee, mortgagee, or encumbrancer, together with the owner's duplicate certificate of title. The registrar receives these documents, checks the signatures with the signature cards, and, when everything is in order, registers the transfer or document. A deed to Torrens registered land does not pass ownership; only the registration transfers title to the grantee. If such property is mortgaged, the registrar of titles issues a duplicate certificate of title to the lender (mortgagee). Torrens registrars usually retain all original documents delivered to them for registration.

The Torrens original certificate of title in the registrar's office reveals the owner of the land and all mortgages, judgments, and similar liens. This record exists because a mortgage judgment or other lien is not valid until it has been entered on the original title certificate by the registrar.

Furthermore, under most state land registration acts, title to Torrens registered property *can never be acquired by possession through a claim of adverse possession.* This gives an owner of registered land protection against such claims.

Under the Torrens system, it may be necessary to verify the payment of taxes and special assessments, since the county treasurer and county collector are not usually required to register their tax liens on the Torrens records. Usually judgments or decrees of the federal courts need not be registered, so a separate federal court search is required. Searches for unpaid taxes, special assessments, and federal liens can be obtained from the registrar of titles.

A certificate of title is issued for Torrens registered properties instead of a title insurance policy. The certificate does not set forth a dollar amount. In the event that a claim or suit regarding title arises, the holder of a Torrens certificate must defend the suit at his or her own expense and be able to prove loss in order to gain a right to any compensation from the registrar. The registrar of titles is not required to go to court to defend a certificate holder. State laws generally provide that a certificate holder who has suffered a loss as a result of a registrar's mistake may file a claim against an indemnity fund established to compensate persons financially for bona fide losses due to registrar errors.

Some state laws permit an owner to remove the title to his or her land from Torrens registration; in other states, land once registered must remain under the Torrens system.

Certificate of Title

In some localities, a certificate of title prepared by an attorney is used, not an abstract. The attorney examines the public records and issues a certificate of title that expresses his or her opinion of the validity of the title. The certificate identifies the title owner and gives the details of all liens and encumbrances against the title. It is not a title insurance policy and does not carry the full protection such a policy carries.

UNIFORM COMMERCIAL CODE

The **Uniform Commercial Code** is a codification of commercial law that has been adopted in practically all states. While this code generally does not apply directly to real estate, it has replaced state laws relating to chattel mortgages, conditional sales agreements, and liens on chattels, crops, or items that are to become fixtures. Some states have made variations in the details of the code's provisions.

To create a security interest in a chattel, including chattels that will become fixtures, the code requires the use of a **security agreement.** A short notice of this agreement is called a *financing statement.* It includes the legal description of the real estate involved, and it *must be filed in the recorder's office.* The recording of the financing statement constitutes notice to subsequent purchasers and mortgagees of the security interest in chattels and fixtures on the real estate. Many mortgagees require the signing and recording of a financing statement when the mortgaged premises include chattels or readily removable fixtures (such as major appliances) as part of the security for the mortgage debt.

Article 6 of the code covers *bulk transfers,* which are defined as the sale of the major part of the materials, supplies, merchandise, or other inventory of an enterprise not made in the ordinary course of the transferor's business. The purpose of this article is to outlaw the fraud perpetrated when a businessperson who is in debt sells the business and all stock in trade (personal property) and disappears without having paid his or her creditors. Under Article 6, a bulk sale does not give the purchaser of such goods a clear title unless the purchaser complies with the article's requirements, which include giving notice of the sale to the seller's creditors.

SUMMARY

The recording acts give legal, public, and *constructive notice* to the world of interests in real estate. The recording provisions have been adopted to create system and order in the transfer of real estate. Without the recording acts, it would be virtually impossible to transfer real estate from one party to another. The interests and rights of the various parties in a particular parcel of land must be recorded so that such rights will be legally effective against third parties who do not have knowledge, or notice, of them. In addition, such records show whether or not a seller is conveying *marketable title*. Marketable title is generally one that is so free from significant defects that the purchaser can be assured that the title will not have to be defended.

Possession of real estate is generally interpreted as notice of the rights of the person in possession. *Actual notice* is firsthand knowledge acquired directly by a person.

Four forms of title evidence are commonly in use throughout the United States: (1) *abstract of title and lawyer's opinion;* (2) *owners' title insurance policy;* (3) *Torrens certificate;* and (4) *certificate of title.*

A deed of conveyance is evidence that a grantor has conveyed his or her interest in real estate to the grantee, but does not prove that the grantor had good and merchantable title—even though the interest is conveyed via a warranty deed containing implied promises or warranties. The grantee should seek evidence of good title prior to accepting any conveyance.

Each form of title evidence bears a date and is evidence up to and including that date. All forms of title evidence show the previous actions that affect the title. A Torrens certificate, title insurance policy, certificate of title, and abstract of title relate to a title based on its history. Each must be *later dated,* or continued or reissued, to cover a more recent date.

Under the Uniform Commercial Code, security interests in chattels must be recorded using a *security agreement* and *financing statement.* The recording of a financing statement gives notice to purchasers and mortgagees of the security interests in chattels and fixtures on the specific parcel of real estate.

QUESTIONS

Please complete all of the questions before turning to the Answer Key.

1. In the process of defending a claim against an insured's property, the title insurance company may acquire certain rights that previously belonged to the insured through the concept of

    a. priority.
    b. subrogation.

    c. registration.
    d. defeasance.

2. Which of the following statements is true regarding the transfer of title under the Torrens system?

    a. All original documents are returned by the registrar to the grantor.
    b. Title to property registered under the Torrens system cannot be acquired through adverse possession.
    c. Title passes to the grantee when the deed is delivered to him or her.
    d. Property may not be simultaneously recorded under the county recorder system.

3. An individual who goes to the county recorder's office and examines the records there has what kind of notice?

    a. Notice of default
    b. Inquiry notice

    c. Actual notice
    d. Constructive notice

4. A condensed history of all of the documents that affect a particular parcel of land is called a(n)

    a. patent.
    b. title insurance policy.

    c. lawyer's opinion.
    d. abstract of title.

5. The presumption of law that makes the buyer responsible for inspecting the property and searching the public records to ascertain the interests of other parties is called

    a. constructive notice.
    b. actual notice.

    c. subrogation.
    d. *caveat emptor.*

6. The principal purpose of requiring title evidence is to show that the grantor is

   a. legally capable of ownership.
   b. competent and of minimum age.
   c. conveying marketable title.
   d. transferring the property unencumbered.

7. All of the following items would constitute evidence of title EXCEPT a(n)

   a. abstract of title and legal opinion.
   b. title insurance policy.
   c. certificate of title.
   d. warranty deed.

8. *J* gives a deed to a parcel of property to *L*, who does not record the deed but who does move onto the property. Later, *J* gives another deed to the same parcel to *T*, who does record that deed. Who is the owner of the property?

   a. *L*   c. *L* and *T* equally
   b. *T*   d. *J*

9. Where must all documents that affect property ownership be recorded to be effective?

   a. In the state where the grantor resides
   b. In the state where the grantee resides
   c. In the county where the grantor resides
   d. In the county where the property is located

10. All of the following statements regarding the Uniform Commercial Code are true EXCEPT

   a. it usually applies to realty mortgages.
   b. it covers bulk transfers of personalty.
   c. it requires a security agreement or financing statement.
   d. it generally applies to chattel mortgages.

6:

KEY TERMS

assignment	multiple listing
bilateral contract	net listing
contract	novation
equitable title	open listing
escrow	specific performance
exclusive-agency listing	statute of limitations
exclusive-right-to-sell listing	unenforceable contract
executed contract	unilateral contract
executory contract	valid contract
expressed contract	voidable contract
implied contract	void contract

Brokers and salespeople use many types of contracts and agreements in the course of their business. Among these documents are listing agreements, sales contracts, option agreements, installment contracts, leases, and escrow agreements. As discussed elsewhere in the text, state laws generally stipulate that such agreements be in writing.

Before studying the specifics of each individual type of agreement, you must first understand the basic principles of *contract law,* the general body of law that governs the operation of such agreements.

CONTRACT LAW

A **contract** may be defined as a voluntary agreement between legally competent parties to perform or refrain from performing some legal act, which is supported by legal consideration. Simply put, two parties exchange promises: one promises to do or not to do something, in exchange for the promise of a second party to do or not to do something else.

Depending on the situation and the nature or language of the agreement, a contract may be: (1) *expressed* or *implied;* (2) *bilateral* or *unilateral;* (3) *executory* or *executed;* and (4) *valid, void, voidable,* or *unenforceable.* These terms are used to describe the type, status and legal effect of a contract.

Expressed and Implied Contracts

Depending on how a contract is created, it may be expressed or implied. In an **expressed contract,** the parties state the terms and show their intentions in words, either orally or in writing. In an **implied contract,** the agreement of the parties is demonstrated by their acts and conduct.

In the usual agency relationship, a listing agreement is an expressed contract between the seller and broker, and it names the broker as the fiduciary representative of the seller. However, the courts have held that a broker may, under certain circumstances, also create an unwanted implied contract to represent a buyer. For example, a broker took a listing for a residence and began to show the property. One serious prospect told the broker to have a physical inspection of the property made. The broker complied, but hired an unqualified person to do it. The party who bought the property discovered a serious physical defect, and subsequently sued the broker. The court ruled that, in complying with the purchaser's request, the broker had by implication accepted an agency agreement to represent the purchaser. By hiring an incompetent inspector, the broker violated a fiduciary duty to the purchaser under this implied agreement.

Bilateral and Unilateral Contracts

According to the nature of the agreement made, contracts may also be classified as either bilateral or unilateral. In a **bilateral contract,** both parties promise to do something; one promise is given in exchange for another. A real estate sales contract is a bilateral contract because the seller promises to sell a parcel of real estate and deliver title to the property to the purchaser, who promises to pay a certain sum of money for the property.

In a one-sided, or **unilateral contract,** one party makes a promise in order to induce a second party to perform. The second party is not legally obligated to act. However, if the second party does comply, the first party is obligated to keep the promise. For example, a real estate owner signed

Table 6.1   Legal Effects of Contracts

Type of Contract	Legal Effect	Example
Valid	Binding and Enforceable on Both Parties	Agreement Complying with Essentials of a Valid Contract
Void	No Legal Effect	Contract for an Illegal Purpose
Voidable	Valid, but May Be Disaffirmed by One Party	Contract with a Minor
Unenforceable	Valid Between the Parties, but Neither May Force Performance	Certain Oral Agreements

an option agreeing to sell her property to a specific purchaser and not to anyone else if that person decided to purchase the property within the time period stated in the agreement. The purchaser made no promise to perform. The seller is bound to act (sell the property to the buyer) only if the buyer performs (exercises the option to purchase) within the agreed-upon time limit.

Executory and Executed Contracts

A contract may be classified as either executory or executed, depending on whether the agreement is completely performed. An **executory contract** exists when something remains to be done by one or both parties. A fully **executed contract** is one in which both parties have fulfilled their promises and thus performed the contract.

Validity of Contracts

The legal effect of any contract may be described as valid, void, voidable, or unenforceable (see Table 6.1), depending on the circumstances.

A **valid contract** complies with all the essentials of a contract and is binding and enforceable on both parties. A **void contract** is one that has no legal force or effect because it does not meet the essential requirements of a contract. For example, one of the essential conditions in order for a contract to be valid is that it be for a legal purpose; thus, a contract to commit a crime is void.

A **voidable contract** is one that seems to be valid on the surface but may be rejected, or disaffirmed, by one of the parties. A contract agreed to under duress is voidable, as is any contract entered into with a minor. A minor is usually permitted to disaffirm a real estate contract within a reasonable period of time after reaching legal age. A voidable contract is considered to be valid if the party who has the option to disaffirm the agreement does not do so within a reasonable period of time, or as set by statute.

An **unenforceable contract** is also one that seems on the surface to be valid; however, neither party can sue the other to force performance. For example, in many states a listing agreement is invalid, or unenforceable, unless it is in writing and signed by the parties. Unenforceable contracts are said to be "valid as between the parties," because once the agreement has been fully executed, and both parties satisfied, neither would have cause to initiate a lawsuit to force performance.

ESSENTIAL ELEMENTS OF A VALID CONTRACT

The essential elements of a valid real estate contract vary somewhat from state to state. Those elements that are uniformly required are (1) competent parties; (2) mutual assent; (3) consideration; (4) legality of object; and (5) special formality.

Competent Parties

For a contract to be valid, all parties entering into it must have the legal capacity to contract. The buyer and seller must be of legal age and not suffering from a mental handicap that would make them incompetent. In most states, 18 is the legal age to enter into binding contracts. A contract entered into by someone who is under the influence of alcohol or drugs *may be* voidable; a contract with a person who is known to have been judged incompetent by the court *is* void.

Attorneys-in-fact.   Persons acting under the dictates of a properly executed power of attorney may acquire the capacity to contract for another person, provided the power of attorney complies with state law. For example, most states require that the power of attorney be in writing, signed and acknowledged by the principal, and recorded, if the act to be performed is the conveyance of title to real property.

Corporations.   A corporation is considered legally capable of contracting. However, the individual signing on behalf of the corporation must have the authority from the board of directors; such authority is normally granted through a *resolution* by the directors. Plus, some states require that the corporate seal be affixed to all contracts entered into by the corporation.

Partnerships. In a general partnership, each general partner usually has the power to enter into agreements on behalf of the entire partnership. With a limited partnership, *only* the general partners may contract on behalf of the partnership, as limited partners may have only a financial interest in the venture.

Mutual Assent

This element (also known as reality of consent, mutual consent, and mutual agreement) requires that all parties must be mutually willing to enter into the contract and that the contract be signed as the "free and voluntary act" of each party. There must be a "meeting of the minds" between the two parties. The wording of the contract must express all of the agreed-upon terms and must be clearly understood by the parties. (The applicability of the mutual assent element to real estate contracts in particular is discussed later in this chapter.)

To arrive at mutual assent, an *offer and acceptance* must be completed, where an offeror makes an offer to an offeree, who then unconditionally accepts the offer and *communicates that acceptance back to the offeror.* If any terms of the original offer are changed, they constitute a total rejection of the original offer, relieve the original offeror of any liability under the original offer, and bring to life a *counteroffer.*

Misrepresentation, fraud and mistake. There must be no misrepresentation, fraud, or mistake. *Misrepresentation* is an innocent misstatement of a material fact upon which someone relies and which causes that person to suffer damages. *Fraud* is a deliberate misstatement of a material fact with the intent to deceive upon which someone relies and which causes him or her to suffer damages. Fraud may also result from failure to disclose vital information such as latent (hidden) defects. A *mistake* is not poor judgment, nor is it ignorance. It generally involves a mutual misunderstanding in negotiations between the parties or is a mistake of fact, such as a party being confused as to which property is under consideration.

Duress, menace and undue influence. There must be no *duress, menace,* or *undue influence.* To be valid, every contract must be signed as the "free and voluntary act" of each party. *Duress, menace,* and *undue influence* cannot be used to obtain the signatures of the parties to the contract.

Consideration

For a contract to be valid, it must show consideration. In a few states, a seal is sufficient, as described below. The consideration given for the entering into of a contract can be either *good* or *valuable* consideration. *Good consideration* is generally recognized only in transactions between loved ones where it can be established that a relationship of "love and affection" exists. *Valuable consideration* is anything that can be expressed in terms of monetary value, such as money, notes, promises, labor, service, real property, or personal property. Other characteristics of valuable consideration are these: (1) the amount of consideration is relatively unimportant, and (2) the consideration need only be stated in the contract to make the contract binding. Only with an option does the law require that the consideration stated must actually change hands.

Consideration should not be confused with earnest money. While consideration is a component of a contract, *earnest money* is given by the buyer with an offer to purchase to show sincerity and an intent to complete the contract if the seller accepts the offer. Earnest money is usually cash, but it may be any other items of value acceptable to the seller.

Seal.   The sealing of a contract requires the placing of the letters S.E.A.L. or the letters L.S. on the signature lines following each party's signature. Under early common law, a seal took the place of the recital of consideration, but this has been abolished in all but a few states. It is still customary to have a corporation use its corporate seal to indicate that the contract is being executed by its authorized officers or agents.

Legality of Object

To be valid, a contract must contemplate a purpose that is not illegal or against public policy.

Special Formality

A statute of frauds has been enacted in every state. This law requires certain types of contracts to be in writing in order to be enforceable. The statute of frauds requires the following formalities in order to prevent fraudulent proof of a fictitious oral contract (perjury): (1) the signatures of the buyers and sellers; (2) a spouse's signature when necessary to release such marital rights as dower, curtesy, and homestead; (3) an agent's signature for a principal if he or she has proper written authority (power of attorney); (4) the signatures of all co-owners selling the property. The courts hold that written contracts supersede oral contracts if there is a conflict between the two. As a matter of fact, the *parol evidence rule* states that oral agreements, promises, and inducements made by the parties prior to the entering into of a written contract may not be used in court to dispute or contradict some written provision expressed in the contract.

Description of the property. In addition to the aforementioned elements, a valid real estate sales contract must contain an accurate description of the property being conveyed. The property should be identified by street address as well as by legal description.

Performance of Contract

Under any contract, each party has certain rights and obligations to fulfill. The question of when a contract must be performed is an important factor. Many contracts call for a specific time at or by which the agreed-upon acts must be completely performed. In addition, many contracts provide that "time is of the essence." This means that the contract must be performed within the limit specified, and any party who has not performed on time is guilty of a breach of contract.

When a contract does not specify a date for performance, the acts it requires should be performed within a reasonable time. The interpretation of what constitutes a reasonable time will depend upon the situation. Generally, if the act can be done immediately—such as payment of money—it should be performed immediately, unless the parties agree otherwise.

Assignment and Novation

Often after a contract has been signed, one party may want to withdraw without actually terminating the agreement. This may be accomplished through either assignment or novation.

Assignment refers to a transfer of rights and/or duties under a contract. Generally speaking, rights may be assigned to a third party unless the agreement forbids such an assignment. Obligations may also be assigned, but the original obligor remains secondarily liable for them (after the new obligor), unless he or she is specifically released from this responsibility by the other party to the contract. A contract that requires some personal quality or unique ability of one of the parties may not be assigned. Most contracts include a clause that either permits or forbids assignment.

A contract may also be performed by **novation,** or the substitution of a new contract for an existing agreement with the intent of extinguishing the old contract. The new agreement may be between the same parties, or a new party may be substituted for either. The parties' intent must be to discharge the old obligation. The new agreement must be supported by consideration and must conform to all the essential elements of a valid contract. For example, when a real estate purchaser assumes the seller's existing mortgage (see Chapter 11), the lender may choose to release the seller and substitute the buyer as the party primarily liable for the mortgage debt.

Discharge of Contract

A contract may be completely performed, with all terms carried out, or it may be breached (broken) if one of the parties defaults. In addition, there are various other methods by which a contract may be discharged (canceled). These include:

1. *Partial performance* of the terms along with a written acceptance by the person for whom acts have not been done or to whom money has not been paid.

2. *Substantial performance,* in which one party has substantially performed the contract but does not complete all the details exactly as the contract requires. Such performance may be sufficient to force payment with certain adjustments for any damages suffered by the other party.

3. *Impossibility of performance,* in which an act required by the contract cannot be legally accomplished.

4. *Mutual agreement* of the parties to cancel.

5. *Operation of law,* as in the voiding of a contract by a minor, as a result of fraud, the expiration of the statute of limitations, or a contract's being altered without the written consent of all parties involved.

Default—Breach of Contract

A *breach* is a violation of any of a contract's terms or conditions without legal excuse, such as when a seller does not deliver title to the buyer under the conditions stated in the sales contract.

If either party to a real estate sales contract clearly shows by his or her actions that he or she intends to breach the contract, or default, the defaulting party assumes certain burdens and the nondefaulting party has certain rights.

If the seller defaults, the buyer has three alternatives:

1. The buyer may *rescind,* or *cancel,* the contract and recover the earnest money.

2. The buyer may file a court suit, known as an action for **specific performance,** to force the seller to perform the contract (*i.e.,* convey the property).

3. The buyer may *sue the seller for compensatory damages.*

A suit for damages seldom is used in this instance, however, because in most cases the buyer would have difficulty proving the extent of damages.

If the *buyer defaults,* the seller may pursue one of the following courses:

1. The seller may *declare the contract forfeited.* The right to forfeit usually is provided in the terms of the contract, and the seller usually is entitled to retain the earnest money and all payments received from the buyer.

2. The seller may *rescind the contract,* that is, cancel or terminate the contract as if it had never been made. In this case the seller must return all payments the buyer has made.

3. The seller may *sue for specific performance.* This may require the seller to offer, or tender, a valid deed to the buyer to show the seller's compliance with the contract terms.

4. The seller may *sue for compensatory damages.*

Statute of limitations.   Laws in every state allow a specific time limit during which parties to a contract may bring legal suit to enforce their rights (for example, within seven years). Any party who does not take steps to enforce his or her rights within this **statute of limitations** may lose the right to do so.

REAL ESTATE CONTRACTS

As mentioned earlier, the types of written agreements most commonly used by brokers and salespeople are listing agreements, real estate sales contracts, option agreements, installment contracts, leases, and escrow agreements.

Broker's Authority to Prepare Documents

In many states, specific guidelines have been drawn, either by agreement between broker and lawyer associations, by court decision, or by statute, regarding the authority of real estate licensees to prepare documents for their clients and customers. As a rule, a real estate broker is not authorized to practice law—that is, to prepare legal documents such as deeds and mortgages. A broker or salesperson may, however, be permitted to fill in the blanks of preprinted documents (such as sales contracts and leases) approved by the state bar association and/or real estate commission. Inquire with state officials or your local real estate board to determine current authority of real estate licensees to prepare documents.

Listing Agreements

Listing agreements are instruments used by the real estate broker in order to legally represent a principal. (See Figure 6.1 for an example of a typical listing agreement.) They are contracts of employment that establish the rights of the broker as agent of a principal. Often a broker is hired to represent a seller, but is now more frequently asked to represent a buyer.

Under the provisions of each state's broker and salesperson licensing laws, only a broker can act as an agent to list, rent, or sell another person's real estate for a fee. While a salesperson has the authority to list, lease, and sell property as well as to provide other services to the principal, these acts are all done in the name of and on behalf of the broker to whom he or she is licensed, never in the name of the salesperson.

Many states provide that a broker cannot institute a court action to collect a commission unless he or she can prove the existence of an agency and the promise on the part of the principal to pay consideration (a commission) in the event of performance. Both of these requirements can be met by submitting into evidence a written listing agreement, signed by the principal, in which the amount of commission to be paid is clearly stated. Thus, in good practice, all listing agreements should be *in writing* and *state the commission* to be earned by the broker.

All listings should specify a *definite period of time* during which the broker is to be employed. The use of automatic extensions of time in exclusive listings has been discouraged by the courts and outlawed in some states. An example of an automatic extension is a listing that provides for a base period of 90 days and "continuing thereafter until terminated by either party hereto by 30 days' notice in writing."

A listing agreement may be *terminated* by: (1) performance by the broker; (2) expiration of the time period stated in it; (3) abandonment by the broker if he or she spends no time on it; (4) revocation by the owner before the broker performs or spends time or money on it (although the

Figure 6.1 Sample Listing Agreement

Type **ER**

RESIDENTIAL LISTING CONTRACT
EXCLUSIVE AUTHORIZATION AND RIGHT TO SELL

Legal I.D. 740880

THIS IS INTENDED TO BE A LEGALLY BINDING CONTRACT. NO REPRESENTATION IS MADE AS TO THE LEGAL VALIDITY OR ADEQUACY OF ANY PROVISION OR THE TAX CONSEQUENCES THEREOF. IF YOU DESIRE LEGAL OR TAX ADVICE, CONSULT YOUR ATTORNEY OR TAX ADVISOR.

1. **EXCLUSIVE RIGHT TO SELL.** In consideration of the acceptance by the undersigned licensed Arizona real estate broker ("Broker") of the terms of this Listing Contract ("Listing") and Broker's promise to endeavor to effect a sale of the property described below ("Property"), I or we, as owner(s) ("Owner"), employ and grant Broker the exclusive and irrevocable right

commencing on _____ , 19___ , and expiring at 11:59 p.m. on _____ , 19___ , to sell, exchange, option or rent the Property described in Paragraph 2.

2. **THE PROPERTY.** For purposes of this Listing, the "Property" means the real property in _____ County, Arizona described below, plus all fixtures and improvements thereon, all appurtenances incident thereto and all personal property described in Paragraphs 4, 5 and 10.

Legal Description _____

Street Address _____   City/Town _____

3. **PRICE.** The listing price shall be $ _____ , to be paid as described in the Owner's Profile Sheet ("Data Entry Form"), or such other price and terms as are accepted by Owner.

4. **FIXTURES AND PERSONAL PROPERTY.** Except as provided in the Data Entry Form, the Property includes the following fixtures or personal property: All existing storage sheds; heating and cooling equipment; built-in appliances; attached light fixtures and ceiling fans; window and door screens; sun screens; storm windows and doors; towel, curtain and drapery rods; draperies and other window coverings; attached carpeting; attached fireplace equipment; pool and spa equipment (including any mechanical or other cleaning systems); garage door openers and controls; attached TV antennas (excluding satellite dishes); watering systems; fire warning and security systems and fences.

5. **ADDITIONAL PERSONAL PROPERTY AND LEASED EQUIPMENT.** The Property includes additional personal property and excludes leased equipment as described in the Data Entry Form.

6. **ACCESS AND LOCKBOX.** Owner ☐ does ☐ does not authorize Broker to install and use a lockbox containing a key to the Property. Owner acknowledges that a lockbox and any other keys left with or available to Broker will permit access to the Property by Broker, Broker's subagents and buyers' agents, with or without potential purchasers, even when Owner is absent. Owner acknowledges that neither the Arizona Regional Multiple Listing Service ("ARMLS"), nor any Board or Association of REALTORS®, nor any broker is insuring Owner against theft, loss or vandalism resulting from any such access. Owner is responsible for obtaining appropriate insurance. If the Property is occupied by someone other than Owner, Owner will provide to Broker the occupant's written permission for the installation of the lockbox and the publication and dissemination of the occupant's name and telephone number.

7. **HOME PROTECTION PLAN.** Owner acknowledges that home protection plans are available and that such plans may provide additional protection and benefits to Owner and any purchaser of the Property. Owner ☐ does ☐ does not agree to provide at his expense a home protection plan for the purchaser that will be effective at the close of escrow.

8. **AGENCY RELATIONSHIPS.** Owner understands that Broker is Owner's agent with respect to this Listing. Owner understands that Broker may also want to serve as a buyer's agent in connection with the purchase of the Property. In that event, Broker would be serving as the agent for both Owner and a potential purchaser. Since Owner does not wish to limit the range of possible purchasers at this time, Owner agrees to work with Broker to resolve any potential agency conflicts that may arise.

9. **COMPENSATION TO BROKER.** Owner agrees to compensate Broker as follows:

   a. **RETAINER.** Broker acknowledges receipt of a non-refundable retainer fee of _____ payable to Broker for initial counseling, consultation and research.

   b. **SALE COMMISSION.** If Broker produces a ready, willing and able purchaser in accordance with this Listing, or if a sale, option or exchange of the Property is made by Owner or through any other agent, or otherwise, during the term of this exclusive listing, for services rendered, Owner agrees to pay Broker a commission of _____ . The same amount of commission shall be payable to Broker if, without the consent of Broker, the Property is withdrawn from this Listing, otherwise withdrawn from sale, or transferred or conveyed by Owner.

   c. **RENTAL COMMISSION.** Owner agrees not to rent the Property during the term of this Listing without Broker's prior knowledge and consent. If the Property is rented, Owner agrees to pay Broker a commission on rentals, including renewals and holdovers, of _____

   d. **PURCHASE BY RENTER.** If during the terms of such rental, including any renewals or holdovers, or within _____ days after its termination, the tenant, or any of such tenant's heirs, executors, or assigns shall buy the Property from Owner, the commission described in Paragraph 9(b)shall be deemed earned by and payable to Broker.

   e. **AFTER EXPIRATION.** After the expiration of this Listing, the same commission, as appropriate, shall be payable, if a sale, exchange, option, or rental is made by Owner to any person to whom the Property has been shown or with whom Owner or any broker has negotiated concerning the Property during the term of this Listing, (1) within _____ days after the expiration of this Listing, unless the Property has been listed on an exclusive basis with another broker, or (2) during the pendency, including the closing, of any purchase contract or escrow relating to the Property that was executed or opened during the term of this Listing, or (3) with respect to any sale covered by Paragraph 9 (d).

   f. **FAILURE TO CLOSE.** If completion of the sale is prevented by default of Owner, or with the consent of Owner, the entire commission shall be paid directly by Owner. If the earnest deposit is forfeited for any other reason, Owner shall pay a brokerage fee equal to the lesser of one-half of the earnest deposit or the full amount of the commission.

   g. **PAYMENT FROM ESCROW.** Owner instructs the escrow company to pay all such compensation to Broker in cash as a condition to closing or upon cancellation of the escrow, and to the extent necessary, irrevocably assigns to Broker all money payable to Owner at the closing or cancellation of the escrow.

   h. **OTHER BROKERS.** Owner authorizes Broker to cooperate with other brokers and to divide all such compensation with other brokers in any manner acceptable to Broker.

   i. **NO LIMITATION.** Nothing in this Listing shall be construed as limiting applicable provisions of law relating to when commissions are earned or payable.

10. **ADDITIONAL TERMS.** _____

11. THE TERMS AND CONDITIONS ON THE REVERSE SIDE HEREOF PLUS ALL INFORMATION ON THE DATA ENTRY FORM ARE INCORPORATED HEREIN BY REFERENCE.

COMMISSIONS PAYABLE FOR THE SALE, LEASING OR MANAGEMENT OF PROPERTY ARE NOT SET BY ANY BOARD OR ASSOCIATION OF REALTORS® OR MULTIPLE LISTING SERVICE OR IN ANY MANNER OTHER THAN BY NEGOTIATION BETWEEN THE BROKER AND THE CLIENT.

BY SIGNING BELOW, OWNER ACKNOWLEDGES THAT HE HAS READ, UNDERSTANDS AND ACCEPTS ALL TERMS AND PROVISIONS CONTAINED HEREIN AND THAT HE HAS RECEIVED A COPY OF THIS LISTING.

Owner's Signature _____   Mo/Da/Yr _____   Owner's Signature _____   Mo/Da/Yr _____

Print Name of Owner _____   Phone _____   Print Name of Owner _____   Phone _____

Street _____   City/Town _____   State _____   Zip _____

In consideration of Owner's representations and promises in this Listing, Broker agrees to endeavor to effect a sale, exchange, option or rental in accordance with this Listing and further agrees to file this Listing for publication by a local Board or Association of REALTORS® and dissemination to the users of ARMLS.

Broker's Listing Office _____   Phone _____

By: _____   Date: _____
    Signature

Copyright© December 1991 by Arizona Regional Multiple Listing Service   For Use With Data Entry Forms Number 1, 2 and 3

For Broker's office use only:

Broker's File/Log No. _____   Manager's Initials _____   Broker's Initials _____   Date _____

BROKER

Figure 6.1 (continued)

12. **MULTIPLE LISTING SERVICE.** Broker is a member of a local Board or Association of REALTORS®, which is a shareholder or client of ARMLS. This listing information will be provided to ARMLS to be published and disseminated to its users. Broker is authorized to offer subagency and to appoint subagents and to report the sale, exchange, option or rental of the Property, and its price, terms and financing, to a local Board or Association of REALTORS® for dissemination to authorized ARMLS users and to the public and for use by authorized ARMLS users.

13. **ROLE OF BROKER.** Owner acknowledges that Broker is not responsible for the custody or condition of the Property or for its management, maintenance, upkeep or repair.

14. **TITLE.** Owner agrees to furnish marketable title by warranty deed and an Owner's policy of title insurance in the full amount of the purchase price.

15. **DOCUMENTS.** In connection with any sale of the Property, Owner consents to the use of the standard form of purchase contract used by Broker and all other standard documents used by the escrow and title companies.

16. **COOPERATION BY OWNER.** Owner agrees to make available to Broker and prospective purchasers all data, records and documents pertaining to the Property. Owner authorizes Broker, and any other broker who is a subagent of Broker, to preview and show the Property at reasonable times and upon reasonable notice and agrees to commit no act which might tend to obstruct Broker's performance hereunder. If the Property is occupied by someone other than Owner, Owner will provide to Broker the occupant's written consent to the showing of the Property. Owner also authorizes Broker to permit a broker who is a buyer's agent to preview and show the Property at such times and on such terms as are acceptable to Owner or Broker. Owner shall not deal directly with any prospective purchaser of the Property during the term of this Listing and shall refer all prospective purchasers to Broker during the term hereof.

17. **SIGN.** Until the close of escrow, Broker is authorized to place Broker's appropriate signs on the Property.

18. **WARRANTIES BY OWNER.** Owner represents and warrants:

    a. **CAPACITY.** Owner has the legal capacity, full power and authority to enter into this Listing and consummate the transactions contemplated hereby on his own behalf or on behalf of the party he represents, as appropriate.

    b. **CORRECT INFORMATION.** All information concerning the Property in this Listing, including the Data Entry Form relating to the Property, or otherwise provided by Owner to Broker or to any prospective purchaser of the Property is, or will be at the time made, and shall be at the closing, true, correct and complete. Owner agrees to notify Broker promptly if there is any material change in such information during the term of this Listing.

    c. **CONDITION OF PROPERTY.** Except as otherwise provided in this Listing, Owner warrants that, at the earlier of possession or the close of escrow: the roof will have no known leaks; all heating, cooling, mechanical, plumbing, watering and electrical systems and built-in appliances will be in working condition; if the Property has a swimming pool and/or spa, the motors, filter systems, cleaning systems and heaters, if so equipped, will be in working condition; and the Property shall otherwise be in substantially the same condition as on the effective date of this Listing. Owner agrees to maintain and repair the Property, as necessary, to fulfill the warranties described in this Paragraph 18(c). Prior to the close of escrow, Owner shall grant the purchaser or purchaser's representatives reasonable access to enter and inspect the Property for purposes of satisfying purchaser that the Property is as warranted by Owner.

    d. **PAYMENTS FOR IMPROVEMENTS AND SEWER.** Prior to the close of escrow, payment in full will have been made for all labor, professional services, materials, machinery, fixtures or tools furnished within the 120 days immediately preceding the close of escrow in connection with the construction, alteration or repair of any structure on or improvement to the Property. The information in this Listing, if any, regarding connection to a public sewer system, septic tank or other sanitation system is correct.

    e. **AVAILABILITY OF UTILITIES.** Owner 's obligated to deliver all utility service equipment and appliance hook-ups in a condition that will enable the purchaser to connect all utility services that are available on the effective date of this listing without repairs or additional improvement expense.

    f. **ADVERSE INFORMATION.** Owner will disclose to any potential purchaser and Broker all information, excluding opinions of value, and all material facts known to him concerning adverse conditions or latent defects in, or affecting the Property.

    g. **WOOD INFESTATION REPORT.** Owner will, at his expense, place in escrow a wood infestation report by a qualified, licensed pest control operator, which, when considered in its entirety, indicates that all residences and buildings attached to the Property are free from evidence of current infestation and damage from wood destroying pests or organisms. Owner agrees to pay up to one percent of the purchase price for the extermination of pests and organisms, the treatment of the Property, the repair of the damage caused by infestation and the correction of any conditions conducive to infestation. If such costs exceed one percent of the purchase price, (1) the purchaser may elect to cancel the sale unless Owner agrees in writing to pay all of such costs, and (2) Owner may elect to cancel the sale unless the purchaser agrees in writing to accept the Premises together with the one percent that the Owner has agreed to pay.

    h. Broker is hereby relieved of any and all liability and responsibility for everything stated in this Paragraph 18.

19. **INDEMNIFICATION.** Owner agrees to indemnify and hold Broker, all Boards or Associations of REALTORS®, ARMLS, and all other brokers harmless against any and all claims, liability, damage or loss arising from any misrepresentation or breach of warranty by Owner in this Listing, any incorrect information supplied by Owner and any facts concerning the Property not disclosed by Owner, including without limitation, any facts known to Owner relating to adverse conditions or latent defects.

20. **OTHER POTENTIAL SELLERS.** Owner understands that other potential sellers may make offers to sell, or may sell, lease, exchange or option property similar to the Property through Broker. Owner consents to any agency representation by Broker of such other potential sellers before, during, and after the expiration of this Listing and understands that the Property may not be presented or shown to every potential purchaser encountered by Broker.

21. **ATTORNEYS' FEES.** In any action or proceeding to enforce any provision of this Listing, or for damages sustained by reason of its breach, the prevailing party shall be entitled to receive from the other party reasonable attorneys' fees, as set by the court or arbitrator and not by a jury, and all other related expenses, such as expert witness fees, fees paid to investigators and court costs. Additionally, if any Broker reasonably hires an attorney to enforce the collection of any commission payable pursuant to this Listing, and is successful in collecting some or all of such commission without commencing any action or proceeding, Owner agrees to pay such Broker's reasonable attorneys' fees and costs and Owner also agrees to pay interest on all compensation and other amounts owed or due to Broker from the time due until paid in full.

22. **DEPOSITS.** Owner authorizes Broker to accept earnest deposits on behalf of Owner and to issue receipts for such earnest deposits.

23. **DISPUTE RESOLUTION.** Owner agrees to request from the purchaser of the Property written confirmation that any dispute or claim arising from or relating to the purchase contract, the breach of the purchase contract or services provided in relation to the purchase contract shall be submitted to mediation in accordance with the Rules and Procedures of the REALTORS® Homesellers/Homebuyers Dispute Resolution System, if such system is reasonably available to the parties. Subject to certain exclusions, disputes subject to mediation shall include, in part, representations made by Owner, purchaser or any broker or other person or entity in connection with the sale, purchase, financing or condition or any other aspect of the Property, including without limitation any allegation of concealment, misrepresentation, negligence or fraud. If the purchaser of the Property consents to mediation, Owner agrees to submit disputes as described in such Rules and Procedures to mediation.

24. **RECOMMENDATIONS.** If Broker recommends a builder, contractor, escrow company, title company, pest control service, appraiser, lender, home inspection company, home warranty company or any other person or entity to Owner for any purpose, such recommendation shall be independently investigated and evaluated by Owner, who hereby acknowledges that any decision to enter into any contractual arrangement with any such person or entity recommended by any Broker will be based solely upon such independent investigation and evaluation. Owner understands that said contractual arrangement may result in a commission or fee to Broker.

25. **FIRPTA.** If applicable, Owner agrees to complete, sign and deliver to escrow company a certificate indicating whether Owner is a foreign person or non-resident alien pursuant to the Foreign Investment in Real Property Tax Act of 1980 (FIRPTA).

26. **SUBSEQUENT OFFER.** Once there is a fully executed purchase contract with respect to the Property, Owner waives his right to receive any subsequent offer with respect to the Property until after forfeiture by the offeror or other nullification of the contract.

27. **ENTIRE AGREEMENT** This Listing, the Data Entry Sheet and any attached exhibits and any addenda or supplements signed by the parties, shall constitute the entire agreement between Owner and Broker and supersede any other written or oral agreements between Owner and Broker. This Listing can be modified only by a writing signed by Owner and Broker.

28. **EQUAL HOUSING OPPORTUNITY.** Properties will be presented in compliance with federal, state and local fair housing laws and regulations.

29. **TIME OF ESSENCE.** Time is of the essence in the performance of the obligations contained in this Listing.

30. **COUNTERPARTS AND FACSIMILE.** This Listing may be executed in any number of counterparts by the parties hereto. All counterparts so executed shall constitute one Listing binding upon all parties hereto, notwithstanding that all parties do not sign the same counterpart. A facsimile copy of the entire Listing which indicates that the Listing was fully executed shall be treated as an original Listing.

31. **CONSTRUCTION OF LANGUAGE AND GOVERNING LAW.** The language of this Listing shall be construed according to its fair meaning and not strictly for or against either party. Words used in the masculine, feminine or neuter shall apply to either gender or the neuter, as appropriate. All singular and plural words shall be interpreted to refer to the number consistent with circumstances and context. The headings or captions of paragraphs in this Listing are for convenience and reference only and do not define, limit or describe the scope or intent of this Listing or the provisions of such paragraphs. If this Listing is used for an exchange, option, or lease instead of a sale of the Property, all language in this Listing relating to the sale of property shall be construed to apply as appropriate, to an exchange, option or lease. For example, Owner shall be deemed to be Exchanger, Optionor, or Landlord respectively. This Listing shall be governed by the laws of the State of Arizona.

Source: Reproduced with permission and copyrighted 1991 by Arizona Regional Multiple Listing Service, Inc.

owner may be liable for damages); (5) cancellation by the broker or by mutual consent; (6) death or insanity of either party; (7) destruction of the property; (8) condemnation of the property; (9) the revocation, suspension, or expiration of the listing broker's license; or (10) transfer of title by operation of law, as in a bankruptcy.

The basic forms of listing agreements are (1) open listing, (2) exclusive-agency listing, and (3) exclusive-right-to-sell listing.

Open listing. In an **open listing,** the seller retains the right to employ any number of brokers to act as his or her agents. These brokers can act simultaneously, and the seller is obligated to pay a commission only to that broker who successfully produces a ready, willing, and able buyer. If the seller personally sells the property without the aid of any of the brokers, he or she is not obligated to pay any of them a commission. If a broker was in any way a procuring cause in the transaction, however, he or she may be entitled to a commission. A listing contract generally creates an open listing unless wording that specifically provides otherwise is included.

Exclusive-agency listing. In an **exclusive-agency listing,** only one broker is specifically authorized to act as the exclusive agent of the principal. The seller under this form of agreement retains the right to sell the property himself or herself without obligation to the broker. Under such circumstances, the seller is not obligated to pay a commission to the broker unless the broker was the procuring cause of the sale.

Exclusive-right-to-sell listing. In an **exclusive-right-to-sell listing,** one broker is appointed as the sole agent of the seller and is given the exclusive right, or authorization, to represent the seller in marketing the property and finding a purchaser. Under this form of contract, the seller gives up the right to find a buyer for the property himself or herself and thereby avoid paying the broker's commission. Regardless of who procures the buyer, the broker is entitled to receive a commission from the seller. Among brokers, the exclusive-right-to-sell listing generally is the preferred type.

Multiple-listing contracts. While not a specific form of listing agreement unto itself, multiple-listing contracts are used by brokers who are members of a **multiple-listing** organization, which consists of a group of brokers within an area who agree to share their listings.

The multiple-listing agreement is, in effect, an exclusive-agency or exclusive-right-to-sell (usually the latter) with an additional authority and obligation given to the listing broker to distribute the listing to other brokers who belong to the multiple-listing organization. The contractual obligations among the member brokers of a multiple-listing organization may differ. Most provide that upon sale of the property, the commission be divided between the listing broker and selling broker (as a subagent for the listing broker). The terms for division of the commission are negotiable between the brokers.

Under most multiple-listing contracts, the broker who secures the listing is not only authorized but usually obligated to turn over the listing to his or her multiple-listing organization within a definite period of time so it can be distributed to the other member brokers. The length of time during which the listing broker can offer the property exclusively without notifying the other member brokers varies widely.

A multiple listing offers advantages to both the broker and the seller. The broker develops a sizable inventory of properties to be sold and is assured of a portion of the commission if he or she lists the property or participates in its sale. The seller also gains under this form of listing agreement, because all members of the multiple-listing organization work to sell his or her property.

Net listing.   A **net listing** is based on the amount of money the seller will receive if the property is sold. The seller's property is listed (under one of the previously discussed types of listings) for this net amount and the broker is free to offer the property for sale at any price higher than the listing price. If the property is sold, the broker pays the seller only the net amount for which the property was listed. This type of listing is outlawed in some states, and is not recommended in most of the other states. The question of fraud is frequently raised because of uncertainty over the sales price set or received by the broker. If a seller offers a net listing, it is recommended that the licensee suggest the property be listed for a full sales price that includes a specified commission.

Sales Contracts

A contract for the sale of real estate (see Figure 6.2) sets forth all details of the agreement between a buyer and seller for the purchase and sale of a parcel of real estate. Depending on the state or locality, this agreement may be known as an *offer to purchase, contract of purchase and sale, earnest money agreement, deposit receipt,* or other variation of these terms. Whatever the contract is called, when it has been prepared and signed by the purchaser, it is an offer to purchase the subject real estate. Later, if the document is accepted and signed by the seller, it then becomes a contract of sale.

Every sales contract requires at least two parties, a seller and a buyer. The same person cannot be both buyer and seller, as a person cannot legally contract with himself or herself. The contract of sale is the most important document in the sale of real estate, because it sets out in detail the agreement between the buyer and seller and establishes both parties' legal rights and obligations. It is more important than the deed itself, because *the contract, in effect, dictates the contents of the deed.* Therefore, once the deed is prepared and delivered from the grantor to the grantee, there is no need for the contract to exist. Through the process of *merger,* when the deed is delivered the contract "merges" into the deed and ceases to exist. This means that neither the buyer nor the seller can ever go back to the contract to enforce any covenant contained in it. Every sales contract merges into the deed upon delivery unless the contract contains a *survival clause.* This clause provides, as the name implies, that the contract will survive the closing of the transaction and not merge into the deed. With the inclusion of the survival clause, either party can enforce any covenant in the contract even after the deed has been delivered.

Details to be included in a real estate sales contract are the price, terms, legal description of the land, kind and condition of the title, form of deed the seller will deliver, kind of title evidence required, who will provide title evidence, and how defects in the title, if any, are to be eliminated. The contract must state all the terms and conditions of the agreement and spell out all contingencies. Any items of personal property (drapes, carpeting, appliances, etc.) that are to be included in the sale should be detailed in the agreement. In situations where the terms of a contract are vague and one party sues the other based on one of these terms, the courts may refuse to make a contract for the parties. The real estate broker must be aware of the responsibilities and legal rights of the parties to a sale and ensure that an adequate contract is prepared.

In a few localities, it is customary to prepare a shorter document, known as a *binder,* for the purchaser to sign. This document states the essential terms of the purchaser's offer and acknowledges receipt of his or her deposit. It also provides that upon the seller's acceptance and signing of the binder, the parties agree to have a more formal and complete contract of sale drawn up by an attorney. Throughout the country, a binder receipt may be used in any situation in which the details of the transaction are too complex for the standard sales contract form.

Figure 6.2   Sample Real Estate Sales Contract

RESIDENTIAL
REAL ESTATE PURCHASE CONTRACT AND RECEIPT FOR DEPOSIT

THE PRINTED PORTION OF THIS CONTRACT HAS BEEN APPROVED BY THE ARIZONA ASSOCIATION OF REALTORS≠. THIS IS INTENDED TO BE A BINDING CONTRACT. NO REPRESENTATION IS MADE AS TO THE LEGAL VALIDITY OR ADEQUACY OF ANY PROVISION OR THE TAX CONSEQUENCES THEREOF. IF YOU DESIRE LEGAL OR TAX ADVICE, CONSULT YOUR ATTORNEY OR TAX ADVISOR

RECEIPT

1. **Received From:** _____ ("Buyer")
2. **Title:** Buyer **will** take title as: ☐ Determined before Close of Escrow   ☐ Community Property   ☐ Joint Tenants with Right of Survivorship
   ☐ Sole and Separate Property   ☐ Tenants in Common   ☐ Other:
3. **Earnest Money Deposit:** Earnest money shall be held by Broker named in Line 7 until offer is accepted, subject to prior sale. Upon acceptance, Broker is
4. authorized to deposit the earnest money with the escrow company to which the check is payable. If the check is payable to Broker, Broker may deposit in
5. Broker's trust account or endorse the check without recourse and deposit it with a duly licensed escrow company. All earnest money is subject to collection
6. and is considered to be part of the purchase price for the Premises described below.

   a. Amount   b. Form of   ☐ Personal Check   c. Deposited ☐ Broker's Trust Account
   of Deposit $ _____   Earnest Money: ☐ Other: _____   With: ☐ Escrow Company: _____

7. **Received By:** _____
      Firm Name   Agent's Signature   Mo/Da/Yr

OFFER

8. **Property Description & Offer:** Buyer agrees to purchase the real property and all fixtures and improvements thereon and appurtenances incident thereto,
9. plus personal property described below (collectively the "Premises")

10. Property Address: _____   Assessor's#: _____
11. City: _____   County: _____   AZ, Zip Code: _____
12. Legal Description: _____

13. **Fixtures and Personal Property:** All existing storage sheds; heating and cooling equipment; built-in appliances; light fixtures; ceiling fans; window and
14. door screens; sun screens; storm windows and doors; towel, curtain and drapery rods; draperies and other window coverings; attached carpeting; attached
15. fireplace equipment; pool and spa equipment (including any mechanical or other cleaning systems); garage door openers and controls; and attached TV
16. antennas, excluding satellite dishes, shall be left upon and included with the Premises.

17. **Additional Personal Property Included:** _____
18. **Fixtures and Leased Equipment NOT Included:** _____

19. **Addenda:** ☐ Gov't. Financing Addendum ☐ Financing Addendum ☐ Mediation Addendum ☐ Addendum: _____

20. $ _____   **Full purchase price**, payable as follows:
21. $ _____   Earnest deposit as indicated above.
22. $ _____
23. $ _____
24. _____
25. _____
26. _____
27. _____

28. **Assumption of Existing Loans:** The balance of any encumbrance being assumed is approximate. Any difference shall be reflected in the
29. ☐ Cash down payment   ☐ Seller Carryback ☐ Other: _____   Buyer shall reimburse Seller for any impounds transferred to Buyer.

30. **Close of Escrow:** Seller and Buyer will comply with all terms and conditions of this Contract and close escrow on or before _____
31. Seller and Buyer hereby agree that close of escrow shall be defined as recordation of the documents. If escrow does not close by such date, this Contract
32. is subject to cancellation as provided on lines 147-154.
33. **Possession:** Possession shall be delivered to Buyer at ☐ Close of Escrow   ☐ Other: _____
34. **Assessments:** The amount of any assessment which is a lien as of the close of escrow shall be   ☐ Paid in Full by Seller   ☐ Prorated and
35. Any assessment that becomes a lien after close of escrow is the Buyer's responsibility.   Assumed by Buyer
36. **Proration and Costs:** Taxes, homeowner association fees, and irrigation fees, and if assumed, insurance premiums, interest on assessments and interest
37. on encumbrances shall be prorated as of ☐ Close of Escrow   ☐ Other: _____
38. **Home Protection Plan:** A home protection plan will be obtained for the Premises at close of escrow ☐ Yes ☐ No   The plan will be obtained at the
39. expense of the ☐ Seller ☐ Buyer Name of Plan: _____   Type of Plan or Maximum Cost: _____
40. **Fire and Extended Insurance Coverage:** ☐ A new policy to be obtained   ☐ Existing policy to be assumed   ☐ Determined in escrow
41. **Escrow Instructions:** ☐ Separate escrow instructions will be executed   ☐ This Contract will be used as escrow instructions
42. The escrow company shall be: _____
43. **Time for Acceptance:** This offer must be accepted by Seller on or before _____. Written acceptance of this Contract
44. given to the Broker named on Line 7 of this Contract shall be notice to Buyer.
45. COMMISSIONS PAYABLE FOR THE SALE, LEASING OR MANAGEMENT OF PROPERTY ARE NOT SET BY ANY BOARD OR ASSOCIATION OF
46. REALTORS® OR MULTIPLE LISTING SERVICE OR IN ANY MANNER OTHER THAN BETWEEN THE BROKER AND CLIENT.
47. **Terms on Reverse:** THE TERMS AND CONDITIONS ON THE REVERSE SIDE HEREOF ARE INCORPORATED HEREIN BY REFERENCE.
48. **Agency Confirmation:** Unless otherwise disclosed in writing, Buyer and Seller understand and agree that Brokers represent the Seller only, and have a
49. duty to treat fairly all parties to the transaction.
50. The undersigned agree to purchase the Premises on the terms and conditions herein stated and acknowledge receipt of a copy hereof.
51.
52. _____   _____   _____   _____
     (Buyer's Signature)   Mo/Da/Yr   (Buyer's Signature)   Mo/Da/Yr

     _____   _____   _____   _____
     Street   City   State   Zip

ACCEPTANCE

53. Seller agrees to sell the Premises as stated herein and for services rendered, agrees to pay a brokerage fee as follows:
54. _____ to _____   ("Broker named in Line 7")
55. _____ to _____   ("Listing Broker")
56. Seller instructs escrow company to pay such fee to Brokers in cash as a condition to closing and, to the extent necessary, irrevocably assigns Seller's
57. proceeds to Brokers at close of escrow. If completion of the sale is prevented by default of Seller, or with the consent of Seller, the entire brokerage fee
58. shall be paid directly by Seller. If the earnest deposit is forfeited for any reason, Seller shall pay a brokerage fee equal to one-half of the earnest deposit.
59. provided such payment shall not exceed the full amount of the brokerage fee. Nothing in this paragraph shall be construed as limiting applicable provisions
60. of law or any listing agreement relating to when commissions are earned or payable. UPON ACCEPTANCE OF THIS CONTRACT, SELLER HEREBY
61. WAIVES HIS RIGHT TO RECEIVE ANY SUBSEQUENT OFFER TO PURCHASE THE PREMISES UNTIL AFTER FORFEITURE BY BUYER OR OTHER
62. CANCELLATION OF THIS CONTRACT.
63. **Seller Receipt of Copy:** The undersigned acknowledge receipt of a copy hereof and grant permission to Broker in Line 7 to deliver a copy to Buyer.
64. ☐ Counter Offer is attached, which is incorporated herein by reference. If there is a conflict between this Contract and the Counter Offer, the provisions of
65. the Counter Offer shall be controlling. (NOTE: If this box is checked, Seller must sign both Contract and Counter Offer.)

66. _____   _____   _____   _____
     (Seller's Signature)   Mo/Da/Yr   (Seller's Signature)   Mo/Da/Yr

67. _____   _____
     (Print Name of Seller)   (Print Name of Seller)

68. _____   _____   _____   _____
     Street   City   State   Zip

☐ For Broker Use Only Brokerage File/Log No. _____   Manager's Initials _____ Broker's Initials _____ Date _____

Arizona Association of REALTORS' 1991 **This Form Available Through Your Local Board of REALTORS**   FORM RREPCRD 11/91

Figure 6.2 (continued)

69. **Time of Essence:** Time is of the essence.

70. **Permission:** Buyer and Seller grant Brokers permission to advise the public of the sale upon execution of this Contract, and Brokers may disclose
71. price and terms herein after close of escrow.

72. **Entire Agreement:** This Contract, any attached exhibits and any addenda or supplements signed by the parties, shall constitute the entire agreement
73. between Seller and Buyer, and shall supersede any other written or oral agreement between Seller and Buyer. This Contract can be modified only by
74. a writing signed by Seller and Buyer. A fully executed facsimile copy of the entire agreement shall be treated as an original Contract.

75. **Title and Title Insurance:** Seller hereby instructs the escrow company to obtain and distribute to Buyer a preliminary title report together with
76. complete and legible copies of all documents which will remain as exceptions to Buyer's policy of title insurance. Title to the real property described
77. in Lines 8-12 of this Contract shall be conveyed by a general warranty deed. Title to the personal property described in Lines 13-17 of this Contract
78. shall be transferred free and clear of any liens or encumbrances. Seller shall furnish to Buyer, at Seller's expense, a Standard Owner's Title
79. Insurance Policy in the full amount of the purchase price issued by a title insurance company, showing good and marketable title to the real property
80. vested in Buyer free from defects and encumbrances except as follows: (1) liens and other matters described in this Contract, (2) building, use and
81. other restrictive covenants of record, (3) claims, title or rights to water (4) zoning regulations, (5) easements and rights-of-way for roadways,
82. canals, laterals, ditches and public utilities, (6) taxes, paving, irrigation and other assessments not delinquent as of the close of escrow, (7) rights of
83. tenants in possession, if any, (8) rights and minerals reserved in patents or otherwise by any entity, (9) printed exceptions contained in the Standard
84. Owner's Title Insurance Policy. If title to the real property otherwise is defective at the time set for close of escrow, Buyer may elect, as Buyer's sole
85. option, either to accept title subject to defects which are not cured or to cancel this Contract whereupon all money paid by Buyer pursuant to this
86. Contract shall be returned to Buyer. Buyer shall furnish to Seller, at Buyer's expense, a Standard Loan Policy in the full amount of any loan carried
87. back by Seller and secured by the real property described in Lines 8-12 of this Contract. Such Standard Loan Policy shall show that Seller's lien has
88. the priority agreed to by the parties. If applicable Seller agrees to complete, sign and deliver to escrow company a certificate indicating whether
89. Seller is a foreign person or non-resident alien pursuant to the Foreign Investment in Real Property Tax Act. (FIRPTA)

90. **Documents and Escrow:** (1) If Seller and Buyer elect to execute escrow instructions to fulfill the terms hereof, they shall deliver the same to escrow
91. company within 15 days of the acceptance of this Contract. (2) All documents necessary to close this transaction shall be executed promptly by
92. Seller and Buyer in the standard form used by escrow company. Seller and Buyer hereby instruct escrow company to modify such documents to the
93. extent necessary to be consistent with the Contract. (3) If any conflict exists between this Contract and any escrow instructions executed pursuant
94. hereto, the provisions of this Contract shall be controlling. (4) All closing and escrow costs shall be allocated between Seller and Buyer in accordance
95. with local custom and applicable laws and regulations. (5) Escrow company is hereby instructed to send to Brokers copies of all notices and
96. communications directed to Seller or Buyer and shall provide to such Brokers access to escrowed materials and information about the escrow upon
97. request. (6) Any documents necessary to close the escrow may be signed in counterparts, each of which shall be effective as an original upon
98. execution and all of which together shall constitute one and the same instrument.

99. **Default and Remedies:** If Buyer defaults in any respect on any material obligations under this Contract, Seller may elect to be released from the
100. obligation to sell the Premises to Buyer. Seller may proceed against Buyer upon any claim or remedy which he may have, in law or equity, or
101. because it would be difficult to fix actual damages in case of Buyer's default, the amount of the earnest deposit may be deemed a reasonable
102. estimate of the damages; and Seller may, at his option retain the earnest deposit, subject to the brokerage fee as provided herein, as his sole right to
103. damages. If Buyer or Seller files suit against the other to enforce any provision of this Contract or for damages sustained by reason of its breach, all
104. parties prevailing in such action, on trial and appeal, shall receive their reasonable attorneys' fees and costs as awarded by the court. In
105. addition, both Seller and Buyer agree to indemnify and hold harmless all Brokers against all costs and expenses, which any Broker may incur or
106. sustain in connection with any lawsuit arising from this Contract and will pay the same on demand unless the court shall grant judgment in such
107. action against the party to be indemnified. Costs shall include, without limitation: attorneys' fees, expert witness fees, fees paid to investigators and
108. court costs.

109. **Warranties:** Except as otherwise provided in this Contract, Seller warrants and shall maintain and repair the Premises so that, at the earlier of
110. possession or the close of escrow: (1) the Premises shall be in substantially the same condition as on the effective date of this Contract, (2) the roof
111. has no known leaks, (3) all heating, cooling, mechanical, plumbing and electrical systems and built-in appliances will be in working condition, (4) if the
112. Premises has a swimming pool and/or spa, the motors, filter systems, cleaning systems, and heaters, if so equipped, will be in working condition.
113. The Seller grants Buyer or Buyer's representative reasonable access to enter and inspect the Premises for the purpose of satisfying Buyer that the
114. items warranted by Seller are in working condition. Buyer shall keep the Premises free and clear of any liens; indemnify and hold Seller and Brokers
115. harmless from all liability, claims, demands and costs; and repair all damages to the Premises caused by said inspection. At the earlier of
116. possession or close of escrow, Buyer acknowledges that all warranties concerning the Premises have been satisfied or extinguished. Any personal
117. property included herein shall be transferred IN AS IS CONDITION AND SELLER MAKES NO WARRANTY of any kind, express or implied (including,
118. without limitation, ANY WARRANTY OF MERCHANTABILITY). Brokers are hereby relieved of any and all liability and responsibility from everything
119. stated in this paragraph and the following paragraph.

120. **Warranties That Survive Closing:** Prior to the close of escrow, Seller warrants that, payment in full will have been made for all labor, professional
121. services, materials, machinery, fixtures or tools furnished within the 120 days immediately preceding the close of escrow in connection with the
122. construction, alteration or repair of any structure on or improvement to the Premises. Seller warrants that the information in the current listing
123. agreement, if any, regarding connection to a public sewer system, septic tank or other sanitation system is correct to the best of his knowledge.
124. Seller warrants that he has disclosed to Buyer and Brokers all material latent defects concerning the Premises that are known to Seller. Seller further
125. warrants that he has disclosed to all parties any information, including physical opinions of value, that he possesses which materially and adversely affects the
126. consideration to be paid by Buyer.

127. **Representations and Releases:** By signing this Contract, Buyer represents that he has or will have prior to close of escrow conducted all
128. independent investigations desired by Buyer of any and all matters concerning this purchase and by closing accepts the Premises. Seller and Buyer
129. hereby release all Brokers from all responsibility and liability regarding the condition, square footage, lot lines or boundaries, value, rent rolls,
130. compliance with building codes or other governmental regulations, or other material matters relating to the Premises; and neither Seller, Buyer, nor
131. any Broker shall be bound by any understanding, agreement, promise or representation, express or implied, not specified herein.

132. **Wood Infestation Report:** Seller will, at his expense, place in escrow a wood infestation report by a qualified licensed pest control operator, which,
133. when considered in its entirety, indicates that all residences and buildings attached to the Premises are free from evidence of current infestation and
134. damage from wood-destroying pests or organisms. Seller agrees to pay up to one percent of the purchase price for the treatment and repair of the
135. damage caused by infestation and correct any conditions conducive to infestation. If such costs exceed one percent of the purchase price: (1)
136. Buyer may elect to cancel this Contract unless Seller agrees in writing to pay such costs, or (2) Seller may elect to cancel this contract unless Buyer
137. agrees in writing to either accept the Premises or to pay such costs in excess of one percent that the Seller has agreed to pay.

138. **Recommendations:** If any Broker recommends a builder, contractor, or any other person or entity to Seller or Buyer for any purpose, such
139. recommendation will be independently investigated and evaluated by Seller or Buyer, who hereby acknowledge that any decision to enter into any
140. contractual arrangements with any such person or entity recommended by any Broker will be based solely upon such independent investigation and
141. evaluation. Seller and Buyer understand that said contractual arrangement may result in a commission or fee to Broker.

142. **Risk of Loss:** If there is any loss or damage to the Premises between the date hereof and the close of escrow, by reason of fire, vandalism, flood,
143. earthquake or act of God, the risk of loss shall be on the Seller, provided, however, that if the cost of repairing such loss or damage would exceed
144. ten percent of the purchase price, (1) Buyer may elect to cancel this Contract unless Seller agrees in writing to pay the cost of repairing all such loss
145. or damage, or (2) Seller may elect to cancel this Contract unless Buyer agrees in writing to accept the Premises and to pay the cost of repair in
146. excess of ten percent of the purchase price that the Seller has agreed to pay.

147. **Cancellation:** Any party who wishes to cancel this Contract because of any breach by another party, or because escrow fails to close by the agreed
148. date, and who is not himself in breach of this Contract, except as occasioned by a breach by the other party, may cancel this Contract by delivering a
149. notice to either the breaching party or to the escrow company stating the nature of the breach and that this Contract shall be cancelled unless the
150. breach is cured within 13 days following the delivery of the notice. If this notice is delivered to the escrow company, it shall contain the address of
151. the party in breach. Any notice delivered to any party must be delivered to the Brokers and the escrow company. Within three days after receipt of
152. such notice, the escrow company shall send the notice by United States Mail to the party in breach at the address contained in the notice. No further
153. notice shall be required. In the event that the breach is not cured within 13 days following the delivery of the notice to the party in breach or to the
154. escrow company, this Contract shall be cancelled.

155. **Brokers' Rights:** If any Broker hires an attorney to enforce the collection of the commission payable pursuant to this Contract, and is successful in
156. collecting some or all of such commission, Seller agrees to pay such Broker's costs including, but not limited to: attorneys' fees, expert witness fees,
157. fees paid to investigators and court costs. The parties agree that any monies deposited in the trust account of the Broker named in line 7 pursuant
158. to this Contract may earn interest, and that the Broker shall be entitled to all of the interest from said interest-bearing trust account as additional
159. compensation. The Seller and the Buyer acknowledge that the Brokers are third-party beneficiaries of this Contract.

160. **FHA or VA:** If applicable, the current language prescribed by FHA or VA pertaining to the value of the Premises shall be incorporated in this
161. Contract by reference as if set forth in full herein, and Seller and Buyer agree to execute any appropriate FHA or VA supplements to this Contract.
162. Buyer is entitled to a return of the earnest deposit if, after a diligent and good faith effort, Buyer does not qualify for a VA or FHA Loan. Buyer
163. acknowledges that prepaid items paid separately from earnest money are not refundable.

164. **Buyer's Loan:** If Buyer is seeking a new loan or an assumption of an existing loan that requires qualification in connection with this transaction.
165. Buyer agrees to file a substantially complete loan application within five business days after the acceptance of this Contract and to promptly supply all
166. documentation required by the lender.

167. **Severability:** If a court of competent jurisdiction makes a final determination that any term or provision of this Contract is invalid or unenforceable, all
168. other terms and provisions shall remain in full force and effect, and the invalid or unenforceable term or provision shall be deemed replaced by a term
169. or provision that is valid and enforceable and comes closest to expressing the intention of the invalid term or provision.

170. **Construction of Language:** The language of this Contract shall be construed according to its fair meaning and not strictly for or against either party
171. Words used in the masculine, feminine or neuter shall apply to either gender or the neuter, as appropriate. This agreement shall be governed by the
172. laws of the State of Arizona.

Arizona Association of REALTORS 1991 **This Form Available Through Your Local Board of REALTORS**   FORM RREPCRD 11/91

Contract in writing.   Under the statute of frauds of every state, no action may be brought on any contract for the sale of land unless the contract is in writing and signed by the parties to the agreement. A written agreement establishes the interest of the purchaser and his or her rights to enforce that interest by court action. It thus prevents the seller from selling the property to another person who might offer a higher price. The signed contract agreement also obligates the buyer to complete the transaction according to the terms agreed upon in the contract.

Offer and acceptance.   One of the essential elements of a valid contract of sale is a meeting of the minds, whereby the buyer and seller agree on the terms of the sale. This is usually accomplished through the process of offer and acceptance.

A broker lists an owner's real estate for sale at the price and under the conditions set by the owner. A prospective buyer is found who wants to purchase the property at those terms or some other terms. A contract of sale is drawn up, signed by the prospective buyer, and presented by the broker to the seller. This is an *offer.* If the seller agrees to the offer exactly as it was made and signs the contract, the offer has been accepted and the contract is valid. The broker must then advise the buyer of the seller's acceptance, or preferably deliver a signed copy of the contract to the buyer.

Any attempt by the seller to change the terms proposed by the buyer creates a *counteroffer.* The buyer is relieved of his or her original offer because the seller has rejected it. The buyer can accept the seller's counteroffer or reject it and possibly make another counteroffer. Any change in the last offer made results in a counteroffer, until one party finally agrees to the other party's last offer and both parties sign the final contract.

An offer or counteroffer may be withdrawn at any time before it has been accepted, and an acceptance may be withdrawn at any time prior to the communication of such action to the offeror. When the parties are communicating through an agent or at a distance, questions may arise regarding whether an acceptance, rejection, or counteroffer has effectively taken place. The real estate broker or salesperson should transmit all offers, acceptances, or other responses as soon as possible in order to avoid such problems.

Equitable title.   When a buyer signs a contract to purchase real estate, he or she does not receive title to the land. Only a deed can actually convey title. However, after both buyer and seller have signed a sales contract, the buyer acquires an interest in the land known as **equitable title.** If the parties decide not to go through with the purchase and sale, the buyer may be required to give the seller a quitclaim deed to release the buyer's equitable interest in the land.

Destruction of the premises.   In many states, once the sales contract is signed by both parties, unless the contract provides otherwise, the buyer must bear the loss if any damage to or destruction of the property occurs by fire or other casualty. If the buyer were given possession prior to closing and the contract was silent on the risk, the court might find the vendee or buyer liable. Through laws and court decisions, however, a growing number of states have placed on the seller the risk of any loss that occurs before the deed is delivered. Quite a few of these states have adopted the *Uniform Vendor and Purchaser Risk Act,* which specifically provides that the seller (vendor) bears any loss that occurs before the title passes or the buyer (vendee) takes possession. In any case, the seller may be made to assume the risk of loss when he or she has been negligent, is unable to deliver good title, or has delayed the closing of the transaction.

Earnest money deposits.   It is customary for a purchaser to put down a cash deposit when making an offer to purchase real estate. This deposit, commonly referred to as earnest money, binds the purchaser and gives evidence of his or her intention to carry out the terms of the contract. The deposit is paid to the broker, and the sales contract usually provides that the broker will hold the deposit for the parties.

The amount of the deposit is agreed upon by the parties. Under the terms of most listing agreements, a real estate broker is required to accept a reasonable amount as earnest money. Generally, the deposit should be sufficient to discourage the buyer from defaulting, compensate the seller for taking property off the market, and cover any expenses the seller might incur if the buyer defaults. In many areas, the standard deposit is not less than 10 percent of the sales price. Most contracts provide that the deposit becomes the seller's property if the buyer defaults.

Under the laws of most states, earnest money must be held by a broker in a special trust account or escrow account. This money cannot be *commingled* (mixed) with a broker's personal funds. In many states a broker is permitted to place a minimal amount of his or her own money into the trust account in order to keep it open. It is not necessary for a broker to open a special trust or escrow account for each earnest money deposit received. One account for all such deposits is sufficient. A broker should maintain full, complete, and accurate records of all earnest money deposits in order to comply with strict state license laws covering these deposits.

OPTIONS

An *option* is a contract by which an optionor (generally an owner) gives an optionee (prospective purchaser or lessee) the right to buy or lease the owner's property at a fixed price within a stated period of time. The optionee pays a fee (the agreed-upon consideration) for this option right and assumes no obligation to make any other payment until he or she decides, within the specified time, either to: (1) exercise the option right (to buy or lease the property) or (2) allow the option right to expire.

For example, for a consideration of a specified amount of money, a present owner (optionor) agrees to give an optionee an irrevocable right for a limited period of time to buy the real estate at a certain price. At the time the option is signed by the parties, the owner does not sell, nor does the optionee buy. They merely agree that the optionee will have the right to buy and the owner will be obligated to sell *if* the optionee decides to exercise the right of option.

The option agreement requires the optionor to act only after the optionee gives notice that he or she elects to execute the option and buy or lease. If the option is not exercised within the time specified, then the optionor's obligation and the optionee's right will expire. The optionee cannot recover the consideration paid for the option right. The option agreement may stipulate that the option fee be applied to the purchase price if the option is exercised.

A common application of an option is a lease that includes an option for the tenant to purchase the property. Options on commercial real estate frequently are made dependent upon the fulfillment of specific conditions, such as the obtaining of a change in zoning or a building permit. The optionee is usually obligated to exercise his or her option if the conditions are met. Similar terms could also be included in a sales contract.

Leases

A lease is a contractual agreement in which the owner agrees to give possession of all or a part of the real estate to another person for a period of time in exchange for a rental fee. (Leases are discussed in detail in Chapter 7.)

Escrow Agreements

An **escrow** is a means by which the parties to a contract carry out the terms of their agreement. The parties appoint a disinterested third party to act as the escrowee, or escrow agent. This escrow agent must be someone who is not party to the contract and will not benefit in any way from the contract.

Any real estate transaction can be closed through an escrow. The parties to the transaction enter into an escrow agreement (usually a separate agreement from the contract) that sets forth the duties of the escrow agent and the obligations and requirements of the parties to the transaction. An escrow agreement may be used in closing such real estate transactions as a sale, mortgage loan, exchange of property, installment contract (contract for deed), or lease.

In a real estate sale, the purpose of an escrow agreement is to close the transaction; therefore, the escrow agreement necessarily follows the terms of the sales contract. An escrow agent is given the responsibility to see that: (1) the transaction is closed as required by the sales contract, or (2) the sale is not closed unless the buyer and seller agree to changes in the contract terms. An escrow agreement requires the seller to deposit with the escrow agent the deed for the buyer and other pertinent documents, such as leases, insurance policies, and a mortgage payment letter, if the existing mortgage is to be paid in full and released of record. It also provides for the buyer to deposit the purchase price and an executed mortgage and note if he or she is securing mortgage funds to purchase the property. The escrow agent is authorized to have the title examined, and if it is found to meet the conditions of the escrow agreement, the sale is concluded. The title then passes to the buyer, and the seller receives the money.

If the title is unacceptable, the escrow agreement usually provides for the escrow agent to forward a copy of the title commitment to the parties, and the seller is given a specified number of days to clear title defects. If the title cannot be cleared and the sale is canceled, the intended purchaser executes a deed that returns the title to the former owner (the seller). This is recorded by the escrow agent and the purchaser's money is refunded. In other words, all of the parties are restored to their original positions. (Escrow agreements as used in the closing of a real estate transaction will be discussed further in Chapter 15.)

SUMMARY

A contract is defined as an agreement made by competent parties, with adequate consideration, to perform or not to perform some proper or legal action. The essentials of a valid real estate contract are (1) *competent parties;* (2) *mutual assent;* (3) *seal or consideration;* (4) *legality of object;* and (5) *special formality.*

Contracts may be classified according to whether the parties' intentions are expressly stated or *implied* by their actions. They may also be classified as *bilateral* if both parties have obligated themselves to act, or *unilateral* if one party is obligated to perform only if the other party acts. Many contracts specify a deadline for performance. In any case, all contracts must be performed within a reasonable time. An *executed* contract is one that has been fully performed. An *executory* contract is one in which some act remains to be performed. In addition, contracts may be classified according to their legal enforceability as either *valid, void, voidable,* or *unenforceable.*

In a number of circumstances, a contract may be canceled before it is fully performed. Furthermore, in many types of contracts, either of the parties may transfer his or her rights and obligations under the agreement by *assignment* of the contract or *novation* (substitution) by a new contract.

If either party to a real estate sales contract defaults, several alternative methods of action are available. Contracts usually provide that the seller has the right to declare the contract canceled through forfeiture if the buyer defaults. In general, if either party has suffered a loss because of the other's default, he or she may sue for damages to cover the loss. If one party insists on completing the transaction, he or she may sue the defaulter for *specific performance* of the terms of the contract. In this way, a court can order the parties to comply with their agreement.

Contracts frequently used in the real estate business include listings, sales contracts, options, installment contracts (contracts for deed), leases, and escrow agreements.

A *real estate sales contract* binds a buyer and seller to a definite transaction, as described in detail in the contract. The buyer is bound to purchase the property for the amount of consideration stated in the agreement. The seller is bound to deliver a good and marketable title, free from liens and encumbrances (except those allowed by the "subject to" clause of the contract).

Under an *option* agreement, the optionee purchases from the optionor, for a limited time period, the exclusive right to purchase or lease the optionor's property. For a potential purchaser or lessee, an option is a means of buying time to consider or complete arrangements for the transaction. An *installment contract,* or *contract for deed,* is a sales/financing agreement under which a buyer purchases a seller's real estate on time with periodic payments. The buyer takes possession of and responsibility for the property, but does not receive the deed until the final installment is paid.

Any real estate transaction may be completed through an *escrow,* a means by which the parties to the contract carry out the terms of their agreement. The parties appoint a third party to act as the *escrowee* or *escrow agent.* In the sale of real estate, the seller's deed and the buyer's money are deposited with an escrow agent under an escrow agreement that sets forth the conditions to be met before the sale will be consummated. The escrow agent records the deed, and when the title conditions and any other requirements of the escrow agreement are met, the title passes and the sale is completed.

QUESTIONS

Please complete all of the questions before turning to the Answer Key.

1. If both a written contract and an oral contract exist between two parties for the same purpose, the written contract will supersede the oral contract because of

    a.   the parol evidence rule.
    b.   the statute of limitations.
    c.   laches.
    d.   *caveat emptor.*

2. A contract that has not been fully performed is

    a.   executed.   c.   implied.
    b.   executory.   d.   void.

3. The creation of a new contract with the intent of replacing a prior contract is known as

    a.   assignment.   c.   novation.
    b.   escrow.   d.   estoppel.

4. The statute of frauds requires that

    a.   legal actions be instituted within a reasonable period of time.
    b.   real estate purchase contracts be in writing.
    c.   a suit for specific performance be filed after any seller default.
    d.   a suit to quiet title be used in every transaction.

5. The type of listing contract most likely to be in the form of a unilateral contract is a(n)

    a.   exclusive-right-to-sell listing.
    b.   exclusive-agency listing.
    c.   open listing.
    d.   multiple listing.

6. If there is no consideration exchanged or promised in a contract, then the agreement is

    a.   void.   c.   expressed.
    b.   voidable.   d.   implied.

7. Obligations or promises under a contract can be discharged by all of the following EXCEPT

   a. partial performance.   c. mutual agreement.
   b. unilateral rescission.   d. operation of law.

8. The seller deliberately misinforms the buyer of his property. The contract between them is

   a. valid and binding on both parties.
   b. void and without effect.
   c. voidable at the option of the buyer.
   d. voidable at the option of either party.

9. An offer is made by *K* to purchase *T*'s property. *T* changes the terms of the offer and returns it to *K* for *K*'s acceptance. All of the following statements regarding this situation are true EXCEPT

   a. this is a rejection of the original offer made by *K*.
   b. this constitutes a counteroffer by *T*.
   c. *K* is released from the original offer.
   d. *T* would not be bound by *K*'s acceptance.

10. During the period of time after a real estate sales contract is signed but before title actually passes, the status of the contract is

    a. voidable.   c. executory.
    b. unilateral.   d. implied.

11. A listing agreement can be terminated for any of the following reasons EXCEPT

    a. performance of the broker.
    b. mutual consent.
    c. destruction of the property.
    d. decision by the owner not to sell.

12. A contract is referred to as a bilateral contract if

    a. all of the parties to the contract are bound to act.
    b. only one party to the contract is bound to act.
    c. the contract has yet to be fully performed.
    d. one of the parties to the contract is a minor.

13. A listing contract in which one broker is specifically authorized to act for the principal and the principal retains the right to sell the property himself without an obligation to pay the broker a commission is called a(n)

    a. exclusive-right-to-sell listing.
    b. exclusive-agency listing.
    c. open listing.
    d. multiple listing.

14. All of the following items are essential elements of a valid contract EXCEPT

    a. consideration.   c. legal purpose.
    b. competent parties.   d. assignment.

15. A contract that is binding on all of the parties to it is what type of contract?

    a. Valid   c. Voidable
    b. Void   d. Unilateral

16. A contract that can be affirmed or disaffirmed by a wronged party is

    a. valid.   c. voidable.
    b. void.   d. executed.

17. The transfer of rights or duties under the terms of a contract is called

    a. novation.   c. substitution.
    b. assignment.   d. rescission.

18. The type of listing contract under which the seller can employ as many brokers as he or she likes but has an obligation to pay a commission to only the broker who produces a buyer is a(n)

    a. exclusive-right-to-sell listing.
    b. exclusive-agency listing.
    c. open listing.
    d. multiple listing.

19. An irrevocable right to purchase a property is called a(n)

    a. option.   c. lease.
    b. right of first refusal.   d. partial performance.

20. The funds the buyer presents along with an offer to purchase that show an intent to complete the terms of any contract that might be created with the seller are known as

    a. commission.   c. consideration.
    b. down payment.   d. earnest money.

21. The type of listing contract that indicates the property will be sold for a specific amount with any proceeds above that amount going to the broker as commission is called a(n)

    a. exclusive-agency listing.   c. multiple listing.
    b. net listing.   d. open listing.

22. All of the following would be found in a typical listing contract EXCEPT the

    a. signature of the seller.
    b. signature of the buyer.
    c. commission rate or fee.
    d. description of the property.

23. All of the following statements regarding options are true EXCEPT

    a. the option must contain an irrevocable right to purchase or lease the property.
    b. the option must be in writing to be enforceable under the statute of frauds.
    c. the optionee must purchase the property within a stipulated time period after the option is granted.
    d. the optionor must honor the terms of the option if the optionee decides to exercise it.

24. A lawsuit initiated by one party to a contract asking the court to force the other party to comply with the terms of the contract is called a suit for

    a. quiet title.   c. specific performance.
    b. partition.   d. restitution.

25. A written contract between two parties is what type of contract?

    a. Expressed   c. Voidable
    b. Implied   d. Executed

26. A contract that cannot be enforced against any of the parties to it is what type of contract?

    a. Valid   c. Voidable
    b. Void   d. Unilateral

27. When a real estate broker mixes his or her personal funds with those of a client, it is called

    a. assignment.   c. commingling.
    b. rescission.   d. compensation.

28. Under the concept of "competent parties" to a contract, which of the following would be considered to be competent?

    a. A minor
    b. A person under the influence of alcohol
    c. A person signing for another without an appropriate power of attorney
    d. A person signing for a corporation under a corporate resolution

29. If the buyer defaults under the terms of a purchase contract and the seller wants only to recover the earnest money that the buyer provided with the offer, which of the following courses of action would the seller pursue?

    a. Declare the contract forfeited
    b. Rescind the contract
    c. Sue for specific performance
    d. Sue for compensatory damages

30. During the period of time after a real estate sales contract is signed but before title actually passes, the buyer of the property has

    a. no interest in the property.
    b. legal title to the property.
    c. personal interest in the property.
    d. equitable title to the property.

7: Landlord and Tenant

KEY TERMS

actual eviction	ground lease
cash rent	index lease
constructive eviction	lease
contract rent	lease option
economic rent	lease purchase
estate at sufferance	lessee
estate at will	lessor
estate for years	net lease
estate from period	percentage lease
to period	sandwich lease
graduated lease	sharecropping
gross lease	sublease

When an owner of real estate does not wish to use the property personally or wants to derive some measure of income from its ownership, he or she can allow another person to use it in exchange for valuable consideration. This is usually accomplished by means of an agreement known as a lease. A **lease** is a contract between a property owner (known as the **lessor**) and a tenant (the **lessee**) that transfers the right to exclusive possession and use of the landlord's property to the tenant for a specified period of time. This agreement sets forth the length of time the contract is to run, the amount to be paid by the lessee for the right to use the property, and other rights and obligations of the parties.

In effect, the lease agreement conveys an interest in the real property and includes a contract to pay rent and assume other obligations. The landlord/lessor grants the tenant/lessee the right to occupy the premises and use them for purposes stated in the lease. In return, the landlord retains the right to receive payment for the use of the premises plus a *reversionary right* to retake possession after the lease term has expired. The lessor's interest in leased property is called a *leased fee plus reversionary right*. The statute of frauds in most states requires that to be enforceable, a lease for a term of more than one year must be in writing and signed by both lessor and lessee.

LEASEHOLD ESTATES

As discussed in Chapter 2, when an owner of real property leases his or her property to a tenant, the tenant's right to occupy the land for the duration of the lease is called a leasehold, or non-freehold, estate. Leasehold estates are *chattels real*. Although they give their owner (the tenant/lessee) an interest in real property, they are in fact personal property and are governed by laws applicable to personal property. When the contract is a lease for life or more than 99 years under which the tenant assumes many of the obligations of the landowner, certain states give the tenant some of the benefits and privileges of a property owner.

The four most important types of leasehold estates are (1) estate for years, (2) estate from period to period (periodic estate), (3) estate at will, and (4) estate at sufferance (see Table 7.1).

Estate for Years

An **estate for years** is a leasehold estate that continues for a *definite* period of time—one month, one year, five years, and so on. When a definite term is specified in a written or oral lease and that period of time expires, the tenant (lessee) is required to vacate the premise and surrender possession to the landlord (lessor), unless the parties agree to renew the lease for another specified term. No notice is required to terminate such an estate; the termination date was established in the lease. This type of leasehold conveys more rights to the tenant than any of the other three.

Estate from Period to Period

An **estate from period to period,** or a periodic estate, is created when the landlord and tenant enter into an agreement that continues for an indefinite number of definite periods. These estates are generally created by agreement or operation of law to run for a certain amount of time; for example, from month to month, quarter to quarter, or year to year. The agreement is automatically renewed for like succeeding periods until one of the parties gives notice to terminate. The notice requirement for both tenant and landlord is governed by state law, and is normally established by the length of the period. For example, a month-to-month periodic

Table 7.1   Leasehold Estates

Type of Estate	Distinguishing Characteristic
Estate for years	For definite period of time
Estate from period to period	Automatically renews
Estate at will	For indefinite period of time
Estate at sufferance	Without landlord's consent

estate would require one month's notice from either the tenant or the landlord to terminate the estate. This type of tenancy is more common in residential than in commercial leases.

Estate at Will

An **estate at will** is an estate of *indefinite* duration. It is created at the will of the landlord and will continue to exist until either landlord or tenant serves proper notice to the other of a desire to terminate the estate. Most states have statutory notice requirements to terminate an estate at will.

Estate at Sufferance

An **estate at sufferance** arises when a tenant who lawfully came into possession of real property continues to hold possession of the premises after his or her rights have expired, without the consent of the landlord. Because the tenant's original possession was legal, however, the tenant is not considered a trespasser. It is an estate of *indefinite* duration because the landlord can institute legal action to regain possession of the property at any time.

STANDARD LEASE PROVISIONS

In determining the validity of a lease, the courts apply the rules governing contracts. If the intention to convey temporary possession of a certain parcel of real estate from one person to another is expressed, the courts generally hold that a lease has been created. Most states require no special wording to establish the landlord-tenant relationship. Likewise, the lease may be written, oral, or implied, depending on the circumstances. However, the provisions of the statutes of the state where the real estate is located must be followed to ensure the validity of the lease.

Once a valid lease has been signed, the lessor, as the owner of the real estate, is usually bound by the implied covenant of quiet possession. Under this covenant, the lessor guarantees that the lessee may take possession of the leased premises and that he or she will not be evicted from these premises by any person who successfully claims to have a title superior to that of the lessor.

Requirements for a Valid Lease

The requirements are essentially the same as those for any other real estate contract. Generally, the essentials of a valid lease are competent parties, mutual assent, legality of object, contract in writing, valuable consideration, description of premises, and signatures.

Competent parties.   The parties must have the legal capacity to contract.

Mutual assent.   The parties must reach a mutual agreement on all the terms of the contract.

Legality of object.   The objectives of the lease must be legal.

Contract in writing.   Most statutes of frauds require that leases that will not be fully performed within one year of the date of making must be in writing in order to be enforceable in court. When the statute of frauds applies but the provisions of the lease do not comply with its terms, the lease is considered unenforceable.

Valuable consideration.   As discussed earlier, the laws of contract control the creation of a landlord-tenant relationship. Every contract must be supported by a valid valuable consideration. In leasing real estate, *rent* is the usual consideration granted for the right to occupy the leased premises; however, the payment of rent is not essential as long as consideration was granted in creation of the lease itself. Some courts have construed rent as being any consideration that supports the lease, thus not limiting its definition to the payment of monthly rent. For example, most ground leases and long-term leases provide that the tenant must pay all property charges—such as real estate taxes, insurance premiums, and the like—in addition to the rent. The courts consider a lease to be a contract. Even if a rent concession reduced the monthly rent to zero for a period of time, the tenant's payment of the property charge would be sufficient consideration to establish the lease as a valid contract. As such, the agreement is not subject to later changes in the rent or other terms unless these changes are in writing and executed in the same manner as the original lease.

The amount of rent the tenant must pay for use of the premises is set forth in the lease contract and is known as the **contract rent.** The amount of rent the property would command in a fully informed competitive marketplace is known as the **economic rent.** When the lease contract is negotiated, the contract rent and the economic rent are normally the same. But as the lease runs its term, the two may come to differ greatly. To prevent this from happening, the lessor, in long-term lease situations, will quite often use a form of lease that provides for adjustments in the amount of rent throughout the term of the lease.

In this regard, if a lease contract does not specify the amount of rent to be paid, the court will usually infer the rent to be what it feels is a "fair and reasonable" amount. Likewise, in making a rental agreement it is important to state specifically when the rent is to be paid to the lessor. If it is to be paid in advance or at any time other than the end of the term, the contract should state that fact. The law states that rent becomes due only at the end of the term unless it is specifically agreed to the contrary. Thus, in the absence of usage or contract to the contrary, rent is payable at the termination of the successive period of the holding—weekly, monthly, or yearly, as the case may be.

Description of the premises.   A description of the leased premises should be clearly stated. If the lease covers land, the legal description of the real estate should be used. If the lease is for a part of the building, such as office space or an apartment, the space itself or the apartment designation should be clearly and carefully described. If supplemental space is to be included, the lease should clearly identify the space.

Signatures.   To be valid, a lease must be signed by the landlord, since the courts consider a lease to be a conveyance of an interest in real estate. When a lessor holds his or her interest in severalty, most states require the spouse to join in signing the lease in order to release any homestead or inheritance rights. The tenant's signature is usually *not essential* if the tenant has actually taken possession. Of course, it is considered better practice for both parties to sign the lease.

Use of Premises

A lessor may restrict a lessee's use of the premises through provisions included in the lease. This is most important in leases for stores or commercial space. For example, a lease may provide that the lease premises are to be used only for the purpose of a real estate office and for no other. In the absence of such limitations, a lessee may use the premises for any lawful purpose.

Term of the Lease

The term of a lease is the period for which the lease will run; thus it should be set out precisely. Good practice requires that the date of the beginning of the term and the date of its ending be stated together with statement of the total period of the lease: for example, "for a term of thirty years beginning June 1, 1996, and ending May 31, 2026." Courts hold that a lease with an indefinite term is not valid unless the language of the lease and the surrounding circumstances clearly indicate that a perpetual lease is the intention of the parties. Leases are controlled by the statutes of the various states and must be in accordance with those provisions. In some states, terms of agricultural leases are limited by statute. Also, the laws of some states prohibit leases of more than 99 years.

Security Deposits

Most leases require the tenant to provide some form of security. This security, which guarantees payment of rent and safeguards against a tenant's destruction of the premises, may be established by: (1) contracting for a lien on the tenant's property; (2) requiring the tenant to pay a portion of the rent in advance; (3) requiring the tenant to post security; and/or (4) requiring the tenant to have some third party guarantee the payment of the rent. Some states have laws that specify how security deposits must be handled and require that lessees receive annual interest on their security deposits.

Judgment Clauses

Judgment clauses are included in many leases to assist the landlord in forcing collection of rent. In such a clause, the tenant authorizes any attorney of record to appear in court in the name of the tenant and to confess judgment, or agree that a judgment be entered against the tenant in favor of the landlord for the delinquent rent, court costs, and attorney's fee. Some states have now declared these judgment clauses to be illegal.

LEGAL PRINCIPLES OF LEASES

Most states provide that leases can be filed for record in the county in which the property is located. Unless the lease is for a relatively long term, it usually is not recorded. Possession of the property by the lessee is constructive notice to the world of his or her rights, and an inspection of the property will result in actual notice of the lessee's leasehold interest.

When a lease runs for a period of three years or longer, recordation is more common. The recording of such a long-term lease places the world on notice of the long-term rights of the lessee. Recordation of such a lease is usually required if the lessee intends to mortgage his or her leasehold interest.

In some states, only a memorandum of lease is filed for record. The terms of the lease are not disclosed to the public by the filing; however, the objective of giving public notice of the rights of the lessee is still accomplished. The memorandum of lease must set forth the names of the parties and a description of the property leased.

Possession of the Leased Premises

Leases carry the implied covenant that the landlord will give the tenant possession of the premises and the right of *quiet enjoyment*. In most states, the landlord must give the tenant actual possession, or occupancy, of the leased premises. Thus, if the premises are occupied by a holdover tenant, or adverse claimant, at the beginning of the new lease period, it is the landlord's duty to bring whatever action is necessary to recover possession as well as to bear the expense of this action. However, in a few states, the landlord is only bound to give the tenant the right of possession. It is the tenant's obligation to bring any court action necessary to secure actual possession.

Maintenance of Premises

Under the principle of *caveat emptor* ("buyer beware"), a landlord is not obligated to make any repairs to leased premises. However, many states now require a lessor to maintain dwelling units in a habitable condition and to make any necessary repairs to common elements, such as hallways, stairs, or elevators. The tenant does not have to make any repairs, but he or she must return the premises in the same condition as they were when received, with certain allowances for ordinary use.

Improvements

The tenant may make improvements with the landlord's permission, but any such alterations generally become the property of the landlord; that is, they become fixtures. However, as discussed in Chapter 1, a tenant may be given the right to install trade fixtures or chattel fixtures by the terms of the lease. Such trade fixtures may be removed by the tenant before the expiration of the lease, provided the tenant restores the premises to the condition they were in when he or she took possession.

Assignment and Subleasing

A lessee may assign the lease or may sublease the premises as long as the terms of the lease contract do not prohibit these actions (see Figure 7.1). An *assignment* is the total transfer to another person (assignee) of all the tenant's (assignor's) right, title, and interest in the leasehold estate. After an assignment is completed, the assignee becomes known as the tenant. The original tenant has no further interest in the leasehold estate, but does remain secondarily liable for the payment of rent.

A **sublease** involves a transfer of only a portion of the rights held under a leasehold estate. Therefore, a sublease may concern only a portion of the leased premises or only a part of the lease term. The party acquiring the rights under a sublease is known as the sublessee, while the original tenant becomes the sublessor. Generally, the sublessee pays rent to the sublessor, who in turn pays rent to the landlord. Since the interest of the original tenant is located between the interest of the property owner (landlord) and the end-user of the property (sublessee), it is known as a **sandwich lease.**

Options

Many leases contain an option that grants the lessee the privilege of renewing the lease but requires that the lessee give notice on or before a specific date of his or her intention to exercise the option. Some leases grant to the lessee the option to purchase the leased premises. The provisions for the option to purchase vary widely.

Destruction of Leased Premises

In land leases involving agricultural land, the courts have held that damage or destruction of the improvements, even if it is not the tenant's fault, does not relieve the tenant from the obligation to pay rent to the end of the term. This ruling has been extended in most states to include ground leases upon which the tenant has constructed a building and, in many instances, leases that give possession of an entire building to the tenant. Since the tenant is leasing an entire building, the courts have held that he or she is also leasing the land upon which that building is located.

In those cases where the leased premises are only a part of the building (such as office or commercial space or an apartment), upon destruction of the leased premises the tenant is not required to continue to pay rent. Furthermore, in some states, if the property was destroyed as a result of the landlord's negligence, the tenant can recover damages from the landlord.

Figure 7.1 Assignment versus Subletting

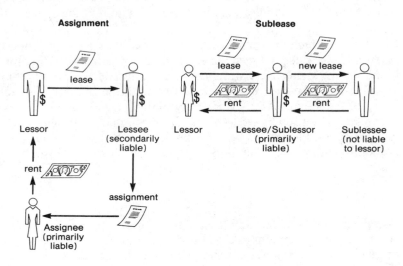

All of these general statements concerning destruction of leased premises are controlled largely by the terms of the lease. Printed lease forms and all individually prepared leases should include a provision covering the subject of destruction of the premises.

Termination of a Lease

A written lease for a definite period of time expires at the end of that time period; no separate notice is required to terminate the lease when it expires. Oral and written leases that do not specify a definite expiration date (such as a month-to-month or year-to-year tenancy or a tenancy at will) may be terminated by giving proper notice in advance as required by state law. Generally, the laws specify a minimum time period or number of days' notice that must be given by the party who wishes to terminate the lease.

When the conditions of a lease are breached (broken), a landlord may terminate the lease and evict the tenant. This kind of action must be handled through a court proceeding according to state law.

It is possible for the parties to a lease to mutually agree to cancel the lease. The tenant may offer to surrender the lease, and acceptance by the landlord will result in termination. A tenant who abandons leased property, however, remains liable for the terms of the lease—including the rent. In such cases, the terms of the specific lease usually dictate whether or not the landlord is obligated to try to rent the space.

In a case in which the owner of leased property dies or the property is sold, the lease does not terminate. The heirs of a deceased landlord are bound by the terms of existing valid leases. In addition, if a landlord conveys leased real estate, the new landlord takes the property subject to the rights of the tenants. However, a lease will be terminated in the event the property is acquired by the government through condemnation, the landlord is declared bankrupt, or the property is foreclosed upon by a lienholder. In some states, that lien must have predated the leases.

Breach of Lease

When a tenant breaches any lease provision, the landlord may sue the tenant to obtain a judgment to cover past due rent, damages to the premises, or other defaults. Likewise, when a landlord breaches any lease provision, the tenant is entitled to similar remedies.

Landlord's remedies/actual eviction.   When a tenant improperly retains possession of leased premises, the landlord may regain possession through a *suit for possession*. This process is known as **actual eviction.** The law requires the landlord to serve notice on the tenant before commencing the suit. Usually at least a ten-day notice is required in case of a default in most lease terms, but in many states, only a five-day notice must be given before filing a suit for possession based on a default in payment of rent. When a court issues a judgment for possession to a landlord, the tenant must peaceably remove himself or herself and his or her belongings, or the landlord can have the judgment enforced by a bailiff or other court officer, who will forcibly remove the tenant.

Tenants' remedies/constructive eviction.   If a landlord breaches any clause of a lease agreement, the tenant has the right to sue, claiming a judgment for damages against the landlord. If an action or omission on the landlord's part results in the leased premises becoming uninhabitable for the purpose intended in the lease, the tenant may have the right to abandon the premises. This action, called **constructive eviction,** terminates the lease agreement if the tenant can prove that the premises have become uninhabitable because of the conscious neglect of the landlord. In order to claim constructive eviction, the *tenant must actually remove himself or herself from the premises while the uninhabitable condition exists.* In some states, the tenant must remove all of his belongings as well.

For example, a lease requires the landlord to furnish heat in the winter. Because of the landlord's failure to repair a defective heating plant, the heat is not provided. If this results in the leased premises being untenable, the tenant may abandon them. Some leases provide that if the failure to furnish heat is accidental and not the fault of the landlord, it does not constitute grounds for constructive eviction.

Tenants' Rights

For the most part, leases are drawn up primarily for the benefit of the landlord. Recent consumer awareness, however, has fostered the belief that a valid lease depends on both parties fulfilling certain obligations. To provide laws outlining such obligations, several states have adopted some variation of the Uniform Residential Landlord and Tenant Act. This model law addresses such issues as the landlord's right of entry, maintenance of premises, response to tenant complaints, and disclosure of the property owners' names and addresses to the tenants. The act further sets down specific remedies available to both the landlord and the tenant if a breach of the lease agreement occurs.

The federal government also took steps to increase tenants' protection with the implementation of the Tenants' Eviction Procedures Act in the late 1970s. This act establishes standardized eviction procedures for persons living in government-subsidized housing. It requires that the landlord have a valid reason for evicting the tenant and that the landlord give the tenant proper notice of eviction. This act does not supersede state laws in this area; however, it does provide recourse for tenants in states that have no protective laws. The act applies only to multiunit residential buildings that are owned or subsidized by the Department of Housing and Urban Development or buildings that have government-backed mortgages.

Americans with Disabilities Act (ADA) and fair housing requirements. The Americans with Disabilities Act (discussed in Chapter 14) has a significant impact on commercial, nonresidential leasing practices. Any property in which public goods or services are provided must be free of architectural barriers or must accommodate individuals with disabilities so that they can enjoy access to those businesses or services. The Fair Housing Act (also discussed in Chapter 14) makes it illegal to discriminate against prospective tenants on the basis of a handicap. Disabled tenants must be permitted to make reasonable modifications to a property (at their own expense), but a landlord may require that rental premises be restored to their original condition at the end of the lease term.

TYPES OF LEASES

The manner in which rent is determined indicates the type of lease in force. The three primary types of leases based upon rentals are (1) gross lease; (2) net lease; and (3) percentage lease (see Table 7.2).

Gross Lease

A **gross lease** provides for a fixed rental. The tenant's obligation is to pay a fixed rental, and the landlord pays all taxes, insurance, mortgage payments, repairs, and the like connected with the property (usually called *property charges*). This type of lease is most often used for residential apartment rentals.

Net Lease

The **net lease** provides that, in addition to the rent, the tenant pays all or part of the property charges except principal and interest on the owner's debt, which remains the owner's responsibility. The monthly rental paid to the landlord is in addition to these charges, so it is net income for the landlord after operating costs have been paid. Leases for entire commercial or industrial buildings (and the land on which they stand), long-term leases, and ground leases (discussed in a later section) are usually net leases.

Percentage Lease

A **percentage lease** provides that the rental is based on a percentage of the gross income received by the tenant doing business on the leased property. This type of lease is usually employed in the rental of retail business locations. The percentage lease usually provides for a minimum fixed rental fee plus a percentage of that portion of the tenant's business income that exceeds a stated minimum.

For example, a lease might provide for a minimum monthly rental of $1,200 with the further agreement that the tenant pay an additional amount each month equivalent to 4 percent of all gross sales in excess of $30,000. (While the $1,200 rental represents 4 percent of $30,000 gross, the percentage feature of this lease will not actually begin to apply until after the tenant has grossed in excess of $30,000.) The percentage charged in such leases varies widely with the nature of the business, and it is negotiable between landlord and tenant. A tenant's bargaining power is determined by the volume of his or her business. Of course,

Table 7.2   Types of Leases

Type of Lease	Lessee	Lessor
Gross lease (residential)	Pays basic rent	Pays property charges (taxes, repairs, insurance, etc.
Net lease (commercial/industrial)	Pays basic rent plus all or most property charges	May pay some property charges
Percentage lease (commercial/industrial)	Pays basic rent plus percent of gross sales (may pay property costs)	May pay some or all property charges

percentages vary with the location of the property and general economic conditions.

Other Lease Types—Variations and Special Circumstances

Several types of leases allow for changes in the fixed rental charge during the lease period.

Graduated leases.   A **graduated lease** begins with rent payments at a fixed, often low, rate with increases at set intervals during the term of the lease. The increases might be based on changes in the value of the land as determined by periodic appraisal. For long-term commercial tenants the advantage is the ability to avoid a heavy financial burden in the early years of business.

Index lease.   The **index lease** calls for an adjustment in the rent based on some designated index, such as the consumer price index or the wholesale price index.

Ground lease.   When a landowner leases his or her land to a tenant who agrees to erect a building on it, the lease is usually referred to as a **ground lease.** Such a lease must be for a term long enough to make the transaction desirable to the tenant making the investment in the building. These leases are generally net leases that require the lessee to pay rent plus real estate taxes, insurance, upkeep, and repairs. Ground leases can run for terms of 50 years or longer, and a lease for 99 years is not impossible.

Oil and gas lease.   When oil companies lease land to explore for oil and gas, a special lease agreement must be negotiated. Usually, the land owner receives a cash payment for executing the lease. If no well is drilled within a year or other period stated in the lease, the lease expires. However, most oil and gas leases provide that the oil company may pay another flat rental fee to continue its rights for another year. Such rentals may be paid annually until a well is produced. If oil and/or gas is found, the landowner usually receives one-eighth of its value as a royalty. In this case, the lease will continue for as long as oil and/or gas is obtained in significant quantities.

Lease option.   A **lease option** allows the tenant the right to purchase the leased property at a predetermined price for a certain time period. Although it is not required, the owner frequently will give the tenant credit toward the purchase price for some of the rent paid. In a lease option the lease is the primary consideration and the option is secondary.

Lease purchase.   A **lease purchase** is used when the tenant wants to purchase the property and is unable to do so presently yet still needs the use of the leased facility. Common reasons for using a lease purchase are current inability to obtain favorable financing or obtain clear title and unfavorable tax consequences of a current purchase. Here the purchase agreement is the primary consideration and the lease is secondary.

Agricultural landowners often lease their land to tenant farmers, who provide the labor to produce and bring in the crop. The owner can be paid by the tenant in one of two ways: as an agreed-on rental amount in cash in advance (**cash rents**) or as a percentage of the profits from the sale of the crop when it is sold (**sharecropping**).

SUMMARY

A *lease* is an agreement that grants one person the right to use the property of another for a certain period in return for valuable consideration. The lease agreement is a combination of a conveyance creating a leasehold interest in the property and a contract outlining the rights and obligations of the landlord (lessor) and the tenant (lessee). A leasehold estate is generally classified as the personal property of the lessee.

The requirements for a valid lease include competent parties, mutual assent, legality of object, signatures, valuable considerations, and a description of the leased property. In addition, state statutes of frauds generally require that any lease that runs longer than one year must be in writing in order to be enforceable in court. Leases also generally include clauses relating to such rights and obligations of the landlord and tenant as the use of the premises, subletting, assignment, judgments, maintenance of the premises, and termination of the lease period.

Leases may be terminated by the expiration of the lease period, the mutual agreement of the parties (*surrender*), or a breach of the lease by either the landlord or the tenant. Neither the death of the landlord nor the landlord's sale of the rented property terminates a lease.

Upon a tenant's default on any of the lease provisions, a landlord may sue for a money judgment or for *actual eviction* when a tenant has improperly retained possession of the premises. If the premises have become uninhabitable due to the landlord's negligence, the tenant may have the right of *constructive eviction;* that is, he or she may have the right to abandon the premises and refuse to pay rent until the premises are repaired.

Several basic types of leases, including *gross leases, net leases, percentage leases, graduated leases,* and *index leases,* are classified according to the method used in determining the rental rate of the property.

QUESTIONS

Please complete all of the questions before turning to the Answer Key.

1. A lease may be terminated by which of the following circumstances

    a.   mutual agreement.   c.   sale of the property.
    b.   death of the landlord.   d.   unilateral rescission.

2. A lease that allows for increases or decreases in the rental amount based on a particular economic indicator is called a(n)

    a.   index lease.   c.   ground lease.
    b.   gross lease.   d.   percentage lease.

3. If the lease does not restrict the use of the premises, the tenant may perform any of the following acts EXCEPT

    a.   assign the lease using an assignment.
    b.   sublease the property with a new lease.
    c.   convey the interest with a warranty deed.
    d.   use the property for any legal purpose.

4. A lease may take on the implication of being a freehold interest rather than a leasehold interest when the term of the lease extends

    a.   10 years.   c.   50 years.
    b.   25 years.   d.   99 years.

5. Leasehold estates that continue for a definite period of time and require no termination notice are called estates

    a.   at will.   c.   from period to period.
    b.   for years.   d.   at sufferance.

6. If an action on the part of the landlord results in the premises becoming uninhabitable, then the tenant may have the right to abandon the premises. This situation is called

    a.   a suit for possession.   c.   actual eviction.
    b.   a judgment lien.   d.   constructive eviction.

7. A lease under which the lessor pays the operating expenses connected with the property and the lessee pays a fixed amount of rent is called a

    a.   gross lease.   c.   graduated lease.
    b.   net lease.   d.   percentage lease.

8. When a tenant takes possession of a property through some legal means but then remains on the property illegally, this is known as a tenancy

    a.   in common.   c.   by the entirety.
    b.   at sufferance.   d.   at will.

9. The amount of rent set forth in the lease agreement is known as

    a.   economic rent.   c.   contract rent.
    b.   gross rent.   d.   net rent.

10. Which of the following statements is true regarding the assignment of a lease?

    a.   A lease can always be assigned.
    b.   The assignee becomes known as the tenant.
    c.   After the assignment, the owner may collect rent only from the assignor.
    d.   The original tenant remains primarily liable for the payment of the rent.

11. Under the terms of a lease, all of the following would be considered to be property charges EXCEPT the

    a.   maintenance expenses for the property.
    b.   real estate taxes due on the property.
    c.   mortgage payment required on the property.
    d.   hazard and liability insurance for the property.

12. All of the following could be considered to be valuable consideration under the terms of a lease EXCEPT

    a.   love and affection.   c.   contributed labor.
    b.   cash.   d.   a percentage of revenues.

13. All of the following items are essential elements of a lease EXCEPT

    a.   legality of object.   c.   valuable consideration.
    b.   competent parties.   d.   option to purchase.

14. If a tenant remains after the expiration of the lease but refuses to pay any rent, that tenant is called a

    a.   resident.   c.   leaseholder.
    b.   tenant at will.   d.   tenant at sufferance.

15. Which of the following statements regarding a sublease is true?

    a.   The sublessee pays rent directly to the owner.
    b.   The sublessee is primarily responsible for meeting the terms of the lease.
    c.   The sublessee holds the sandwich portion of the lease.
    d.   The sublessee is financially responsible to the lessee.

16. The type of lease that calls for regularly scheduled increases in the rental amount due by the lessee is the

    a.   percentage lease.   c.   graduated lease.
    b.   index lease.   d.   gross lease.

17. A lease that automatically renews itself every week is a tenancy

    a.   at will.   c.   at sufferance.
    b.   for years.   d.   from period to period.

18. Which of the following statements concerning leasehold estates is true?

    a.   The property owner is called the lessee.
    b.   The leasehold interest is personal property.
    c.   The tenant's interest is called a leased fee.
    d.   The tenant must record the lease for it to be valid.

8:   Real Estate Brokerage

KEY TERMS

agent
antitrust laws
broker
coinsurance clause
commission
franchise
fraud
independent
   contractor

law of agency
principal
property manager
puffing
real estate commission
real estate license law
salesperson
special agent
subagent

The business of bringing buyers and sellers together in the marketplace is called *brokerage*. Buyers and sellers in many fields employ the services of brokers to facilitate complex business transactions. The term "broker" can be traced back to the Norman French word *brocour* meaning "wine dealer." At that time the local pub was the central meeting place of each village, and it was common practice to inform the wine dealer about items desired. The wine dealer would then pass this information on to other customers. If a sale was made, the *brocour* would receive a fee for his services.

REAL ESTATE BROKERAGE DEFINED

In the real estate business, a **broker** is defined as any person who is licensed to buy, sell, exchange, or lease real property for others in exchange for a fee. Working on behalf of, and licensed to represent the broker, is the real estate **salesperson.**

The person who employs the broker is called a **principal;** the principal (client) may be a seller, a prospective buyer, an owner who wishes to lease his or her property, or a person who seeks property to rent. The real estate broker acts as an agent of the principal, who usually compensates the broker in the form of a **commission,** usually an agreed-upon percentage of the sales or rental price. The commission is contingent upon the broker's successfully performing the service for which he or she was employed—negotiating a transaction with a prospective purchaser, seller, lessor, or lessee who is ready, willing, and able to complete the contract.

Real Estate License Law

Every state and Canadian province requires real estate brokers and salespeople to be licensed. Knowledge of the state's **real estate license law** is essential to the understanding of the legal authorities and responsibilities of brokers and salespeople. The purposes of such laws are to: (1) protect the public from dishonest or incompetent brokers and salespeople; (2) prescribe standards and qualifications for licensing brokers and salespeople; and (3) maintain high standards in the real estate profession.

The authority that controls the licenses of real estate brokers and salespeople is generally the state real estate commission. The commission usually has the power to issue, deny, suspend or revoke licenses, make real estate information available to licensees, and otherwise enforce the license law. Generally, each state's commission has adopted a set of rules and regulations that further define the basic real estate license law and have the same power and effect as the law itself.

Generally, each state law stipulates who must be licensed and who is exempt from licensure, as well as certain operating standards to which brokers and salespeople must adhere. In addition, the license laws establish certain licensing procedures and requirements. License applicants are generally required to pass an examination designed to test their knowledge of real estate principles and laws, including the state license law.

If an applicant does not already have a copy of his or her state license law, he or she should obtain one immediately. Each state's real estate commission will test the applicant's knowledge of that state's particular license law and require real estate brokers and salespeople to operate under its provisions, *which must be known well.*

AGENCY RELATIONSHIPS

The role of a broker as the agent of his or her principal is a fiduciary relationship that falls within the requirements of the **law of agency.** Most fre-

Figure 8.1   Traditional Agency Relationship

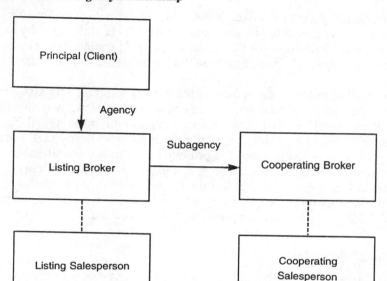

quently this agency is between the seller of a parcel of real estate (the principal) and the real estate broker (the agent), although brokers are increasingly establishing agency relationships with buyers as well. In this relationship, the seller hires the broker to find a suitable buyer (the customer) for the seller's property. In other cases, a broker may be hired by a buyer to find that person a suitable parcel of real estate. In this instance, the buyer is the principal and the seller is the customer. In addition, each of these agency situations generally involves a fourth party, a real estate salesperson who works on behalf of the broker and is, therefore, the broker's agent. A fifth party, another real estate broker, the selling broker, acting as a **subagent** of the listing brokers, may also be involved (see Figure 8.1). Agency law reforms in many states are eliminating subagency as they codify the traditionally common-law agency relationships to ensure greater protections and representation, particularly for buyers.

It must be emphasized that *the payment of a commission by one party does not create an agency relationship.* Such relationships are created by contract, regardless of who might be obligated to pay a commission.

Types of Agencies

A licensed real estate broker is hired by a principal to become his or her agent. In the purest sense, an **agent** is one who is authorized by another to negotiate contracts for that person. An agent is classified as a *general agent* or a *special agent,* based on the extent of his or her authority.

General agents are authorized to perform any and all acts associated with a particular, limited activity. For instance, a property manager might be the general agent of the owner of an apartment building. A special agent, on the other hand, has extremely limited authority and is authorized normally to represent the principal only in one specific transaction or piece of business. Therefore, a real estate broker is a **special agent,** most often hired by a seller to find a ready, willing, and able buyer for the seller's property. As a special agent, the broker is not authorized to sell the property or to bind the principal to any contract.

Creation of Agency

A broker-seller relationship is created by an agreement of the parties. Although a written contract of employment, commonly referred to as a *listing agreement,* is preferred, it is not necessary in all states. As discussed in Chapter 6, these agreements include *open, exclusive-agency,* and *exclusive-right-to-sell* listings. Some states recognize agency relationships that are created by: (1) oral agreement; (2) implication; or (3) ratification.

Oral agreement.   Some states construe an oral open listing as binding. All that is technically necessary is that the client expresses willingness to be represented in a transaction by the broker and the broker expresses willingness to carry out the client's directions.

Implication.   This relationship is created when one party gives another reason to believe that the broker is his or her agent. For example, suppose owner *A* knows that broker *B* is showing her unimproved property to prospective buyers without the authority to do so. If *A* does not stop the broker's unauthorized showings, the law construes that all persons dealing with *B* on the property have reason to believe, based on the actions of the broker and the seller, that an agency exists. Such an agency is known as an *ostensible agency* (on the surface it appears to exist). Once this agency is created, the law prevents the principal from denying its existence by the legal doctrine of *estoppel,* under which a person may not assert rights or facts contrary to his or her actions or silence.

Ratification.   This broker-seller relationship is created when the broker has acted without authority and without the seller's knowledge of his or her acts, but the seller later approves all of the broker's previous unauthorized acts. For example, suppose owner *A* has no idea that broker *B* is showing her property to prospective buyers, but when an offer to purchase is presented by the broker to *A,* she accepts the offer and agrees to pay *B* a commission. By her acceptance of the offer, *A* has accepted all of *B*'s previously unauthorized acts and created an agency relationship with the broker through this ratification.

Because of the special nature of a real estate broker's responsibility, many states have enacted laws similar to the statute of frauds or have incorporated provisions into the statute of frauds that require listing agreements to be in writing when a commission is to be paid for securing a person who is ready, willing, and able to buy, sell, or rent. A wise real estate broker does not rely on an oral agreement from his or her principal, but rather requires that all agreements be in writing and signed by the principal.

Again, remember that the payment of a commission by one party does not create an agency relationship. Agency relationships are created by contract, regardless of who might be obligated to pay a commission, or by the actions of the party.

Termination of Agency

An agency relationship may be terminated by the actions of either principal or agent or through the operation of law in a number of ways, as listed in Figure 8.2.

C - CARE
O - OBEDIENCE
A - ACCOUNTING
L - LOYALTY
D - DISCLOSURE

Figure 8.2   Ways an Agency May Be Terminated

Act of the parties	Operation of law
1. Full performance by the agent	1. Death of either party
2. Expiration of the listing period	2. Incapacity of either
3. Abandonment by the agent	3. Destruction of the property
4. Revocation by the principal	4. Bankruptcy of either
5. Cancellation by the agent	5. Condemnation of the property
6. Mutual agreement by the parties	6. Revocation of the agent's license

Please note that abandonment by the agent occurs when neither time nor money has been spent to market the property. If the principal revokes the agency, he or she may be responsible for damages or expenses or both. In addition, the agent may cancel the listing if given illegal instructions by the principal.

Agent's Responsibilities to Principal   C. O. A L. D.

The broker, as an agent, owes his or her principal certain duties. These duties are clear and specific; they are neither simply moral nor merely ethical. They are the law—the law of agency. An agent has a fiduciary relationship with his or her principal; that is, a relationship of trust and confidence as between employer and employee. This confidential relationship carries with it certain duties that the broker must perform—the duties of care, obedience, accounting, loyalty, and disclosure (see Figure 8.3). These duties may be more easily remembered by the acronym COALD.

Care.   The broker, as an agent, must exercise a reasonable degree of care while transacting business entrusted to him or her by the principal. Brokers are liable to their principals for any loss resulting from negligence or carelessness.

Obedience.   Brokers are at all times obligated to act in good faith and in conformity with their principals' instructions and authority. Again, a broker is liable for any losses incurred by the principal due to the broker's performance of acts that are not within his or her scope of authority.

Accounting.   Brokers must be able to report the status of all funds entrusted to them by their principals. Most state real estate license laws require brokers to give accurate copies of all documents to all parties affected by them and to keep copies of such documents on file for a specified period of time. In addition, the license laws generally require brokers to deposit immediately all funds entrusted to them in a special trust or escrow account and make it illegal for brokers to *commingle* such monies with personal funds.

All states forbid brokers or salespeople to buy property listed with them for their own accounts, or for accounts in which they have a personal interest, without first notifying and receiving the consent of the principal of such interest. Likewise, by law, neither brokers nor salespeople may sell property in which they have an interest without informing the purchaser of their personal interest.

Figure 8.3   Agent's Responsibilities

Loyalty.   Loyalty is a must—brokers owe their employers 100 percent, the utmost in loyalty. An agent must always place a principal's interests above those of the other persons he or she is dealing with. Thus, an agent cannot disclose such information as the principal's financial condition, the fact that the principal (if the seller) will accept a price lower than the listing price for his or her real estate, or any similar confidential facts that might damage the principal's bargaining position.

Disclosure.   Along with these four responsibilities goes the duty of disclosure, sometimes called *notice*. It is the broker's responsibility to keep the principal fully informed at all times of all facts the broker obtains that could affect the transaction. A broker who fails to disclose such information may be held liable for any damages that result.

The broker may also be responsible for facts he or she *should have known* and revealed to the principal but did not. This *duty of discovery* includes facts both favorable and unfavorable, even if their disclosure might terminate the transaction.

Broker-Buyer Relationship

As mentioned previously, in the brokerage business, a buyer can be either the principal or the customer of a broker.

Buyer as principal.   Not so long ago, the principal of "caveat emptor" (let the buyer beware) ruled the real estate industry. Brokers always represented sellers, and buyers were expected to look out for themselves. Today, however, many residential brokers are discovering the opportunities available to them by having buyers rather than sellers as their clients. Real estate commissions across the country have developed rules and procedures to regulate such **buyer-brokers,** and REALTOR® organizations are developing forms for their use. Professional associations have been created, such as the Real Estate Buyer's Agent Council (REBAC) and the National Association of Exclusive Buyer's Agents (NAEBA), to offer assistance, certification, training and networking opportunities for buyer's agents.

An agency relationship is not dependent on who pays the commission, but on the terms of the agency agreements. For example, in some buyer-brokerage relationships, the buyer-client pays the broker an up-front fee for services. In other arrangements, the buyer's broker will split a commission with the listing agent. In both instances, the buyer is the broker's principal, and is owed the traditional duties of care, obedience, accounting, loyalty, and disclosure discussed above.

It is easy for a buyer to believe that the agent who shows them a property represents them in subsequent negotiations. This natural misunderstsanding may arise out of the amount of time an agent typically spends with the buyer, and the professionally cordial relationship the agent properly seeks to build. The buyer may confide confidential financial information to the agent and feel he or she is being represented in the negotiations as well; however, if the agent represents the seller, he or she is obliged to pass on all relevant information, and to represent only the seller's best interests.

To avoid problems with the issue of whom the agent represents, most states have enacted or are planning to enact statutes that address some form of mandatory agency disclosure. Whether the disclosure is on a separate written form or is part of a contract, whether it is made at first contact with the nonclient or customer or at some other time is not the concern. Public policy demands a level playing field: nonclients or customers must somehow be informed that they do *not* have representation, and real estate commissions have been charged with implementing that policy. The statutes typically establish which forms of agency are legal in the state: buyer and seller agency, for instance, or disclosed dual agency may be permitted; many states have abolished the practice of subagency altogether. Within a single real estate office, a broker may be required to designate one or more agents as "buyer's agents" and "seller's agents" for a transaction in which both the selling and buying sides are represented by the same company. Some brokers avoid the whole issue by becoming transactional or facilitating brokers: their job is simply to help with the necessary paperwork and formalities; the buyer and seller negotiate the sale on their own. Transactional brokers must disclose known defects in a property, but may not negotiate for either side. A real estate licensee must be knowledgeable about his or her state's particular disclosure requirements in order to provide effective representation and to avoid liability.

Buyer as customer.   In dealing with a buyer, a broker, as an agent of the seller, must be aware of the laws and ethical considerations that affect this relationship. For example, brokers must be careful of the statements they or their staff members make about a parcel of real estate. Statements of opinion **(puffing)** are permissible as long as they are offered as opinions and without any intention to deceive. An example would be the statement, "In my opinion, this house has the best view in the city."

Statements of fact, however, must be accurate. The broker must be alert to ensure that none of his or her statements in any way can be interpreted as involving fraud. **Fraud** consists of all deceitful or dishonest practices intended to harm or take advantage of another person. In addition to false statements about a property, the concept of fraud also includes concealment or nondisclosure of important facts. If a contract to purchase real estate is obtained as a result of misstatements made by a broker or his or her salespeople, the contract may be disaffirmed or renounced by a purchaser. In such a case, the broker will lose the commission. If either party suffers loss because of a broker's misrepresentations, the broker can be held liable for damages. If the broker's misstatements are based upon the owner's own inaccurate statements to the broker, however, the broker may be entitled to a commission even if the buyer rescinds the sales contract.

Brokers and salespeople should be aware that, despite the principle of *caveat emptor* (let the buyer beware), which relates to *patent defects* (defects readily seen and understood by the buyer), the courts have ruled that a seller is responsible for revealing to a buyer any hidden or latent defects in a property. A *latent defect* is one that is known to the seller but not the buyer, and is not discoverable by ordinary inspection. Buyers have been able to either rescind a sales contract or receive damages in such instances. Cases in which the seller neglected to reveal violations of zoning or building codes have also been ruled in favor of the buyer. The use of the phrase *"as is"* in a sales contract has no effect on the duty to disclose latent defects. The courts have ruled that "as is" relates solely to defects that are open and obvious.

Dual agency.   In dealing with buyers, brokers must be careful of any situation that might be considered a dual agency. Sometimes a broker may have the opportunity to receive compensation from both the buyer and seller in a transaction. Theoretically, however, an agent cannot be loyal to two or more distinct principals in the same transaction. Thus, the state real estate license laws generally prohibit a broker from representing and collecting compensation from both parties to a transaction without their prior mutual knowledge and consent. Some courts reject the consent exception altogether because of public policy considerations. In fact, basically the only transaction in which the agent may generally act as a dual agent without being subject to possible rejection of commission rights in a court action is when the agent is representing two parties in an exchange agreement. In such cases, there are in essence two buyers, two sellers, and two parcels of real estate. Therefore, the earning of two commissions is proper.

In situations in which the agent has represented the seller, a charge of undisclosed dual agency may be filed if the buyer mistakenly believes the agent represented him and later finds that was not the case.

To avoid problems with the issue of whom the agent represents, most states have enacted or are planning to enact statutes that address some form of mandatory agency disclosure. Whether the disclosure is on a separate written form or is part of a contract, whether it is made at first contact with the nonclient or customer or at a more convenient time is not the concern. Public policy indicates that nonclients or customers must somehow be informed that they do *not* have representation, and real estate commissions have been charged with implementing that policy. An informed real estate licensee will be knowledgeable about such disclosure requirements. Until that time, however, each licensee must be careful not to create false impressions on the part of the nonclient or customer.

Transaction Broker.   A relatively recent development is the emergence of transaction brokers, whose practice is limited to neutrally facilitating a real estate transaction between a buyer and a seller. Because he or she represents neither party's interest, a transaction broker is not an agent for either the buyer or the seller, and is not bound by rules of confidentiality. A transaction broker is generally expected to treat all parties honestly and competently, to locate qualified buyers or suitable properties, to work with both the buyer and the seller to arrive at mutually-acceptable terms, and to assist in the closing of the transaction. Agency laws do not usually govern transaction brokers, but all parties should clearly understand the nature of the services being offered.

NATURE OF THE REAL ESTATE BUSINESS

A real estate broker is an independent businessperson who sets the policies of his or her own office. A broker engages employees and salespeople, determines their compensation, and directs their activities. He or she is free to accept or reject agency relationships with principals. This is an important characteristic of the brokerage business: a broker has the right to reject agency contracts that in his judgment violate the ethics or standards of the office. However, once a brokerage relationship has been established, the broker represents the person who engaged him or her. The broker owes that person, the principal, the duty to exercise care, skill, and integrity in carrying out instructions.

Broker-Salesperson Relationship

A person licensed to perform any of the real estate activities discussed at the beginning of this chapter on behalf of a licensed real estate broker is known as a real estate salesperson. The salesperson is responsible only to the broker under whom he or she is licensed, and the salesperson can carry out only those responsibilities assigned by that broker.

A broker is licensed to act as the principal's agent and can thus collect a commission for performing his or her assigned duties. A salesperson, on the other hand, has no authority to make contracts or receive compensation directly from a principal. The broker pays a commission to the salesperson and is fully responsible for the acts of all salespeople licensed under him or her. All of a salesperson's activities must be performed in the name of his or her supervising broker.

Employee status versus independent-contractor status.   Salespeople are engaged by brokers as either employees or **independent contractors.** The agreement between a broker and a salesperson may be set down in a written contract that defines the obligations and responsibilities of the relationship. Whether a salesperson is employed by the broker or operates under the broker as an independent contractor affects the broker's relationship with the salesperson and the broker's liability to pay and withhold taxes from that salesperson's earnings (see Figure 8.4).

The nature of the employer-employee relationship allows a broker to exercise certain controls over salespeople who are *employees.* The broker may require an employee to adhere to regulations concerning such matters as working hours, office routine, and dress or language standards. As an employer, a broker is required by the federal government to withhold social security tax and income tax from wages paid to employees. He or she is also required to pay unemployment compensation tax on wages paid to one or more employees, as defined by state and federal laws. In addition, a broker may provide his or her employees with such benefits as health insurance and profit-sharing plans.

A broker's relationship with an independent contractor is very different. The independent contractor-salesperson operates more independently

Figure 8.4   Employee vs. Independent Contractor

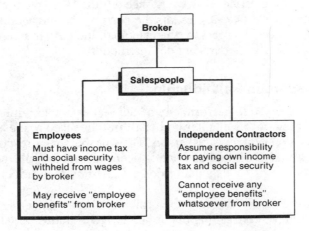

than an employee, and the broker may not control his or her activities in the same way. Basically, the broker may control what the independent contractor does, but not how it is done. An independent contractor assumes responsibility for paying his or her own income and social security taxes and must provide his or her own health insurance, if such coverage is desired. An independent contractor receives nothing from his or her brokers that could be construed as an employee benefit.

The Internal Revenue Service often investigates the independent contractor/ employee situation in real estate offices. Under the "qualified real estate agent" category in the Internal Revenue Code, meeting three requirements can establish an independent contractor status: (1) The individual must have a current real estate license. (2) He or she must have a written contract with the broker containing the following clause: "The salesperson will not be treated as an employee with respect to the services performed by such salesperson as a real estate agent for federal tax purposes." (3) Ninety percent or more of the individual's income as a licensee must be based on sales production and not on the number of hours worked. The broker should have a standardized agreement drawn or reviewed by an attorney to ensure its compliance with these federal dictates. The broker should also be aware that written agreements mean little to an IRS auditor if the actions of the parties are contrary to the document's provisions.

Broker-Subagent Relationship

A principal may expressly authorize his or her agent to appoint a sub-agent and establish a new contractual and fiduciary relationship directly between the principal and the subagent. When this occurs, the subagent represents the principal in the same way the agent does. The latter is liable for the acts of the subagent only when negligent in the selection of the subagent. In the absence of express or implied authorization by the principal to appoint a subagent, the general rule is that an agent may not establish a new agency relationship between the principal and a third person. If the agent does attempt to employ a subagent without the authority to do so, the agency between the principal and the purported subagent does not exist.

The subagent, normally a cooperating broker, may not, as a general rule, sue the seller of the property for a commission. It would appear to follow that the cooperating broker would thus not be liable to the seller, having no privity of contract with the seller. However, recent court decisions show a trend to hold a cooperating broker to be the agent of the seller and to owe certain obligations to this principal. Cooperating brokers acting with the express permission of the listing broker have been held liable for damages sustained by the seller on account of their misrepresentations.

An agent, unless specifically forbidden by the principal to do so, can delegate the agent's powers to another person in any of the following cases, but in no others: (1) when the act is purely mechanical; (2) when it is an act the agent cannot do alone and the subagent can lawfully perform; (3) when it is typical of the local market area to delegate such powers; or (4) when the principal authorized the delegation. However, discretionary powers may not be delegated unless authorized by the principal. Most listing contracts now in use authorize the listing broker to delegate to cooperating brokers much of the work of procuring a buyer.

Broker's Compensation

The broker's compensation is specified in the listing agreement, management agreement, or other contract with the principal. Compensation is usually in the form of a commission or brokerage fee negotiable between broker and seller and computed as a percentage of the total amount of money involved. Such commission is usually considered to be earned when the broker has accomplished the work for which he or she was hired, and is due at the closing. Most sales commissions are payable when the sale is consummated by delivery of the seller's deed. This provision is generally included in the listing agreement or the real estate sales contract. The broker's commission is generally *earned* when a completed

Figure 8.5 Broker's Compensation

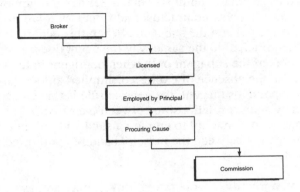

sales contract has been signed by a ready, willing, and able buyer and accepted by the seller.

In order to be entitled to a sales commission, a broker must be able to show that he or she: (1) was a licensed broker; (2) was the procuring cause of the sale; and (3) was employed by the client to cause the transaction (see Figure 8.5). In order to be considered the *procuring cause,* the broker must have taken action that started or caused a chain of events that resulted in the sale. A broker who causes or completes an action without a promise or contract to be paid is termed a volunteer and has no legal claim for compensation. In order to collect a sales commission from a seller, a broker must be able to prove that the seller agreed to pay the broker a commission for the sale.

Once a seller accepts an offer from a ready, willing, and able buyer, the seller is technically liable for the broker's commission regardless of whether or not the buyer completes the purchase. A *ready, willing, and able buyer* is one who is prepared to buy on the seller's terms and is ready to take positive steps toward consummation of the transaction. The modern courts, however, tend to prevent a broker from seeking a commission from the seller if the broker knew or should have known that the buyer was not financially able to complete the purchase.

A broker who has produced a buyer ready, willing, and able to meet the listing terms is usually still entitled to a commission if the transaction is not consummated for any of the following reasons:

1. The owner changes his or her mind and refuses to sell.
2. The owner's spouse refuses to sign the deed.

3. The owner's title contains uncorrected defects.

4. The owner commits fraud during the transaction.

5. The owner is unable to deliver possession within a reasonable time.

6. The owner insists on terms not in the listing, such as the right to restrict the use of the property.

7. The owner and the buyer agree to cancel the transaction.

The rate of a broker's commission is *negotiable* in every case. Any attempt by members of the profession, no matter how subtle, to impose uniform commission rates would be a clear violation of state and federal antitrust laws (which will be discussed later in this chapter). If no amount or percentage rate of commission is stated in the listing contract, then the broker is entitled to no commission. If such a case is taken to court, the court might assign a reasonable amount of commission based on the custom in that community.

Most license laws make it illegal for a broker to share a commission with someone who is not licensed as a salesperson or broker. This has been construed to include personal property (for instance, a broker giving a new TV to "a friend" for providing a valuable lead) and other premiums (vacations and the like) as well as finder's fees and actual percentages of the commission paid to the broker.

Salesperson's Compensation

The compensation of a salesperson is set by agreement between the broker and salesperson. A broker may agree to pay a salary or a share of the commissions from transactions originated by a salesperson. A salesperson may have a drawing account against his or her earned share of commissions. Some brokers require salespeople to pay all or part of the expenses of advertising listed properties.

A recent innovation in salespeople's compensation is the 100-percent commission plan. In a brokerage firm where this system has been adopted, all salespeople who achieve a predetermined sales quota pay a monthly service charge to their broker (to cover the costs of office space, telephones, and supervision) and receive 100 percent of the commissions from the sales they negotiate. Needless to say, such salespeople are hired as independent contractors rather than as employees. One of the advantages of the 100-percent commission plan to the broker is that only top-producing salespeople can survive in such a situation. The necessity of

maintaining a high level of productivity eliminates part-timers and reduces the turnover rate of salespeople. The broker, of course, also enjoys
a steady income, regardless of fluctuations in the real estate market, and
benefits from the independent-contractor status of his or her associates
for reasons mentioned earlier in this chapter. The salespeople's benefits
are obvious—they never again have to split a commission with the broker
for services they have personally rendered. However, the salespersons
pay for their monthly share of office expense, regardless of their earnings, as well as advertising, sign costs, and other expenses.

Real Estate Franchises

A recent development in real estate brokerage operations is the fran-
chised brokerage. Basically, a **franchise** refers to a private contractual
agreement to run a business using a designated trade name and operating
procedures. Such firms as Century 21, Red Carpet, and Gallery of Homes
are real estate franchisors, affiliated with thousands of brokerages nationwide. As franchisors, these companies neither own nor operate the offices
of the individual franchisees. Rather, they "lease" their trade names, reputations, and services to independent brokers for either a flat fee or a percentage of the office's gross commissions.

From a broker's point of view, the advantages of franchising include
good market identification; strong business image resulting from the franchisor's trade name, trademark, and national advertising; a nationwide referral network, which can aid contacts in planning long-distance moves;
and services such as training programs and management assistance.
Among the disadvantages are: the fees paid may be proportionately
greater than the services or benefits derived from the franchisor; possible
loss of local, individual identity; implementation of bookkeeping procedures that would not ordinarily be necessary; and difficulties such as ten-
sions among referring brokers.

Antitrust Laws

The real estate industry is subject to federal (Sherman Antitrust Act and
Clayton Antitrust Law) and state **antitrust laws.** These laws prohibit mo-
nopolies and contracts, combinations, and conspiracies that unreasonably
restrain trade. The most common antitrust violations in the real estate
business are price fixing and allocation of customers or markets.

Illegal *price fixing* occurs when brokers conspire to set prices for the services they perform (sales commissions, management rates), rather than
letting those prices be established through competition in the open market.

Allocation of customers or markets involves an agreement among brokers to divide their markets and refrain from competing for each other's business. Allocations might take place on a geographic basis, with brokers agreeing to specific territories within which they will operate exclusively. The division might also take place along other lines. For example, two brokers might agree that one will handle only residential properties under $75,000 in value, while another will handle only residential properties over $75,000 in value.

The penalties for such violations are severe. Under the Sherman Antitrust Act, individuals who fix prices or allocate markets may be found guilty of a misdemeanor punishable by a maximum $100,000 fine and three years in prison. For corporations, the penalty may be as much as $1 million. In a civil suit, a person who has suffered a loss because of the antitrust activities of a guilty party may recover triple the value of the actual damages, plus attorney's fees and costs.

REAL ESTATE SPECIALIZATIONS

In addition to bringing buyers and sellers together in a typical real estate transaction, brokers often engage in related specializations such as appraisal, property management, and insurance.

Appraisal

The process of estimating the value of a parcel of real estate is called *appraisal*. Although real estate licensees must possess some understanding of valuation as part of the training, state-licensed or state-certified appraisers must be employed when the property is involved in any federally related transaction, such as a loan from a bank or an appraisal for estate tax purposes. The appraiser must have sound judgment and experience as well as a detailed knowledge of the methods of valuation. Appraisal is covered in more detail in Chapter 10.

Property Management

A real estate broker who operates income-producing property on behalf of a principal is a **property manager.** The property manager is usually responsible for soliciting tenants, collecting rents, altering or constructing new space for tenants, ordering repairs, and generally maintaining the property. The manager's basic responsibility is to protect the owner's investment and maximize the owner's return on investment. The property manager, as agent of the property owner, is charged with the same agency responsibilities as a listing broker—care, obedience, accounting, loyalty, and disclosure.

The written agreement that establishes the agency relationship between the principal and the property manager is called a *management agreement*. The management agreement defines the manager's authority and responsibilities and establishes the manager's rate of compensation, generally a fixed percentage of all rents collected. Most states require a property manager to be a real estate licensee.

Insurance

Among the major services of the real estate broker's business, insurance is sometimes included. In many offices, the real estate broker is also an insurance broker. Insurance brokerage, however, is a separate business that requires a *separate state license*.

Types of coverage.   The real estate/insurance broker may offer many different types of property insurance to his or her customers. Some of the more common types include:

1. *Homeowners' insurance:* A standard coverage homeowners' policy covers the insured against fire, theft, and windstorm damage, as well as losses or damage to persons on the owner's property. Such coverage can usually be extended to include protection against losses due to hail, explosion, civil unrest, glass breakage, damage to trees and shrubs, and other less common types of perils. Through a policy provision called a **coinsurance clause,** a homeowner is generally required to carry fire insurance in an amount equal to at least *80 percent of the replacement cost* of the building.

2. *Renters' or condominium owners' insurance:* This policy insures a tenant or condominium unit owner against loss due to fire, windstorm, theft, and public liability within the apartment or unit.

3. *Income-property insurance:* Generally, insurance protecting an owner of income-producing property against losses is similar in nature to homeowners' and renters' insurance, and usually includes fire, hazard, public liability, and casualty coverage. However, such insurance packages, often referred to as *multiperil policies,* are generally more inclusive than homeowners' policies and can be extended to protect the owner against losses re-

sulting from business interruption as well as criminal or negligent acts of employees.

SUMMARY

Real estate brokerage is the bringing together, for a fee or commission, of people who wish to buy, sell, exchange, or lease (and in some states mortgage or finance) real estate. A broker may hire salespeople to assist him or her in this work. The salesperson works on the broker's behalf as either an employee or as an *independent contractor.*

An important part of real estate brokerage is the law of agency, which controls the complex interrelationships of duties, rights, and liabilities among three people: the principal, the *agent,* and the *third party* with whom the agent deals. A real estate broker is a *special agent* in that he or she is normally authorized to act for the principal only in regard to one specific piece of property. The broker may be hired by either a buyer or a seller of real estate to sell or find a particular parcel of real estate. The person who hires the broker is the *principal.* The principal and agent have a *fiduciary relationship,* under which the agent owes the principal the duties of care, obedience, accounting, loyalty, and disclosure. The person with whom the broker interacts in performing the duties of his agency is the *third party* to whom the broker owes the obligation of fair and honest business practices.

The broker's compensation in a real estate sale generally takes the form of a *commission,* which is a percentage of the real estate's selling price or an agreed-upon fee. The broker is considered to have earned a commission when he or she procures a buyer who is *ready, willing,* and *able* to buy under the seller's terms.

A growing number of real estate brokerages are affiliated with franchises. Many of the general operations of a real estate brokerage are regulated by state law, including the real estate license law. In addition, state and federal *antitrust laws* prohibit brokers from conspiring to fix prices or allocate customers or markets.

Although selling is the most widely recognized activity of a real estate broker's business, the broker may also engage in a number of specializations, including property management and insurance brokerage.

QUESTIONS

Please complete all of the questions before turning to the Answer Key.

1. A real estate broker who is employed by a principal to market a specific parcel of property is classified as a

   a. general agent.   c. subagent.
   b. special agent.   d. client.

2. All of the following activities require a person to have a real estate license EXCEPT

   a. listing property.   c. selling property.
   b. appraising property.   d. managing property.

3. A broker may lose the right to receive a commission in a real estate transaction if he or she

   a. did not advertise the property.
   b. was not licensed when employed as an agent.
   c. did not personally market and sell the listing.
   d. accepted a commission from another client.

4. In a traditional real estate relationship among the seller, the buyer, and the broker, the

   a. seller is the customer.   c. seller is the client.
   b. buyer is the principal.   d. buyer is the fiduciary.

5. An employment contract between the seller and the broker may be created by any of the following situations EXCEPT

   a. a written listing agreement.
   b. an oral agreement.
   c. implication.
   d. operation of law.

6. A real estate salesperson can receive a commission check directly from the

   a. employing broker.   c. seller.
   b. cooperating broker.   d. buyer.

7. A broker is employed by a listing contract with the seller. During the sales process, the buyer tells the broker how pleased he is with the way the broker negotiated the price. The broker allows the buyer to continue to think that he is represented by the broker, although there is no written contract or other agreement with the buyer. In this situation, the broker might be charged with

   a. puffing.
   b. misrepresentation.
   c. undisclosed dual agency.
   d. fraud.

8. A real estate broker employed by a property owner to market a parcel of real estate must comply with

   a. any instructions of the owner.
   b. any instructions of the buyer.
   c. the concept of *caveat emptor.*
   d. the law of agency.

9. A real estate salesperson who makes a statement of opinion concerning a parcel of property is probably

   a. puffing.
   b. guilty of fraud.
   c. making a misrepresentation.
   d. liable to the buyer for damages.

10. A broker who deposits a customer's earnest money into his or her personal account is guilty of

    a. dual agency.
    b. violation of fiduciary obligations.
    c. commingling.
    d. misrepresentation.

11. Broker *J* has secured a listing from the seller and then offers to share the commission with any other broker who helps to procure a ready, willing, and able buyer. Unless indicated otherwise, which of the following relationships exists?

    a. Broker *J* is the subagent of the seller.
    b. Broker *J* is the fiduciary of the other broker.
    c. The other broker is the subagent of the seller.
    d. The other broker is the fiduciary of the seller.

12. A salesperson acts as an independent contractor for the broker who holds the salesperson's real estate license. As an independent contractor, the salesperson is

    a.   not responsible to the broker for what he or she does.
    b.   responsible for paying all of his or her income taxes.
    c.   allowed to receive employee benefits such as health insurance.
    d.   told what specific hours he or she must work for the broker.

13. The responsibilities of the broker to the principal include all of the following EXCEPT

    a.   care.   c.   obedience.
    b.   loyalty.   d.   courtesy.

14. A real estate licensee must disclose the fact that he or she has a real estate license in all of the following situations EXCEPT when

    a.   offering a seller's property for purchase.
    b.   offering an owner's property for rent.
    c.   purchasing an automobile for business use.
    d.   purchasing real estate as a personal investment.

15. At which of the following events will the real estate broker have earned his or her commission?

    a.   At the signing of the listing contract
    b.   At the presentation of the offer to purchase
    c.   At the acceptance of the offer to purchase
    d.   At the completion of the transaction

16. While in the employ of a real estate broker, the salesperson has the authority to

    a.   act as an agent for the seller.
    b.   assume responsibilities assigned by the broker.
    c.   accept a commission from another broker.
    d.   advertise the property on his or her own behalf.

17. The real estate commissions that are paid to the broker are

  a. fixed by law.
  b. set by local custom.
  c. determined by the real estate board.
  d. established through negotiation.

18. A principal may authorize his or her agent to appoint another broker to act on the principal's behalf. This other broker would be called the

  a. listing broker.   c. client.
  b. subagent.   d. fiduciary.

19. When the broker has acted without the principal's knowledge or authority, but the principal later approves all of the broker's unauthorized acts, this is known as agency by

  a. implication.   c. ratification.
  b. estoppel.   d. disclosure.

20. An agent is employed by the buyer. Which of the following obligations would she have to a seller?

  a. Honesty   c. Obedience
  b. Accounting   d. Loyalty

21. A person who employs a broker to act on his or her behalf by securing a buyer for real property could be referred to by any of the following names EXCEPT

  a. client.   c. fiduciary.
  b. principal.   d. seller.

22. When the broker has been employed by the seller under a listing contract, it would be appropriate for the broker to disclose all of the following items to a prospective buyer EXCEPT the

  a. lowest price that the seller would accept for the property.
  b. lowest interest rate that the buyer could obtain on a loan.
  c. location of the nearest public and private schools.
  d. location of the nearest houses of worship.

23. A transaction is voided because the seller misrepresented the property to both the broker and the buyer. The broker would be entitled to

   a. partial commission.   c. half commission.
   b. full commission.   d. no commission.

24. The agency obligation that requires a broker to be responsible for funds and documents entrusted to him or her on behalf of a client is

   a. care.   c. accounting.
   b. loyalty.   d. disclosure.

25. For a broker to prove that he or she is entitled to receive a commission, all of the following conditions must be met EXCEPT that the broker was

   a. a disclosed dual agent.
   b. employed by the principal.
   c. properly licensed.
   d. the procuring cause.

26. All of the following concerning real estate brokerage are true EXCEPT that the

   a. agent has a fiduciary obligation to the principal.
   b. real estate broker acts as an agent for the principal.
   c. real estate salesperson acts on behalf of the employing broker.
   d. customer generally pays the real estate commission to the broker.

27. A broker would have the right to dictate which of the following to an independent contractor who was working for him or her?

   a. The number of hours that the person would have to work
   b. The schedule that the person would have to follow
   c. The minimum acceptable dress code for the office
   d. The commission rate that the broker would earn

28. A broker is entitled to collect a commission from both the seller and the buyer when

   a. the seller holds a real estate license.
   b. the buyer and the seller are related.
   c. both parties agree to such a transaction.
   d. both parties have attorneys.

9:   Real Estate Taxation

KEY TERMS

adjusted basis	equalization factor
ad valorem tax	exchange
appropriation	installment sale
basis	mill
capital gain	special assessment
cost recovery	transfer tax

As discussed in Chapter 2, the ownership of real estate is subject to certain government powers. One of these powers is the right to levy taxes for the support of governmental functions. Because the location of real estate is permanently fixed, the government can levy taxes with a high degree of certainty that the taxes will be collected.

State and local governments levy annual real estate taxes on all but certain exempt parcels of land within their jurisdictions. These taxes usually have priority over other previously recorded liens. Such liens may be enforced by the court sale of the real estate free of any other liens.

In addition to taxes on real estate ownership, the federal government (and most state governments) imposes an income tax on all profits resulting from the ownership and/or sale of real estate. However, federal income taxes are generally reduced by certain provisions in the tax laws that are designed to encourage ownership of and investment in real estate.

STATE AND LOCAL PROPERTY TAXATION

Real estate taxes can be divided into two types: (1) general real estate tax, or ad valorem tax; and (2) special assessments, or improvement tax. Both of these taxes are levied against specific parcels of property and automatically become liens on those properties. In addition, there is a third category of state and local taxation that affects parcels of real estate when they are sold, the real estate transfer tax.

General Tax (Ad Valorem Tax)

The general real estate tax is made up of the taxes levied on real estate by various governmental agencies and municipalities. These include cities, towns, villages, and counties. Other taxing bodies are the school districts or boards (including local elementary and high schools, junior colleges, and community colleges), drainage districts, water districts, and sanitary districts. Municipal authorities operating recreational preserves such as forest preserves and parks are also authorized by the legislatures of the various states to levy real estate taxes.

General real estate taxes are levied for the general support or operation of the governmental agency authorized to impose the levy. These taxes are known as **ad valorem taxes** (from the Latin, "to value") because the amount of the tax varies in accordance with the value of the property being taxed.

Exemptions from general taxes.   Under most state laws, certain real estate is exempt from real estate taxation. For example, property owned by cities, various municipal organizations (such as schools, parks, or playgrounds), the state and federal governments, and religious organizations, hospitals, or educational institutions is tax exempt. Usually, the property must be used for tax-exempt purposes by the exempted group or organization, or it will be subject to tax.

Many state laws also allow special exemptions to reduce real estate tax bills for certain property owners or land uses. Homeowners and senior citizens are frequently granted set reductions in the assessed value of their homes. Some states offer real estate tax reductions to attract industries, and many states offer tax reductions for agricultural land to encourage the continuation of agricultural uses.

Assessment.   Real estate is valued, or assessed, for tax purposes by county or township assessors. The land is usually appraised separately from the building. The building value is usually determined from a manual or set of rules covering unit-cost prices and rates of depreciation. Some states require assessments to be a certain percentage of true (market) value. State laws may provide for property to be reassessed periodically.

Property owners who claim that errors were made in determining the assessed value of their property may present their objections to a local board of appeal or board of review. Protests or appeals regarding tax assessments may ultimately be taken to court. Such cases generally involve a proceeding whereby the court reviews the certified assessment records of the tax assessment official.

Equalization. In some jurisdictions, when it is necessary to correct general inequalities in statewide tax assessments, uniformity may be achieved by use of an **equalization factor.** Such a factor may be provided for use in counties or districts where the assessments are to be raised or lowered. The assessed value of each property is multiplied by the equalization factor, and the tax rate is then applied to the equalized assessment. For example, the assessments in one county are determined to be 20 percent lower than the average assessments throughout the rest of the state. This underassessment can be corrected by the application of an equalization factor of 125 percent to each assessment in that county. Thus, a parcel of land assessed for tax purposes at $63,000 would be taxed based upon an equalized assessment of $78,750 in this county ($63,000 × 1.25 = $78,750).

Tax rates. The process of arriving at a real estate tax rate begins with the adoption of a budget by each county, city, school board, or other taxing district. Each budget covers the financial requirements of the taxing body for the coming fiscal year, which may be the January to December calendar year or some other 12-month period designated by statute. The budget must include an estimate of all expenditures for the year and indicate the amount of income expected from all fees, revenue sharing, and other sources. The net amount remaining to be raised from real estate taxes is then determined from these figures.

The next step is **appropriation,** the action taken by each taxing body that authorizes the expenditure of funds and provides for the sources of such monies. Appropriation generally involves the adoption of an ordinance or the passage of a law setting forth the specifics of the proposed taxation.

The amount to be raised from the general real estate tax is then imposed on property owners through a *tax levy,* the formal action taken to impose the tax, by a vote of the taxing district's governing body.

The tax rate for each individual taxing body is computed separately. To arrive at a tax rate, the total monies needed for the coming fiscal year are divided by the total assessments of all real estate located within the jurisdiction of the taxing body. For example, a taxing district's budget indicates that $300,000 must be raised from real estate tax revenues, and the assessment roll (assessor's record) of all taxable real estate within this district equals $10 million. The tax rate is computed as follows:

$$\$300,000 \div \$10,000,000 = \mathbf{0.03} \text{ (or 3 percent)}$$

The tax rate may be expressed in a number of different ways. In many areas it is expressed in mills. A **mill** is 1/1000 of a dollar, or $.001. The tax rate of the preceding example could be expressed as:

$3 per $100 assessed value
or
30 mills ($30 per $1,000 of assessed value)

Tax bills.   A property owner's tax bill is computed by applying the tax rate to the assessed valuation of the property. For example, on a property assessed for tax purposes at $90,000 at a tax rate of 3 percent, or 30 mills, the tax will be $2,700 ($90,000 × 0.030 = **$2,700**). If an equalization factor is used, the computation on a property with an assessed value of $75,000 and a tax rate of 2½ percent, with an equalization factor of 120 percent, would be as follows:

$$\$75,000 \times 1.20 = \$90,000 \times 0.025 = \mathbf{\$2,250 \text{ tax}}$$

Generally, one tax bill for each property incorporates all real estate taxes levied by the various taxing districts. In some areas, however, separate bills are prepared by different taxing bodies. Sometimes the taxing bodies operate on different budget years, so that the taxpayer will receive separate bills for various taxes at different times during the year.

Due dates for payment of taxes are usually set by statute. In many areas, taxes are payable in two installments. Collection procedures vary; in some areas, taxes become due during the current tax year; in others, they are payable in arrears during the year after the taxes are levied; and in still others, a partial payment is due in the year of the tax, with the balance due the following year. Knowledge of local tax-payment schedules is especially important in computing the proration of current taxes when the property is sold.

Some states offer discounts to encourage prompt payment of real estate taxes. Penalties in the form of monthly interest charges are added to all taxes that are not paid when due. The due date is also called the *penalty date*.

Enforcement of tax liens. To be enforceable, real estate taxes must be valid, which means they must be (1) properly levied; (2) for a legal purpose; and (3) applied equitably to all affected property. Tax liens are generally given priority over all other liens against a property; that is, they must be satisfied before all of a property owner's other debts. Real estate taxes delinquent for a period of time specified by state law can be collected by either tax foreclosure (similar to mortgage foreclosure) or tax sale. While there are substantial differences in the methods and details of the various states' tax-sale procedures, the results are the same.

A tax sale is usually held after a court has rendered a judgment for the tax and penalties and ordered that the property be sold and a notice of sale be published. The sale is usually conducted by the tax collector at an annual public sale. Since there is a definite amount of delinquent tax and penalty to be collected, the purchaser must pay at least this amount. Since a defaulted owner has the right to redeem (buy back) the real estate, in many areas bidding takes place on the percentage of interest the bidder may receive from the defaulted owner if and when the property is redeemed. In this type of bidding, the person bidding the lowest interest rate becomes the successful purchaser. A certificate of sale or similar document is usually given to the successful bidder when he or she pays the delinquent tax amount.

Generally, the delinquent taxpayer can redeem the property at any time before the tax sale by paying the delinquent taxes plus interest and charges (court costs and attorney's fees). Most state laws also grant a period of redemption after the tax sale during which the defaulted owner or other lienholders (creditors of the defaulted owner) may redeem the property by paying the amount paid at the tax sale plus interest and charges (including any taxes levied since the sale). If no redemption is made within this statutory redemption period, the certificate holder can apply for a *tax deed.* The quality of the title conveyed by a tax deed varies from state to state according to statutory provisions.

In some states, titles to tax-delinquent land are sold or conveyed to the state or a taxing authority. At the expiration of the redemption period, titles to these lands are then sold at auction to the highest bidder. The tax deeds issued to purchasers in such cases are regarded as conveying good title, because they are considered conveyances by the state of state-owned land. In some jurisdictions, tax-delinquent land that is not sold at a tax sale due to lack of buyers is forfeited to the state. The state may then either use the land for its own purposes or sell it to the highest bidder.

Special Assessments, or Improvement Taxes

Special assessments are special taxes levied on real estate that require property owners to pay for improvements that benefit the real estate they own. Taxes are often levied to pay for such improvements as streets, alleys, street lighting, and curbs, and are enforced in the same manner as general real estate taxes. The procedures for making a special assessment vary widely from state to state, but usually include the following steps.

Specific improvement recommended.   The authority to recommend or initiate the specific improvement is vested in either the property owners, who may petition for an improvement, or in a proper legislative authority, such as the city council or board of trustees, who may initiate the proposal for an improvement. Hearings are held and notices are given to the owners of the property affected.

Ordinance passed.   After the preliminary legal steps have been taken, the legislative authority authorized by statute to act in such cases adopts an ordinance that sets out the nature of the improvement, its cost, and a description of the area to be assessed.

Assessment roll spread.   The proper authority spreads the assessment (called the assessment roll) over the various parcels of real estate to benefit. The assessment for each parcel is determined by one of these methods: (1) estimated benefit each tract will receive by reason of the assessment and (2) front footage. Regardless of the basis used, the assessment usually varies from parcel to parcel, because all do not benefit equally from the improvement.

Petition and approval.   After hearing the benefits and nature of improvements to be made, and hearing any objections from members of the local community affected by the improvements, the local authority, usually a court of record, either approves or rejects the proposal. This is called *confirming the assessment roll.*

Special assessment warrant.   Finally, the assessment becomes a lien on the land assessed. When the contract has been let and the improvement completed, a warrant is usually issued by the clerk of the court that approved the roll. This warrant gives the local collector the authority to issue special assessment bills and begin collection.

Lien.   In most states, an assessment becomes a lien following the confirmation of the roll. Special assessments are usually due and payable in equal annual installments over a period of five to ten years. Interest is also charged each property owner on the total amount of his or her assessment. The first installment generally becomes due during the year following confirmation. The bill includes yearly interest on the entire assessment. As subsequent installments are billed in following years, each bill will include a year's interest on the unpaid balance. Property owners usually have the right to prepay any or all installments, thus stopping the interest charges.

Real Estate Transfer Tax

Some states have enacted laws providing for a tax on conveyances of real estate, usually referred to as the state **transfer tax.** These states usually require state revenue stamps to be affixed to deeds and conveyances before the document can be recorded.

The transfer tax is usually paid by the seller. A tax rate of 50 or 55 cents for each $500 or fraction thereof of taxable consideration is common and may be divided between the state and county. State statute will indicate whether the transfer tax is paid by the seller or buyer or by either party. However, in most states, the seller pays the transfer tax. In many states, when real estate is transferred subject to the unpaid balance of an existing mortgage made by the seller before the time of transfer and being assumed by the buyer, the amount of the assumed mortgage may be deducted from the full consideration to determine the taxable consideration.

When the deed is recorded, the tax is paid to the county recorder in form of tax stamps. In addition, an increasing number of municipalities have enacted transfer taxes.

In many states, a transfer declaration form must be signed by both the buyer and the seller or their agents. This form must detail the full sales price of the property; the legal description of the property conveyed; the address, date, and type of deed; the type of improvement; and whether the transfer is between relatives or is a compulsory transaction in accordance with a court order.

Certain deeds may be exempted from the tax, such as gifts of real estate; deeds not made in connection with a sale (such as a change of joint tenants); conveyances to, from, or between governmental bodies; deeds by charitable, religious, or educational institutions; deeds securing debts or releasing property as security for a debt; partitions; tax deeds; deeds pursuant to mergers of corporations; correction deeds; and deeds from subsidiary to parent corporations for cancellation of stock.

FEDERAL INCOME TAX ON REAL ESTATE

The federal government imposes an income tax on all profits resulting from the ownership and/or sale of real estate. However, both homeowners and real estate investors may have their tax burdens reduced through use of *tax shelters*.

Unlike ad valorem tax liens, a federal income tax lien (one administered by IRS) does not attach to a specific parcel of real estate. An IRS tax lien resulting from a failure to pay federal income taxes (whether or not the tax pertains to real estate ownership) is a general lien that attaches to all real and personal property held by the delinquent taxpayer.

Due to the complexity of federal tax laws, the following material is limited to the concepts the real estate practitioner will be expected to recognize. The licensee must be current in all areas that can affect property and its value, such as zoning, land use, and tax implications of purchase and sale. As with potential legal problems, the practitioner should realize when customers or clients need to consult a tax advisor; and he or she should raise the issues, but not make decisions concerning legal or accounting matters.

Income Tax Deductions

At the time of this writing, IRS rules for deductions have changed, homeowners may deduct mortgage interest, mortgage origination fees, prepayment penalties, and real estate taxes on their principal residence.

Taxpayers may deduct interest paid on residential mortgage loans used to acquire a principal residence and a second home, as long as the total residential acquisition debt does not exceed $1 million. Acquisition debt is what it cost to buy, build, or substantially improve the residence, and it must be secured by that home.

Items that may *not* be deducted include any payments into escrow to cover fire or homeowner's insurance premiums; any insurance premiums paid other than through escrow; depreciation; utility or service fees and assessments; and amounts paid toward reducing the mortgage principal. However, if a penalty is imposed for early pay-off of a mortgage, that amount is considered deductible interest by the IRS. If points are paid at closing, they may not be deducted in that year, but must be amortized over the life of the mortgage.

Interest may also be deducted on home equity loans up to $100,000. Home equity debt is debt other than acquisition debt, and total of acquisition and home equity debt may not exceed the fair market value of the home.

If a homeowner borrows money to make substantial improvements to a house, it is considered acquisition debt and subject to the million-dollar limit, not the $100,000 cap on home equity loans.

In addition, interest on mortgages for mobile homes and boats used as second homes might qualify for interest-rate deductions. A tax advisor should be consulted to determine if the property meets IRS requirements.

Capital Gains

Under tax regulations, a **capital gain** is the profit realized from the sale or exchange of property held for personal use. More specifically, the capital gain on the sale of a personal residence is the difference between its *tax basis* (acquisition or construction cost of the home plus the cost of the lot) and the *adjusted sales price*. The adjusted sales price is the amount received minus the broker's commission and other sales expenses (such as legal fees or repairs needed to prepare a house for sale).

The amount of gain a taxpayer must recognize is determined by the adjusted sales price of the old residence and the cost of the new home. For example, if Roger Johnson purchased a vacant lot three years ago for $15,000 and built a house on it for $60,000, his tax basis would be $75,000 ($60,000 + $15,000 = $75,000). This year he sold the property for $120,000, eventually paying a $9,000 commission to his broker and $300 to an attorney. This means the adjusted sales price on this transaction would be $110,700; Johnson would realize a gain of $35,700. The computations are as follows:

Sales price:		$120,00
commission	$9,000	
attorney's fee	300	
Less expenses:		−9,300
Adjusted sales price:		$110,700
Less tax basis of residence sold:		−75,000
Capital gain:		$ 35,700

Deferment of tax on capital gain.   The gain or profit on the sale of a personal residence is exempt from immediate taxation if another residence is bought for the same or a higher price within either 24 months before or after the sale of the old residence. In this situation, the capital gains tax is not avoided but rather is *deferred* until the property is later sold in a taxable transaction—such as when another home is not purchased, when the purchase price of the new home is less than the sales price of the previous home, or when the owner dies and the property is passed on to his or her heirs.

In our example, if Johnson were to buy a new home within the allotted time for $100,000, his taxable gain, deferred gain, and a new tax basis would be as follows:

Old residence

adjusted sales price:		$110,700
Less cost of newly acquired home:		−100,000
Taxable gain:		**$ 10,700**
Cost of newly acquired home:		$100,000
Less		
gain from old home:	$35,700	
minus taxable gain:	−10,700	
	$25,000	
Deferred gain:		$25,000
Tax basis of new home:		$75,000

Once-in-a-lifetime exclusion.   A homeowner who sells or exchanges his or her principal residence and (1) was 55 or older before the date of sale or exchange, and (2) owned and used the property sold or exchanged as a principal residence for a period totaling at least three years within the five-year period ending on the date of the sale may exclude from his or her gross income part or all of the capital gain on that sale or exchange. Taxpayers who meet these requirements can exclude the first *$125,000* of gain. However, each homeowner may elect to exclude gains under the "over-55" provision *only once in a lifetime,* even if the total gain excluded is less than the $125,000 limit. In the case of a married couple, only one spouse need be 55 or older in order to qualify for this deduction. However, both spouses will be credited with claiming the deduction; the younger spouse will not be able to claim the deduction in the future, even if divorced or widowed.

Thus, if Johnson, the homeowner in our example, were over 55 and chose to take advantage of his once-in-a-lifetime exemption, his taxable gain would be zero.

TAX BENEFITS FOR INVESTORS

One of the main reasons real estate investments are so popular—and profitable—is that federal law allows investors to shelter portions of their incomes from taxation. Some of the more common methods of sheltering real estate profits are exchanges, depreciation, and installment sales.

The taxable gain on real estate held for investment is determined by two factors, the basis and the adjusted basis. **Basis** usually refers to the initial cost an investor pays for a parcel of real estate. Generally, the **adjusted basis** represents the basis plus the cost of any physical improvements to the property minus depreciation. The gain is the *difference between the adjusted basis and the net selling price* (less any depreciation for tax purposes claimed on the property).

The discussions and examples used in this section are designed to introduce the reader to general tax concepts—a tax attorney or CPA should be consulted for further details on specific regulations. Internal Revenue Service regulations are subject to frequent change; again, a tax expert should be consulted for up-to-date information.

Exchanges

In an **exchange** of one property for another, an investor can further reduce, defer, or even eliminate capital-gains tax. Tax laws generally provide that an investor's capital gains are not taxed when he or she exchanges the property for real estate of like kind with the same or greater selling value. *The tax is deferred, not eliminated* (this is similar to the deferment benefit allowed homeowners). If the investor ever sells the property (or subsequently exchanges properties), he or she will be required to pay tax on the difference between the sales price and the carryover basis. Therefore, an investor can keep exchanging upward in value, adding to his or her assets for a lifetime without ever having to pay any capital-gains tax.

To qualify as a tax-deferred exchange, the properties involved must be of *like kind*—basically, real estate for real estate or personal property for personal property. Any additional capital or personal property included with the transaction to even out the exchange is considered a *boot* and is taxed at the time of the exchange. In addition, the value of the boot is added to the basis of the property with which it is given in exchange to form a new basis for the investor giving the boot. To the extent that liabilities are given up in excess of liabilities assumed, the difference is taxed at the time of the exchange and the basis is increased by the gain.

Cost Recovery (Depreciation)

Cost recovery.   The term also known as *depreciation* is a statutory concept that allows an investor to recover in tax deductions the basis of an asset over the period of its useful life. **Cost recovery** is an accounting concept, and may have very little relationship to the actual physical deterioration of the real estate. Cost recovery deductions may be taken only on improvements to land or personal property, and only if they are used in a trade or business or for the production of income. *Land cannot be depreciated*—technically it never wears out or becomes obsolete. In addition, an individual cannot claim a cost recovery deduction on his or her own personal residence.

Basis.   The value of the improvements represents a property's basis only—it is not the total value of the real estate. Real estate tax statements usually separate land from improvements for tax purposes; this is helpful to an investor in determining the basis for calculating recovery deductions.

Installment Sales

An investor may defer federal income tax on a capital gain, provided he or she does not receive all cash for the asset at the time of sale, but instead receives payments in two or more periods. This transaction is an **installment sale.** This method of reporting is now automatic, unless the taxpayer elects not to use it. As the name implies, the seller receives payment in installments and pays income tax each year based only on the amount received during that year. (This can be accomplished by selling through a contract for deed, purchase-money mortgage, or similar instrument.) Besides avoiding tax payments on money not yet collected, the installment method often saves an investor money by spreading the gain over a number of years. The gain may be subject to a lower tax than if it were received in one lump sum. Internal Revenue Service regulations on installment sales are quite complicated, and the sale should be planned with the seller's tax advisor.

SUMMARY

Ad valorem real estate taxes are levied annually by local taxing authorities. Such tax liens are generally given priority over other liens. Payments are required before stated dates, after which penalties accrue. An owner may lose title to his or her property for nonpayment of taxes because tax-delinquent property can be sold to pay the taxes. Some states allow a time period during which a defaulted owner can redeem his or her real estate from a tax sale.

Special assessments are levied to spread the cost of improvements such as new sidewalks, curbs, or paving to the real estate that benefits from the improvements. Assessments are usually payable annually over a period of five to ten years, together with interest due on the balance of the assessment. In addition, if required by state law, conveyances of real estate are subject to state *transfer taxes*.

One of the federal *income-tax benefits* available to homeowners allows them to deduct mortgage interest payments and property taxes from their income tax returns. Income tax on the gain from the sale of a personal residence may be deferred if the homeowner purchases another residence within a set period of time. Homeowners over the age of 55 are given additional benefits.

By *exchanging* one property for another with an equal or greater selling value, an investor can *defer* paying tax on the gain realized until a sale is made. *Cost recovery* is a statutory concept that allows an investor to recover in tax deductions the basis of an asset over the period of its useful life. Only costs of improvements to land may be recovered, not costs for the land itself. An investor may also defer federal income taxes on gain realized from the sale of an investment property through an *installment sale*. In this situation the investor pays income tax only on the portion of the total gain he or she receives in any one year.

QUESTIONS

Please complete all of the questions before turning to the Answer Key.

1. When it is necessary to correct general dissimilarities in statewide tax assessments, uniformity may be achieved with the use of a(n)

    a. levy.   c. appropriation.
    b. equalization factor.   d. mill.

2. A specific parcel of real estate has a market value of $80,000 and is assessed for tax purposes at 25 percent of market value. The tax rate for the county in which the property is located is 30 mills. The annual tax bill will be

    a. $300.   c. $600.
    b. $550.   d. $850.

3. Taxes levied based on the value of the property are known as

    a. ad valorem taxes.   c. capital gain taxes.
    b. special assessments.   d. cost recovery.

4. The initial cost of an investment property to an investor is called its

    a. basis.   c. sales price.
    b. adjusted basis.   d. adjusted sales price.

5. For tax purposes, in an installment sale of real estate, the taxable gain is received and must be reported as income by the seller

    a. in the year the sale is initiated.
    b. in the year the final installment payment is received.
    c. in each year the installment payments are being received.
    d. at any one time during the period that installment payments are being received.

6. What is the annual real estate tax on a property valued at $135,000 and assessed for tax purposes at $47,250 with an equalization factor of 125 percent and a tax rate of 25 mills?

    a. $1,181   c. $3,375
    b. $1,477   d. $4,219

7. After real estate has been sold by the state or county to satisfy a delinquent real estate tax lien, the owner usually has the right to

    a. refinance the parcel of property sold.
    b. remain in possession of the property indefinitely.
    c. redeem the property within the time period set by law.
    d. have the sale canceled by partial payment of the taxes due.

8. The type of tax based on the sales price of a property and charged when the property is conveyed is the

    a. capital gain tax.   c. transfer tax.
    b. cost recovery tax.   d. special assessment.

9. Which of the following statements is true regarding the once-in-a-lifetime exclusion?

    a. The exclusion may be used each time a homeowner 55 years old or older sells a personal residence.
    b. The first $175,000 of capital gain can be excluded from tax liability.
    c. When two spouses each own property, they may use the exclusion again if they become divorced or widowed and later remarry.
    d. If one spouse has previously used the exclusion, it cannot be used by the couple again.

10. All of the following entities would probably receive an exemption from the payment of real estate taxes EXCEPT a

    a. government office building.
    b. commercial office building.
    c. hospital.
    d. church.

11. The taxes on the profit from the sale of a personal residence for $80,000 may be deferred EXCEPT if the seller

    a. rents a condominium for three years following the sale.
    b. purchases a $90,000 home within 24 months before the sale.
    c. constructs an $85,000 home within 24 months after the sale.
    d. qualifies for and uses his once-in-a-lifetime exclusion.

12. All of the following types of liens attach to a specific parcel of real estate
EXCEPT a

   a. mechanic's lien.   c. special assessment lien.
   b. federal income tax lien.   d. general assessment lien.

13. Which of the following statements is true regarding the calculation of
depreciation?

   a. Only the improvements can be depreciated.
   b. Only the land can be depreciated.
   c. The improvements can be fully depreciated and the land can be
       partially depreciated.
   d. The improvements and the land can both be partially depreciated.

14. When comparing 1 mill to 1 percent, 1 mill is

   a. ten times as large as 1 percent.
   b. one hundred times as large as 1 percent.
   c. one-tenth of 1 percent.
   d. one-hundredth of 1 percent.

15. The initial cost of an investment property, plus the cost of any subsequent
improvements, minus any depreciation represents the investment's

   a. adjusted sales price.   c. basis.
   b. adjusted basis.   d. salvage value.

16. The type of tax levied and collected for improvements that benefit the
owners of real estate in the taxing area is a(n)

   a. ad valorem tax.   c. general assessment.
   b. capital gain tax.   d. special assessment.

17. Homeowners' tax deductions could include any of the following EXCEPT

   a. mortgage interest.
   b. real estate taxes.
   c. hazard insurance premiums.
   d. mortgage prepayment penalties.

10:

KEY TERMS

appraisal
capitalization rate
competitive market
    analysis (CMA)
cost approach
depreciation
gross rent multiplier
income approach

market value
plottage
reconciliation
replacement cost
reproduction cost
sales comparison approach
substitution
value

An **appraisal** is an *estimate* or *opinion of value*. Appraisals are frequently used for pricing, financing, protecting, or leasing property.

The appraisal profession is now regulated apart from the real estate business. With the passage of the Financial Institutions Reform, Recovery, and Enforcement Act of 1989 (FIRREA), appraisals performed as part of a federally related transaction must comply with state standards and be performed by state-licensed or state-certified appraisers. Although the federal compliance date already has been changed at least twice, most states have implemented programs requiring that appraisal applicants meet certain education, experience, and examination criteria. State appraisal standards and appraiser licensing and certification requirements must meet at least the minimum levels set by the Appraisal Standards Board and the Appraiser Qualifications Board of The Appraisal Foundation, a national body composed of representatives of the major appraisal and related industry organizations.

Not all estimates of real estate value are made by professional appraisers, however. Everyone engaged in the real estate business must have at least a fundamental knowledge of real estate valuation. Often a real estate agent must help a seller arrive at an asking price or a buyer determine an offering price for property without the aid of a formal appraisal report. The agent may prepare a **competitive market analysis (CMA),** which simply compares the selling prices of homes that are similar to a particular property in location, style, and amenities. While the CMA may help a seller determine the best price for his or her home, however, it must not be confused with a formal appraisal.

VALUE

Value is an abstract word with many acceptable definitions. In a broad sense, value may be defined as the relationship between an object desired and a potential purchaser. It is the *power of a good or service to command other goods or services in exchange.* In terms of appraisal, value may be described as the *present worth of future benefits arising from the ownership of real property.*

To have value in the real estate market, property must have these characteristics:

1. *Demand.* The need or desire for possession or ownership backed up by the financial means to satisfy that need.

2. *Utility.* The capacity to satisfy human needs and desires.

3. *Scarcity.* A finite supply.

4. *Transferability.* The relative ease with which ownership rights are transferred from one person to another.

Market Value

A given parcel of real estate may have many different kinds of value at the same time, such as market value (used to estimate selling price), assessed value (used for property taxes), insured value, book value, mortgage value, salvage value, condemnation value, and depreciated value. Generally the goal of an appraiser is to estimate **market value** (see Figure 10.1). The market value of real estate is the most probable price that a property will bring in a competitive and open market, allowing a reasonable time to find a purchaser who knows all the purposes to which it can be adapted and for which it is capable of being used. Included in this definition are the following key points:

1. Market value is the *most probable* price a property will bring— not the average price or the highest price.

Figure 10.1   Market Value

DEFINITION OF MARKET VALUE: The most probable price which a property should bring in a competitive and open market under all conditions requisite to a fair sale, the buyer and seller, each acting prudently, knowledgeably and assuming the price is not affected by undue stimulus. Implicit in this definition is the consummation of a sale as of a specified date and the passing of title from seller to buyer under conditions whereby: (1) buyer and seller are typically motivated; (2) both parties are well informed or well advised, and each acting in what he considers his own best interest; (3) a reasonable time is allowed for exposure in the open market; (4) payment is made in terms of cash in U.S. dollars or in terms of financial arrangements comparable thereto; and (5) the price represents the normal consideration for the property sold unaffected by special or creative financing or sales concessions* granted by anyone associated with the sale.

*Adjustments to the comparables must be made for special or creative financing or sales concessions. No adjustments are necessary for those costs which are normally paid by sellers as a result of tradition or law in a market area; these costs are readily identifiable since the seller pays these costs in virtually all sales transactions. Special or creative financing adjustments can be made to the comparable property by comparisons to financing terms offered by a third party institutional lender that is not already involved in the property or transaction. Any adjustment should not be calculated on a mechanical dollar for dollar cost of the financing or concession but the dollar amount of any adjustment should approximate the market's reaction to the financing or concessions based on the appraiser's judgment.

Source: FHLMC Form 439 JUL 86/FNMA Form 1004 B July 86

2. Payment must be made in *cash* or its equivalent.

3. Buyer and seller must be unrelated and acting without *undue pressure.*

4. A *reasonable length of time* must be allowed for the property to be exposed in the *open market.*

5. Both buyer and seller must be well informed of the property's use and potential, including its assets and defects.

Market value versus market price.   Market value is an estimate based on an analysis of comparable sales and other pertinent market data. Market price, on the other hand, is what a property has *actually* sold for—its sales price. Theoretically the market price would be the same as market value. Market price can be taken as accurate evidence of current market value, however, only after considering all of the factors listed above. A sale from father to daughter, for instance, might well have been designed to favor one of the parties.

Market value versus cost.   One of the most common errors made in valuing property is the assumption that cost represents market value. Cost and market value may be equal when the improvements on a property are new and represent the highest and best use of the land. However, more often, cost does not equal market value. For example, two homes are identical in every respect except that one is located on a street with heavy traffic, the other on a quiet, residential street. The value of the former may be less than the latter, although the cost of each may be exactly the same.

Externalities: Forces That Influence Value

Real estate value is created, changed, and destroyed, in part by the interaction of four forces: physical, political, economic, and social. Because these exist outside the property and are thus beyond the property owner's control, they are referred to as *externalities*.

Physical externalities.   The climate, the topography of the land, the proximity to rivers and streams, the availability of water, and water quality are examples of physical forces that can influence property value.

Political externalities.   Government controls over money and credit, government-insured or government-guaranteed loan programs, health and safety codes, building codes, zoning ordinances, the availability of public housing, rent controls, the quality of schools and education, the quantity and quality of parks, and tax burdens are examples of government influences on property value.

Economic externalities.   The availability of employment, wage and salary levels, and the broadness of the economic base or the dependence on one major industry as an employer are typical of economic externalities.

Social externalities.   These include population growth and decline, birth rates and death rates, attitudes toward marriage and family size, divorce rates, life-styles, and life-style changes.

Value Principles

Whether an appraiser observes them or not, a number of economic principles are always at work affecting the value of real estate. The more important of these principles are defined in the following sections.

Highest and best use.   This is the most profitable use to which the property can be adapted or the use that is likely to be in demand in the reasonably near future. For example, a highest-and-best-use study may show that a parking lot in a busy downtown area should be replaced by an office building. To place a value on the property based on its present use would be erroneous, because a parking lot is not the highest and best use of the land. In appraising a residential location, amenities and owner satisfaction become important.

Substitution.   This appraisal principle states that the *maximum value of a property tends to be set by the cost of purchasing an equally desirable and valuable substitute property.*

Supply and demand. This principle holds that the value of a property will increase if the supply decreases and the demand either increases or remains constant (seller's market)—and vice versa (buyer's market). For example, the last available lot in a residential area where the demand for homes is high would probably sell for more than the first lot sold in the area.

Balance. Balance is achieved when the addition of improvements to the land and structures increases the property value.

Conformity. This principle holds that maximum value is realized if the use of land conforms to existing neighborhood standards. In areas of single-family houses, for example, buildings should be similar in design, construction, size, and age. Deed restrictions rely on the principle of conformity to assure maximum future value.

Regression and progression. When dissimilar properties exist in the same neighborhood, the worth of the better-quality properties is adversely affected by the presence of the lesser-quality properties. This is known as *regression.* Conversely, *progression* states that the worth of a lesser property tends to increase if it is located among better properties.

Anticipation. This principle holds that value can increase or decrease in anticipation of some future benefit or detriment affecting the property. For example, the value of a house may be affected if rumors are circulating that an adjacent property will be rezoned to commercial use in the near future.

Plottage. The **plottage** principle holds that the merging of adjacent parcels of property into one larger parcel may increase its utility and, thus, its value. For example, two parcels of land might be worth $20,000 each, but when combined, they might be worth $50,000 because more can be done with the larger parcel. The process of merging the parcels is known as *assemblage.*

Increasing and decreasing returns. This principle states that improvements to land and structures eventually reach a point at which they have no effect on property values. If money spent on such improvements produces an increase in income or value, the law of increasing returns is applicable. Where additional improvements do not produce a proportionate increase in income or value, the law of decreasing returns applies.

Contribution. This principle holds that the value of any component of a property consists of what its addition contributes to the value of the whole or what its absence detracts from that value. For example, the cost of installing an air-conditioning system and remodeling an older office building may be greater than is justified by the rental increase that could result from the improvement to the property.

Competition.   This principle states that excess profits attract competition and competition often destroys profits. For example, the success of a retail store may attract investors to open similar stores in the area. This tends to mean less profit for all stores concerned, unless purchasing power in the area increases substantially.

Change.   This principle holds that no physical or economic condition remains constant. Real estate is subject to natural phenomena, such as tornadoes, fires, and routine wear and tear from the elements. The real estate business is also subject to the demands of its market, just as is any business. It is an appraiser's job to be knowledgeable about the past and predictable effects of natural phenomena as well as about the vagaries of the marketplace.

THE THREE APPROACHES TO VALUE

To arrive at an accurate estimate of value, three basic approaches, or techniques, are used by appraisers: the sales comparison approach, the cost approach, and the income approach. Each method serves as a check against the others and narrows the ranges within which the final estimate of value will fall. For specific types of property, one method is generally selected as the most reliable.

The Sales Comparison, or Market Data, Approach to Value

In the **sales comparison approach,** an estimate of value is obtained by comparing the *subject property* (the property under appraisal) with recent sales of *comparable properties* (properties similar to the subject). No two parcels of real estate are exactly alike, so each comparable property must be compared to the subject property and the sales prices adjusted for any dissimilar features. This approach is most often used by brokers and salespeople helping a seller to set a price for residential real estate. The principal factors for which adjustments must be made fall into four basic categories:

1. *Sales or financing concessions.* This consideration becomes important if a sale is not financed by a standard mortgage procedure.

2. *Date of sale.* An adjustment must be made if economic changes have occurred since the comparable property was sold.

3. *Location.* An adjustment may be necessary to compensate for locational differences. For example, similar properties might differ in price from neighborhood to neighborhood, or even within the same neighborhood.

4. *Physical features and amenities.* Physical features that may cause adjustments include age of building, size of lot, landscaping, construction, number of rooms, square feet of living space, interior and exterior condition, presence or absence of a garage, fireplace, central air conditioning, and so forth.

After a careful analysis of the differences between comparable properties and the subject property, the appraiser assigns a dollar value to each of these differences. The value of a feature present in the subject property but not in the comparable property is *added* to the sales price of the comparable property. The value of a feature present in the comparable but not in the subject property is *subtracted.* The *adjusted sales price* represents the probable value range of the subject property. From this range, a single market value estimate can be selected. In this way, the properties, at least on paper, can be made equivalent.

The sales comparison approach is considered essential in almost every appraisal of real estate. It is thought to be the most reliable of the three approaches in appraising *residential* property, in which the amenities (intangible benefits) are difficult to measure. An example of the sales comparison approach is shown in Table 10.1.

The Cost Approach to Value

The cost approach is based on the principle of **substitution,** which states that the maximum value of a property tends to be set by the cost of acquiring an equally desirable and valuable substitute property, assuming that no costly delay is encountered in making the substitution. It is most appropriate in the valuation of properties for which no comparable structures readily exist, such as schools, courthouses, churches, and cemeteries. The **cost approach** consists of five steps:

1. Estimate the value of the land as if it were vacant and available to be put to its highest and best use.

2. Estimate the current cost of constructing the building(s) and site improvements.

Table 10.1 Sales Comparison Approach to Value

| | Subject Property | Comparables | | | | |
		A	B	C	D	E
Sale Price		$118,000	$112,000	$121,000	$116,500	$110,000
Financing Concessions	none	none	none	none	none	none
Date of Sale		current	current	current	current	current
Location	good	same	poorer +6,500	same	same	same
Age	6 years	same	same	same	same	same
Size of Lot	60' × 135'	same	same	larger −5,000	same	larger −5,000
Landscaping	good	same	same	same	same	same
Construction	brick	same	same	same	same	same
Style	ranch	same	same	same	same	same
No. of Rooms	6	same	same	same	same	same
No. of Bedrooms	3	same	same	same	same	same
No. of Baths	1½	same	same	same	same	same
Sq. Ft. Living Space	1500	same	same	same	same	same
Other Space (basement)	full basement	same	same	same	same	same
Condition—Exterior	average	better −1,500	poorer +1000	better −1,500	same	poorer +2,000
Condition—Interior	good	same	same	better −500	same	same
Garage	2-car attached	same	same	same	same	none +5,000
Other Improvements	none	none	none	none	none	none
Net Adjustments		−1,500	+7,500	−7,000	-0-	+2,000
Adjusted Value		$116,500	$119,500	$114,000	$116,500	$112,000

Note: Because the value range of the properties in the comparison chart (excluding comparable B) is close, and comparable D required no adjustment, an appraiser might conclude that the indicated market value of the subject is $116,500.

3. Estimate the amount of accrued depreciation resulting from physical deterioration, functional obsolescence, and/or external obsolescence.

4. Deduct accrued depreciation from the estimated construction cost of new building(s) and site improvements.

5. Add the estimated land value to the depreciated cost of the building(s) and site improvements to arrive at the total property value.

For example, assume the value of the land (Step 1) is $25,000. The current cost of replacing the building and improving the site is $100,000, and the accrued depreciation is $16,000 (Steps 2 and 3). Step 4 would be $84,000 ($100,000 − $16,000). The total property value (Step 5) would be $84,000 + $25,000, or $109,000.

Land value. (Step 1) This estimate uses the sales comparison approach; that is, the location and site improvements of the subject property are compared with those of similar nearby sites, and adjustments are made for significant differences. When the sales comparison approach is used to determine land value in the cost approach, a basis of comparison must be established. This is necessary because, unlike homes that are basically similar and easily compared, tracts of land might not share such similarity. Comparison of large tracts of land may be made by establishing a *per acre* value from comparables and applying it to the subject land; comparison of subdivided lots zoned for commercial or industrial usage may be made by establishing a *square foot* value from comparables and applying it to the subject lot; and comparison of land zoned for retail business usage may be made by establishing a *front foot* value from comparables and applying it to the subject land.

Reproduction cost and replacement cost. (Step 2) There are two ways to look at the construction cost of a building for appraisal purposes. **Reproduction cost** is the dollar amount required to duplicate the subject building at current prices. Replacement cost of the subject property would be the construction cost at current prices of a property that is not necessarily a duplicate, but serves the same purpose or function as the original. **Replacement cost** is most often used in appraising, since it eliminates obsolete features and takes advantage of current construction materials and techniques. An example of the cost approach to value is shown in Table 10.2.

In determining the replacement cost of the improvement as if it were new, the appraiser generally uses one of the following methods:

1. *Quantity survey method.* An estimate is made of the quantities of raw materials needed to replace the subject structure (lumber, plaster, brick, and so forth) as well as their current prices and installation costs. These factors are added to indirect costs (such as building permits, surveys, payroll taxes, and builder's profit to arrive at the total replacement cost of the structure. This method is extremely detailed and time-consuming and usually is used only for historical and dedicated-use properties.

2. *Unit-in-place method.* The replacement cost of the structure is estimated based on the construction cost per unit of measure of individual building components, such as materials, labor, overhead, and profit. Although some components are measured and costed-out in square feet, some, like plumbing fixtures and heating and air-conditioning units, are estimated by unit cost.

Table 10.2 Cost Approach to Value

Land Valuation: Size 60′ × 135′ @ $450 per front foot		= $27,000
Plus site improvements: driveway, walks, landscaping, etc.		= 8,000
Total Land Valuation		$35,000
Building Valuation: Replacement Cost		
1,500 sq. ft. @ $65 per sq. ft. =		$97,500
Less Depreciation:		
Physical depreciation,		
curable		
(items of deferred maintenance)		
exterior painting and roof repair	$4,000	
incurable (structural deterioration)	5,200	
Functional obsolescence	2,000	
External obsolescence	–0–	
Total Depreciation		11,200
Depreciated Value of Building		$ 86,300
Indicated Value by Cost Approach		$121,300

3. *Square-foot method.* The cost-per-square-foot of a recently built comparable structure is multiplied by the number of square feet of the subject improvements. This is the most common method of cost estimation. For some properties, such as warehouses and industrial facilities, the cost-per-cubic-foot of a recently built comparable structure is multiplied by the number of cubic feet of the subject structure.

4. *Index method.* A factor representing a percentage increase in construction costs to the present time is applied to the original cost of the subject property. Because this method fails to account for individual property variables, it is useful only as a check of the estimate reached by one of the other methods.

Depreciation.   (Step 3) In a real estate appraisal, **depreciation** refers to any condition that adversely affects the value of an *improvement*. (Land is said to retain its value indefinitely, except in such rare instances as mis-used farmland.) Depreciation for appraisal purposes is divided into three classes according to its cause:

1. *Physical deterioration:* This form of depreciation results from "wear and tear" due to everyday use and the action of natural elements such as sun, wind, rain, heat, and cold. Physical deterioration is within the property owner's control and is most often *curable.* This means that necessary repairs are economically feasible, considering the remaining years of life of the building. For example, a new roof would be a justifiable expense even on a 40-year-old brick building that is otherwise in good condition. When necessary repairs would not contribute a comparable value to a building—for instance, near the end of a building's useful life—such deterioration would be considered *incurable.*

2. *Functional obsolescence:* This form of depreciation results from outmoded function or poor design. An example would be a four-bedroom, one-bath house, or a house with old-fashioned kitchen and bathroom fixtures and an inadequate electrical system. As with physical deterioration, functional obsolescence exists within the property, is within the property owner's control, and is often curable. This means that the physical or design features that are no longer considered desirable by property buyers could be replaced or redesigned at reasonable cost. For example, outmoded plumbing fixtures are usually easily replaced. Room function might be redefined at no cost if the basic room layout allows for it, as in the case of a bedroom adjacent to a kitchen that might easily be converted to a family room. When currently undesirable physical or design features cannot be easily remedied because of cost or other factors, such obsolescence would be considered incurable.

3. *External (economic) obsolescence:* This form of depreciation results from adverse factors outside the subject property and thus beyond the property owner's control. Therefore, external obsolescence is always incurable. For example, proximity to a nuisance like a polluting factory or a noisy airport would be an unchangeable factor that could not be cured by the owner of the subject property.

Depreciation is difficult to measure because much of functional obsolescence and all of locational obsolescence can be evaluated only by considering the actions of buyers in the marketplace.

The Income Approach to Value

The **income approach** is based on the *present worth of the future rights to income.* It assumes that the income derived from a property, to a large extent, will control the value of the property. The income approach is used primarily for valuation of income-producing properties—apartment buildings, shopping centers, and the like. In estimating value via the income approach, an appraiser must go through the following steps:

1. Estimate annual *potential gross income,* including both rental income and income from other sources, such as concessions and vending machines.

2. Based on market experience, deduct an appropriate allowance for vacancy and collection losses to arrive at *effective gross income.*

3. Based on appropriate operating standards, deduct the annual *operating expenses* of the real estate from the effective gross income to arrive at the annual *net operating income.* Management costs are always included as operating expenses, even if the current owner also manages the property. Mortgage payments, however (including principal and interest), are debt service and *not* considered operating expenses.

4. Estimate the price a typical investor would pay for the income produced by this particular type and class of property. This is done by estimating the rate of return (or yield) that an investor will demand for the investment of capital in this type of building. This rate of return is called the **capitalization** (or "cap") **rate** and is determined by comparing the relationship of net operating income with the sales prices of similar properties that have sold in the current market. For example, a comparable property that is producing an annual net income of $15,000 is sold for $187,500. The capitalization rate is $15,000 ÷ 187,500, or 8 percent. If other comparable properties sold at prices that yielded substantially the same rate, the appraiser should apply an 8 percent rate to the subject property.

5. Finally, the capitalization rate is applied to the property's annual net income, resulting in the appraiser's estimate of the property value.

With the appropriate capitalization rate and the projected annual net income, the appraiser can obtain an indication of value by the income approach in the following manner:

Table 10.3 Income Approach to Value

Potential Gross Annual Income	
Market Rent	$60,000
Income from other sources	
(vending machines and pay phones)	+ 600
	$60,600
Less vacancy and collection losses (estimated) @ 4%	– 2,424
Effective Gross Income	$58,176
Expenses:	
Real estate taxes	$ 9,000
Insurance	1,000
Heat	2,800
Maintenance	6,400
Utilities, electricity, water, gas	800
Repairs	1,200
Decorating	1,400
Replacement of equipment	800
Legal and accounting	600
Management	3,000
Total Expenses	$27,000
Annual Net Operating Income	$31,176

Capitalization Rate = 10%

Capitalization of annual net income: $\dfrac{\$31,176}{.10}$

Indicated Value by Income Approach = $311,760

Net Income ÷ Capitalization Rate = Value
Example: $15,000 income ÷ 10% cap rate = $150,000 value

This formula and its variations are important in dealing with income property.

$$\frac{\text{Income}}{\text{Rate}} = \text{Value} \qquad \frac{\text{Income}}{\text{Value}} = \text{Rate} \qquad \text{Value} \times \text{Rate} = \text{Income}$$

A simplified version of the computations used in applying the income approach appears in Table 10.3.

Gross rent or income multipliers.   Sometimes, single-family homes are purchased for their income. As a substitute for the income approach, the **gross rent multiplier** (GRM) method is often used in appraising such properties. The GRM relates the sale price of a property to its rental price and can be determined by the following formula:

Table 10.4 Gross Rent Multiplier

Comparable No.	Sale Price	Monthly Rent	GRM
1	$70,000	$500	140.0
2	68,500	490	139.8
3	70,500	505	139.6
4	67,900	485	140.0
Subject	?	495	?

Note: Based on an analysis of these comparisons, a GRM of 140 seems reasonable for homes in this area. In the opinion of an appraiser, then, the estimated value of the subject property would be $495 × 140, or $69,300.

$$\frac{\text{Sale Price}}{\text{Monthly Rental Income}} = \text{GRM}$$

For example, a home recently sold for $50,000. The monthly rental income was $425. The GRM for the property would be

$$\$50,000 \div \$425, \text{ or } 117.6$$

To establish an accurate GRM, an appraiser must have recent sales and rental data from at least four properties that are similar to the subject property. The resulting GRM could then be applied to the estimated fair market rental of the subject property in order to arrive at its market value. The formula would then be

$$\text{Monthly Rental Income} \times \text{GRM} = \text{Estimated Market Value}$$

Table 10.4 shows some examples of GRM comparisons.

Generally, gross annual income is used in appraising industrial and commercial properties. The ratio to convert annual income into market value is then called a gross income multiplier (GIM).

Much skill is required to use multipliers accurately because there is no fixed multiplier for all areas or all types of properties. Therefore, many appraisers view the technique simply as a quick way to check the validity of a property value obtained by the three accepted appraisal methods: sales comparison, cost, and income.

Reconciliation

When the three approaches are applied to the same property, they will usually produce three separate indications of value. **Reconciliation** is the art of analyzing and effectively weighing the findings from the three approaches.

Although each approach may serve as an independent guide to value, all three approaches should be used as a check on the final estimate of value. The process of reconciliation is more complicated than simply taking the average of the three value estimates. An average implies that the data and logic applied in each of the approaches are equally valid and reliable, and should therefore be given equal weight. In fact, however, certain approaches are more valid and reliable with some kinds of properties than with others.

For example, in appraising a home the income approach is usually given little weight, and the cost approach is of limited value unless the home is relatively new. Therefore, the sales comparison approach is usually given greatest weight in valuing single-family residences. In the appraisal of income or investment property, the income approach would normally be given the greatest weight. In the appraisal of churches, libraries, museums, schools, and other special-use properties where there is no income and few, if any, sales, the cost approach would usually be assigned the greatest weight. From this reconciliation, a single estimate of market value is produced.

Reconciliation for a single-family residence might be weighted as follows:

Sales comparison approach	$75,000 × 70%	=	$52,500
Cost approach	$72,000 × 20%	=	$14,400
Income approach	$70,000 × 10%	=	$ 7,000
Estimate of total market value		=	**$73,900**

THE APPRAISAL PROCESS

The key to an accurate appraisal lies in the methodical collection of data. The appraisal process is an orderly set of procedures used to collect and analyze data to arrive at an ultimate value conclusion. The data are divided into two basic classes:

Figure 10.2   The Appraisal Process

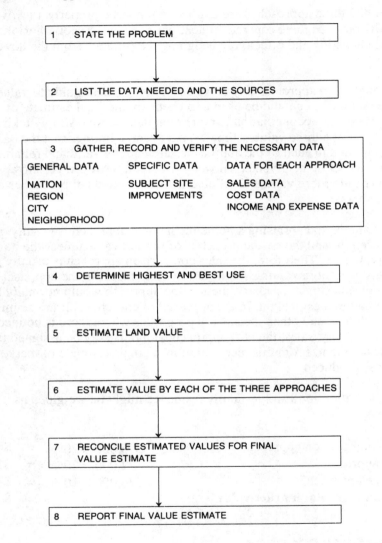

Source: *Fundamentals of Real Estate Appraisal*, Fifth Edition, by William L. Ventolo, Jr., and Martha R. Williams, p. 17, © 1990 by Dearborn Financial Publishing, Inc. Used with permission.

1. *General data,* covering the nation, region, city and neighborhood. Of particular importance is the neighborhood, where an appraiser finds the physical, economic, social and political influences that directly affect the value and potential of the subject property.

2. *Specific data,* covering details of the subject property as well as comparative data relating to costs, sales and income and expenses of properties similar to and competitive with the subject property.

Figure 10.2 outlines the steps an appraiser takes in carrying out an appraisal assignment. The numbers in the following list correspond to the numbers on the flowchart.

1. *State the problem.* The kind of value to be estimated must be specified, and the valuation approach(es) most valid and reliable for the kind of property under appraisal must be selected.

2. *List the data needed and the sources.* Based on the approach(es) the appraiser will be using, the types of data needed and the sources to be consulted are listed.

3. *Gather, record and verify the necessary data.* Detailed information must be obtained concerning the economic, political, and social conditions of the nation, region, city, and neighborhood, and comments on the effects of these data on the subject property also must be obtained.

   Specific data about the subject site and improvements must be collected and verified.

   Depending on the approach(es) used, comparative information relating to sales, income and expenses, and construction costs of comparable properties must be collected. All data should be verified, usually by checking the same information against two different sources. In the case of sales data, one source should be a person directly involved in the transaction.

4. *Determine highest and best use.* The appraiser analyzes market forces such as competition and current versus potential uses to determine the reasonableness of the property's present use in terms of its profitability.

5. *Estimate land value.* The features and sales prices of comparable sites are compared to the subject to determine the value of the land alone.

6. *Estimate value by each of the three approaches.* The *sales comparison, cost,* and *income capitalization* approaches are used to estimate the value of the subject property.

7. *Reconcile estimated values for final value estimate.* The appraiser makes a definite statement of conclusions reached, usually in the form of a value estimate of the property.

8. *Report final value estimate.* After the three approaches have been reconciled and an opinion of value reached, the appraiser prepares a formal written report for the client. The statement may be a completed *form,* a *letter* or a lengthy written *narrative.* The most complete appraisal report would contain the following information:

   a. the estimate of value and the date to which it applies;
   b. the purpose for which the appraisal was made;
   c. a description of the neighborhood and the subject property;
   d. factual data covering costs, sales, and income and expenses of similar, recently sold properties;
   e. an analysis and interpretation of the data collected;
   f. a presentation of one or more of the three approaches to value in enough detail to support the appraiser's final value conclusion;
   g. any qualifying condition;
   h. supportive material, such as charts, maps, photographs, floor plans, leases and contracts; and
   i. the certification and signature of the appraiser.

SUMMARY

To *appraise* real estate means to *estimate its value.* Although there are many types of value, the most common objective of an appraisal is to estimate *market value,* the most probable sale price of a property.

Appraisals are concerned with values, prices, and costs. *Value* is an estimate of future benefits, *cost* represents a measure of past expenditures, and *price* reflects the actual amount of money paid for a property.

Basic to appraising are certain underlying economic principles, such as highest and best use, substitution, supply and demand, balance, conformity, regression and progression, anticipation, plottage, increasing and decreasing returns, contribution, competition, and change.

Figure 10.3   Uniform Residential Appraisal Report

Property Description & Analysis   **UNIFORM RESIDENTIAL APPRAISAL REPORT**   File No.

SUBJECT

Property Address	Census Tract
City	County	State	Zip Code
Legal Description	
Owner/Occupant	Map Reference
Sale Price $	Date of Sale
Loan charges/concessions to be paid by seller $	
R.E. Taxes $	Tax Year	HOA $/Mo.
Lender/Client	

LENDER DISCRETIONARY USE
Sale Price $
Date
Mortgage Amount $
Mortgage Type
Discount Points and Other Concessions
Paid by Seller $

PROPERTY RIGHTS APPRAISED
☐ Fee Simple
☐ Leasehold
☐ Condominium (HUD/VA)
☐ De Minimis PUD

NEIGHBORHOOD

LOCATION	☐ Urban	☐ Suburban	☐ Rural
BUILT UP	☐ Over 75%	☐ 25-75%	☐ Under 25%
GROWTH RATE	☐ Rapid	☐ Stable	☐ Slow
PROPERTY VALUES	☐ Increasing	☐ Stable	☐ Declining
DEMAND/SUPPLY	☐ Shortage	☐ In Balance	☐ Over Supply
MARKETING TIME	☐ Under 3 Mos.	☐ 3-6 Mos.	☐ Over 6 Mos.

PRESENT LAND USE	%	LAND USE CHANGE	PREDOMINANT	SINGLE FAMILY HOUSING
Single Family		Not Likely	OCCUPANCY	PRICE / AGE
2-4 Family		Likely	☐ Owner	$ (000) (yrs)
Multi-family		In process	☐ Tenant	
Commercial		To:	☐ Vacant (0-5%)	Low
Industrial			☐ Vacant (over 5%)	High
Vacant				Predominant

NEIGHBORHOOD ANALYSIS	Good	Avg.	Fair	Poor
Employment Stability	☐	☐	☐	☐
Convenience to Employment	☐	☐	☐	☐
Convenience to Shopping	☐	☐	☐	☐
Convenience to Schools	☐	☐	☐	☐
Adequacy of Public Transportation	☐	☐	☐	☐
Recreation Facilities	☐	☐	☐	☐
Adequacy of Utilities	☐	☐	☐	☐
Property Compatibility	☐	☐	☐	☐
Protection from Detrimental Cond.	☐	☐	☐	☐
Police & Fire Protection	☐	☐	☐	☐
General Appearance of Properties	☐	☐	☐	☐
Appeal to Market	☐	☐	☐	☐

Source

Note: Race or the racial composition of the neighborhood are not considered reliable appraisal factors.
COMMENTS:

SITE

Dimensions	Topography
Site Area	Size
Zoning Classification	Corner Lot	Shape
HIGHEST & BEST USE: Present Use	Zoning Compliance	Drainage
	Other Use	View

UTILITIES	Public	Other	SITE IMPROVEMENTS	Type	Public	Private
Electricity	☐		Street		☐	☐
Gas	☐		Curb/Gutter		☐	☐
Water	☐		Sidewalk		☐	☐
Sanitary Sewer	☐		Street Lights		☐	☐
Storm Sewer	☐		Alley		☐	☐

Landscaping
Driveway
Apparent Easements
FEMA Flood Hazard Yes*☐ No☐
FEMA* Map/Zone

COMMENTS (Apparent adverse easements, encroachments, special assessments, slide areas, etc.):

IMPROVEMENTS

GENERAL DESCRIPTION	EXTERIOR DESCRIPTION	FOUNDATION	BASEMENT	INSULATION
Units	Foundation	Slab	Area Sq. Ft.	Roof ☐
Stories	Exterior Walls	Crawl Space	% Finished	Ceiling ☐
Type (Det./Att.)	Roof Surface	Basement	Ceiling	Walls ☐
Design (Style)	Gutters & Dwnspts.	Sump Pump	Walls	Floor ☐
Existing	Window Type	Dampness	Floor	None ☐
Proposed	Storm Sash	Settlement	Outside Entry	Adequacy
Under Construction	Screens	Infestation		Energy Efficient Items:
Age (Yrs.)	Manufactured House			
Effective Age (Yrs.)				

ROOM LIST

ROOMS	Foyer	Living	Dining	Kitchen	Den	Family Rm.	Rec. Rm.	Bedrooms	# Baths	Laundry	Other	Area Sq. Ft.
Basement												
Level 1												
Level 2												

Finished area above grade contains: Rooms;   Bedroom(s):   Bath(s):   Square Feet of Gross Living Area

Figure 10.3 (continued)

INTERIOR	SURFACES	Materials/Condition	HEATING		KITCHEN EQUIP.		ATTIC		IMPROVEMENT ANALYSIS	Good	Avg.	Fair	Poor
	Floors		Type		Refrigerator		None		Quality of Construction				
	Walls		Fuel		Range/Oven		Stairs		Condition of Improvements				
	Trim/Finish		Condition		Disposal		Drop Stair		Room Sizes/Layout				
	Bath Floor		Adequacy		Dishwasher		Scuttle		Closets and Storage				
	Bath Wainscot		COOLING		Fan/Hood		Floor		Energy Efficiency				
	Doors		Central		Compactor		Heated		Plumbing-Adequacy & Condition				
			Other		Washer/Dryer		Finished		Electrical-Adequacy & Condition				
			Condition		Microwave				Kitchen Cabinets-Adequacy & Cond.				
	Fireplace(s) #		Adequacy		Intercom				Compatibility to Neighborhood				
AUTOS	CAR STORAGE: Garage		Attached		Adequate		House Entry		Appeal & Marketability				
	No. Cars Carport		Detached		Inadequate		Outside Entry		Estimated Remaining Economic Life				Yrs.
	Condition None		Built-In		Electric Door		Basement Entry		Estimated Remaining Physical Life				Yrs.

COMMENTS	
Additional features:
Depreciation (Physical, functional and external inadequacies, repairs needed, modernization, etc.):
General market conditions and prevalence and impact in subject/market area regarding loan discounts, interest buydowns and concessions:

Freddie Mac Form 70 10/86 12Ch.   AO   Forms and Worms Inc.,° 315 Whitney Ave., New Haven, CT 06511 1/(800) 243-4546   Item #111710   Fannie Mae Form 1004 10/86

Valuation Section   **UNIFORM RESIDENTIAL APPRAISAL REPORT**   **File No.**

Purpose of Appraisal is to estimate Market Value as defined in the Certification & Statement of Limiting Conditions.

COST APPROACH

BUILDING SKETCH (SHOW GROSS LIVING AREA ABOVE GRADE)
If for Freddie Mac or Fannie Mae, show only square foot calculations and cost approach comments in this space.

ESTIMATED REPRODUCTION COST-NEW-OF IMPROVEMENTS:

Dwelling _____ Sq. Ft. @ $ _____	= $ _____
_____ Sq. Ft. @ $ _____	= _____
Extras _____	= _____
_____	= _____
Special Energy Efficient Items _____	= _____
Porches, Patios, etc. _____	= _____
Garage/Carport _____ Sq. Ft. @ $ _____	= _____
Total Estimated Cost New	= $ _____

	Physical	Functional	External
Less			
Depreciation			= $ _____

Depreciated Value of Improvements .... = $ _____
Site Imp. "as is" (driveway, landscaping, etc.) . = $ _____
ESTIMATED SITE VALUE .... = $ _____
(If leasehold, show only leasehold value.)
INDICATED VALUE BY COST APPROACH .... = $ _____

(Not Required by Freddie Mac and Fannie Mae)
Does property conform to applicable HUD/VA property standards? ☐ Yes ☐ No
If No, explain: _____

Construction Warranty ☐ Yes ☐ No
Name of Warranty Program _____
Warranty Coverage Expires _____

Figure 10.3 (continued)

SALES COMPARISON ANALYSIS

The undersigned has recited three recent sales of properties most similar and proximate to subject and has considered these in the market analysis. The description includes a dollar adjustment, reflecting market reaction to those items of significant variation between the subject and comparable properties. If a significant item in the comparable property is superior to, or more favorable than, the subject property, a minus (–) adjustment is made, thus reducing the indicated value of subject; if a significant item in the comparable is inferior to, or less favorable than, the subject property, a plus (+) adjustment is made, thus increasing the indicated value of the subject.

ITEM	SUBJECT	COMPARABLE NO. 1		COMPARABLE NO. 2		COMPARABLE NO. 3	
Address							
Proximity to Subject							
Sales Price	$		$		$		$
Price/Gross Liv. Area	$ ☐	$ ☐		$ ☐		$ ☐	
Data Source							
VALUE ADJUSTMENTS	DESCRIPTION	DESCRIPTION	+(–)$ Adjustment	DESCRIPTION	+(–)$ Adjustment	DESCRIPTION	+(–)$ Adjustment
Sales or Financing Concessions							
Date of Sale/Time							
Location							
Site/View							
Design and Appeal							
Quality of Construction							
Age							
Condition							
Above Grade Room Count	Total Bdrms Baths	Total Bdrms Baths		Total Bdrms Baths		Total Bdrms Baths	
Gross Living Area	Sq. Ft.	Sq. Ft.		Sq. Ft.		Sq. Ft.	
Basement & Finished Rooms Below Grade							
Functional Utility							
Heating/Cooling							
Garage/Carport							
Porches, Patio, Pools, etc.							
Special Energy Efficient Items							
Fireplace(s)							
Other (e.g. kitchen equip., remodeling)							
Net Adj. (total)		☐ + ☐ –	$	☐ + ☐ –	$	☐ + ☐ –	$
Indicated Value of Subject			$		$		$

Comments on Sales Comparison: ____________________

INDICATED VALUE BY SALES COMPARISON APPROACH .... $ ________

INDICATED VALUE BY INCOME APPROACH (If Applicable) Estimated Market Rent $ ________ /Mo. x Gross Rent Multiplier ________ = $ ________

RECONCILIATION

This appraisal is made ☐ "as is" ☐ subject to the repairs, alterations, inspections or conditions listed below ☐ completion per plans and specifications.

Comments and Conditions of Appraisal: ____________________

Final Reconciliation: ____________________

This appraisal is based upon the above requirements, the certification, contingent and limiting conditions, and Market Value definition that are stated in

☐ FmHA, HUD &/or VA instructions.

☐ Freddie Mac Form 439 (Rev. 7/86)/Fannie Mae Form 1004B (Rev. 7/86) filed with client ________ 19 ___ ☐ attached.

I (WE) ESTIMATE THE MARKET VALUE, AS DEFINED, OF THE SUBJECT PROPERTY AS OF ________ 19 ___ to be $ ________

I (We) certify: that to the best of my (our) knowledge and belief the facts and data used herein are true and correct; that I (we) personally inspected the subject property, both inside and out, and have made an exterior inspection of all comparable sales cited in this report; and that I (we) have no undisclosed interest, present or prospective therein.

Appraiser(s) SIGNATURE ________ NAME ________

Review Appraiser (if applicable) SIGNATURE ________ NAME ________ ☐ Did ☐ Did Not Inspect Property

Freddie Mac Form 70 10/86 12Ch Forms and Worms Inc.,® 315 Whitney Ave. New Haven, CT 06511 1(800) 243-4545 Fannie Mae Form 1004 10/86

A professional appraiser analyzes a property through three approaches to value. In the *sales comparison approach,* the subject property is compared with others like it that have sold recently. Since no two properties are exactly alike, adjustments must be made to account for any differences. With the *cost approach,* an appraiser calculates the cost of building a similar structure on a similar site. Then the appraiser subtracts *depreciation* (loss in value), which reflects the differences between new properties of this type and the subject property in its present condition. The *income approach* is an analysis based on the relationship between the rate of return that an investor requires and the net income that a property produces.

An offshoot of the income approach, the *gross rent multiplier* (GRM), is often used to estimate the value of single-family residential properties that are not usually rented but could be. The GRM is computed by dividing the sales price of a property by its gross monthly rent.

Normally, the application of the three approaches results in three different estimates of value. In the process of *reconciliation,* the validity and reliability of each approach are weighed objectively to arrive at the single best and most supportable conclusion of value.

QUESTIONS

Please complete all of the questions before turning to the Answer Key.

1. The rental home owned by the *D*s rents for $9,000 per year in a community where the gross rent multiplier is 140. What is the value of the *D*s' property?

    a. $98,000   c. $108,000
    b. $105,000   d. $126,000

2. When an appraiser has used all three approaches to value, the analysis and effective weighing of the findings to develop the final value estimate is called

    a. reproduction.   c. reconsideration.
    b. rehabilitation.   d. reconciliation.

3. The loss in property value because of the lack of sufficient parking facilities in a four-bedroom home would be called

    a. physical deterioration.   c. functional obsolescence.
    b. physical obsolescence.   d. external obsolescence.

4. When using the cost approach to value, an appraiser would consider all of the following items EXCEPT the

    a. reproduction or replacement cost.
    b. price the seller paid for the property.
    c. value of the land parcel.
    d. depreciation from all sources.

5. When determining the effective gross income of a property, the appraiser would consider all of the following items EXCEPT

    a. potential gross income.   c. management fees.
    b. vacancies.   d. collection losses.

6. When a improvement is new and represents the highest and best use of the property, cost would usually equal

    a. mortgage value.   c. market value.
    b. salvage value.   d. assessed value.

7. An increase in value caused by combining several properties into one large contiguous property is called

   a. plottage.
   b. progression.
   c. reconciliation.
   d. regression.

8. All of the following elements are essential for value EXCEPT

   a. demand.
   b. balance.
   c. transferability.
   d. utility.

9. Using a capitalization rate of 9 percent, a property has a value of $270,000. If a new rate of 10 percent is used, what will the value of the property become?

   a. $243,000
   b. $270,000
   c. $300,000
   d. $315,000

10. The duplication of both the function and the form of an improvement would be called

    a. reproduction.
    b. reconciliation.
    c. replacement.
    d. renovation.

11. To calculate net operating income, an appraiser would subtract which of the following items from the effective gross income?

    a. Real estate taxes
    b. Mortgage interest
    c. Principal repayment
    d. Vacancy allowances

12. The appraisal principle that holds that the maximum value of a property tends to be set by the cost of purchasing an equally desirable and valuable property is

    a. plottage.
    b. contribution.
    c. substitution.
    d. anticipation.

13. Which of the following types of depreciation is always incurable?

    a. Physical deterioration
    b. Physical obsolescence
    c. Functional obsolescence
    d. External obsolescence

14. If the cost of upgrading the electrical system in a rented building could not be justified by the anticipated rent increases, this work would not be done because of the principle of

    a. balance.
    b. increasing and decreasing returns.
    c. conformity.
    d. contribution.

15. With the cost approach to value, the most common method of cost estimation is the

    a. quantity survey method.   c. square-foot method.
    b. unit-in-place method.   d. index method.

16. When dissimilar properties exist in the same neighborhood, the values of the better-quality properties will be harmed because of the impact of

    a. contribution.   c. increasing returns.
    b. regression.   d. progression.

17. The concept of market value includes all of the following assumptions EXCEPT

    a. payment must be made in cash or its equivalent.
    b. both the seller and the buyer must be well informed about the property.
    c. the property must be sold as quickly as possible.
    d. both the seller and the buyer must be unrelated and acting without undue pressure.

18. The forces beyond the control of the property owner that affect the value of the property are called

    a. approaches to value.
    b. externalities.
    c. increasing and decreasing returns.
    d. depreciation.

19. Value may be described by all of the following phrases EXCEPT the

    a.   relationship between an object desired and a potential purchaser.
    b.   power of a good or service to command other goods or services in exchange.
    c.   present worth of future benefits arising from property ownership.
    d.   price paid by the original purchaser of a property.

20. Which approach to value would be given the greatest weight in the appraisal of a church?

    a.   Income approach   c.   Sales comparison approach
    b.   Cost approach   d.   Gross income multiplier

11: Real Estate Financing Instruments

KEY TERMS

acceleration clause	lien theory
adjustable-rate mortgage	mortgage
alienation clause	mortgagee
assumption	mortgagor
conventional loan	power-of-sale clause
deed of trust	prepayment penalty
defeasance clause	promissory note
deficiency judgment	redemption
discount points	satisfaction
equitable right of redemption	statutory redemption
FHA-insured loan	subordination
foreclosure	title theory
interest	usury
junior lien	VA loan

Real estate sales are seldom made for cash; most transactions involve some kind of financing. Thus, an understanding of real estate financing is of great importance to brokers and salespeople. In most transactions, the buyer must borrow most of the purchase price by obtaining a loan and pledging the real property involved as *security* (collateral) for the loan. This is generally known as a *mortgage loan*.

The mortgage loan is but one method of financing real estate. In some states, the deed of trust is used in place of a mortgage to finance real estate transactions. In addition, many variations of the terms of these two instruments exist as forms of "alternative financing," often used in times of tight mortgage money. This chapter will discuss in detail mortgage and deed of trust documents as used to finance a typical real estate purchase. The following chapter, "Real Estate Financing Market," will detail the various sources of mortgage money and the government's role in the financing market, as well as many of the forms of alternative financing available to real estate purchasers in the marketplace.

MORTGAGE THEORY

From their inception American courts of equity have considered a mortgage a voluntary lien on real estate, given to secure the payment of a debt or the performance of an obligation. Some states recognize a lender as the owner of mortgaged land. This ownership is subject to defeat upon full payment of the debt or performance of the obligation. These states are called **title theory** states. Under title theory a **mortgagee** (lender) has the right to possession of and rents from the mortgaged property immediately upon default by the **mortgagor** (borrower).

Those states that interpret a mortgage purely as a lien on real property are called **lien theory** states. In such states, if a mortgagor defaults, the lender may foreclose (generally through a court action), offer the property for sale and apply the funds received from the sale to reduce or extinguish the obligation. As protection to the borrower, some states allow a statutory redemption period during which a defaulted mortgagor can redeem the property.

Today a number of states have modified the strict interpretation of title and lien theories. These *intermediary,* or *modified lien theory,* states allow a lender to take possession of the mortgaged real estate upon default.

SECURITY AND DEBT

What Property May Be Mortgaged

Generally, any interest in real estate that may be sold also may be pledged as security for a debt. The basic principle of property law, that a person cannot convey greater rights in property than he or she actually has, applies equally to the right to mortgage. Therefore, the owner of a fee simple estate can mortgage the fee, and the owner of a leasehold or subleasehold can mortgage that leasehold interest. For example, a large retail corporation renting space in a shopping center may mortgage its leasehold interest to finance remodeling work.

Figure 11.1   Mortgage

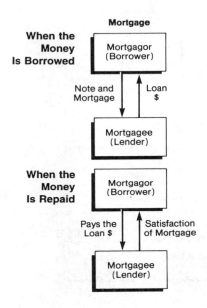

Loan Instruments

The two most commonly used instruments of pledging real estate as collateral for a loan are the mortgage and the trust deed.

Mortgages.   There are two parts to a mortgage loan—the debt itself and the security for the debt. When a property is to be mortgaged, the owner must execute, or sign, two separate instruments:

1. The **promissory note,** or *financing document,* is the written promise to repay a debt in definite installments.

2. The **mortgage,** or *security document,* is the document that creates the lien, or conveys the property to the mortgagee as *security* for the debt.

By itself, a mortgage document is basically a pledge of property to secure a loan. Since a pledge of security is not legally effective unless there is a debt to secure, the promissory note is fundamental to the transaction. Both documents must be executed to create an enforceable mortgage loan (see Figure 11.1). Note that the lender is the giver of the loan monies, but

Figure 11.2   Deed of Trust

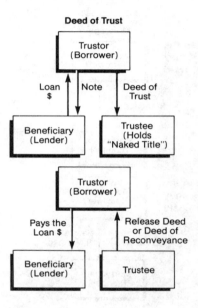

the recipient of the mortgage. The borrower, therefore, is called the mortgagor, and the lender, the mortgagee.

Deeds of trust.   In some states lenders use a three-party instrument known as a **deed of trust,** or *trust deed,* rather than a mortgage. As with mortgages, deeds of trust involve two separate instruments: a *note* (detailing the terms of the loan), and a *trust deed.* A deed of trust conveys the real estate as a security for the loan to a third party, called the *trustee.* The trustee then holds title on behalf of the lender, known as the *beneficiary,* who is the legal owner and holder of the note (see Figure 11.2). The wording of the conveyance sets forth actions that the trustee may take if the borrower, known as the *trustor,* defaults under any of the trust deed's terms. In states where deeds of trust are preferred, foreclosure procedures for defaulted deeds of trust are usually simpler and speedier than those for mortgage loans.

Usually the lender chooses the trustee and reserves the right of substitution if a trustee dies or is dismissed. In the financing of a commercial or industrial real estate venture that involves a large loan and several lenders, the borrower generally executes a deed of trust rather than a mortgage because deeds of trust can be used to secure several notes, one note held by each lender.

PROVISIONS OF THE NOTE

In general, the promissory note executed by a borrower (maker) states the amount of the debt (principal) and the method of payment. If the note is used with a mortgage, it names the mortgagee as the payee; if it is used with a deed of trust, the note is usually made payable to the bearer. It may also refer to or repeat several of the clauses that appear in the mortgage document or deed of trust. The note, like the mortgage or deed of trust, should be signed by all parties who have an interest in the property. In states where dower and curtesy are in effect or homestead or community property is involved, both spouses have an interest in the property and must sign the note.

A note is said to be a *negotiable instrument;* that is, a written promise or order to pay a specific sum of money. A document is said to be negotiable when its holder, known as the payee, may transfer his or her right to payment to a third party by assigning the document to the third party or by delivering the document to that individual. The transferee, or new holder of the note, is known as a *holder in due course.* Other negotiable instruments include checks and bank drafts.

To be negotiable, or freely transferable, a document must meet certain requirements of the Uniform Commercial Code. The note must be in writing, made by one person to another, and signed by the maker. It must contain an unconditional promise to pay a sum of money on demand or at a set date in the future. In addition, the note must be payable to the order of a specifically named person or to the bearer (the person who has possession of the note). Notes that are payable to order must be transferred by endorsement; those payable to bearer must be transferred by delivery.

Payment Plans

Most mortgage and deed of trust loans are *amortized loans.* This means that regular payments are applied first to the interest owed and then to the principal amount, over a specified term. By the end of the term, the full amount of the principal due is reduced to zero.

Most amortized mortgage or deed of trust loans are payable in monthly installments; some, however, are payable quarterly or semiannually.

These payments may be computed by a number of different payment plans, which tend to alternately gain and lose favor in the market as the cost and availability of mortgage money fluctuate (see Figure 11.3). Such payment plans include the following:

1. A borrower may choose a *straight loan* that calls for periodic payments of interest, with the *principal to be paid in full at the end of the loan term.* This is also known as a *term loan.* Such plans are often used for home improvement loans and second mortgages rather than for residential first mortgage loans. Straight loans are nonamortizing loans.

2. The borrower may pay a *different amount for each installment,* with each payment consisting of a fixed amount credited toward the principal, plus an additional amount for the interest due on the balance of the principal outstanding since the last payment was made. This is called an *installment loan.*

3. The most frequently used plan requires the borrower to pay a *constant amount,* usually each month. The lender *first credits each payment to the interest due and then applies the balance to reduce the principal of the loan.* Thus, while each payment is the same, the portion applied toward repayment of the principal grows and the interest due declines as the unpaid balance of the loan is reduced. This is known as a *fully amortized loan.*

4. When a mortgage or trust deed requires periodic payments that will not fully amortize the loan by the time the final payment is due, the final payment is an amount larger than the others called a *balloon payment;* this type of loan is known as a *partially amortized loan.* Balloon payments are frequently used in second mortgages (to keep installments low when paying off two loans at one time) and owner financing (where the seller needs to finance the property to expedite a sale, but does not want to be involved as lender for more than a few years).

Interest

Interest is a charge for the use of money. A lender will charge a borrower a percentage of the principal as interest for each year the debt is outstanding. The amount of interest due on any one installment payment date is calculated by computing the total yearly interest based on the unpaid balance and dividing that figure by the number of payments made each year. For example, if the current outstanding loan balance is $50,000, with interest at the rate of 12 percent per annum and constant

Figure 11.3   Payment Plans

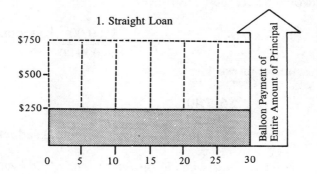

1. Straight Loan

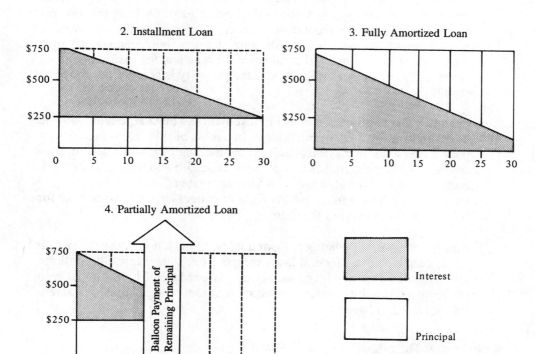

2. Installment Loan

3. Fully Amortized Loan

4. Partially Amortized Loan

Interest

Principal

monthly payments of $617.40, the interest and principal due on the next payment would be computed as follows:

$50,000 $500.00 **one month's interest**
 × .12   12)$6,000.00
$6,000.00 **annual interest**

                              $617.40
                              −500.00
                              $117.40 this month's principal reduction

Interest is customarily due and charged at the end of each month or payment period; this is known as *payment in arrears.* Since mortgage loan payments are customarily made at the beginning of each month, the interest portion of each payment covers the charge for using the borrowed money during the previous month. Some lenders, however, specify in the note that interest is charged in advance. In practice, the distinction between the two becomes important if the property is sold before the debt is repaid.

Usury.   The maximum rate of interest that may be charged on loans may be set by state law. Charging interest in excess of this rate is called **usury,** and lenders may be penalized for making usurious loans. In some states, a lender who makes a usurious loan is allowed to collect interest on the borrowed funds, but only at the legal rate of interest. In other states, such a lender may lose the right to collect any interest or may forfeit the entire amount of the loan.

Enacted to protect consumers from unscrupulous lenders, usury laws are state laws. However, federal law exempts from state interest limitations all residential first mortgage loans made after March 31, 1980, that were made by a federally chartered institution or that were insured or guaranteed by a federal agency.

Adjustable-Rate Mortgages (ARMs)

Adjustable-rate mortgages are generally originated at one rate of interest, with the rate fluctuating up or down during the loan term based on a certain economic indicator. Because the interest may change, so may the mortgagor's loan payments. Details of how and when the rate of interest on the loan will change are included in the provisions of the note. Common components of an ARM include the following.

Index.   The rate of the loan is tied to the movement of an index, such as the cost-of-funds index for federally chartered lenders. Most indexes are tied to U.S. Treasury securities.

Margin.   Usually the interest rate on the loan is the index rate plus a premium called the *margin.* For example, the loan rate may be 2 percent over the U.S. Treasury bill rate.

Interest rate caps.   Rate caps limit the amount the interest rate may change. Most ARMs have both periodic rate caps, which limit the amount the rate may increase at any one time, and aggregate rate caps, which limit the amount the rate may increase over the entire life of the loan.

Payment cap.   The mortgagor is protected against the possibility of individual payments that he or she cannot afford by the payment cap, which sets a maximum amount for payments. With a payment cap, a rate increase could result in negative amortization—an increase in the loan balance.

Adjustment period.   This establishes how often the loan rate may be changed. Common adjustment periods are monthly, quarterly and annually.

Prepayment

When a loan is amortized over a long term, the total interest paid by the borrower will add up to more money than the principal of the loan. If an amortized loan is paid off ahead of its full term, the lender will collect less interest from the borrower. For this reason, many mortgage and trust deed notes require the borrower to pay a **prepayment penalty** against the unearned portion of the interest with any payments made ahead of schedule. However, a *repayment privilege* ("or more" clause) allows the borrower to prepay the debt without penalty.

Any penalty charged will depend on the terms of the loan. Some lenders allow the borrower to pay off 20 percent of the original loan in any one year without paying a penalty; if the loan is paid off in full, however, the borrower may be charged a percentage of the principal paid in excess of that allowance. Some states either limit penalties or do not allow lenders to charge penalties on prepaid residential mortgage or deed of trust loans. Lenders will generally allow prepayment after five years without penalty.

PROVISIONS OF THE MORTGAGE DOCUMENT OR DEED OF TRUST

The mortgage document or deed of trust refers to the terms of the note and establishes that the conveyance of land is security for the debt. It identifies the lender as well as the borrower, and it includes an accurate legal description of the property. It should be signed by all parties who have an interest in the real estate. In addition, the instrument sets forth the obligations of the borrower (mortgagor) and the rights of the lender (mortgagee).

When a mortgage document is used to convey real property as security, both the mortgage and the note must include the name of the mortgagee as the lender. The mortgage document must name as the mortgagee the same person who is named in the note as the payee. It cannot name a third party.

Duties of the mortgagor or trustor.   The borrower is required to fulfill many covenants (promises). They usually include the following:

1. payment of the debt in accordance with the terms of the note;

2. payment of all real estate taxes on the property given as security;

3. maintenance of adequate insurance to protect the lender if the property is destroyed or damaged by fire, windstorm, or other hazard;

4. maintenance of the property in good repair at all times; and

5. in some situations, obtainment of the lender's authorization before making any major alterations on the property.

Failure to meet any of these obligations can result in a borrower's default. When this happens, the mortgage or deed of trust usually provides for a grace period (30 days, for example) during which the borrower can meet the obligation and cure the default. If he or she does not do so, the lender has the right to foreclose the mortgage or deed of trust. The most frequent cause of default is the borrower's failure to make the monthly payments.

Provisions for Default

The provisions of a mortgage may include an **acceleration clause** to assist the lender in a foreclosure. If a borrower defaults, the lender has the right to accelerate the maturity of the debt—to declare the entire debt due and owing immediately—even though the terms of the mortgage allow the borrower to amortize the debt in regular payments over a period of years. Without the acceleration clause, the lender would have to foreclose the debt every time a payment became due and owing.

Other clauses in a mortgage or deed of trust enable the lender to take care of the property in the event of the borrower's negligence or default. If the borrower does not pay taxes or insurance premiums or make necessary repairs on the property, the lender may step in and do so to protect the real estate held as security. Any money advanced by the lender to cure such defaults is either added to the unpaid debt or declared immediately due and owing from the borrower.

Assignment

When a note is sold to a third party, the mortgagee will endorse the note to the third party and also execute an *assignment of mortgage* or an *assignment of deed of trust*. The assignee becomes the new owner of the debt and security instrument. This assignment must be recorded. Upon payment in full, or satisfaction of the debt, the assignee is required to execute the satisfaction, or release, of the security instrument, as discussed in the following section.

Release of the Lien

When all mortgage loan payments have been made and the note paid in full, the mortgagor wants the public record to show that the debt has been paid and the mortgage released. Under the provisions of the **defeasance clause** in the typical mortgage, the mortgagee is required to execute a **satisfaction** of mortgage, when the note is fully paid. This document returns to the mortgagor all interest in the real estate that was transferred to the mortgagee by the original recorded mortgage document. Having this satisfaction entered into the public record shows that the debt has been paid and the mortgage released and canceled. If a mortgage has been assigned by a recorded assignment, the release must be executed by the assignee mortgagee.

When a real estate loan secured by a deed of trust has been completely repaid, the beneficiary requests in writing that the trustee convey the property back to the grantor. The trustee then executes and delivers to the grantor a *deed of reconveyance*. This deed reconveys the rights and powers that the trustee was given under the deed of trust. The deed should be acknowledged and recorded in the county where the property is located.

Recording

Mortgages or deeds of trust must be recorded in the recorder's office of the county in which the real estate is located. Recordation gives constructive notice to the world of the borrower's obligations and establishes the priority of the lien. If the property is registered in Torrens, notice of the lien must be entered on the original certificate of title on file at the registrar's office.

First and Second

[handwritten margin note: SUBROGATION insurance company = right to recover a claim.]

Mortgages and other liens normally have priority in the order in which they have been recorded. A mortgage or deed of trust on land that has no prior mortgage lien on it is a first mortgage or first deed of trust. When the owner of this land later executes another mortgage for additional funds, the new mortgage becomes a second mortgage (deed of trust), or **junior lien,** when recorded. The second mortgage is subject to the first; the first mortgage has prior claim to the value of the land pledged as security.

The priority of mortgage or deed of trust liens may be changed by the execution of a **subordination** agreement in which the first lender subordinates the lien to that of the second lender. To be valid, such an agreement must be signed by both lenders.

Tax and Insurance Reserves

Many lenders require borrowers to provide a reserve fund, called an *impound* or *trust* or *escrow account,* to meet future real estate taxes and insurance premiums. When the mortgage or deed of trust loan is made, the borrower starts the reserve by depositing funds to cover the amount of unpaid real estate taxes. If a new insurance policy has just been purchased, the insurance premium reserve will be started with the deposit of one-twelfth of the annual tax and insurance premium liability. Thereafter the monthly loan payments required of the borrower will include principal, interest and tax and insurance reserves (PITI).

RESPA, the federal Real Estate Settlement Procedures Act (discussed in Chapter 12), limits the total amount of reserves that may be required by a lender.

Federal flood insurance program.   This subsidized program, authorized by Congress, requires property owners in certain areas to obtain flood-damage insurance on properties financed by mortgages or other loans, grants, or guarantees obtained from federal agencies and federally insured or regulated lending institutions. The program seeks to improve future management and planning of floodplain areas through land-use and control measures.

Assignment of Rents

The borrower may make an assignment of rents to the lender, to be effective upon the borrower's default. The rent assignment may be included in the mortgage or deed of trust, or it may be made as a separate document. In either case the rent assignment should be drafted in language that clearly indicates that the parties intend to assign the rents and not merely to pledge them as security for the loan. In title theory states the lender is, in most cases, automatically entitled to any rents if the borrower defaults.

Buying Subject to or Assuming a Seller's Mortgage

A person who purchases real estate that has an outstanding mortgage or deed of trust on it may take the property subject to the mortgage or deed of trust, or may assume it and agree to pay the debt (called **assumption**). This technical distinction becomes important if the buyer defaults and the mortgage or deed of trust is foreclosed.

When the property is sold *subject to* the mortgage, the courts frequently hold that the purchaser is not personally obligated to pay the debt in full. The purchaser has bought the real estate knowing that he or she must make the loan payments and that, upon default, the lender will foreclose and the property will be sold by court order to pay the debt. However, when the grantee not only purchases the property subject to the mortgage, but *assumes and agrees to pay* the debt, then the grantee becomes personally obligated for the payment of the entire debt. If the mortgage is foreclosed in such a case, and if the court sale does not bring enough money to pay the debt in full, a **deficiency judgment** against both the assumer and the original borrower can be obtained for the unpaid balance of the note. Most states recognize this distinction. In certain cases, however, the lender will relieve the seller from continued liability by way of a novation. Therefore, an assumption with novation would be an advantage to sellers as they are released from future liability on the loan. When a mortgage is assumed, most lending institutions charge a transfer or assumption fee to cover the costs of changing their records. This charge is customarily borne by the purchaser.

Alienation clause.   Frequently, lenders wish to prevent some future purchaser from being able to assume real estate loans, particularly at old rates of interest. For this reason, some lenders may include an **alienation**

clause (also known as a *due-on-sale clause*) in the note. An alienation clause provides that upon the sale of the property by the borrower, the lender has the choice of declaring the entire debt immediately due or permitting a qualified buyer to assume the loan at current market interest rates.

FORECLOSURE

When a borrower defaults in making payments or fulfilling any of the obligations set forth in the mortgage or deed of trust, lenders can enforce their rights through **foreclosure.** A foreclosure is a legal procedure whereby the property that is pledged as security in the mortgage document or deed of trust is sold to satisfy the debt. The foreclosure procedure brings the rights of all parties to a conclusion and passes title in the subject property to either the person holding the mortgage document or deed of trust or a third party who purchases the realty at a foreclosure sale. Property thus sold is free of the mortgage and all junior liens.

Methods of Foreclosure

The three general types of foreclosure proceedings are judicial, nonjudicial, and strict. The specific provisions of each vary from state to state.

MASS.

Judicial foreclosure.   In this proceeding, the property pledged as security may be sold by court order after the mortgagee gives sufficient public notice. Upon a borrower's default, the lender may accelerate the due date of all remaining monthly payments. The lender's attorney then files a suit to foreclose the lien. After presentation of the facts in court, the property is ordered sold. A public sale is advertised and held, and the real estate is sold to the highest bidder.

Nonjudicial foreclosure.   Some states allow nonjudicial foreclosure procedures to be used when a **power-of-sale clause** is contained in the loan document. In those states that recognize deed of trust loans, the trustee is generally given the power of sale, although nonjudicial foreclosure is not allowed in a few states that permit deeds of trust. In addition, some states allow a similar power of sale to be used with a mortgage loan. To foreclose, the trustee (or mortgagee) must record a notice of default at the county recorder's office within a designated time period in order to give notice to the public of the intended auction. This official notice is generally accompanied by advertisements published in local newspapers that state the total amount due and the date of the public sale. After selling the property, the trustee (or mortgagee) may be required to file a copy of a notice of sale or affidavit of foreclosure.

Strict foreclosure.   Although the judicial and nonjudicial foreclosure procedures are the prevalent practices today, in some states it is still possible for a lender to acquire the mortgaged property by a strict foreclosure process. After appropriate notice has been given to the delinquent borrower and the proper papers have been prepared and filed, the court establishes a specific time period during which the balance of the defaulted debt must be paid in full. If this is not done, the court usually awards full legal title to the lender.

Deed in Lieu of Foreclosure

An alternative to foreclosure would be for the lender to accept a deed in lieu of foreclosure from the borrower. This is sometimes known as a "friendly foreclosure," because it is by agreement rather than by civil action. The major disadvantage of this manner of default settlement is that the mortgagee takes the real estate subject to all junior liens, while foreclosure eliminates all such liens. Also, by accepting a deed in lieu of foreclosure, the lender usually loses any rights pertaining to FHA insurance, VA guarantees, or private mortgage insurance.

Redemption

Most states give defaulting borrowers a chance to redeem their property. Historically the right of **redemption** is inherited from the old common law proceedings in which the court sale ended the **equitable right of redemption.** Carried over to statutory law, this concept provides that if, during the course of a foreclosure proceeding but *before the foreclosure sale,* the borrower or any other person who has an interest in the real estate (such as another creditor) pays the lender the amount currently due, plus costs, the debt will be reinstated. In some cases the person who redeems may be required to repay the accelerated loan in full. If some person other than the mortgagor or trustor redeems the real estate, the borrower becomes responsible to that person for the amount of the redemption.

Certain states also allow defaulted borrowers a period in which to redeem their real estate *after the sale*. During this **statutory redemption** period (which may be as long as one year) the court may appoint a receiver to take charge of the property, collect rents, pay operating expenses and so forth. The mortgagor or trustor who can raise the necessary funds to redeem the property within the statutory period pays the redemption money to the court. Because the debt was paid from the proceeds of the sale, the borrower then can take possession free and clear of the former defaulted loan.

Deed to Purchaser at Sale

If redemption is not made, or if no redemption period is allowed by state law, then the successful bidder at the sale receives a deed to the real estate. This is a statutory form of deed (sheriff's, master's, or referee's deed) that may be executed by a sheriff or master-in-chancery to convey such title as the borrower had to the purchaser at the sale. There are no warranties with this deed; the title passes as is, but free of the defaulted debt.

Deficiency Judgment

If the foreclosure sale does not produce enough cash to pay the loan balance in full after the deduction of expenses and accrued unpaid interest, the mortgagee may be entitled to a *deficiency judgment* against the signer of the note for the unpaid balance. It may be obtained against any endorsers or guarantors of the note and any owners of the mortgaged property who have assumed the debt by written agreement. If any proceeds remain after expenses are deducted, they are paid to the borrower. A lender who accepts a deed in lieu of foreclosure (as discussed earlier) cannot seek a deficiency judgment against the mortgagor.

CONVENTIONAL, INSURED, AND GUARANTEED LOANS

Mortgage and deed of trust loans are generally classified as conventional, insured, or guaranteed loans. Loans are classified as *conventional* when the payment of the debt rests solely upon the ability of the borrower to pay, with security provided by the mortgage or deed of trust. Repayment of *insured* and *guaranteed loans* is additionally secured by insurance issued by a private insurer or the Federal Housing Administration (FHA) or by a guarantee made by the Department of Veterans Affairs (VA).

Conventional Loans

In making **conventional loans,** lenders rely primarily on their own appraisal of the security and their own credit reports and other information concerning the reliability of the prospective borrower. Because such loans are sold in the secondary market (discussed in Chapter 12), borrower qualifications are somewhat stricter than those for an FHA-insured or a VA-guaranteed loan.

In conventional loans, the ratio of the debt to the value of the property is generally lower than with insured and guaranteed loans. In the conventional loan market, this loan-to-value (LTV) ratio usually does not exceed 80 percent, and some conventional lenders are restricted by state law to granting loans not exceeding 75 percent of the appraised value of the real estate given as the loan's security. (In contrast, the VA allows 100 percent loans, and the FHA allows 97 percent loans.) For example, if a conventional lender requires an 80 percent LTV ratio and the property appraises for $90,000, then the maximum loan would be $72,000.

However, under the provisions of private mortgage insurance (PMI), home purchasers can obtain conventional mortgage or deed of trust loans for up to 95 percent of the appraised property value. For example, on a 95 percent loan, the borrower is charged a premium consisting of a fee at the closing (usually 1 percent of the original loan balance) plus an additional percentage (usually ¼ percent) of the outstanding balance each year the insurance is in force. PMI insures only the top 20 or 25 percent of the loan, so when the LTV ratio drops below a certain percentage (usually 75 or 80 percent), the borrower can request that the lender terminate the coverage.

FHA-Insured Loans

The Federal Housing Administration (FHA) was created in 1934 under the National Housing Act to encourage improvement in housing standards and conditions, provide an adequate home financing system through insurance of housing credit, and exert a stabilizing influence on the mortgage market.

The FHA, which operates under the Department of Housing and Urban Development (HUD), *insures loans on real property made by approved lending institutions*. It does not insure the property, but it does insure the lender against loss. The maximum interest rates charged on **FHA-insured loans** are allowed to rise and fall with the market. The most popular FHA program is Section 203(b), which applies to loans on one-family to four-family residences.

Technical requirements established under congressional authority must be met before the FHA will issue the insurance. Three of these requirements are:

1. The borrower is charged 2.25 percent of the loan amount as a one-time premium for the FHA insurance that protects the lender from loss. In addition, a monthly premium must be paid.

This premium is one-half of 1 percent of the average outstanding loan balance per year, prorated into a monthly amount. For example, on a loan with an average outstanding balance of $72,000, one-half of 1 percent would be $360 per year. As a result, the borrower would pay an additional premium for that year of $30 per month for the protection of the lender.

2. The mortgaged real estate *must be appraised by an approved FHA appraiser*, and the ratio of possible mortgage debt to the appraised value of the property decreases as the appraised value of the property increases. The maximum loan amount cannot exceed the lesser of: (A) 97 percent of the first $25,000 of appraised value; 95 percent of the amount between $25,000 and $125,000; and 90 percent of any amount over $125,000; or (B) 97.75 percent of the sales price or appraisal value.

This means that a family using an FHA-insured loan to purchase a home appraised at $70,000 must make a $3,000 down payment. They will pay 3 percent of the first $25,000 or $750, plus 5 percent of the remaining $45,000, or $2,250, for a total of $3,000. Maximum loan amounts are set for various regions of the country; check with the local FHA office or a lender to determine the limit in your area.

3. The FHA regulations set general standards for type and construction of buildings, quality of neighborhood, and credit requirements of borrowers.

A buyer cannot assume, however, that if the FHA inspects, appraises and agrees to insure the loan on a parcel of real estate, the property is physically sound. HUD has approved the use of forms to be signed by the buyer and seller. These include such statements and warranties as: (1) the buyer has examined the entire premises; (2) the property is sold "as is"; and (3) no special fees or kickbacks have been paid beyond the customary commission or charges. These forms should be completed when the buyer makes an offer to purchase property. The broker must be familiar with the forms to explain them to the buyer and the seller. In some metropolitan areas, the FHA insists that heating, plumbing, and electrical systems be inspected and that needed repairs be completed before the loan is approved.

The FHA changes its regulations from time to time; check with the local HUD office to determine current provisions.

Loan origination fee and discount points.   The FHA purchaser pays a loan origination fee equal to 1 percent of the loan amount. Any discount points required may be paid by the buyer or seller or shared between them. There is, however, a 6 percent ceiling on seller contributions; anything exceeding 6 percent is considered a reduction in sales price.

Prepayment privileges.   When a mortgage or deed of trust loan is insured by the FHA, the borrower retains the privilege of prepaying the debt without penalty. On the first day of any month before the loan matures, the borrower may pay the entire debt or an amount equal to one or more monthly payments on the principal. The borrower must give the lender at least 30 days' written notice of intent to exercise this prepayment privilege.

The FHA also insures loans made to finance a number of other types of real estate improvements, some of which have provisions for prepayment penalties. When a loan is made to finance the purchase of a home, however, *the lender cannot charge a prepayment penalty.*

FHA loan assumptions.   The assumption rules for FHA-insured loans vary, depending on the date that the loan was originated.

- FHA loans originated prior to December 1986 generally have no restrictions on their assumption.

- For FHA loans originated between December 1, 1986, and December 15, 1989, a creditworthiness review of the person proposing to assume is required. If the original loan was for the purchase of a principal residence, this review is required during the first 12 months of the loan's existence. If the original loan was for the purchase of an investment property, the review is required during the first 24 months of the loan.

- For FHA loans originated after December 15, 1989, there are no assumptions without complete buyer qualification, and there are no longer any investor loans; all FHA loans made under the 203(b) program will be for owner-occupied properties only.

203(a) are FHA loans for investors

VA-Guaranteed (GI) Loans

Under the Servicemen's Readjustment Act of 1944 and subsequent federal legislation, the Department of Veterans Affairs is authorized to guarantee loans to purchase or construct homes for eligible veterans—those who have served a minimum of 181 days' active service since September 16, 1940 (90 days for veterans of World War II, the Korean War, the Viet

Nam conflict, and the Persian Gulf War; two full years for those serving during any peacetime period after September 7, 1980); or six or more years of continuous active duty as a reservist in the Army, Navy, Air Force, Marine Corps, and Coast Guard, or as a member of the Army or Air National Guard. The VA also guarantees loans to purchase mobile homes and plots on which to place them. GI loans assist veterans in financing the purchase of homes with little or no down payments, at comparatively low interest rates. Rules and regulations are issued from time to time by the VA, setting forth the qualifications, limitations and conditions under which a loan may be guaranteed.

Like the term *FHA loan,* **VA loan** is something of a misnomer. The VA does not normally lend money; it guarantees loans made by lending institutions approved by the agency. The term *VA loan* refers to a loan that is not made by the agency but guaranteed by it.

There is no VA limit on the amount of the loan a veteran can obtain; this is determined by the lender. The VA does, however, set a limit on the amount of the loan that it will guarantee—currently 50 percent of the loan amount less than $45,000; up to $22,500 for amounts between $45,000 and $56,250; 40 percent (or $36,000, whichever is less) for amounts between $56,250 and $203,000; and 25 percent (or $50,750, whichever is less) for amounts over $203,000. Note that these figures refer to the amount the lender would receive from the VA in the case of a default and foreclosure if the sale did not bring enough to cover the outstanding balance.

To determine what portion of a mortgage loan the VA will guarantee, the veteran must apply for a *certificate of eligibility.* This certificate does not mean that the veteran will automatically receive a mortgage. It merely sets forth the maximum guarantee the veteran is entitled to.

The VA will also issue *a certificate of reasonable value* (CRV) for the property being purchased, stating its current market value based on a VA-approved appraisal. The CRV places a ceiling on the amount of a VA loan allowed for the property; if the purchase price is greater than the amount cited in the CRV, the veteran may pay the difference in cash.

The VA purchaser will pay a loan origination fee to the lender, as well as a funding fee to the Department of Veterans Affairs. Reasonable discount points may be charged on a VA-guaranteed loan, and either the veteran or the seller may pay them.

VA loans may be assumed by purchasers who are not veterans, with prior approval from the VA for loans made after March 1, 1988. The original veteran borrower remains liable for the loan unless he or she obtains a release of liability, which must be approved by the VA. If the purchaser is a veteran, the seller may require the substitution of the buyer's entitlement, allowing the seller to reuse his or her entitlement in another home.

VA mortgage or deed of trust loans do not penalize borrowers for prepaying the entire loan balance at any time. All prepayments must be credited to the unpaid principal balance of the loan as of the due date of the next installment. In addition, under the Veterans Housing Act of 1974, any veteran who paid a prior veteran's loan in full and disposed of the property is entitled to take out another VA-guaranteed loan.

Only in certain situations (such as in isolated rural areas) where financing is not easily available does the VA itself lend money. Otherwise, a veteran applies for and obtains a loan from a VA-approved lending institution.

Discount Points

From a borrower's point of view, a mortgage or deed of trust loan is a means of financing a purchase; from a lender's point of view, it is an investment. FHA-insured and VA-guaranteed loans are made by approved lending institutions, such as mortgage banking companies, and then sold to investors, such as insurance companies. By selling the loans instead of collecting the principal and interest over the long term, lending institutions can continuously replenish their supplies of funds.

Discount points are usually charged by a lending institution when the FHA or VA interest rate is less than the market, or conventional, rate. One point equals 1 percent of the loan amount.

If an FHA or VA mortgage loan made at a fixed interest rate is compared to a similar conventional mortgage loan at a higher rate of interest, the FHA or VA loan yields less. If both loans were offered to an investor at the same price, he or she would choose to buy the loan with the higher yield. The only way to sell the lower-rate loan is to reduce its price (discount it) to bring up its yield.

Discount points represent the percentage by which the face amount of a mortgage loan is discounted, or reduced, when it is sold to an investor to make its fixed interest-rate yield competitive in the current money market. Without this discount, investors would not be interested in such loans and would rather make conventional loans to earn the higher market rate of interest on the investment.

At the closing of a purchase financed by a VA or FHA loan, the seller is usually charged the discount amount, which is paid to the lender. This discount makes up the difference between the amount the loan costs the lender and the amount the lender can expect to sell it for in the market.

Loan Origination Fees

When a mortgage or deed of trust is originated, the mortgage company's commission is figured in points. For example, a charge of two points on a $50,000 mortgage loan would be 2 percent of $50,000, or $1,000. The maximum loan origination fee allowed under an FHA or a VA loan is 1 percent. This fee is generally charged to the borrower on any loan, whether conventional, insured, or guaranteed.

SUMMARY

Mortgage and deed of trust loans provide the principal sources of financing for real estate operations. Mortgage loans involve a borrower, called the *mortgagor*, and a lender, called the *mortgagee*. Deed of trust loans involve a third party, called the *trustee*, in addition to the borrower (the *trustor*) and the lender (the *beneficiary*).

Some states, known as *title theory states*, recognize the lender as the owner of mortgaged property. Others known as *lien theory states* recognize the borrower as the owner of mortgaged property. A few *intermediary states* recognize modified versions of these theories.

After a lending institution has received, investigated, and approved a loan application, it issues a commitment to make the loan. The borrower is required to execute a *note*, agreeing to repay the debt, and a *mortgage* or *deed of trust*, placing a lien on the real estate to secure the note. The mortgage or deed of trust is recorded in the public record in order to give notice of the lender's interest.

The note for the amount of the loan usually provides for *amortization* under one of a number of plans. The note also sets the rate of *interest* at which the loan is made and which the mortgagor or trustor must pay as a charge for borrowing the money. Charging more than the maximum interest rate allowed by state statute is called *usury* and is illegal. The mortgage or deed of trust secures the debt and sets forth the obligations of the borrower and the rights of the lender. Payment in full of the note by its terms entitles the borrower to a satisfaction, or *release*, which is recorded to clear the lien from the public records. Default by the borrower may result in *acceleration* of payments, a *foreclosure* sale, and, after the *redemption period* (if provided by state law), *loss of title*. If the property is sold at foreclosure for an amount not sufficient to cover the debt, the lender may seek a *deficiency judgment* against the borrower to cover the difference, plus costs.

Mortgage and deed of trust loans include *conventional loans* and loans *insured by the FHA or an independent mortgage insurance company or guaranteed by the VA*. FHA and VA loans must meet certain requirements for the borrower to obtain the benefits of the government backing that induces the lender to lend its funds. To make these loans attractive to investors, lenders may charge *discount points*, which traditionally have been paid by the seller.

QUESTIONS

Please complete all of the questions before turning to the Answer Key.

1. Which of the following documents would be used as security for a promissory note?

    a.   Power of attorney
    b.   Deed in lieu of foreclosure
    c.   Deed of trust
    d.   Personal check

2. A lien might not take priority from its date of recordation if it contains a(n)

    a.   acceleration clause.   c.   defeasance clause.
    b.   alienation clause.   d.   subordination clause.

3. When the borrower pays interest only on the funds borrowed during the life of the loan and then pays the full principal balance at its end, this is called a(n)

    a.   straight loan.   c.   subordinated loan.
    b.   amortized loan.   d.   partially amortized loan.

4. All of the following features regarding discount points are true EXCEPT that they

    a.   are considered prepaid interest.
    b.   are paid to the lender.
    c.   increase the effective yield.
    d.   reduce the term of the loan.

5. Which of the following documents would contain a power of sale?

    a.   Certificate of reasonable value
    b.   Deed of trust
    c.   Promissory note
    d.   Certificate of eligibility

6. The mortgage theory that recognizes a mortgage as a conveyance of real property is called the

    a.   title theory.   c.   lien theory.
    b.   intermediary theory.   d.   modified lien theory.

7. All of the following statements regarding conventional loans are true EXCEPT that

a. they can be insured by private mortgage insurance.
b. they often require more down payment than FHA and VA loans.
c. their rates are generally lower than FHA and VA rates.
d. their repayment periods are generally longer than those of FHA and VA loans.

8. When a defaulted borrower can redeem the property before a foreclosure sale, this is called a(n)

a. statutory right.   c. power of sale.
b. equitable right.   d. power of attorney.

9. The quickest foreclosure process occurs in states that permit which of the following clauses?

a. Acceleration   c. Power of attorney
b. Alienation   d. Power of sale

10. All of the following are negotiable instruments EXCEPT a

a. promissory note.   c. cashier's check.
b. personal check.   d. certificate of eligibility.

11. In a real estate loan, the borrower may be referred to by which of the following names?

a. Trustee   c. Beneficiary
b. Mortgagor   d. Mortgagee

12. Which of the following statements regarding real estate loans is true?

a. The mortgage or deed of trust is the security for the debt.
b. The lender under a deed of trust is known as the trustor.
c. A loan with no principal paid until its end is an amortized loan.
d. Conventional loans are backed by the federal government.

13. All of the following statements regarding the interest paid on a real estate loan are true EXCEPT that the interest is

    a. generally paid in arrears.
    b. simple interest.
    c. limited by usury laws in some states.
    d. not deductible for income tax purposes.

14. A loan under which the monthly payment decreases because the interest on the unpaid balance decreases is called a(n)

    a. term loan.   c. amortized loan.
    b. installment loan.   d. partially amortized loan.

15. Which of the following components of an adjustable-rate mortgage loan causes the interest rate to increase or decrease?

    a. Interest rate cap   c. Index
    b. Adjustment period   d. Margin

16. All of the following statements regarding a VA-guaranteed loan are true EXCEPT that the

    a. loans do not contain prepayment penalties.
    b. buyers and the property must be qualified or approved.
    c. VA will guarantee loans to purchase mobile homes and condominium units.
    d. loans generally have lower loan-to-value ratios than do conventional loans.

17. The obligations created by a mortgage or deed of trust include all of the following EXCEPT

    a. payment of the real estate taxes on the property.
    b. maintenance of the property in good repair at all times.
    c. provision of adequate hazard insurance to protect the lender.
    d. payment of the debt as the borrower believes is proper.

18. When a note is sold to a third party, this is called

    a. sale and leaseback.   c. acceleration.
    b. subordination.   d. assignment.

19. The priority of a first mortgage over a second mortgage is based on the first mortgage's

   a.   principal amount.   c.   interest rate.
   b.   date of recordation.   d.   loan term.

20. Which of the following statements is true when a buyer takes over a loan "subject to" the existing mortgage?

   a.   The buyer becomes fully responsible for the loan.
   b.   The seller remains fully liable for the loan.
   c.   The buyer and the seller share liability for the loan equally.
   d.   The seller incurs secondary liability for the loan.

21. Which of the following situations would require the filing of a lawsuit?

   a.   Deed in lieu of foreclosure
   b.   Judicial foreclosure
   c.   Foreclosure under a power of sale
   d.   Nonjudicial foreclosure

22. A lender might refuse a deed in lieu of foreclosure because the

   a.   right to a deficiency judgment would be lost.
   b.   FHA or VA would make up any difference.
   c.   collateral had increased in value.
   d.   borrower had prepaid the loan.

23. The highest loan-to-value ratio is found in which of the following types of loans?

   a.   FHA-insured   c.   Conventional
   b.   VA-guaranteed   d.   Insured conventional

24. Which of the following persons is protected by the insurance in an FHA-insured loan?

   a.   The seller   c.   The lender
   b.   The borrower   d.   The FHA

25. The VA indicates the market value of the property to be purchased in the

  a. certificate of reasonable value.
  b. certificate of eligibility.
  c. power of attorney.
  d. power-of-sale clause.

26. In a VA-guaranteed loan, the funding fee is paid by the veteran purchaser
     to the

  a. VA.   c. seller.
  b. lender.   d. escrow agent.

27. How much would a mortgage company's loan origination fee be on a
     loan of $98,000 at 7.75 percent interest and with the maximum points al-
     lowed for an FHA-insured loan?

  a. $775   c. $2,940
  b. $980   d. $7,595

28. After a foreclosure sale, the defaulted borrower may have a right to re-
     cover the property through which of the following?

  a. Strict foreclosure   c. Equitable redemption
  b. Judicial foreclosure   d. Statutory redemption

29. If a foreclosure sale does not produce enough money to repay the loan
     balance and expenses, the lender may be entitled to a(n)

  a. deed in lieu of foreclosure.
  b. deficiency judgment.
  c. acceleration clause.
  d. prepayment privilege.

12:   Real Estate Financing Market

KEY TERMS

balloon payment
blanket loan
buydown
commercial banks
construction loan
Equal Credit Opportunity Act
(ECOA)
Farmer's Home Administration
(FmHA)
Federal Reserve System
Federal Home Loan Mortgage
Corporation (FHLMC,
Freddie Mac)
Federal National Mortgage
Association (FNMA, Fannie
Mae)
Government National Mortgage
Association (GNMA, Ginnie
Mae)
graduated-payment mortgage
growing-equity mortgage

home equity loan
installment contract
mortgage banking companies
mortgage brokers
mutual savings banks
open-end loan
package loan
primary market
purchase-money loan
real estate investment trust
(REIT)
Regulation Z
Real Estate Settlement
Procedures Act (RESPA)
reverse-annuity mortgage
sale and leaseback
savings and loan associations
secondary mortgage market
shared-appreciation mortgage
wraparound loan

The real estate finance market is one of the most important centers of monetary activity in the country. Buyers, sellers, lenders, developers, real estate licensees, and even the federal government participate in this important market. Chapter 11 discussed the basic instruments involved in real estate financing; the following pages examine mortgage lending from a marketplace perspective. This will include discussions of the various sources of real estate financing, the federal government's participation in the money market, the special creative lending plans that have evolved to address specific needs, and the various federal laws that affect the participants in the market for real estate finance.

SOURCES OF REAL ESTATE FINANCING

Most loans to finance real estate purchases are obtained from financial institutions specifically designed to hold individuals' savings. These institutions lend out the savings to earn interest, some of which is directed back to the savers and some of which is retained by the institution as income. As discussed in Chapter 11, the most common form of real estate financing is the first, or primary, mortgage. As the name implies, it is the first mortgage taken out on a property, as opposed to a second, or junior, mortgage, which is a mortgage on already financed property. First mortgages have priority over all subsequent liens except tax liens. Mortgage loans can be made by savings and loan associations, commercial banks, mutual savings banks, life insurance companies, mortgage banking companies, and mortgage brokers.

Savings and Loan Associations

Savings and loan associations are active participants in the home loan mortgage market, specializing in long-term residential loans. A savings and loan earns money by paying less for the funds it receives than it charges for the loans it makes. Loan income includes more than interest, however—there are loan origination, loan assumption and other fees.

Traditionally, savings and loan associations are the most flexible of all the lending institutions with regard to their mortgage lending procedures, and they are generally local in nature. In addition, they participate in FHA-insured and VA-guaranteed loans, though only to a limited extent.

All savings and loan associations must be chartered, either by the federal government or by the states in which they are located. The *Financial Institutions Reform, Recovery and Enforcement Act of 1989 (FIRREA),* enacted in response to the savings and loan association crisis of the 1980s, was intended to ensure the continued viability of the savings and loan industry. FIRREA restructured the savings and loan association regulatory system as well as the insurance system that protects its depositors. The *Federal Deposit Insurance Corporation (FDIC)* now manages the insurance funds for both savings and loan associations and commercial banks. Savings and loan deposits are insured through the *Savings Association Insurance Fund (SAIF),* and bank deposits are insured through the Bank Insurance Fund (BIF).

FIRREA also created the *Office of Thrift Supervision (OTS)* to monitor and regulate the savings and loan industry and the *Resolution Trust Corporation (RTC)* to liquidate the assets of failed savings and loan associations.

Because of their performance record of the 1980s, savings and loans are now subject to stricter capital requirements than before, as well as new housing loan requirements. Effective July 1, 1991, savings and loan associations are required to maintain 70 percent of their loan portfolios in housing-related loans, such as residential mortgage loans, residential construction loans and home equity loans.

Mutual Savings Banks

These institutions, which operate like savings and loan associations, are located primarily in the northeastern section of the United States. They issue no stock and are mutually owned by their investors. Although **mutual savings banks** do offer limited checking account privileges, they are primarily savings institutions and are highly active in the mortgage market, investing in loans secured by income property as well as residential real estate. In addition, because mutual savings banks usually seek low-risk loan investments, they often prefer to originate FHA-insured or VA-guaranteed loans.

Commercial Banks

Commercial banks are an important source of real estate financing. Bank loan departments primarily handle such short-term loans as construction, home improvement and mobile-home loans. In some areas, however, commercial banks are originating an increasing number of home mortgages. Commercial banks play a significant role in issuing VA and FHA loans. Like the savings and loan associations, banks must be chartered by the state or federal government.

Insurance Companies

Insurance companies amass large sums of money from the premiums paid by their policyholders. While a certain portion of this money is held in reserve to satisfy claims and cover operating expenses, much of it is invested in profit-earning enterprises, such as long-term real estate loans.

Most insurance companies like to invest their money in large, long-term loans that finance commercial and industrial properties. They also invest in residential mortgage and deed of trust loans by purchasing large blocks of FHA-insured and VA-guaranteed loans from the Federal National Mortgage Association and other agencies that warehouse such loans for resale in the secondary mortgage market (discussed later in this chapter).

In addition, many insurance companies seek to further ensure the safety of their investments by insisting on equity positions (known as *equity kickers*) in many projects they finance. This means that the company requires a partnership arrangement with, for example, a project developer or subdivider as a condition of making a loan. This is called *participation financing*.

Mortgage banking companies.   **Mortgage banking companies** use money borrowed from other institutions and funds of their own to make real estate loans that may later be sold to investors (with the mortgage company receiving a fee for servicing the loans). Mortgage bankers are involved in all types of real estate loan activities and often serve as middlemen between investors and borrowers, but they are not mortgage brokers.

Mortgage banking companies are usually organized as stock companies. As a source of real estate financing they are subject to considerably fewer lending restrictions than are commercial banks or savings and loans.

Credit unions.   *Credit unions* are cooperative organizations in which members place money in savings accounts. In the past most credit unions made only short-term consumer and home improvement loans, but they have been branching out to originating longer-term first and second mortgage and deed of trust loans.

Mortgage brokers.   **Mortgage brokers** are not lenders but are often instrumental in obtaining financing. Mortgage brokers are individuals who are licensed to act as intermediaries in bringing borrowers and lenders together. They locate potential borrowers, process preliminary loan applications and submit the applications to lenders for final approval. Frequently they work with or for mortgage banking companies in these activities. They are not involved in servicing a loan once it is made. Many mortgage brokers are also real estate brokers who offer these financing services in addition to their regular brokerage activities.

Pension funds.   *Pension funds* have begun to participate actively in financing real estate projects. Most of the real estate activity for pension funds is handled through mortgage bankers and mortgage brokers.

Investment group financing.   Large real estate projects, such as high-rise apartment buildings, office complexes, and shopping centers, are often financed as a joint venture through group financing arrangements such as syndicates, limited partnerships and real estate investment trusts.

Application for Credit

All mortgage lenders require a prospective borrower to file an application that provides the lender with the basic information necessary to evaluate the acceptability of the proposed loan. The application includes information regarding the purpose of the loan, the amount, and the proposed terms of repayment. This is considered a preliminary offer of a loan agreement; final terms may require substantial negotiations.

A prospective borrower must submit personal information including employment, earnings, assets, and financial obligations. Details of the real estate that will be the security for the loan must be provided, including legal description, improvements, title, and taxes. For loans on income property or loans made to corporations, additional information is required, such as financial and operating statements, schedules of leases and tenants, and balance sheets. Applications must be signed and must include a certificate that the information provided is true and complete.

The loan officer will carefully investigate the application information, using credit reports and an appraisal of the property to help him or her decide whether or not to grant the loan. The lender's acceptance of the application is written in the form of a loan commitment, which creates a contract to make a loan and sets forth the details.

GOVERNMENT PARTICIPATION IN THE FINANCE MARKET

Aside from FHA and VA loan programs, the federal government influences mortgage lending practices through the Federal Reserve System as well as through various federal agencies, such as the Farmer's Home Administration (FmHA). It also deals in the secondary mortgage market through the Government National Mortgage Association, the Federal Home Loan Mortgage Corporation, and the Federal National Mortgage Association.

Federal Reserve System

Established in 1913, the **Federal Reserve System ("the Fed")** operates to maintain sound credit conditions, help counteract inflationary and deflationary trends, and create a favorable economic climate. The system divides the country into 12 federal reserve districts, each served by a Federal Reserve bank. All nationally chartered banks must join the Federal Reserve and purchase stock in its district reserve banks.

The Federal Reserve indirectly regulates the flow of money in the marketplace through its member banks by controlling their reserve requirements and discount rates. In addition, the Federal Reserve tempers the economy through its open-market operations.

Reserve requirements. The Federal Reserve requires each member bank to keep a certain amount of its assets on hand as reserve funds unavailable for loans or any other use. This requirement was designed primarily to protect customer deposits, but it also provides a means of manipulating the flow of cash in the money market. By increasing its reserve requirements, the Federal Reserve, in effect, limits the amount of money that member banks can use to make loans, thus causing interest rates to increase.

In this manner, the government can slow down an overactive economy by restricting the number of loans that would have been directed toward major purchases of goods and services. The opposite is also true—by decreasing the reserve requirements, the Federal Reserve can allow more loans to be made, thus increasing the money circulated in the marketplace and causing interest rates to decline.

Discount rates. Member banks are permitted to borrow money from the district reserve banks to expand their lending operations. The interest rate that the district banks charge for the use of this money is called the *discount rate*. This rate is the basis on which the banks determine the percentage rate of interest that they, in turn, charge their loan customers. Theoretically, when the Federal Reserve discount rate is high, bank interest rates are high; therefore, fewer loans will be made and less money will circulate in the marketplace. Conversely, a lower discount rate results in lower interest rates, more bank loans, and more money in circulation.

Government Participation in the Secondary Market

Mortgage lending takes place in both the **primary market,** where loans are originated, and the **secondary mortgage market,** where loans are bought and sold only after they have been funded. A lender may wish to sell a number of loans to raise immediate funds when it needs more money to meet the mortgage demands in its area. Secondary market

Figure 12.1   Primary and Secondary Mortgage Markets

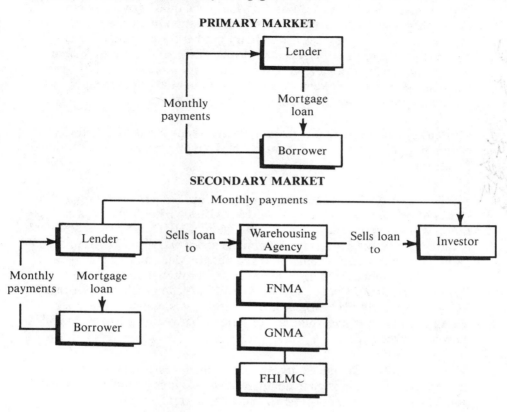

PRIMARY MARKET

SECONDARY MARKET

activity is especially desirable when money is in short supply, because it provides a great stimulant to the housing construction market as well as to the mortgage market (see Figure 12.1).

When a loan has been sold, the original lender may continue to collect the payments from the borrower. The lender then passes the payments along to the investor who has purchased the loan and charges the investor a fee for servicing the loan.

A major source of secondary mortgage market activity is a warehousing agency, which purchases a number of mortgage loans and assembles them into one or more packages of loans for resale to investors. The major warehousing agencies are discussed in the following paragraphs.

Can call 800# for a bank that will let you assume a FNMA Mtge on a foreclosed FNMA property

Federal National Mortgage Association.   The **Federal National Mortgage Association (FNMA, "Fannie Mae")** is a quasi-governmental agency organized as a privately owned corporation that issues its own common stock and provides a secondary market for mortgage loans—conventional as well as FHA and VA loans. FNMA will buy a *block* or *pool* of mortgages from a lender in exchange for *mortgage-backed securities* that the lender may keep or sell. FNMA guarantees payment of all interest and principal to the holder of the securities.

Mortgage banking firms are generally actively involved with FNMA, originating loans and selling them to FNMA while retaining the servicing functions.

Government National Mortgage Association.   The **Government National Mortgage Association (GNMA, "Ginnie Mae")** exists as a corporation without capital stock and is a division of HUD. GNMA is designed to administer special assistance programs and work with FNMA in secondary market activities. Fannie Mae and Ginnie Mae can join forces in times of tight money and high interest rates through their tandem plan. Basically the *tandem plan* provides that FNMA can purchase high-risk, low-yield (usually FHA) loans at full market rates, with GNMA guaranteeing payment and absorbing the difference between the low yield and current market prices.

Ginnie Mae also guarantees investment securities issued by private offerors (such as banks, mortgage companies and savings and loan associations) and backed by pools of FHA and VA mortgage loans. The *Ginnie Mae pass-through certificate* is a security interest in a pool of mortgages that provides for a monthly "pass-through" of principal and interest payments directly to the certificate holder. Such certificates are guaranteed by Ginnie Mae.

Federal Home Loan Mortgage Corporation.   The **Federal Home Loan Mortgage Corporation (FHLMC, "Freddie Mac")** provides a secondary market for mortgage loans, primarily conventional loans. Freddie Mac has the authority to purchase mortgages, pool them and sell bonds in the open market with the mortgages as security. Note, however, that FHLMC does not guarantee payment of Freddie Mac mortgages.

Many lenders use the standardized forms and follow the guidelines issued by Freddie Mac, because use of FHLMC forms is mandatory for lenders who wish to sell mortgages in the agency's secondary mortgage market. The standardized documents include loan applications, credit reports and appraisal forms.

Farmer's Home Administration.   The **Farmer's Home Administration (FmHA)** is a federal agency of the Department of Agriculture. FmHA offers programs to help purchase or operate family farms. It also provides loans to help purchase or improve single-family homes in rural areas (generally areas with a population of fewer than 10,000). Loans are made to low- and moderate-income families, and the interest rate charged can be as low as 1 percent, depending on the borrower's income.

FmHA loan programs fall into two categories: guaranteed loans, made and serviced by a private lender and guaranteed for a specific percentage by the FmHA, and a direct loan program by the FmHA.

SPECIALIZED FINANCING TECHNIQUES

As discussed in Chapter 11, a mortgage or deed of trust is nothing more than a string of individual clauses, the combination of which effect a desired result—a parcel of real estate is given as security for a loan. As has been illustrated in the previous discussions of variable and renegotiable loans, by altering the terms and provisions of a mortgage or deed of trust document, a borrower and lender can tailor these financing instruments to best suit the type of transaction and the financial needs of both parties. In addition, these terms can be changed to reflect certain economic conditions in the marketplace. In times of tight and expensive mortgage money, such forms of creative financing gain prominence. In addition, real estate can be financed using instruments other than mortgages and deeds of trust, as will be discussed on the pages that follow.

Purchase-Money Loans   *owner financing*

A **purchase-money loan** is given at the time of purchase to facilitate the sale. The term is used in two ways—to refer to *any* security instrument originating at the time of sale and (most often) to refer to the instrument *given by the purchaser to a seller who "takes back" a note for part or all of the purchase price.* It may be a first or second mortgage, and it becomes a lien on the property when the title passes.

Blanket Loans

A **blanket loan** covers *more than one parcel or lot* and is usually used to finance subdivision developments (though it can be used to finance the purchase of improved properties as well). It usually includes a provision, known as a *partial release clause,* that the borrower may obtain the release of any one lot or parcel from the lien by repaying a definite amount of the loan. The lender issues a partial release for each parcel released from the mortgage lien. This release form includes a provision that the lien will continue to cover all other unreleased lots.

Package Loans

A **package loan** includes not only the real estate but also *all fixtures and appliances installed on the premises.* In recent years this kind of loan has been used extensively in financing furnished condominium units. Such loans usually include the kitchen range, refrigerator, dishwasher, garbage disposal unit, washer and dryer, food freezer and other appliances, as well as furniture, drapes and carpets.

Open-End Loans

The **open-end loan,** which is being used with increasing frequency, secures a *note* executed by the borrower to the lender as well as any future *advances* of funds made by the lender to the borrower or to the borrower's successors in title. The interest rate on the initial amount borrowed is fixed, but interest on future advances may be the market rate then in effect.

Open-end mortgages, or *equity lines of credit,* frequently are used by borrowers to obtain additional funds to improve their property. The borrower "opens" the mortgage or deed of trust to increase the debt to its original amount—after the debt has been reduced by payments over a period of time. The mortgage or deed of trust usually includes a statement of the maximum amount to be secured. The terms of an open-end mortgage usually limit the increase in debt to either the original amount of the debt or a stipulated amount set forth in the mortgage or deed of trust. The lender is not obligated to advance the additional funds.

Construction Loans

A **construction loan** is made *to finance the construction of improvements* on real estate (homes, apartments, office buildings and so forth). Under a construction loan the lender commits the full amount of the loan but makes partial *progress payments* as the building is being constructed.

Progress payments (also known as *draws)* are made to the *general contractor* for that part of the construction work that has been completed since the previous payment. Prior to each payment the lender inspects the work. The general contractor must provide the lender with adequate waivers of lien releasing all mechanics' lien rights for the work covered by the payment. This kind of loan generally bears a higher-than-market interest rate because of the risks assumed by the lender—inadequate releasing of mechanics' liens, possible delays in completing the building or financial failure of the contractor or subcontractors. This type of financing is generally *short-term, or interim, financing.* The borrower is expected to arrange for a permanent loan (also known as an *end loan* or *take-out loan*) that will repay or "take out" the construction financing lender when the work is completed.

Wraparound Loans

A **wraparound loan,** also known as an *overriding* or *all-inclusive mortgage* or *deed of trust,* enables a borrower who is paying off an existing mortgage or deed of trust loan to obtain additional financing from a second lender. *The new lender assumes payment of the existing loan and gives the borrower a new, increased loan at a higher interest rate.* The total amount of the new loan includes the existing loan as well as the additional funds needed by the borrower. The borrower makes payments to the new lender on the larger loan, and the new lender makes the payments on the original loan.

For example, a buyer purchases a property for $100,000 with $15,000 down. The seller gives the buyer a wraparound note for $85,000 at 13 percent, and the buyer makes payments to the seller of $920.83 There is already a $50,000 mortgage at 10 percent on the property with payments of $438.79. The seller continues to make these payments to the lender and realizes a net monthly income of $482.04 ($920.83 – $438.79).

A wraparound mortgage is frequently used as a method of refinancing real property or financing the purchase of real property when an existing mortgage cannot be prepaid. It is also used to finance the sale of real estate when the buyer wishes to put up a minimum of initial cash for the sale. The buyer executes a wraparound document to the seller, who will collect payments on the new loan and continue to make payments on the old loan. The buyer should require a protective clause in the document granting the right to make payments directly to the original lender in the event of a potential default on the old loan by the seller.

Shared-Appreciation Mortgages

In a **shared-appreciation mortgage** the lender originates a mortgage or deed of trust loan at a favorable interest rate (several points below the current rate) in return for a guaranteed share of the gain (if any) the borrower will realize when the property is eventually sold. This type of loan was originally made to developers of large real estate projects, but in times of expensive mortgage money it has appeared in the residential financing market. The specific details of the shared-appreciation agreement are set forth in the mortgage or deed of trust and note documents.

Reverse-Annuity Mortgages

With a **reverse-annuity mortgage** regular monthly payments are made *to the borrower,* based on the equity the homeowner has invested in the property given as security for the loan. A reverse loan allows senior citizens on fixed incomes to realize the equity buildup in their homes without having to sell. The borrower is charged a fixed rate of interest, and the loan is eventually paid from the sale of the property or from the borrower's estate upon his or her death.

Installment Contracts

Real estate can be purchased under an *installment contract,* also known as a *contract for deed, land contract,* or *agreement of sale.* Real estate is often sold *on contract* in one of two situations: (1) when mortgage financing is not available; and (2) when the purchaser does not have a sufficient down payment to cover the difference between a mortgage or trust deed loan and the selling price of the real estate.

Under an installment contract the seller (the *vendor*) retains fee ownership, while the buyer (the *vendee*) secures possession and an equitable interest in the property. The buyer agrees to give the seller a down payment and pay regular monthly payments of principal and interest over a number of years. The buyer also agrees to pay real estate taxes, insurance premiums, repairs, and upkeep on the property. While the buyer obtains possession when the contract is signed by both parties, the seller is not obligated to execute and deliver a deed to the buyer until the terms of the contract have been satisfied. Under most installment contracts, the buyer is entitled to a deed as soon as he or she is able to complete the terms of the contract. This frequently occurs when the buyer has made a sufficient number of payments to obtain a mortgage loan and pay off the balance due on the contract.

The installment contract is really another means of seller-financing. It is not a mortgage or deed of trust. With this form of financing, the seller/vendor remains in strong control of the transaction. Real estate is occasionally sold with the new buyer assuming an existing installment contract from the original buyer/vendee. Generally, when a buyer assumes an existing contract, the original buyer/vendee must assign or convey his or her interest to the new buyer, and the original seller/vendor must approve the new purchaser.

Default—termination of the contract.   Installment contracts usually include a provision that a default by the buyer permits the seller to forfeit the contract, retain all payments already made, and evict the buyer. In some states, however, laws have been enacted that require the seller to refund to the buyer any payments received in excess of a reasonable rental or use value of the property. In other states, a defaulted installment contract must be foreclosed like a mortgage. There is usually no redemption period during which a buyer in default may redeem an installment contract and retain possession of the property.

Sale and Leaseback

Sale-and-leaseback arrangements are used as a means of financing large commercial or industrial plants. The land and building, usually used by the seller for business purposes, are sold to an investor, such as an insurance company. The real estate is then leased back by the buyer (the investor) to the seller, who continues to conduct business on the property as a tenant. The buyer becomes the lessor, and the original owner becomes the lessee. This enables a business firm that has money invested in a plant to free that money so it can be used as working capital.

Graduated-Payment Mortgages

A *flexible-payment plan,* such as a **graduated-payment mortgage,** allows a mortgagor to make lower monthly payments for the first few years of the loan (typically the first five years) and larger payments for the remainder of the term, when the mortgagor's income is expected to have increased. Generally this type of loan is used to enable first-time buyers and buyers in times of high interest rates to purchase real estate. However, the monthly payments made generally are less than the interest due, resulting in negative amortization. As each payment is made, the unpaid interest is added to the principal balance, resulting in an increasing loan balance for the first few years.

Balloon Payment Loans

When a mortgage or deed of trust loan requires periodic payments that will not fully amortize the amount of the loan by the time the final payment is due, the final payment is larger than the others. This is called a **balloon payment,** and this type of loan is a *partially amortized loan.* For example, a loan made for $80,000 at 11½ percent interest may be computed on a 30-year amortization schedule but paid over a 20-year term with a final balloon payment due at the end of the 20th year. In this case each monthly payment would be $792.24 (the amount taken from a 30-year amortization schedule), with a final balloon payment of $56,340 (the amount of principal still owing after 20 years). It is frequently assumed that if the payments are made promptly the lender will extend the balloon payment for another limited term. The lender, however, is not legally obligated to grant this extension and can require payment in full when the note is due.

Growing-Equity Mortgages

The **growing-equity mortgage**, or *rapid-payoff mortgage,* makes use of a fixed interest rate, but payments of principal are increased according to an index or a schedule. The total payment thus increases, but the borrower's income is expected to keep pace, and the loan is paid off more quickly.

Buydowns

In a **buydown** some of the mortgage loan interest is donated or "repaid" in advance to the lender on the borrower's behalf for the purpose of temporarily reducing the interest rate. That is, the original interest rate is effectively "bought down" for a period of time by the advance payment. Typical buydown arrangements provide for a reduced interest rate of 1 to 3 percent over the first one to three years of the loan term.

Common sources of buydown funds include home builders who wish to sell their stock of houses by offering the lower rate, parents or other relatives wanting to assist the buyers in purchasing a home, and sellers seeking to help the buyers qualify for a loan at the lower interest rate, thus closing the sale on their property.

Home Equity Loans

Home equity loans are a new source of funds for homeowners who wish to finance the purchase of expensive items; consolidate existing installment loans on credit card debt; or pay for medical, educational, home improvement, or other expenses. This type of financing has been used increasingly in the past few years, partly because recent tax laws have ended the deductibility of interest on debts not secured by real estate ("consumer interest"). Home equity loans are secured by the borrower's residence, and the interest charged is deductible up to a loan limit of $100,000.

A home equity loan can be taken out as a fixed loan amount or as an equity line of credit. With the home equity line of credit the lender extends a line of credit that the borrowers can use whenever they want. The borrowers can receive their money by a check sent to them, deposits made in a checking or savings account, or a book of drafts the borrowers can use up to their credit limit.

Investment Group Financing (Syndicates)

A group of investors is called a *syndicate,* and the person who organizes the project and recruits the investors—usually a real estate broker, accountant, or lawyer who specializes in real estate—is called the *syndicator.* Syndication can take many different legal forms, from tenancy in common and joint tenancy to various kinds of partnerships, corporations, and trusts. Private syndication, which involves a small group of closely associated and widely experienced investors, is distinguished from public syndication, which involves a much larger group of investors who may or may not be knowledgeable about real estate as an investment. The distinction between the two, however, is based on the nature of the arrangement between the syndicator and the investors and not on the type of syndicate. For this reason, any pooling of individuals' funds raises questions of definition and registration of securities under state security laws, commonly referred to as *blue sky laws.* In addition, securities must be registered with the federal *Securities and Exchange Commission (SEC)* prior to public offering.

The concept of group financing offers advantages for the entire real estate business. Since investors can pool capital to finance real estate investments they could not otherwise afford, this arrangement stimulates the industry by providing a source of capital for all kinds of real estate projects. Syndicates purchase buildings and finance construction projects that might be considerably delayed if they were forced to wait for a single investor. As discussed in Chapter 4, among the most popular kinds of syndicates are limited partnerships and real estate investment trusts.

Limited partnerships.   *Limited partnerships* are composed of general partners and limited partners. The general partners have complete charge of the operation and management of the partnership business, and they can have extensive liability for the obligations of the partnership. The limited partners agree to contribute a definite amount of capital for which they can be held liable, but they have no voice in the actual operation of the business. They can share in the profits of the venture, if any, but their liabilities or potential losses are limited to the amount of their original subscription. The general partners assume all liability beyond the capital contributions of the limited partners. Typically, when the profits are distributed, the general partners are paid after the limited partners receive their share.

Real Estate Investment Trusts.   Sometimes called a common law trust, a **real estate investment trust (REIT)** is unincorporated and involves 100 or more persons who make investments by purchasing shares. The capital is used to purchase, develop, and/or sell real estate. The trustees are the managers who conduct the business of the venture. Title to the real estate is taken in the name of the trustees. REITs have grown in popularity, partly because they do not have to pay corporate income tax if they distribute 95 percent of their income to the shareholders. After the property is developed and sold, the trustees distribute the profits, if any, to the shareholders as return of capital or capital gains.

FINANCING LEGISLATION

The federal government regulates the lending practices of mortgage lenders through the Truth-in-Lending Act, Equal Credit Opportunity Act, and the Real Estate Settlement Procedures Act.

Truth-in-Lending Act and Regulation Z

The National Consumer Credit Protection Act, referred to as the *Truth-in-Lending Act,* went into effect on July 1, 1969, under **Regulation Z** of the Federal Reserve Board. Regulation Z requires credit institutions to disclose to borrowers the true cost of obtaining credit so that the borrower can compare the costs of various lenders and avoid the uninformed use of credit. Regulation Z applies when credit is extended to individuals for personal, family, or household uses and the amount of credit is $25,000 or less. Regardless of the amount, Regulation Z always applies when a credit transaction is secured by a residence. The regulation does not apply to business or commercial loans or to agricultural loans over $25,000.

The regulation requires that the consumer be fully informed of all finance charges, as well as the true annual interest rate, before a transaction is consummated. The finance charges must include any loan fees, finders' fees, service charges, and points, as well as interest. In the case of a mortgage loan made to finance the purchase of a dwelling the lender must compute and disclose the *annual percentage rate (APR)* but does not have to indicate the total interest payable during the term of the loan. Also, the lender does not have to include as part of the finance charge such actual costs as title fees, legal fees, appraisal fees, credit reports, survey fees, and closing expenses.

Creditor. A *creditor,* for purposes of Regulation Z, is a person who extends consumer credit more than 25 times a year or more than five times a year if the transaction involves a dwelling as security. The credit must be subject to a finance charge or payable in more than four installments by written agreement.

Three-day right of rescission. In the case of most consumer credit transactions covered by Regulation Z the borrower has three days in which to rescind the transaction by merely notifying the lender. This right of rescission does not apply to residential purchase-money or first mortgage or deed of trust loans. In an emergency the right to rescind may be waived in writing to prevent a delay in funding.

Advertising. Regulation Z provides strict regulation of real estate advertisements that include mortgage financing terms. General phrases like "liberal terms available" may be used, but if specifics are given they must comply with this act. By the provisions of the act the APR—which includes all charges—rather than the interest rate alone *must be stated.* The total finance charge must be specified as well.

Specific credit terms, such as down payment, monthly payment, dollar amount of the finance charge, or term of the loan, may not be advertised unless the following information is set forth as well: cash price; required down payment; number, amounts and due dates of all payments; and annual percentage rate. The total of all payments to be made over the term of the mortgage must also be specified unless the advertised credit refers to a first mortgage or deed of trust to finance acquisition of a dwelling.

Penalties. Regulation Z provides penalties for noncompliance. The penalty for violation of an administrative order enforcing Regulation Z is $10,000 for each day the violation continues. A fine of up to $10,000 may be imposed for engaging in an unfair or deceptive practice. In addition, a creditor may be liable to a consumer for twice the amount of the finance charge, for a minimum of $100 and a maximum of $1,000, plus court costs, attorney's fees and any actual damages. Willful violation is a misdemeanor punishable by a fine of up to $5,000 or one year's imprisonment or both.

Federal Equal Credit Opportunity Act

Since 1975, legislation has been enacted in an attempt to ensure fair and equal treatment of credit applications by lenders. The **Federal Equal Credit Opportunity Act (ECOA)** prohibits lenders and others who grant credit to consumers from discriminating against credit applicants on the basis of race, color, religion, national origin, sex, marital status, age (provided the applicant is of legal age), or dependence upon public assistance. In addition, lenders and other creditors must now inform all rejected credit applicants in writing within 30 days of the principal reasons why credit was denied or, in some cases, terminated.

Real Estate Settlement Procedures Act Requirements

The Real Estate Settlement Procedures Act (RESPA) was created to ensure that the buyer and seller in a residential real estate transaction have knowledge of all settlement costs. RESPA requirements apply when the purchase is *financed by a federally related mortgage loan.* Federally related loans include those: (1) made by banks, savings and loan associations, or other lenders whose deposits are insured by federal agencies; (2) insured by the FHA or guaranteed by the VA; (3) administered by HUD; or (4) intended to be sold by the lender to Fannie Mae, Ginnie Mae, or Freddie Mac.

RESPA regulations apply only to *transactions involving new first mortgage loans.* A transaction financed solely by a purchase-money mortgage taken back by the seller, by an installment contract (land contract of sale, contract for deed), or by the buyer's assumption of the seller's existing loan would not be covered by RESPA. RESPA requires that when a transaction is covered by the act, the following regulations must be met for compliance.

Special information booklet.   Lenders must give a copy of the HUD booklet *Settlement Costs and You* to every person from whom they receive or for whom they prepare a loan application, within three days after making a loan application. This booklet provides the borrower with general information about settlement (closing) costs and explains the various RESPA provisions, including a line-by-line discussion of the Uniform Settlement Statement.

Good-faith estimate of settlement costs.   At the time the loan application is made, the lender must provide the borrower with a good-faith estimate of the settlement costs the borrower is likely to incur. This estimate may be a specific figure or a range of costs based upon comparable past transactions in the area. In addition, if the lender requires use of a particular attorney or title company to conduct the closing, the lender must state whether it has any business relationship with that firm and must estimate the charges for this service.

Uniform Settlement Statement (HUD Form 1).   RESPA provides that loan closing information must be prepared on a special HUD form designed to detail all financial particulars of a transaction. Chapter 15 contains a copy of HUD's Uniform Settlement Statement. The completed statement must itemize all charges imposed by the lender. Charges incurred by the buyer and seller that are contracted for separately and outside the closing do not have to be disclosed. Items paid for prior to the closing must be clearly marked as such on the statement and are omitted from the totals. Upon the borrower's request, *the closing agent must permit the borrower to inspect the settlement statement, to the extent that the figures are available, one business day before the closing.*

Prohibition against kickbacks.   RESPA explicitly prohibits the paying of kickbacks (unearned fees), for example, when an insurance agency pays a lender for referring one of its recent customers to the agency. This prohibition does not, however, cover fee splitting between cooperating brokers, brokerage referral arrangements, or a broker's dividing commissions with his or her salespeople.

SUMMARY

The major sources of real estate financing are savings and loan associations, mutual savings banks, commercial banks, insurance companies, mortgage banking companies, credit unions, mortgage brokers, pension funds, and investment groups.

The federal government exercises its influence over the real estate finance market through the *Federal Reserve Board* as well as through various agencies, such as the Farmer's Home Administration. The Federal Reserve regulates the *reserve requirements* and *discount rates* of federally chartered banks and its member banks.

Mortgage loan operations are generally referred to as being in either the primary or secondary market. *Primary market* operations involve the origination of investment papers. This field includes such companies as mortgage houses, banks, and savings and loan associations. The *secondary market* is generally composed of the investors who ultimately purchase and hold the loans as investments. These include insurance companies, investment funds, and pension plans. *Fannie Mae* (Federal

National Mortgage Association), *Ginnie Mae* (Government National Mortgage Association, and *Freddie Mac* (Federal Home Loan Mortgage Corporation) take an active role in creating a secondary market by regularly purchasing mortgage and trust deed loans from originators and retaining, or warehousing, them until investment purchasers are available.

Specialized financing instruments include purchase-money, blanket, package, open-end, wraparound, shared-appreciation, and reverse-annuity mortgages/deeds of trust, as well as construction, sale-and-leaseback, graduated-payment, balloon-payment, growing-equity, and home equity loans.

Other real estate financing is arranged through *installment contracts* (contracts for deed, land contracts), under which the seller retains title to the property until he or she receives the full purchase price, which is generally paid in installments. Firms that own and operate large plants are able to release funds invested in such real estate for use in their businesses through *sale-and-leaseback* transactions.

Syndication is the financing of real estate transactions and investments by groups of investors. There are many forms of syndication, including *limited partnerships* and *real estate investment trusts* (REITs). Laws regulating the sale of securities are known as *blue sky laws,* and their provisions may require that real estate interests be registered as securities or that salespeople who offer such interests be licensed.

Regulation Z, the federal Truth-in-Lending Act, requires lenders to inform prospective borrowers who use their homes as security for credit of *all finance charges* involved in such a loan. Severe penalties are provided for noncompliance. The *Federal Equal Credit Opportunity Act* prohibits creditors from discriminating against credit applicants on the basis of race, color, religion, national origin, sex, marital status, age or dependency upon public assistance. In addition, the *Real Estate Settlement Procedures Act* requires lenders to inform both buyers and sellers in advance of all fees and charges required for the settlement or closing of a residential real estate transaction that is financed by a federally related mortgage or trust deed loan.

QUESTIONS

Please complete all of the questions before turning to the Answer Key.

1. A buyer who wanted to purchase one lot for the construction of a house and the adjacent lot for the construction of a swimming pool would probably use what type of loan?

    a. Package loan
    b. Wraparound loan
    c. Blanket loan
    d. Purchase-money loan

2. The primary purpose of the Truth-in-Lending Act (Regulation Z) is to

    a. set maximum mortgage interest rates.
    b. disclose the costs of borrowing funds.
    c. protect lenders.
    d. allow fair credit reporting.

3. Which of the following agencies is involved in the primary mortgage market?

    a. FmHA
    b. FNMA
    c. GNMA
    d. FHLMC

4. Under RESPA, the lender must perform all of the following acts EXCEPT

    a. give the borrower a copy of *Settlement Costs and You.*
    b. give the borrower a copy of the appraisal.
    c. give the borrower a good-faith estimate of settlement costs.
    d. use the Uniform Settlement Statement.

5. All of the following statements regarding an installment contract are true EXCEPT

    a. it is a method of financing.
    b. it is completed when it is signed by the vendee.
    c. the vendee has an equitable interest in the property.
    d. the vendee pays for the property in regular installments.

6. All of the following statements regarding purchase-money mortgages are true EXCEPT

   a. such mortgages are extensions of credit from individuals.
   b. the seller carries back some or all of the purchase price of the property.
   c. such mortgages are generally junior mortgages.
   d. the seller is entitled to a deficiency judgment in the event of a foreclosure.

7. In which of the following types of loans would an economic indicator be used to determine the upward and downward changes in mortgage interest?

   a. Adjustable-rate loan
   b. Graduated payment loan
   c. Reverse-annuity mortgage
   d. Shared-appreciation mortgage

8. In a sale-and-leaseback arrangement, the

   a. lessee is the investor.
   b. lessor can deduct rental payments from his or her taxes as expense items.
   c. lessee can depreciate the building.
   d. lessor can negotiate a long-term lease.

9. Securities regulations are least likely to apply to a

   a. joint tenancy.
   b. joint venture.
   c. limited partnership.
   d. general partnership.

10. All of the following entities are owned by the government EXCEPT

   a. FHA.
   b. Fannie Mae.
   c. Ginnie Mae.
   d. Freddie Mac.

11. In a loan that requires periodic payments that do not fully amortize the loan, the final payment would best be described as a(n)

   a. balloon payment.
   b. acceleration payment.
   c. variable payment.
   d. adjustment payment.

12. A loan that encompasses an existing loan from one lender plus an additional loan from a second lender would be called a

   a. blanket loan.
   b. package loan.
   c. wraparound loan.
   d. shared-appreciation loan.

13. All of the following functions are inherent in Fannie Mae EXCEPT that it

   a. lends money to residential purchasers.
   b. buys FHA, VA, and conventional loans.
   c. warehouses seasoned loans.
   d. sells mortgage-backed securities to investors.

14. The Equal Credit Opportunity Act prohibits lenders from discriminating against potential borrowers on the basis of all of the following criteria EXCEPT

   a. race.
   b. sex.
   c. source of income.
   d. amount of income.

15. Which of the following characteristics is true about a fixed-rate loan?

   a. The amount of interest to be paid is predetermined.
   b. The loan cannot be sold in the secondary market.
   c. The monthly payment amount will change each month.
   d. The interest rate change will be based on an index.

16. All of the following loan situations are regulated by the Truth-in-Lending Act (Regulation Z) EXCEPT

   a. personal loans for $25,000 or less.
   b. home improvement loans.
   c. business and commercial loans.
   d. loans secured by residential real estate.

17. Which of the following statements describes the secondary mortgage market?

   a. Lenders who deal exclusively in second mortgages
   b. Where loans are bought and sold after they have been originated
   c. The major lender for residential mortgages and deeds of trust
   d. The major lender for FHA-insured and VA-guaranteed loans

18.   The inclusion of any of the following phrases in a print advertisement would require full disclosure under the Truth-in-Lending Act (Regulation Z) EXCEPT

   a.   "Low monthly payments."
   b.   "No down payment."
   c.   "Easy financing available."
   d.   "Own in less than 15 years."

19.   The term *interim financing* is usually associated with

   a.   sales and leasebacks.
   b.   shopping center financing.
   c.   take-out lending.
   d.   construction financing.

20.   For an individual to sell interests in a limited partnership, that person would need a

   a.   real estate license.
   b.   securities license.
   c.   development license.
   d.   limited partnership license.

21.   Under the provisions of the Truth-in-Lending Act (Regulation Z), the annual percentage rate (APR) of a finance charge includes all of the following components EXCEPT the

   a.   discount points.   c.   loan origination fee.
   b.   broker's commission.   d.   loan interest rate.

22.   All of the following entities are included as part of the primary mortgage market EXCEPT

   a.   savings and loan associations.
   b.   commercial banks.
   c.   credit unions.
   d.   government agencies.

23. A borrower obtains a loan to make repairs to her property. The loan documents secure the loan, as well as any future funds advanced to the borrower by the lender. This is called a(n)

    a. wraparound loan.
    b. conventional loan.
    c. open-end loan.
    d. growing-equity loan.

24. The most common type of loan when purchasing a new home is the

    a. wraparound loan.
    b. open-end loan.
    c. blanket loan.
    d. package loan.

25. With a fully amortized mortgage or deed of trust loan,

    a. interest is usually charged in arrears.
    b. the interest portion of each payment remains the same throughout the loan term.
    c. interest only is paid each period.
    d. the balloon payment will be the last payment made.

26. When a lender offers a below-market interest rate in exchange for an equity position in the property, this is known as a(n)

    a. shared appreciation loan.
    b. growing-equity loan.
    c. open-end loan.
    d. installment loan.

27. A graduated-payment mortgage

    a. allows for smaller payments to be made in the early years of the loan.
    b. allows for the interest rate to periodically increase or decrease.
    c. is also known as a growing-equity mortgage.
    d. must be administered by the Federal Housing Administration.

28. Which of the following events is specifically prohibited by RESPA?

    a. Brokerage referral arrangements
    b. A broker's dividing commission with his or her salespeople
    c. Fee splitting between cooperating brokers
    d. Non-real estate referral fees

29. When a homeowner receives a monthly check from a lender under the terms of a loan, this type of loan is called a(n)

    a. buydown.
    b. shared-appreciation mortgage.
    c. reverse-annuity mortgage.
    d. adjustable-rate mortgage.

30. When a buyer agrees to pay not only the seller's original loan but also an additional loan to the seller, this second loan is called a

    a. purchase-money loan.   c. package loan.
    b. wraparound loan.   d. blanket loan.

13: Control and Development of Land

KEY TERMS

conditional-use permit   nonconforming use
developer   property report
enabling acts   subdivider
Interstate Land Sales   subdivision
     Full Disclosure Act   variance
master plan   zoning ordinances

The control and development of land is accomplished through: (1) public land-use controls, (2) private ownership, and (3) public ownership of land—including parks, schools, and expressways—by government.

PUBLIC LAND-USE CONTROLS

Under *police power,* each state and its municipalities have the inherent authority to adopt regulations necessary to protect the public health, safety, and general welfare. This includes limitations on the use of privately owned real estate. Although the courts have traditionally been conservative in extending the scope of police power, changing social and economic conditions have influenced the courts toward making broader interpretations of this power in recent years—and the trend is likely to continue.

Growing urban populations, new types of industry, and the increasing complexity of civilization make it necessary for cities and towns to increase their controls over the private use of real estate. Currently, police power in many areas is being increased to include controls over noise, air, water, and environmental pollution.

The governmental authority that regulates privately owned real estate includes

1. city plan specifications;

2. subdivision regulations;

3. zoning;

4. building codes; and

5. environmental protection legislation.

City Plan Specifications

City planning includes the drafting of a **master plan.** Such a plan gives advice on planning and scheduling public works programs (especially those concerning traffic facilities and public buildings), controlling subdivision development, and preparing, modifying, and administering zoning ordinances and regulations. In most cases a city, county, or regional planning commission is created for these purposes. A combination of residential, commercial, and industrial property is usually included in master plans to spread the tax base and provide employment for local residents.

City planning helps to meet the social and economic needs of ever-changing communities. Both economic and physical surveys are essential in preparing a master plan. Also, plans must include the coordination of numerous civic plans so that orderly city growth and stabilized property values can be assured.

Subdivision Regulations

Subdivision regulations have been adopted by most communities, often as part of a master plan. Subdivision regulations usually provide for the following:

1. location, grading, alignment, surfacing, and widths of streets, highways, and other rights of way;

2. installation of sewers and water mains;

3. building and setback lines;

4. areas to be reserved or dedicated for public use, such as parks or schools; and

5. easements for public utilities.

Subdivision regulations, like all other forms of land-use regulation, cannot be static. These regulations must remain flexible to meet the changing needs of society.

Zoning

Zoning ordinances are laws of local governmental authorities that regulate the use of land. Zoning powers are conferred on municipal governments by state **enabling acts;** there are no state or national zoning ordinances. The ordinances usually regulate the height, bulk, and use of buildings; the use of land; and the density of population.

Zoning ordinances generally divide land use into three broad classifications: (1) residential; (2) commercial; and (3) industrial. A fourth use now included by many communities is called *cluster zoning,* or *multiple-use zoning,* which permits construction of *planned unit developments (PUDs).*

To ensure adequate control, land-use areas are further divided into subclasses. For example, residential areas may be divided to provide for detached single-family dwellings, structures containing not more than four dwelling units, high-rise apartments, and so forth. Some special types of zoning are listed in Table 13.1.

Adoption of zoning ordinances. Today, almost all cities with populations in excess of 10,000 have comprehensive zoning ordinances governing the utilization of land located within corporate limits. Many states have enacted legislation that provides that the use of land located within one to five miles of an incorporated area must receive the approval and consent of the incorporated area, even if the property is not contiguous to that area.

Zoning ordinances must not violate the rights of individuals as property holders, as provided under the due process provisions of the Fourteenth Amendment of the U.S. Constitution or provisions of the constitution of the state in which the real estate is located. If the legislation used to regulate the use of property is destructive, unreasonable, arbitrary, or confiscatory, such legislation is usually considered void. Tests applied in determining the validity of ordinances require that:

1. the power must be exercised in a reasonable manner;

2. the provisions must be clear and specific;

3. the ordinance must be free from discrimination;

Table 13.1   Special Types of Zoning

Type of Zoning	Primary Purpose
Bulk Zoning	To control density and avoid overcrowding through restrictions on setback, building height, and percentage of open areas
Aesthetic Zoning	To require that new buildings conform to specific types of architecture
Incentive Zoning	To require that street floors of office buildings be used for retail establishments

   4. the ordinance must promote public health, safety, and general welfare under the police power concept; and

   5. the ordinance must apply to all property in a similar manner.

Planned Unit Development (PUD).   Zoning for a PUD permits a higher density of dwellings, mixed uses, and greater utilization of open space. Because residential, shopping, office, and other uses are planned simultaneously, the result can be a harmonious combination that provides residents and workers with greater convenience. Occasionally, research facilities or light industrial uses are included, all with ready access to major highways and rail lines. A PUD can be possible in a resort area as well.

There may be one or more community organizations, e.g., one for homeowners and one for retailers. When the developer records the plat of subdivision with its restrictions, provision for such associations is usually included.

The PUD concept is useful whenever variations on the setback or density regulations are desired, such as a development with zero lot lines (no setback from the lot line necessary for structures). Like condominium property, PUDs generally have common areas and more structures per acre than codes would otherwise permit. Condo owners generally own a block of air, whether the condo concept is for residential, office, or commercial purposes. However, the PUD owner owns the land underlying the structure plus a surrounding lot. The PUD common-area association is structured as a nonprofit corporation, and individual owners have no interest in the common areas.

Nonconforming use. In the enforcement of zoning, a frequent problem is a building that does not conform to the zoning because it was erected prior to the enactment of the zoning law. Such a building is not a violation because when it was built, there was no prohibitive zoning ordinance. It is referred to as a **nonconforming use,** and the use is allowed to continue. If the building is destroyed or torn down, any new structure must comply with the current zoning ordinance.

Zoning exceptions. Each time a plan is created or a zoning ordinance enacted, some owners are inconvenienced and want to change the allowed uses of their properties. Generally, such owners may appeal for either a conditional-use permit or a variance to allow a use that does not meet zoning requirements.

A **conditional-use permit** is generally granted a property owner to allow a special use of property that is in the public interest. Schools, hospitals, teen centers and country clubs are some examples of permitted special uses.

A **variance,** a permanent exception to zoning, may be sought by a property owner who has suffered undue hardship as a result of a zoning ordinance. For example, if an owner's lot drops off to 30 feet below street level at the midway depth of the lot, the zoning board may be willing to allow a variance so the owner can build closer to the road than would normally be allowed. However, the board could refuse to allow a change if there was another use available for the same parcel and the only hardship that would result from using the alternate site was a longer driveway that would cost more money.

Zoning boards of appeal. Zoning appeal boards have been established in most communities to hear complaints about the effect of zoning ordinances on specific parcels of property. Petitions may be presented to the appeal board for changes or exceptions in the zoning law.

Building Codes

Most cities have enacted ordinances known as *building codes,* which specify construction standards that must be met when repairing or erecting buildings. Building codes set the requirements for kinds of materials, sanitary equipment, electrical wiring, and fire prevention standards, for example.

Most communities require a building permit to be issued by the city clerk (or other official) before a person can build, alter, or repair a structure on property within the corporate limits of the municipality. Through the permit requirement, city officials are made aware of construction or alterations and can verify compliance with both building codes and zoning ordinances by examination of the plans and inspection of the work. Once the structure has been inspected and found to be satisfactory, the city inspector issues a certificate of occupancy.

If the construction of a building or an alteration violates a deed restriction, the issuance of a building permit will not cure this violation. A building permit is merely evidence of the applicant's compliance with municipal regulations. When a conflict arises, rights of adjoining owners in a subdivision to enforce *deed restrictions* usually prevail over the police power legislation of the community if the restrictions are more limiting.

Environmental Protection Legislation

Federal and state legislators have passed a number of *environmental protection laws* in an attempt to respond to the growing public concern over the improvement and preservation of America's natural resources. Table 13.2 contains a brief summary of significant federal environmental legislation.

States have also responded to these issues by passing a variety of localized environmental protection laws regarding various types of pollution—air, water, noise, and solid-waste. For example, many states have enacted laws that prevent builders or private individuals from constructing septic tanks or other effluence disposal systems in certain areas, particularly near public bodies of water. In addition, cities and counties also pass environmental legislation of their own.

PRIVATE OWNERSHIP AND DEVELOPMENT

Land use may be controlled by private parties as well as by governmental authorities. Land developers and subdividers, as well as individual owners, can dictate land use for future generations.

Subdividers and Developers

Land in large tracts must receive special attention before it can be converted into sites for homes, stores, or other uses. As cities and towns grow, additional land is required for their expansion. For new areas to develop soundly, the services of competent subdividers and developers working closely with city planners are required. A **subdivider** is someone who buys undeveloped acreage, divides it into smaller usable lots, and sells the lots. A **developer** is someone who builds homes or other buildings on the lots and sells them. A developer may use his or her own sales organization or may act through local real estate brokerage firms. City planners, working with land developers, plan whole communities, which later are incorporated into cities or towns.

Regulation of Land Development

No uniform city-planning or land-development legislation affects the entire country. Laws governing subdividing and land planning are controlled by state and local governmental bodies where the land is located. However, through the regulations that have been developed by various governmental agencies such as the FHA, *minimum standards* exist as usable guides. These are minimum standards only and not mandatory, except for those developers who are seeking FHA approval of their subdivision in anticipation of making FHA financing available to purchasers. These regulations are not uniform throughout the entire country. They are flexible and subject to review by regional officers, who have the authority to modify the regulations to meet customs and local climate, health, and hazard conditions.

Land Planning

Although a plat map usually must be recorded prior to public sale for residential or commercial use, land planning precedes the actual subdividing process. The land-development plan must comply with the overall local plan if a *master plan* has been adopted by the county, city, or town. In complying with this local plan, the developer must take into consideration the zoning laws and land-use restrictions that have been adopted for health and safety purposes. Although the basic city plan and zoning requirements are not inflexible, long, expensive, and frequently complicated hearings are usually required before alterations can be authorized.

Most incorporated areas have planning committees or commissioners. Depending upon how the particular group was organized, such a committee or commission may have only an advisory status. In other instances, it can have authority to approve or disapprove plans. Communities establish strict criteria before approving new subdivisions, frequently including: (1) *dedication* of land for streets, schools, parks, and easements for drainage, utilities, and so forth; (2) assurance by *bonding* that sewer and street costs will be paid; and (3) *compliance with zoning ordinances* governing use and lot size, along with fire and safety ordinances.

Table 13.2   Recent Federal Environmental Legislation

Legislation	Major Purpose
National Environmental Policy Act—1970	To establish a Council for Environmental Quality for land-use planning; in addition, created the Environmental Protection Agency (EPA) to enforce federal environmental legislation
Clean Air Amendment—1970	To create more stringent standards for automotive, aircraft, and factory emission
Water Quality Improvement Act—1970	To strengthen water pollution standards
Resource Recovery Act—1970	Expanded the solid waste disposal program
Water Pollution Control Act Amendment—1972	To create standards for cleaning navigable streams and lakes by the mid-1980s
Clean Water Act—1974	To establish standards for water suppliers
Resource Conservation & Recovery Act—1976	To regulate potentially dangerous solid waste disposal
Clean Water Act Amendment—1977	To update the list of potentially dangerous water pollutants under the 1974 act
Comprehensive Environmental Response, Compensation and Liability Act (Superfund)—1980	To provide gigantic sums of money for hazardous waste disposal and charge cleanup costs to the parties responsible for the waste
Superfund Amendment and Reauthorization Act—1986	To clarify regulations regarding hazardous waste and to limit liability for some parties, including real estate brokers

Because of the fear they may pollute water sources, septic systems are no longer authorized in some areas, and an approved sewerage-disposal arrangement must be included in the land-development plan. The shortage of water has caused great concern, and local authorities usually require land planners to submit information on how they intend to satisfy sewerage-disposal and water-supply requirements. Frequently, a planner also has to submit an environmental impact statement.

When property to be subdivided is located outside the limits of incorporated areas, most state laws require that the proposed land plan be submitted to county authorities (borough or parish) for approval, and also to all incorporated communities located within a radius of one to five miles. If there is more than one such incorporated area, each must review and approve the plan. Local officials are not quick to approve such plans unless they comply with the community's ordinances and requirements. This is the main reason that developers now have less freedom in planning an outlying suburban development than one located in a city or town.

Subdividing

The process of subdivision generally involves three distinct stages of development: (1) initial planning; (2) final planning; and (3) disposition, or start-up.

During the *initial planning stage,* the subdivider seeks out raw land in a suitable area that can be profitably subdivided. Once the land is located, the property is analyzed for its highest and best use, and preliminary subdivision plans are drawn up. Close contact is initiated between the subdivider and local planning and zoning officials; if the project requires zoning variances, negotiations begin along these lines. The subdivider also locates financial backers and initiates marketing strategies at this point.

The *final planning stage* is basically a follow-up of the initial stage—final plans are prepared, approval is sought from local officials, permanent financing is obtained, land is purchased, final budgets are prepared, and marketing programs are designed.

The *disposition,* or *start-up,* carries the subdividing process to a conclusion. Subdivision plans are recorded with local officials, and streets, sewers, and utilities are installed. Buildings, open parks, and recreational areas are constructed and landscaped if they are part of the subdivision plan. The marketing programs are then initiated, and title to the individual parcels of subdivided land is transferred as the lots are sold.

Subdivision plans.   In plotting out a subdivision according to local planning and zoning controls a subdivider usually determines the size as well as the location of the individual lots. The size of the lots, both in front footage and in depth, together with the total amount of square footage, is generally regulated by local ordinances and must be considered carefully. Frequently, ordinances regulate both the minimum and the maximum sizes of a lot.

The land itself must be studied, usually in cooperation with a surveyor, so that the subdivision can be laid out with consideration of natural drainage and land contours. A subdivider should provide *utility easements* as well as easements for water and sewer mains.

Most subdivisions are laid out by use of *lots and blocks*. An area of land is designated as a block, and the area making up this block is divided into lots.

Although subdividers customarily designate areas reserved for schools, parks, and future church sites, this is usually not considered good practice. Once a subdivision has been recorded, the purchasers of the lots have a vested interest in those areas reserved for schools, parks, and churches. If for any reason in the future any such purpose is not appropriate, it will become difficult for the developer to abandon the original plan and use that property for residential purposes. To get around this situation many developers designate such areas as *out-lot A, out-lot B,* and so forth. Such a designation does not vest any rights in these out-lots in the purchasers of the homesites. If one of these areas is to be used for church purposes, it can be so conveyed and so used. If, on the other hand, the out-lot is not to be used for such a purpose, it can be resubdivided into residential properties without the burden of securing the consent of the lot owners in the area.

Plat of subdivision.   The subdivider's completed plat of subdivision must contain all necessary approvals of public officials and must be recorded in the county where the land is located.

Because the plat will be the basis for future conveyances, the subdivided land should be measured carefully, with all lot sizes and streets noted by the surveyor and entered accurately on the document. Survey monuments should be established, and measurements should be made from these monuments, with the location of all lots carefully marked.

Covenants and restrictions.   Deed restrictions are originated and recorded by a subdivider as a means of *controlling and maintaining the desirable quality and character of the subdivision.* These restrictions can be included in the subdivision plat, or they may be set forth in a separate recorded instrument, commonly referred to as a *declaration of restrictions.*

Development costs.   Most homeowners are not aware of the costs of developing land. The subdivider, developer, and builder frequently invest many hundreds of thousands of dollars (and in larger developments, several millions of dollars) before the subdivision is even announced to the public. The difference between the raw land cost on a per-acre basis and the asking price per front foot of subdivided lot surprises the average homeowner. An analysis of development costs substantiates the sale price of a building lot in an average subdivision that is four to six times the cost of the raw land. These costs, of course, vary from area to area and according to the nature of the development.

A finished lot's sale price generally reflects such expenses as cost of land; installation of sewers, water mains, storm drains, landscaping, and street lights; earthworks (mass dirt removal, site grading, and similar operations); paving; engineering and surveying fees; brokers' commissions; inspections; bonding costs; filing and legal fees; sales costs; and overhead. In certain areas, a subdivider may also be required to give financial assistance to school districts, park districts, and the like, in the form of either donated school or park sites or a fixed subsidy per subdivision lot. Should such further costs be incurred, they must be added proportionately to the sale price of each building site.

Subdivided land sales.   To protect consumers from "overenthusiastic sales promotions" in interstate land sales Congress passed the **Interstate Land Sales Full Disclosure Act.** The law requires those engaged in the interstate sale or leasing of 25 or more lots to file a statement of record and *register* the details of the land with HUD.

The seller is also required to furnish prospective buyers a **property report** containing all essential information about the property, such as distance over paved roads to nearby communities, number of homes currently occupied, soil conditions affecting foundations and septic systems, type of title a buyer will receive, and existence of liens. The property report must be given to a prospective purchaser at least three business days before any sales contract is signed.

Any contract to purchase a lot covered by this act may be revoked at the purchaser's option until midnight of the seventh day following the signing of the contract. If a contract is signed for the purchase of a lot covered by the act and a property report is not given to the purchaser, an action to revoke the contract may be brought by the purchaser within two years.

If the seller misrepresents the property in any sales promotion, a buyer induced by such a promotion is entitled to sue the seller for civil damages. Failure to comply with the law may also subject a seller to criminal penalties of fines and imprisonment.

Many state legislatures have enacted their own subdivided-land sales laws. Some affect only the sale of land located outside the state to state residents, while others affect sales of land located both inside and outside the state. Generally these state land sales laws tend to be stricter and more detailed than the federal law.

Private Deed Restrictions

A real estate owner can control future use of his or her property by using deed restrictions. A deed restriction is created by including a provision for it in the deed when the property is conveyed. Deed restrictions are discussed in Chapter 2.

DIRECT PUBLIC OWNERSHIP

Over the years, the government's general policy has been to encourage private ownership of land. But the government must own a certain amount of land for such uses as municipal buildings, state legislative houses, schools, and military stations. Public ownership is also a means of land control.

There are other examples of necessary public ownership. Urban renewal efforts, especially government-owned housing, are one way that public ownership serves the public interest. Publicly owned streets and highways perform a necessary function for the entire population. In addition, public land is often used for recreational purposes. National and state parks and forests create areas for public use and recreation, and at the same time help to conserve natural resources. Through direct public ownership, the government can put land to use in ways that will benefit all the people.

SUMMARY

Any effective control of land requires an overall *master plan* to be developed based upon a local economic survey of the community.

Subdivision regulations are necessary to maintain control of the development of expanding community areas so that growth will be harmonious with community standards. *Zoning ordinances* segregate residential areas from business and industrial zones, and control not only land use but also height and bulk of buildings and density of population. Zoning enforcement problems involve boards of appeal, *variances,* and exceptions, as well as nonconforming uses.

Building codes are different from zoning ordinances. While zoning ordinances control use, building codes control construction of buildings by specifying standards for construction, plumbing, sewers, electrical wiring, and equipment.

In addition to land-use control on a local level, the state and federal governments have occasionally intervened when necessary to preserve natural resources through *environmental legislation.*

Land development must generally comply with master land plans adopted by counties, cities, villages, or towns. This may entail approval of land-use plans by local planning committees or commissions.

The process of subdivision includes dividing the tract of land and providing for utility easements, as well as laying out street patterns and widths. A subdivider must generally record a completed *plat of subdivision* with all necessary approvals of public officials in the county where the land is located. Subdividers usually place *restrictions* upon the use of all lots in a subdivision as a general plan for the benefit of all lot owners.

Subdivisions that are to be submitted for approval for FHA loan insurance must meet certain FHA *minimum standards.* Subdivided land sales are regulated on the federal level by the *Interstate Land Sales Full Disclosure Act.*

QUESTIONS

Please complete all of the questions before turning to the Answer Key.

1. A property owner who wants to use his or her real estate in a manner other than that allowed by local ordinance may appeal for a

    a.   variance.   c.   building permit.
    b.   nonconforming use.   d.   certificate of occupancy.

2. Someone who buys undeveloped acreage, splits it into smaller usable parcels, and then sells those parcels to a potential user is called a

    a.   developer.   c.   builder.
    b.   subdivider.   d.   syndicator.

3. Police power is the government's right to enact regulations to protect the public health, safety, and welfare. This power includes the right to institute all of the following items EXCEPT

    a.   master plan specifications.
    b.   subdivision regulations.
    c.   environmental protection laws.
    d.   deed restrictions.

4. In which of the following situations would building codes be taken into account?

    a.   The development of the area master plan
    b.   The construction of a new structure
    c.   The subdivision of a large tract of land
    d.   The demolition of a partially destroyed building

5. Municipal governments receive the power to enact zoning ordinances through

    a.   federal statutes.   c.   court precedent.
    b.   common law.   d.   enabling acts.

6. The Interstate Land Sales Full Disclosure Act was enacted to

   a. protect the public from unscrupulous subdividers.
   b. encourage the interstate sales of land parcels.
   c. help the public purchase government-owned property.
   d. develop land for retirement and recreation purposes.

7. Deed restrictions are enforceable by affected property owners through

   a. zoning ordinances.
   b. building codes.
   c. boards of appeal.
   d. court injunctions.

8. Police power permits the regulation of all of the following items EXCEPT

   a. the number of buildings.
   b. the size of buildings.
   c. building ownership.
   d. building occupancy.

9. The goals of a planning commission include all of the following activities EXCEPT

   a. formulation of policy.
   b. determination of land uses.
   c. conservation of natural resources.
   d. education of the public.

10. To protect the public, the Interstate Land Sales Full Disclosure Act requires that a developer involved in the interstate land sales of 25 or more lots must

    a. provide each prospective buyer with a copy of the property report.
    b. pay the prospective buyer's expenses to see the property involved.
    c. provide preferential financing to such buyers.
    d. include the deed restrictions for such buyers.

11. Boards of appeal are established to hear complaints about

    a. deed restrictions.
    b. building codes.
    c. the effects of a zoning ordinance.
    d. the effects of public ownership.

12. A new zoning ordinance is enacted. A structure is permitted to continue in its former use, even though that use conflicts with the new zoning. This is an example of

    a. inverse condemnation.
    b. eminent domain.
    c. a nonconforming use.
    d. a variance.

13. Which of the following situations may be properly regulated through deed restriction?

    a. The right to convey the property
    b. The use of the property
    c. Who the next purchaser can be
    d. Who may occupy the property

14. To determine whether a certain location can be put to future use as a retail store, one would examine the

    a. building codes for that location.
    b. zoning ordinances for that location.
    c. lists of permitted nonconforming uses.
    d. list of obtainable variances.

15. All of the following items would be properly addressed by deed restriction EXCEPT the

    a. types of buildings that may be constructed.
    b. minimum sizes of buildings to be constructed.
    c. activities prohibited on the property.
    d. permitted religious preferences of purchasers.

16. Which of the following entities would be responsible for taking action against a property owner who violated a deed restriction?

    a. The local sheriff
    b. The local court
    c. The homeowners' association
    d. The property owner's personal attorney

17. When the local zoning authority wants to grant an exception to zoning because it would be in the public interest, it grants a

    a. conditional-use permit.
    b. variance.
    c. nonconforming use.
    d. violation.

18. All of the following features regarding land planning are true EXCEPT that land planning

     a. precedes the actual process of subdividing the land.
     b. must comply with whatever master plan is in effect, if any.
     c. must consider zoning ordinances and deed restrictions.
     d. must enforce compliance with applicable building codes.

19. Which of the following statements is true regarding the Interstate Land Sales Full Disclosure Act?

     a. Compliance is required for those who sell or lease a minimum of 15 lots.
     b. A buyer cannot cancel a purchase agreement after signing it.
     c. The seller must furnish the prospective buyer with a property report.
     d. There is a 30-day rescission period after any contract is signed.

20. All of the following items would be addressed on the plat map filed for a new subdivision EXCEPT

     a. easements for water and sewer lines.
     b. land to be dedicated for public facilities.
     c. land set aside for roadbeds and rights of way.
     d. prices of the available residential lots.

14: Fair Housing Laws and Ethical Practices

KEY TERMS

blockbusting
Civil Rights Act of 1866
Department of Housing and
    Urban Development
Fair Housing Amendments Act of 1988
Federal Fair Housing Act of 1968

Housing and Community
    Development Act of 1974
protected class
redlining
steering

EQUAL OPPORTUNITY IN HOUSING

Real estate licensees who offer *residential* property for sale must be aware of the federal, state, and local laws pertaining to civil rights and nondiscrimination. These laws, under such titles as open housing, fair housing, and equal opportunity housing, prohibit undesirable and discriminatory activities. Their provisions affect every phase of the real estate sales process, from listing to closing, and *all brokers and salespeople must comply with them.*

The goal of legislators who have enacted these laws and regulations is to create an unbiased housing market—one in which all home seekers have the opportunity to buy any home they choose, provided the home is within their financial means. As a potential licensee the student of real estate must be able to recognize illegal housing practices to avoid them. Failure to comply with fair housing practices is not only grounds for license revocation but also a criminal act.

Federal Fair Housing Laws

The efforts of the federal government to guarantee equal housing opportunities to all U.S. citizens began over one hundred years ago with the passage of the **Civil Rights Act of 1866.** This law prohibits any type of

Table 14.1 Summary of Federal Fair Housing Laws

Law	Purpose
Civil Rights Act of 1866	Prohibits discrimination in housing based on race without exception
Executive Order No. 11063 (1962)	Prohibits discrimination in housing funded by FHA or VA loans
Civil Rights Act of 1964	Prohibits discrimination in federally funded housing programs
Title VIII of the Civil Rights Act of 1968 (Federal Fair Housing Act)	Prohibits discrimination in housing based on race, color, religion or national origin, with certain exceptions
Housing and Community Development Act of 1974	Extends prohibitions to discrimination in housing based on sex
Fair Housing Amendments Act of 1988	Extends protection to cover persons with handicaps and families with children, with certain exceptions

discrimination based on race. The law states "All citizens of the United States shall have the same right in every state and territory as is enjoyed by white citizens thereof to inherit, purchase, lease, sell, hold, and convey real and personal property." A summary of federal fair housing laws appears in Table 14.1.

Aside from a few isolated court decisions, however, there was little effort to enforce the principles of fair housing until 1962 when President John Kennedy issued Executive Order No. 11063. This order guaranteed nondiscrimination in all housing financed by FHA or VA loans. Because of the relatively small percentage of housing affected by Executive Order No. 11063, however, it had limited impact.

The scope of the federal government's fair housing regulation was expanded by the *Civil Rights Act of 1964,* which prohibited discrimination in any housing program that receives whole or partial federal funding. Since only a very small percentage of housing is government-funded, this law also had little impact on the housing industry.

Fair Housing Act of 1968. In 1968 two major events greatly encouraged the progress of guaranteeing fair housing. The first of these was the passage of the **Federal Fair Housing Act of 1968,** which is contained in *Title VIII of the Civil Rights Act of 1968.* This law provides that it is unlawful to discriminate on the basis of *race, color, religion, or national* *origin* when selling or leasing residential property. (The second major event, the Supreme Court decision in *Jones v. Mayer,* is discussed later.)

The *Housing and Community Development Act of 1974* added *sex* (gender) as a **protected class.** The *Fair Housing Amendments Act of 1988* then added as protected classes those with mental or physical *handicaps* and families with children *(familial status).*

Additional federal fair housing laws.   Drug abusers are not protected as handicapped, nor are those who pose a threat to the health or safety of others. Housing intended for older persons is exempt if: (1) it is occupied solely by persons 62 and older; or (2) 80 percent of its units are occupied by at least one person 55 or older and special facilities for the elderly are provided.

Individual states may name the same protected classes as the federal laws and may protect additional classes as well. Prospective licensees should be sure they are aware of all classes protected in their state.

The Federal Fair Housing Act (along with the 1974 and 1988 acts) covers houses and apartments as well as vacant land acquired for the construction of residential buildings, and it prohibits the following discriminatory acts:

1. Refusing to sell, rent, or negotiate with any person or otherwise making a dwelling unavailable to any person

2. Changing terms, conditions, or services for different individuals as a means of discrimination

3. Practicing discrimination through any statement or advertisement that restricts the sale or rental of residential property

4. Representing to any person, as a means of discrimination, that a dwelling is not available for sale or rental

5. Making a profit by inducing owners of housing to sell or rent because of the prospective entry into the neighborhood of persons of a particular race, color, religion, national origin, handicap, or familial status

6. Altering the terms or conditions for a home loan to any person who wishes to purchase or repair a dwelling or otherwise denying such a loan as a means of discrimination

7. Denying people membership or limiting their participation in any multiple-listing service, real estate brokers' organization, or

other facility related to the sale or rental of dwellings as a means of discrimination.

The following exemptions to the Federal Fair Housing Act are provided:

1. The sale or rental of a single-family home is exempted when the home is owned by an individual who does not own more than three such homes at one time and when a broker or salesperson is not used and discriminatory advertising is not used. If the owner is not living in the dwelling at the time of the transaction or was not the most recent occupant, only one such sale by an individual is exempt from the law within any 24-month period.

2. The rental of rooms or units is exempted in an owner-occupied one-family to four-family dwelling.

3. Dwelling units owned by religious organizations may be restricted to people of the same religion if membership in the organization is not restricted on the basis of race, color, national origin, handicap, or familial status.

4. A private club that is not open to the public may restrict the rental or occupancy of lodgings that it owns to its members as long as the lodgings are not operated commercially.

Jones v. Mayer.   The second significant fair housing development of 1968 was the Supreme Court decision in the case of *Jones v. Alfred H. Mayer Company, 392, U.S. 409 (1968)*. In its ruling, the Court upheld the previously discussed Civil Rights Act of 1866, which "prohibits all racial discrimination, private or public, in the sale and rental of property."

The importance of this decision rests in the fact that while the 1968 federal law exempts individual homeowners and certain groups, the 1866 law *prohibits all racial discrimination without exception.* So despite any exemptions in the 1968 law, an aggrieved person may seek a remedy for racial discrimination under the 1866 law against any homeowner, regardless of whether or not the owner employed a real estate broker and/or advertised the property. Where race is involved, no exceptions apply.

Equal housing poster.   An amendment to the Federal Fair Housing Act of 1968 instituted the use of an equal housing opportunity poster, Figure 14.1. This poster, which can be obtained from the **Department of Housing and Urban Development (HUD)**, features the equal housing opportunity slogan, an equal housing statement pledging adherence to the fair housing act and support of affirmative marketing and advertising programs, and the equal housing opportunity logo (Figure 14.1).

Figure 14.1   Equal Housing Opportunity Poster*

U.S.. Department of Housing and Urban Development

**EQUAL HOUSING
OPPORTUNITY**

We Do Business in Accordance With the Federal Fair Housing Law

(The Fair Housing Amendments Act of 1988)

It is Illegal to Discriminate Against Any Person Because of Race, Color, Religion, Sex, Handicap, Familial Status, or National Origin

- ■ In the sale or rental of housing or residential lots

- ■ In advertising the sale or rental of housing

- ■ In the financing of housing

- ■ In the provision of real estate brokerage services

- ■ In the appraisal of housing

- ■ Blockbusting is also illegal

Anyone who feels he or she has been discriminated against may file a complaint of housing discrimination:

1-800-424-8590 (Toll Free)
1-800-424-8529 (TDD)

**U.S. Department of Housing and Urban Development
Assistant Secretary for Fair Housing and Equal Opportunity
Washington, D.C. 20410**

form HUD-928.1 (3-89)

*Previous editions are obsolete.

When HUD investigates a broker for discriminatory practices, it may consider failure to display the poster in the broker's place of business prima facie evidence of discrimination.

The Americans with Disabilities Act

The Americans with Disabilities Act is a civil rights law that guarantees individuals with certain disabilities an equal opportunity in the areas of employment, public accommodations, and telecommunications. Real estate licensees will most likely be affected by Titles I and III, which deal with employment and public accommodations.

Although the real estate brokerage business may not be affected immediately, licensees will soon need to become familiar with specific areas of the law. Consideration will have to be given to the properties that the licensee is marketing or managing, as well as to the licensee's own real estate office. For example, the owners or managers of structures to which those confined to wheelchairs would need access must be concerned with accessibility (ramps, wide doorways, wide hallways), interior movement (low-pile carpeting, rearranged furniture, accessible light switches and electrical outlets), and restroom facilities (wide stalls, grab bars, lowered sinks). For those with visual or hearing impairments, other types of accommodations must be made.

The Americans with Disabilities Act is vague in many areas, particularly those that address what is a reasonable attempt to comply with the law. As a result, many lawsuits are anticipated for the purpose of clarifying the requirements for compliance. However, the real estate professional must obtain as much education in this area as possible. The licensee needs to assure his or her personal compliance as well as be able to relate information to the client.

Blockbusting and Steering

Blockbusting and steering are undesirable housing practices frequently discussed in connection with fair housing. While they are not mentioned by name in the Federal Fair Housing Act of 1968, both are prohibited by that law.

Blockbusting, also known as "panic peddling," means *inducing homeowners to sell by making representations regarding the entry or prospective entry into the neighborhood of members of a protected class, usually a racial consideration.* The blockbuster frightens homeowners into selling and makes a profit by buying the homes cheaply and selling them at considerably higher prices to minority group persons. This practice is specifically prohibited by the Federal Fair Housing Act.

Steering is the channeling of home seekers to particular areas on the basis of race, religion, country of origin, or other protected class. On these grounds it is prohibited by the provisions of the Federal Fair Housing Act. Steering is often difficult to detect, however, because the steering tactics can be so subtle that the home seeker is unaware that his or her choices have been limited. Steering may be done unintentionally by agents who are not aware of their own unconscious assumptions.

Redlining

Refusing to make mortgage loans or issue insurance policies in specific areas without regard to the economic qualifications of the applicant is known as **redlining.** This practice, which often contributes to the deterioration of older, transitional neighborhoods, is frequently based on racial grounds rather than on any real objections to the applicant. However, a lending institution that refuses a loan solely on sound economic grounds cannot be accused of redlining.

Advertising

Any printed or published advertisement of property for sale or rent cannot include language that indicates any discriminatory preference or limitation, regardless of how subtle the choice of words. HUD's regulations cite examples of discriminatory and nondiscriminatory language. For example, the phrases "master bedroom," "mother-in-law suite" and "walk-in closet" are not discriminatory, while "white neighborhood," "nice Christian home," and "no wheelchairs" suggest a discriminatory intent. Pictures of people in advertisements should be as clearly representative of the entire population as reasonably possible, and should not exclude anyone. The selective choice of media, whether by language or geographic coverage, may also be discriminatory. For instance, advertising a property only in Spanish-language newspapers or over a cable service available only to white suburbanites may be construed as discriminatory.

Enforcement

A person who believes illegal discrimination has occurred has up to one year after the alleged act to file a charge with HUD or he or she may bring a federal suit within two years. HUD will investigate, and if the department believes a discriminatory act has occurred it may issue a charge. Any party involved (or HUD) may choose to have the charge heard in a federal district court. If no one requests the court procedure, the charge will be heard by an administrative law judge within HUD itself.

The administrative judge has the authority to issue an *injunction.* The injunction would order the offender to do something—rent to the complaining party, for example—or to refrain from doing something. In addition, penalties can be imposed, ranging from $10,000 for a first violation to $25,000 for a second violation within five years and $50,000 for further violations within seven years. If the case is heard in federal court, an injunction, actual damages, and punitive damages are possible, with no dollar limit. In addition to offended parties the Department of Justice may itself sue anyone who seems to show a pattern of illegal discrimination. Dollar limits on penalties in such cases are set at $50,000, with a $100,000 penalty for repeat violations.

Complaints brought under the Civil Rights Act of 1866 must be taken directly to a federal court. The only time limit for action would be the state's statute of limitation for *torts,* injuries done by one individual to another.

Substantially Equivalent State Laws

Whenever a state or municipality has a fair housing law that has been ruled "substantially equivalent to the federal law," all complaints in that state or locality, including those filed with HUD, are referred to and handled by the state enforcement agencies. To be considered substantially equivalent, the local law and its related regulations must contain prohibitions comparable to the federal law. In addition, the state or locality must show that its local enforcement agency is taking sufficient affirmative action in processing and investigating complaints and in finding remedies for discriminatory practices.

Threats or Acts of Violence

The Federal Fair Housing Act of 1968 contains criminal provisions protecting the rights of those who seek the benefits of the open housing law as well as owners, brokers, or salespeople who aid or encourage the enjoyment of open housing rights. Unlawful actions involving threats, coercion, and intimidation are punishable by civil action. In such cases the victim should immediately report the incident to the local police and to the nearest office of the Federal Bureau of Investigation.

Implications for Brokers and Salespeople

To a large extent the laws place the burden of responsibility for effecting and maintaining fair housing on real estate licensees. The laws are clear and widely known. *The complainant does not have to prove guilty knowledge or specific intent—only the fact that discrimination occurred.*

When a broker is charged with discrimination, it is *no defense* that the offense was unintentional. Citing past service to members of the same minority group also is of little value as a defense. The licensee's best course is to study fair housing law, develop sensitivity on the subject, and follow routine practices designed to reduce the danger of unintentionally hurting any member of the public. These practices include careful record keeping for each customer: financial analysis, properties suggested, houses shown, check-back phone calls. Using a standard form for all qualifying interviews is helpful. Special care should be taken to be on time for appointments and to follow through on returning all phone calls. Besides helping to avoid civil rights violations, these practices are simply good business and should result in increased sales.

In addition, HUD offers guidelines for nondiscriminatory language and illustrations for use in real estate advertising, to help licensees comply with the laws and make that policy known to the public.

From time to time real estate offices may be visited by testers, undercover volunteers who want to see whether customers and clients are being treated equally and are being offered the same free choice within a given price range. The courts have held that such practice is permissible as it is the only way to test compliance with the fair housing laws.

STANDARDS OF PROFESSIONAL PRACTICE

Years ago, real estate brokers realized the need for an organization to assist them in improving their business abilities and to educate the public to the value of qualified real estate brokers. The National Association of REALTORS® was organized in 1908 (as the National Association of Real Estate Boards) to meet this need. This association has grown with the business, and today is one of the leading trade organizations in the country. It is the parent organization of the majority of local real estate boards that operate throughout the United States, and the professional activities of all REALTORS®—active members of state associations and local boards affiliated with the national association—are governed by the association's Code of Ethics. To be a member of the national association, a licensee must hold membership in a state association and local board.

Figure 14.2   Code of Ethics and Standards of Practice

Code of Ethics and Standards of Practice
of the
NATIONAL ASSOCIATION OF REALTORS®

Effective January 1, 1995

Where the word REALTORS® is used in this Code and Preamble, it shall be deemed to include REALTOR-ASSOCIATE®s.

While the Code of Ethics establishes obligations that may be higher than those mandated by law, in any instance where the Code of Ethics and the law conflict, the obligations of the law must take precedence.

Preamble...

Under all is the land. Upon its wise utilization and widely allocated ownership depend the survival and growth of free institutions and of our civilization. REALTORS® should recognize that the interests of the nation and its citizens require the highest and best use of the land and the widest distribution of land ownership. They require the creation of adequate housing, the building of functioning cities, the development of productive industries and farms, and the preservation of a healthful environment.

Such interests impose obligations beyond those of ordinary commerce. They impose grave social responsibility and a patriotic duty to which REALTORS® should dedicate themselves, and for which they should be diligent in preparing themselves. REALTORS®, therefore, are zealous to maintain and improve the standards of their calling and share with their fellow REALTORS® a common responsibility for its integrity and honor.

In recognition and appreciation of their obligations to clients, customers, the public, and each other, REALTORS® continuously strive to become and remain informed on issues affecting real estate and, as knowledgeable professionals, they willingly share the fruit of their experience and study with others. They identify and take steps, through enforcement of this Code of Ethics and by assisting appropriate regulatory bodies, to eliminate practices which may damage the public or which might discredit or bring dishonor to the real estate profession.

Realizing that cooperation with other real estate professionals promotes the best interests of those who utilize their services, REALTORS® urge exclusive representation of clients; do not attempt to gain any unfair advantage over their competitors; and they refrain from making unsolicited comments about other practitioners. In instances where their opinion is sought, or where REALTORS® believe that comment is necessary, their opinion is offered in an objective, professional manner, uninfluenced by any personal motivation or potential advantage or gain.

NATIONAL ASSOCIATION
OF REALTORS®
430 North Michigan Avenue
Chicago, Illinois 60611-4087

The term REALTOR® has come to connote competency, fairness, and high integrity resulting from adherence to a lofty ideal of moral conduct in business relations. No inducement of profit and no instruction from clients ever can justify departure from this ideal.

In the interpretation of this obligation, REALTORS® can take no safer guide than that which has been handed down through the centuries, embodied in the Golden Rule, "Whatsoever ye would that others should do to you, do ye even so to them."

Accepting this standard as their own, REALTORS® pledge to observe its spirit in all of their activities and to conduct their business in accordance with the tenets set forth below.

Duties to Clients and Customers

Article 1

When representing a buyer, seller, landlord, tenant, or other client as an agent, REALTORS® pledge themselves to protect and promote the interests of their client. This obligation of absolute fidelity to the client's interests is primary, but it does not relieve REALTORS® of their obligation to treat all parties honestly. When serving a buyer, seller, landlord, tenant or other party in a non-agency capacity, REALTORS® remain obligated to treat all parties honestly. *(Amended 1/93)*

- **Standard of Practice 1-1**
  REALTORS®, when acting as principals in a real estate transaction, remain obligated by the duties imposed by the Code of Ethics. *(Amended 1/93)*

- **Standard of Practice 1-2**
  The duties the Code of Ethics imposes on agents/representatives are applicable to REALTORS® acting as agents, transaction brokers, facilitators, or in any other recognized capacity except for any duty specifically exempted by law or regulation. *(Adopted 1/95)*

- **Standard of Practice 1-3**
  REALTORS®, in attempting to secure a listing, shall not deliberately mislead the owner as to market value.

- **Standard of Practice 1-4**
  REALTORS®, when seeking to become a buyer/tenant representative, shall not mislead buyers or tenants as to savings or other benefits that might be realized through use of the REALTOR®'s services. *(Amended 1/93)*

- **Standard of Practice 1-5**
  REALTORS® may represent the seller/landlord and buyer/tenant in the same transaction only after full disclosure to and with informed consent of both parties. *(Adopted 1/93)*

- **Standard of Practice 1-6**
  REALTORS® shall submit offers and counter-offers objectively and as quickly as possible. *(Adopted 1/93, Amended 1/95)*

- **Standard of Practice 1-7**
  When acting as listing brokers, REALTORS® shall continue to submit to the seller/landlord all offers and counter-offers until closing or execution of a lease unless the seller/landlord has waived this obligation in writing. REALTORS® shall not be obligated to continue to market the property after an offer

Figure 14.2 (continued)

has been accepted by the seller/landlord. REALTORS® shall recommend that sellers/landlords obtain the advice of legal counsel prior to acceptance of a subsequent offer except where the acceptance is contingent on the termination of the pre-existing purchase contract or lease. *(Amended 1/93)*

- **Standard of Practice 1-8**
  REALTORS® acting as agents of buyers/tenants shall submit to buyers/tenants all offers and counter-offers until acceptance but have no obligation to continue to show properties to their clients after an offer has been accepted unless otherwise agreed in writing. REALTORS® acting as agents of buyers/tenants shall recommend that buyers/tenants obtain the advice of legal counsel if there is a question as to whether a pre-existing contract has been terminated. *(Adopted 1/93)*

- **Standard of Practice 1-9**
  The obligation of REALTORS® to preserve confidential information provided by their clients continues after the termination of the agency relationship. REALTORS® shall not knowingly, during or following the termination of a professional relationship with their client:
  1) reveal confidential information of the client; or
  2) use confidential information of the client to the disadvantage of the client; or
  3) use confidential information of the client for the REALTOR®'s advantage or the advantage of a third party unless the client consents after full disclosure except where the REALTOR® is:
     a) required by court order; or
     b) it is the intention of the client to commit a crime and the information is necessary to prevent the crime; or
     c) necessary to defend the REALTOR® or the REALTOR®'s employees or associates against an accusation of wrongful conduct. *(Adopted 1/93, Amended 1/95)*

- **Standard of Practice 1-10**
  REALTORS® shall, consistent with the terms and conditions of their property management agreement, competently manage the property of clients with due regard for the rights, responsibilities, benefits, safety and health of tenants and others lawfully on the premises. *(Adopted 1/95)*

- **Standard of Practice 1-11**
  REALTORS® who are employed to maintain or manage a client's property shall exercise due diligence and make reasonable efforts to protect it against reasonably foreseeable contingencies and losses. *(Adopted 1/95)*

Article 2
REALTORS® shall avoid exaggeration, misrepresentation, or concealment of pertinent facts relating to the property or the transaction. REALTORS® shall not, however, be obligated to discover latent defects in the property, to advise on matters outside the scope of their real estate license, or to disclose facts which are confidential under the scope of agency duties owed to their clients. *(Amended 1/93)*

- **Standard of Practice 2-1**
  REALTORS® shall be obligated to discover and disclose adverse factors reasonably apparent to someone with expertise in only those areas required by their real estate licensing authority.

Article 2 does not impose upon the REALTOR® the obligation of expertise in other professional or technical disciplines. *(Amended 11/86)*

- **Standard of Practice 2-2**
  When entering into listing contracts, REALTORS® must advise sellers/landlords of:
  1) the REALTOR®'s general company policies regarding cooperation with subagents, buyer/tenant agents, or both;
  2) the fact that buyer/tenant agents, even if compensated by the listing broker, or by the seller/landlord will represent the interests of buyers/tenants; and
  3) any potential for the listing broker to act as a disclosed dual agent, e.g. buyer/tenant agent. *(Adopted 1/93)*

- **Standard of Practice 2-3**
  When entering into contracts to represent buyers/tenants, REALTORS® must advise potential clients of:
  1) the REALTOR®'s general company policies regarding cooperation with other firms; and
  2) any potential for the buyer/tenant representative to act as a disclosed dual agent, e.g. listing broker, subagent, landlord's agent, etc. *(Adopted 1/93)*

- **Standard of Practice 2-4**
  REALTORS® shall not be parties to the naming of a false consideration in any document, unless it be the naming of an obviously nominal consideration.

- **Standard of Practice 2-5**
  Factors defined as "non-material" by law or regulation or which are expressly referenced in law or regulation as not being subject to disclosure are considered not "pertinent" for purposes of Article 2. *(Adopted 1/93)*

Article 3
REALTORS® shall cooperate with other brokers except when cooperation is not in the client's best interest. The obligation to cooperate does not include the obligation to share commissions, fees, or to otherwise compensate another broker. *(Amended 1/95)*

- **Standard of Practice 3-1**
  REALTORS®, acting as exclusive agents of sellers/landlords, establish the terms and conditions of offers to cooperate. Unless expressly indicated in offers to cooperate, cooperating brokers may not assume that the offer of cooperation includes an offer of compensation. Terms of compensation, if any, shall be ascertained by cooperating brokers before beginning efforts to accept the offer of cooperation. *(Amended 1/94)*

- **Standard of Practice 3-2**
  REALTORS® shall, with respect to offers of compensation to another REALTOR®, timely communicate any change of compensation for cooperative services to the other REALTOR® prior to the time such REALTOR® produces an offer to purchase/lease the property. *(Amended 1/94)*

- **Standard of Practice 3-3**
  Standard of Practice 3-2 does not preclude the listing broker and cooperating broker from entering into an agreement to change cooperative compensation. *(Adopted 1/94)*

Figure 14.2 (continued)

- **Standard of Practice 3-4**

  REALTORS®, acting as listing brokers; have an affirmative obligation to disclose the existence of dual or variable rate commission arrangements (i.e., listings where one amount of commission is payable if the listing broker's firm is the procuring cause of sale/lease and a different amount of commission is payable if the sale/lease results through the efforts of the seller/landlord or a cooperating broker). The listing broker shall, as soon as practical, disclose the existence of such arrangements to potential cooperating brokers and shall, in response to inquiries from cooperating brokers, disclose the differential that would result in a cooperative transaction or in a sale/lease that results through the efforts of the seller/landlord. If the cooperating broker is a buyer/tenant representative, the buyer/tenant representative must disclose such information to their client. *(Amended 1/94)*

- **Standard of Practice 3-5**

  It is the obligation of subagents to promptly disclose all pertinent facts to the principal's agent prior to as well as after a purchase or lease agreement is executed. *(Amended 1/93)*

- **Standard of Practice 3-6**

  REALTORS® shall disclose the existence of an accepted offer to any broker seeking cooperation. *(Adopted 5/86)*

- **Standard of Practice 3-7**

  When seeking information from another REALTOR® concerning property under a management or listing agreement, REALTORS® shall disclose their REALTOR® status and whether their interest is personal or on behalf of a client and, if on behalf of a client, their representational status. *(Amended 1/95)*

- **Standard of Practice 3-8**

  REALTORS® shall not misrepresent the availability of access to show or inspect a listed property. *(Amended 11/87)*

Article 4

REALTORS® shall not acquire an interest in or buy or present offers from themselves, any member of their immediate families, their firms or any member thereof, or any entities in which they have any ownership interest, any real property without making their true position known to the owner or the owner's agent. In selling property they own, or in which they have any interest, REALTORS® shall reveal their ownership or interest in writing to the purchaser or the purchaser's representative. *(Amended 1/91)*

- **Standard of Practice 4-1**

  For the protection of all parties, the disclosures required by Article 4 shall be in writing and provided by REALTORS® prior to the signing of any contract. *(Adopted 2/86)*

Article 5

REALTORS® shall not undertake to provide professional services concerning a property or its value where they have a present or contemplated interest unless such interest is specifically disclosed to all affected parties.

Article 6

When acting as agents, REALTORS® shall not accept any commission, rebate, or profit on expenditures made for their principal, without the principal's knowledge and consent. *(Amended 1/92)*

- **Standard of Practice 6-1**

  REALTORS® shall not recommend or suggest to a client or a customer the use of services of another organization or business entity in which they have a direct interest without disclosing such interest at the time of the recommendation or suggestion. *(Amended 5/88)*

- **Standard of Practice 6-2**

  When acting as agents or subagents, REALTORS® shall disclose to a client or customer if there is any financial benefit or fee the REALTOR® or the REALTOR®'s firm may receive as a direct result of having recommended real estate products or services (e.g., homeowner's insurance, warranty programs, mortgage financing, title insurance, etc.) other than real estate referral fees. *(Adopted 5/88)*

Article 7

In a transaction, REALTORS® shall not accept compensation from more than one party, even if permitted by law, without disclosure to all parties and the informed consent of the REALTOR®'s client or clients. *(Amended 1/93)*

Article 8

REALTORS® shall keep in a special account in an appropriate financial institution, separated from their own funds, monies coming into their possession in trust for other persons, such as escrows, trust funds, clients' monies, and other like items.

Article 9

REALTORS®, for the protection of all parties, shall assure whenever possible that agreements shall be in writing, and shall be in clear and understandable language expressing the specific terms, conditions, obligations and commitments of the parties. A copy of each agreement shall be furnished to each party upon their signing or initialing. *(Amended 1/95)*

- **Standard of Practice 9-1**

  For the protection of all parties, REALTORS® shall use reasonable care to ensure that documents pertaining to the purchase, sale, or lease of real estate are kept current through the use of written extensions or amendments. *(Amended 1/93)*

Duties to the Public

Article 10

REALTORS® shall not deny equal professional services to any person for reasons of race, color, religion, sex, handicap, familial status, or national origin. REALTORS® shall not be parties to any plan or agreement to discriminate against a person or persons on the basis of race, color, religion, sex, handicap, familial status, or national origin. *(Amended 1/90)*

- **Standard of Practice 10-1**

  REALTORS® shall not volunteer information regarding the racial, religious or ethnic composition of any neighborhood and shall not engage in any activity which may result in panic selling. REALTORS® shall not print, display or circulate any statement or advertisement with respect to the selling or renting of a property that indicates any preference, limitations or discrimination based on race, color, religion, sex, handicap, familial status or national origin. *(Adopted 1/94)*

Figure 14.2   (continued)

Article 11

The services which REALTORS® provide to their clients and customers shall conform to the standards of practice and competence which are reasonably expected in the specific real estate disciplines in which they engage; specifically, residential real estate brokerage, real property management, commercial and industrial real estate brokerage, real estate appraisal, real estate counseling, real estate syndication, real estate auction, and international real estate.

REALTORS® shall not undertake to provide specialized professional services concerning a type of property or service that is outside their field of competence unless they engage the assistance of one who is competent on such types of property or service, or unless the facts are fully disclosed to the client. Any persons engaged to provide such assistance shall be so identified to the client and their contribution to the assignment should be set forth. *(Amended 1/95)*

- **Standard of Practice 11-1**

  The obligations of the Code of Ethics shall be supplemented by and construed in a manner consistent with the Uniform Standards of Professional Appraisal Practice (USPAP) promulgated by the Appraisal Standards Board of the Appraisal Foundation. *(Adopted 1/95)*

- **Standard of Practice 11-2**

  The obligations of the Code of Ethics in respect of real estate disciplines other than appraisal shall be interpreted and applied in accordance with the standards of competence and practice which clients and the public reasonably require to protect their rights and interests considering the complexity of the transaction, the availability of expert assistance, and, where the REALTOR® is an agent or subagent, the obligations of a fiduciary. *(Adopted 1/95)*

Article 12

REALTORS® shall be careful at all times to present a true picture in their advertising and representations to the public. REALTORS® shall also ensure that their professional status (e.g., broker, appraiser, property manager, etc.) or status as REALTORS® is clearly identifiable in any such advertising. *(Amended 1/93)*

- **Standard of Practice 12-1**

  REALTORS® shall not offer a service described as "free of charge" when the rendering of a service is contingent on the obtaining of a benefit such as a listing or commission.

- **Standard of Practice 12-2**

  REALTORS® shall not represent that their services are free or without cost if they expect to receive compensation from any source other than their client. *(Adopted 1/95)*

- **Standard of Practice 12-3**

  The offering of premiums, prizes, merchandise discounts or other inducements to list, sell, purchase, or lease is not, in itself, unethical even if receipt of the benefit is contingent on listing, selling, purchasing, or leasing through the REALTOR® making the offer. However, REALTORS® must exercise care and candor in any such advertising or other public or private representations so that any party interested in receiving or otherwise benefiting from the REALTOR®'s offer will have clear,

thorough, advance understanding of all the terms and conditions of the offer. The offering of any inducements to do business is subject to the limitations and restrictions of state law and the ethical obligations established by any applicable Standard of Practice. *(Amended 1/95)*

- **Standard of Practice 12-4**

  REALTORS® shall not offer for sale/lease or advertise property without authority. When acting as listing brokers or as subagents, REALTORS® shall not quote a price different from that agreed upon with the seller/landlord. *(Amended 1/93)*

- **Standard of Practice 12-5**

  REALTORS® shall not advertise nor permit any person employed by or affiliated with them to advertise listed property without disclosing the name of the firm. *(Adopted 11/86)*

- **Standard of Practice 12-6**

  REALTORS®, when advertising unlisted real property for sale/lease in which they have an ownership interest, shall disclose their status as both owners/landlords and as REALTORS® or real estate licensees. *(Amended 1/93)*

- **Standard of Practice 12-7**

  Only REALTORS® as listing brokers, may claim to have "sold" the property, even when the sale resulted through the cooperative efforts of another broker. However, after transactions have closed, listing brokers may not prohibit successful cooperating brokers from advertising their "cooperation," "participation," or "assistance" in the transaction, or from making similar representations.

  Only listing brokers are entitled to use the term "sold" on signs, in advertisements, and in other public representations. *(Amended 1/90)*

Article 13

REALTORS® shall not engage in activities that constitute the unauthorized practice of law and shall recommend that legal counsel be obtained when the interest of any party to the transaction requires it.

Article 14

If charged with unethical practice or asked to present evidence or to cooperate in any other way, in any disciplinary proceeding or investigation, REALTORS® shall place all pertinent facts before the proper tribunals of the Member Board or affiliated institute, society, or council in which membership is held and shall take no action to disrupt or obstruct such processes. *(Amended 1/90)*

- **Standard of Practice 14-1**

  REALTORS® shall not be subject to disciplinary proceedings in more than one Board of REALTORS® or affiliated institute, society or council in which they hold membership with respect to alleged violations of the Code of Ethics relating to the same transaction or event. *(Amended 1/95)*

- **Standard of Practice 14-2**

  REALTORS® shall not make any unauthorized disclosure or dissemination of the allegations, findings, or decision developed in connection with an ethics hearing or appeal or in connection with an arbitration hearing or procedural review. *(Amended 1/92)*

Figure 14.2   (continued)

- **Standard of Practice 14-3**

  REALTORS® shall not obstruct the Board's investigative or disciplinary proceedings by instituting or threatening to institute actions for libel, slander or defamation against any party to a professional standards proceeding or their witnesses. *(Adopted 11/87)*

- **Standard of Practice 14-4**

  REALTORS® shall not intentionally impede the Board's investigative or disciplinary proceedings by filing multiple ethics complaints based on the same event or transaction. *(Adopted 11/88)*

Duties to REALTORS®

Article 15

REALTORS® shall not knowingly or recklessly make false or misleading statements about competitors, their businesses, or their business practices. *(Amended 1/92)*

Article 16

REALTORS® shall not engage in any practice or take any action inconsistent with the agency of other REALTORS®.

- **Standard of Practice 16-1**

  Article 16 is not intended to prohibit aggressive or innovative business practices which are otherwise ethical and does not prohibit disagreements with other REALTORS® involving commission, fees, compensation or other forms of payment or expenses. *(Adopted 1/93, Amended 1/95)*

- **Standard of Practice 16-2**

  Article 16 does not preclude REALTORS® from making general announcements to prospective clients describing their services and the terms of their availability even though some recipients may have entered into agency agreements with another REALTOR®. A general telephone canvass, general mailing or distribution addressed to all prospective clients in a given geographical area or in a given profession, business, club, or organization, or other classification or group is deemed "general" for purposes of this standard.

  Article 16 is intended to recognize as unethical two basic types of solicitations:

  First, telephone or personal solicitations of property owners who have been identified by a real estate sign, multiple listing compilation, or other information service as having exclusively listed their property with another REALTOR®; and

  Second, mail or other forms of written solicitations of prospective clients whose properties are exclusively listed with another REALTOR® when such solicitations are not part of a general mailing but are directed specifically to property owners identified through compilations of current listings, "for sale" or "for rent" signs, or other sources of information required by Article 3 and Multiple Listing Service rules to be made available to other REALTORS® under offers of subagency or cooperation. *(Amended 1/93)*

- **Standard of Practice 16-3**

  Article 16 does not preclude REALTORS® from contacting the client of another broker for the purpose of offering to provide, or entering into a contract to provide, a different type of real estate service unrelated to the type of service currently being provided (e.g., property management as opposed to brokerage). However, information received through a Multiple Listing Service or any other offer of cooperation may not be used to target clients of other REALTORS® to whom such offers to provide services may be made. *(Amended 1/93)*

- **Standard of Practice 16-4**

  REALTORS® shall not solicit a listing which is currently listed exclusively with another broker. However, if the listing broker, when asked by the REALTOR®, refuses to disclose the expiration date and nature of such listing; i.e., an exclusive right to sell, an exclusive agency, open listing, or other form of contractual agreement between the listing broker and the client, the REALTOR® may contact the owner to secure such information and may discuss the terms upon which the REALTOR® might take a future listing or, alternatively, may take a listing to become effective upon expiration of any existing exclusive listing. *(Amended 1/94)*

- **Standard of Practice 16-5**

  REALTORS® shall not solicit buyer/tenant agency agreements from buyers/tenants who are subject to exclusive buyer/tenant agency agreements. However, if a buyer/tenant agent, when asked by a REALTOR®, refuses to disclose the expiration date of the exclusive buyer/tenant agency agreement, the REALTOR® may contact the buyer/tenant to secure such information and may discuss the terms upon which the REALTOR® might enter into a future buyer/tenant agency agreement or, alternatively, may enter into a buyer/tenant agency agreement to become effective upon the expiration of any existing exclusive buyer/tenant agency agreement. *(Adopted 1/94)*

- **Standard of Practice 16-6**

  When REALTORS® are contacted by the client of another REALTOR® regarding the creation of an agency relationship to provide the same type of service, and REALTORS® have not directly or indirectly initiated such discussions, they may discuss the terms upon which they might enter into a future agency agreement or, alternatively, may enter into an agency agreement which becomes effective upon expiration of any existing exclusive agreement. *(Amended 1/93)*

- **Standard of Practice 16-7**

  The fact that a client has retained a REALTOR® as an agent in one or more past transactions does not preclude other REALTORS® from seeking such former client's future business. *(Amended 1/93)*

- **Standard of Practice 16-8**

  The fact that an agency agreement has been entered into with a REALTOR® shall not preclude or inhibit any other REALTOR® from entering into a similar agreement after the expiration of the prior agreement. *(Amended 1/93)*

- **Standard of Practice 16-9**

  REALTORS®, prior to entering into an agency agreement, have an affirmative obligation to make reasonable efforts to determine whether the client is subject to a current, valid exclusive agreement to provide the same type of real estate service. *(Amended 1/93)*

Figure 14.2   (continued)

- **Standard of Practice 16-10**

  REALTORS®, acting as agents of buyers or tenants, shall disclose that relationship to the seller/landlord's agent at first contact and shall provide written confirmation of that disclosure to the seller/landlord's agent not later than execution of a purchase agreement or lease. *(Amended 1/93)*

- **Standard of Practice 16-11**

  On unlisted property, REALTORS® acting as buyer/tenant agents shall disclose that relationship to the seller/landlord at first contact for that client and shall provide written confirmation of such disclosure to the seller/landlord not later than execution of any purchase or lease agreement.

  REALTORS® shall make any request for anticipated compensation from the seller/landlord at first contact. *(Amended 1/93)*

- **Standard of Practice 16-12**

  REALTORS®, acting as agents of sellers/landlords or as subagents of listing brokers, shall disclose that relationship to buyers/tenants as soon as practicable and shall provide written confirmation of such disclosure to buyers/tenants not later than execution of any purchase or lease agreement. *(Amended 1/93)*

- **Standard of Practice 16-13**

  All dealings concerning property exclusively listed, or with buyer/tenants who are exclusively represented shall be carried on with the client's agent, and not with the client, except with the consent of the client's agent. *(Adopted 1/93)*

- **Standard of Practice 16-14**

  REALTORS® are free to enter into contractual relationships or to negotiate with sellers/landlords, buyers/tenants or others who are not represented by an exclusive agent but shall not knowingly obligate them to pay more than one commission except with their informed consent. *(Amended 1/94)*

- **Standard of Practice 16-15**

  In cooperative transactions REALTORS® shall compensate cooperating REALTORS® (principal brokers) and shall not compensate nor offer to compensate, directly or indirectly, any of the sales licensees employed by or affiliated with other REALTORS® without the prior express knowledge and consent of the cooperating broker.

- **Standard of Practice 16-16**

  REALTORS®, acting as subagents or buyer/tenant agents, shall not use the terms of an offer to purchase/lease to attempt to modify the listing broker's offer of compensation to subagents or buyer's agents nor make the submission of an executed offer to purchase/lease contingent on the listing broker's agreement to modify the offer of compensation. *(Amended 1/93)*

- **Standard of Practice 16-17**

  REALTORS® acting as subagents or as buyer/tenant agents, shall not attempt to extend a listing broker's offer of cooperation and/or compensation to other brokers without the consent of the listing broker. *(Amended 1/93)*

- **Standard of Practice 16-18**

  REALTORS® shall not use information obtained by them from the listing broker, through offers to cooperate received through Multiple Listing Services or other sources authorized by the listing broker, for the purpose of creating a referral prospect to a third broker, or for creating a buyer/tenant prospect unless such use is authorized by the listing broker. *(Amended 1/93)*

- **Standard of Practice 16-19**

  Signs giving notice of property for sale, rent, lease, or exchange shall not be placed on property without consent of the seller/landlord. *(Amended 1/93)*

Article 17

In the event of a contractual dispute between REALTORS® associated with different firms, arising out of their relationship as REALTORS®, the REALTORS® shall submit the dispute to arbitration in accordance with the regulations of their Board or Boards rather than litigate the matter.

In the event clients of REALTORS® wish to arbitrate contractual disputes arising out of real estate transactions, REALTORS® shall arbitrate those disputes in accordance with the regulations of their Board, provided the clients agree to be bound by the decision. *(Amended 1/94)*

- **Standard of Practice 17-1**

  The filing of litigation and refusal to withdraw from it by REALTORS® in an arbitrable matter constitutes a refusal to arbitrate. *(Adopted 2/86)*

- **Standard of Practice 17-2**

  Article 17 does not require REALTORS® to arbitrate in those circumstances when all parties to the dispute advise the Board in writing that they choose not to arbitrate before the Board. *(Amended 1/93)*

The Code of Ethics was adopted in 1913. Amended at the Annual Convention in 1924, 1928, 1950, 1951, 1952, 1955, 1956, 1961, 1962, 1974, 1982, 1986, 1987, 1989, 1990, 1991, 1992, 1993 and 1994.

EXPLANATORY NOTES

The reader should be aware of the following policies which have been approved by the Board of Directors of the National Association:

In filing a charge of an alleged violation of the Code of Ethics by a REALTOR®, the charge must read as an alleged violation of one or more Articles of the Code. Standards of Practice may be cited in support of the charge.

The Standards of Practice serve to clarify the ethical obligations imposed by the various Articles and supplement, and do not substitute for, the Case Interpretations in **Interpretations of the Code of Ethics**.

Modifications to existing Standards of Practice and additional new Standards of Practice are approved from time to time. Readers are cautioned to ensure that the most recent publications are utilized.

NATIONAL ASSOCIATION OF REALTORS®
430 North Michigan Avenue
Chicago, Illinois 60611-4087

Many independent real estate boards and other professional associations have been organized to set high standards for their members, promote their members' best interests, and educate the public about the real estate profession. The National Association of Real Estate Brokers (Realtists) was founded in 1947. Its membership includes individual members, as well as brokers, who belong to state and local real estate boards that are affiliated with the organization. The members also subscribe to a code of ethics that sets professional standards for all Realtists.

Code of Ethics

The National Association of REALTORS® adopted the Code of Ethics for its members in 1913. The NAR also publishes interpretations of the Code known as Standards of Practice (see Figure 14.2). Because the real estate business is only as good as its reputation, and reputations are built on fair dealings with the public, licensees are obligated to conduct themselves in an ethical manner.

SUMMARY

Federal regulations regarding equal opportunity in housing are contained principally in two laws. The *Civil Rights Act of 1866* prohibits all racial discrimination, and the *Federal Fair Housing Act* (Title VIII of the Civil Rights Act of 1968) prohibits discrimination on the basis of race, color, religion, national origin, sex (1974), handicap (1988), or the presence of children in a family (1988) in the sale or rental of residential property. Discriminatory actions include refusing to deal with an individual or a specific group, changing any terms of a real estate or loan transaction, changing the services offered for any individual or group, making statements or ads that indicate discriminatory restrictions, or otherwise attempting to make a dwelling unavailable to any person or group because of membership in a protected class. Some exceptions apply to owners but none to brokers and none when the discriminatory act is based on race.

Complaints under the Federal Fair Housing Act may be reported to and investigated by the Department of Housing and Urban Development and may be taken to a U.S. district court. Complaints under the Civil Rights Act of 1866 must be taken to a federal court. The law also prohibits *steering, blockbusting* and *redlining*. Compliance is occasionally monitored by undercover testers. The National Association of REALTORS® Code of Ethics suggests a set of standards for all members to follow.

QUESTIONS

Please complete all of the questions before turning to the Answer Key.

1. The primary goal of fair housing laws is to

   a. create fair sales prices.
   b. encourage home purchases.
   c. create an unbiased housing market.
   d. promote discriminatory activities.

2. The Civil Rights Acts of 1866 prohibits any type of discrimination based on

   a. national origin.   c. race.
   b. religion.   d. sex.

3. Inducing homeowners to sell by making representations regarding the entry or potential entry of minority group members into the neighborhood is called

   a. steering.   c. channeling.
   b. blockbusting.   d. equal opportunity housing.

4. Under the Federal Fair Housing Act of 1968, an aggrieved person has how long after the alleged act of discrimination occurs to file a complaint with the Secretary of the Department of Housing and Urban Development?

   a. Thirty days   c. Six months
   b. Ninety days   d. One year

5. If a state has a fair housing law that is substantially equivalent to the federal law, all complaints in that state concerning the Federal Fair Housing Act should be directed to the

   a. state enforcement agency.
   b. federal courts.
   c. Office of Equal Opportunity.
   d. Secretary of HUD.

6. The law places the burden of responsibility for fair housing laws on

    a. municipalities.   c. brokers and salespeople.
    b. open housing groups.   d. the public.

7. The Civil Rights Act of 1866 is unique because it

    a. has been broadened to protect the aged.
    b. adds welfare recipients as a protected class.
    c. contains "choose your neighbor" provisions.
    d. provides no exceptions to racial discrimination.

8. The act of channeling home seekers to a particular area, either to maintain or to change the character of a neighborhood, is known as

    a. steering.   c. redlining.
    b. blockbusting.   d. testing.

9. Complaints brought under the Civil Rights Act of 1866 must be taken directly to

    a. federal court.
    b. state court.
    c. the Secretary of HUD.
    d. the state enforcement agency.

10. The practice of refusing to make mortgage loans in a specific area without regard to the economic qualifications of the applicant is called

    a. steering.   c. blockbusting.
    b. redlining.   d. channeling.

11. The Fair Housing Amendments Act of 1988 added which of the following classes as new protected classes under fair housing laws?

    a. Occupation and source of income
    b. Handicap and familial status
    c. Political affiliation and country of origin
    d. Marital status and prison record

12. Which of the following acts is permitted under the Federal Fair Housing Act?

    a.   Advertising property for sale only to a special group
    b.   Altering the terms of a loan for a member of a minority group
    c.   Refusing to sell a home to an individual because of poor credit history
    d.   Telling an individual that an apartment has been rented when in fact it has not

13. Undercover investigation to determine whether fair housing practices are being followed is sometimes made by

    a.   testers.   c.   operatives.
    b.   evaluators.   d.   appraisers.

14. A black real estate broker's practice of offering a special discount to black clients is

    a.   satisfactory.   c.   legal but ill-advised.
    b.   illegal.   d.   not important.

15. "I hear they're moving in; there goes the neighborhood. Better sell to me today!" is an example of

    a.   panic peddling.   c.   testing.
    b.   redlining.   d.   steering.

16. Under the federal law, families with children may be refused rental or purchase in buildings where occupancy is reserved exclusively for those at least how many years old?

    a.   55   c.   62
    b.   60   d.   65

17. The seller who requests prohibited discrimination in the showing of a house should be told

    a.   "I'll need those instructions in writing to protect my company."
    b.   "I'll do what I can, but I can't guarantee anything."
    c.   "You'll have to clear that with my broker."
    d.   "We're not allowed to obey such instructions."

18. Which of the following activities would NOT be permitted under the Federal Fair Housing Act?

   a. The Harvard Club in New York will rent rooms only to graduates of Harvard who belong to the club.
   b. The owner of a 20-unit apartment building rents only to women.
   c. A Catholic convent refuses to furnish housing for a Jewish man.
   d. An owner refuses to rent the other side of her duplex home to families with children.

19. The fine for a first violation of the Federal Fair Housing Act could be as much as

   a. $1,000.   c. $10,000.
   b. $5,000.   d. $25,000.

20. Guiding prospective buyers to a particular area because the licensee feels they belong there may lead to a charge of

   a. blockbusting.   c. redlining.
   b. steering.   d. panic peddling.

21. An insurance company refuses to insure properties located within certain zip code zones in an urban area. This is an example of

   a. steering.   c. blockbusting.
   b. panic peddling.   d. redlining.

22. If a case brought under the Federal Fair Housing Act is heard in a federal court, what is the maximum dollar award that can be ordered for actual damages and punitive damages?

   a. $50,000
   b. $100,000
   c. $1,000,000
   d. There is no dollar limit for such damages.

23.   If an individual feels that he or she has been threatened as a result of complying with or encouraging the open housing laws, such threats should be immediately reported to the

    a.   Secretary of the Department of Housing and Urban Development.
    b.   Federal Bureau of Investigation.
    c.   state real estate licensing authority.
    d.   state fair housing authority.

24.   The Federal Fair Housing Act of 1968 prohibited discrimination based on all of the following criteria EXCEPT

    a.   race.   c.   national origin.
    b.   sex.   d.   religion.

25.   A property owner places a handpainted sign in front of his 12-unit apartment building that says, "Rooms for rent—only to Christians and people who are not attorneys." Which of the following statements is true regarding his action under the Federal Fair Housing Act of 1968?

    a.   The owner may advertise as he pleases, but must rent the rooms to anyone capable of paying the rent.
    b.   The owner may restrict the rooms he rents by religion only.
    c.   The owner may restrict the rooms he rents by occupation only.
    d.   The owner may restrict the rooms he rents by both religion and occupation.

15:　Closing the Real Estate Transaction

KEY TERMS

accrued items

closing statement

credit

debit

prepaid items

prorations

Uniform Settlement

　　Statement (HUD-1)

The moment when a real estate transaction is finalized is known by many names, including *closing, settlement,* and *transfer* (of title). In the Northeast, where the parties to the transaction sit around a single table and exchange a variety of documents, the process is known as *passing papers.* In the West, where buyer and seller may never meet and paperwork is handled by an escrow agent, the process is known as *closing escrow.* Whether the closing occurs face-to-face or through escrow, main concerns are that the buyer receive the marketable title, that the seller receive the purchase price, and that certain other items be adjusted properly between the two.

Though real estate licensees seldom conduct the proceedings at a closing, they usually attend and therefore should be thoroughly familiar with the process.

It is also in the broker's interest that a transaction in which he or she has been instrumental be finalized successfully and smoothly. In addition, in some states a closing statement problem is part of the broker's licensing examination. Although the salesperson's examination does not usually include completion of a closing statement problem, most states require an applicant to compute prorations, and many include the completion of a sales contract and listing agreement from the description of a sample transaction.

FACE-TO-FACE CLOSING

A face-to-face closing of a real estate transaction involves a gathering of interested parties at which the promises made in the *real estate sales contract* are kept, or *executed*. In many sales transactions two closings actually take place at this time: the closing of the buyer's loan—the disbursal of mortgage funds by the lender—and the closing of the sale.

As discussed in Chapter 6, a sales contract is the blueprint for the completion of a real estate transaction. Before completing the exchange of documents and funds the parties should assure themselves that the various stipulations of their sales contract have been met.

The buyer will want to be sure that the seller is delivering good title and that the property is in the promised condition. This involves inspecting the title evidence, the deed the seller will give, any documents representing the removal of undesired liens and encumbrances, the survey, the termite report, and any leases if there are tenants on the premises. The seller will want to be sure that the buyer has obtained the stipulated financing and has sufficient funds to complete the sale. Both parties will wish to inspect the closing statement to make sure that all monies involved in the transaction have been accounted for properly. In many areas the parties are usually accompanied by their *attorneys*.

When the parties are satisfied that everything is in order, the exchange is made, and all pertinent documents are then recorded. The documents must be recorded in the correct order to avoid creating a defect in the title. For example, if the seller is paying off an existing loan and the buyer is obtaining a new loan, the seller's satisfaction of mortgage must be recorded before the seller's deed to the buyer. The buyer's new mortgage or deed of trust must then be recorded after the deed, because the buyers cannot pledge the property as security for the loan until they own it.

Where Closings are Held and Who Attends

Face-to-face closings may be held at a number of locations, including the offices of the title insurance company, the lending institution, one of the parties' attorneys, the broker, the county recorder (or other local recording official), or the escrow company. Those attending a closing may include any of the following interested parties:

1. Buyer
2. Seller
3. Real estate licensees (brokers and salespeople)

4. Attorney(s) for the seller and/or buyer

5. Representatives of lending institutions involved with the buyer's new mortgage loan, the buyer's assumption of the seller's existing loan, or the seller's payoff of an existing loan

6. Representative of the title insurance company

Closing agent.   One person usually conducts the proceedings at a closing and calculates the official settlement, or division of incomes and expenses between the parties. In some areas real estate brokers preside, but more commonly the closing agent is an escrow agent, the buyer's or seller's attorney, a representative of the lender, or a representative of a title company. Some title companies and law firms employ paralegal assistants, called *closers,* who conduct all closings for their firms. The closer is the person in such offices who arranges the closing with the parties involved, prepares the closing statements, compares figures with lenders and orders title evidence, surveys and other miscellaneous items needed.

CLOSING IN ESCROW

Although there are a few states where transactions are never closed in escrow, escrow closings are used to some extent in most states, especially in the West.

An *escrow* is a method of closing in which a disinterested third party is authorized to act as escrow agent and coordinate the closing activities. The escrow agent may also be called the *escrow holder.* The escrow agent may be an attorney, a title company, a trust company, an escrow company or the escrow department of a lending institution. While many brokerages do offer escrow services, a broker cannot be a disinterested party in a transaction from which he or she expects to collect a commission. Because the escrow agent is placed in a position of great trust, many states have laws regulating escrow agents and limiting who may serve in this capacity.

The Escrow Procedure

When a transaction will be closed in escrow, the buyer and seller choose an escrow agent and execute escrow instructions to the escrow agent after the sales contract is signed. Once the contract is signed, the broker turns over the earnest money to the escrow agent, who deposits it in a special trust, or escrow, account.

Buyer and seller deposit all pertinent documents and other items with the escrow agent before the specified date of closing. The seller will usually deposit:

1. the *deed* conveying the property to the buyer;
2. title *evidence* (abstract, title insurance policy, or Torrens certificate);
3. existing hazard *insurance* policies;
4. a letter from the lender and an estoppel certificate stating the exact principal remaining if the buyer is assuming the seller's loan;
5. *affidavits of title* (if required);
6. a reduction certificate (payoff statement) if the seller's loan is to be paid off; and
7. other instruments or documents necessary to clear the title or to complete the transaction.

The buyer will deposit:

1. the balance of the *cash needed* to complete the purchase, usually in the form of a certified check;
2. loan documents if the buyer is securing a new loan;
3. proof of hazard insurance, including, where required, flood insurance; and
4. other necessary documents.

The escrow agent is given the authority to examine the title evidence. When marketable title is shown in the name of the buyer and all other conditions of the escrow agreement have been met, the agent is authorized to disburse the purchase price—minus all charges and expenses—to the seller and record the deed and mortgage or deed of trust (if a new loan has been obtained by the purchaser).

If the escrow agent's examination of the title discloses liens against the seller or a lien for which the seller is responsible, the escrow instructions usually provide that a portion of the purchase price can be withheld from the seller and used to pay such liens as are necessary to clear the title so the transaction can be closed.

If the seller cannot clear the title, or if for any reason the sale cannot be consummated and the buyer will not accept the title as is, then the escrow instructions usually provide that the parties be returned to their former status. To accomplish this the purchaser reconveys title to the seller and the escrow agent restores all purchase money to the buyer. Because the escrow depends on specific conditions being met before the transfer becomes binding on the parties, the courts have held that the parties can be reinstated to their former status.

IRS Reporting Requirements

Every real estate transaction must be reported to the Internal Revenue Service by the closing agent on a Form 1099. Information includes the sales price and the seller's social security number.

If the closing agent does not notify the IRS, the responsibility for filing the Form 1099 then falls on the mortgage lender, although the brokers or the parties to the transaction ultimately could be held liable.

Broker's Role at Closing

Depending on the locality, the broker's role at a closing can vary from simply collecting the commission to conducting the proceedings. As discussed earlier in the text, a real estate broker is not authorized to give legal advice or otherwise engage in the practice of law. In some areas of the country, principally in some of the eastern states, this means that a broker's job is essentially finished when the sales contract is signed; at that point the attorneys take over. Even so, a broker's service generally continues after the contract is signed in that the broker advises the parties on practical matters and makes sure all the details are taken care of so that the closing can proceed smoothly. In this capacity the broker might make arrangements for such items as title evidence, surveys, appraisals, termite inspections, and repairs or might recommend sources of these services to the parties.

Lender's Interest in Closing

Whether a buyer is obtaining new financing or assuming the seller's existing loan, the lender wants to protect its security interest in the property—to make sure that the buyer is getting good, marketable title and that tax and insurance payments are maintained so that there will be no liens with greater priority than the mortgage lien and the insurance will be paid up if the property is damaged or destroyed. For this reason the lender will frequently require a title insurance policy; a fire and hazard insurance policy, with receipt for the premium; additional information, such as a survey, a termite or other inspection report, or a certificate of occupancy (for newly constructed buildings); establishment of a reserve, or escrow, account for tax and insurance payments; and possibly representation by its own attorney at the closing.

RESPA Requirements

The federal *Real Estate Settlement Procedures Act (RESPA)* was created to ensure that the buyer and seller in a residential real estate sale or transfer have knowledge of all settlement costs. In this context residential real estate includes one-family to four-family homes, cooperatives, and condominiums. *RESPA requirements apply when the purchase is financed by a federally related mortgage loan.* Federally related loans include those made by banks, savings and loan associations, or other lenders whose deposits are insured by federal agencies (FDIC); those insured by the FHA or guaranteed by the VA; those administered by HUD; and those intended to be sold by the lender to Fannie Mae, Ginnie Mae, or Freddie Mac.

RESPA regulations apply only to transactions involving *new first mortgage loans.* A transaction financed solely by seller financing an installment contract (land contract, contract for deed) or the buyer's assumption of the seller's existing loan would *not* be covered by RESPA unless the terms of the assumed loan are modified or the lender imposes charges of more than $50 for the assumption. When a transaction is covered by RESPA, the following requirements must be complied with:

1. *Special information booklet:* Lenders must give a copy of the HUD booklet *Settlement Costs and You* to every person from whom they receive or for whom they prepare a loan application. This booklet provides the borrower with general information about settlement (closing) costs and explains the various RESPA provisions, including a line-by-line discussion of the Uniform Settlement Statement (see item 3).

2. *Good-faith estimate of settlement costs:* At the time of the loan application, or within three business days, the lender must provide the borrower with a good-faith estimate of the settlement costs the borrower is likely to incur. This estimate may be a specific figure or a range of costs based on comparable past transactions in the area. In addition, if the lender requires use of a particular attorney or title insurance company to conduct the closing, the lender must state whether it has any business relationship with that firm and must estimate the charges for this service.

3. *Uniform Settlement Statement (HUD Form 1):* RESPA provides that loan closing information must be prepared on a special HUD form, the **Uniform Settlement Statement (HUD-1)** (Figure 15.1), designed to detail all financial particulars of a transaction. This form can be found on page 318. The completed statement must itemize all charges imposed by the lender. Charges incurred by the buyer and seller, contracted for separately and outside the closing, do not have to be disclosed. Items paid for prior to the closing must be marked clearly as such on the statement and are omitted from the totals. This statement must be made available for inspection by the borrower *at or before* the closing. Upon the borrower's request the closing agent must permit the borrower to inspect the settlement statement, to the extent that the figures are available, one business day before the closing. The Uniform Settlement Statement may be altered to allow for local custom, and certain lines may be deleted if they do not apply in the area.

4. *Prohibition against kickbacks:* RESPA explicitly prohibits the payment of kickbacks, or unearned fees, such as when an insurance agency pays a kickback to a lender for referring one of the lender's recent customers to the agency. This prohibition does *not* include fee splitting between cooperating brokers or members of multiple-listing services, brokerage referral arrangements, or the division of a commission between a broker and his or her salespeople.

RESPA is administered by the U.S. Department of Housing and Urban Development (HUD).

THE TITLE PROCEDURE

The principle of *caveat emptor* requires the purchaser and the purchaser's lender to assure themselves that the seller's property and title comply with the contract requirements. The sales contract usually includes time limitations for the parties to obtain and present title evidence and remove any objections to the title. A contract that includes the provision "time is of the essence" expresses the agreement of the parties that all *time limitations are to be met as stated.*

The seller is usually required to show proof of ownership by producing a current abstract or *title commitment* from the title insurance company. When an abstract of title is used, the purchaser's attorney examines it and issues an opinion of title. This opinion, like the title commitment, sets

forth the status of the seller's title, showing liens, encumbrances, easements, conditions, or restrictions that appear on the record and to which
the seller's title is subject.

On the date when the sale is actually completed (the date of delivery of
the deed), the buyer has a title commitment or an abstract that was issued
several days or weeks before the closing. For this reason the title or abstract company is usually required to make two searches of the public
records. The first shows the status of the seller's title on the date of the
sales contract; the seller usually pays the charges for this report. The second search is made after the closing and covers the date when the deed is
recorded to the purchaser; the purchaser generally pays to "bring the title
down" to the closing date.

In this later search the seller is usually required to execute an *affidavit of
title*. This is a sworn statement in which the seller assures the title insurance company (and the buyer) that since the date of the title examination
there have been no judgments, bankruptcies, or divorces involving the
seller, no unrecorded deeds or contracts made, no repairs or improvements that have not been paid for, and no defects in the title that the seller
knows of. The seller also assures that he or she is in possession of the
premises. This form is always required by the title insurance company before it will issue an owner's policy, particularly an extended-coverage policy, to the buyer. Through this affidavit the title insurance company
obtains the right to sue the seller if his or her statements in the affidavit
prove incorrect.

In some areas where real estate sales transactions are customarily closed
through an escrow the escrow instructions usually include provision for
an extended-coverage policy to be issued to the buyer as of the date of
closing. In such cases there is no need for the seller to execute an affidavit of title.

Checking the Premises

It is important for the buyer to inspect the property to determine the interests of any parties in possession or other interests that cannot be determined from inspecting the public record. A *survey* is frequently required
so that the purchaser will know the location and size of the property. The
contract will specify who is to pay for this. It is usual for the survey to
"spot" the location of all buildings, driveways, fences, and other improvements located primarily on the premises being purchased, as well as any
such improvements located on adjoining property that may encroach on

the premises being bought. The survey also sets out, in full, any existing easements and encroachments.

Shortly before the closing takes place the buyer will usually make a *final inspection* of the property (often called the *walk-through*) with the broker. Through this inspection the buyer can make sure that necessary repairs have been made, that the property has been well maintained (both inside and outside), that all fixtures are in place, and that there has been no un-authorized removal or alteration of any part of the improvements.

Releasing Existing Liens

When the purchaser is paying cash or is obtaining a new loan to purchase the property, the seller's existing loan is paid in full and released of record. To know the exact amount required to pay the existing loan the seller secures a current *payoff statement* from the lender. This payoff statement sets forth the unpaid amount of principal, interest due through the date of payment, the fee for issuing the certificate of satisfaction or re-lease deed, credits (if any) for tax and insurance reserves, and penalties that may be due because the loan is being prepaid before its maturity. The same procedure would be followed for any other liens that must be re-leased before the buyer takes title.

When the buyer is assuming the seller's existing loan, the buyer will want to know the exact balance of the loan as of the closing date. In some areas it is customary for the buyer to obtain a *mortgage reduction certifi-cate* from the lender, stating the exact balance due and the last interest payment made.

PREPARATION OF CLOSING STATEMENTS

A typical real estate transaction involves expenses for both parties in addi-tion to the purchase price. These include items prepaid by the seller for which he or she must be reimbursed (such as insurance premiums and prepaid taxes) and items of expense the seller has incurred but the buyer will be billed for (such as mortgage interest paid in arrears). The financial responsibility for these items must be prorated (adjusted or divided) be-tween the buyer and the seller. In closing a transaction it is customary to account for all these items by preparing a written statement to determine how much money the buyer needs and how much the seller will net after expenses. There are many different formats of closing statements, or set-tlement statements, but all are designed to achieve the same results.

The broker should possess the necessary knowledge to prepare statements to give the seller an accurate estimate of sale costs. In addition, the buyer must be prepared with the proper amount of money to complete the purchase, and again, the broker should be able to assist by making a reasonably accurate estimate.

How the Closing Statement Works

The completion of a **closing statement** involves an accounting of the parties' debits and credits. A **debit** is a charge, an amount that the party being debited owes and must pay at the closing. A **credit** is an amount entered in a person's favor—either an amount that the party being credited has already paid, an amount that he or she must be reimbursed for, or an amount the buyer promises to pay in the form of a loan.

To determine the amount the buyer needs at the closing the buyer's debits are totaled—any expenses and prorated amounts for items prepaid by the seller are added to the purchase price. Then the buyer's credits are totaled. These would include the earnest money (already paid), the balance of the loan the buyer is obtaining or assuming, and the seller's share of any prorated items that the buyer will pay in the future. Finally the total of the buyer's credits is subtracted from the total amount the buyer owes (debits) to arrive at the actual amount of cash the buyer must bring to the closing. Usually the buyer brings a cashier's check or a certified check.

A similar procedure is followed to determine how much money the seller will actually receive. The seller's debits and credits are each totaled. The credits would include the purchase price, plus the buyer's share of any prorated items that the seller has prepaid. The seller's debits would include expenses, the seller's share of prorated items to be paid later by the buyer, and the balance of any mortgage loan or other lien that the seller is paying off. Finally the total of the seller's charges is subtracted from the total credits to arrive at the amount the seller will receive.

Expenses

In addition to the payment of the sales price and the proration of taxes, interest, and the like, a number of other expenses and charges may be involved in a real estate transaction.

Broker's commission.   The broker's commission is usually paid by the seller because the broker is usually the seller's agent. When the buyer has employed the broker, the buyer pays the commission, unless other arrangements have been made.

Attorney's fees.   If either of the parties' attorneys will be paid from the closing proceeds, that party will be charged with the expense in the closing statement.

Recording expenses.   The charges for recording different types of documents vary widely. These charges are established by law and are based on the number of pages included in the instrument.

The *seller* usually pays for recording charges (filing fees) necessary to clear all defects and furnish the purchaser with a marketable title in accordance with the contract. Items customarily charged to the seller would include the recording of release deeds or satisfaction of mortgages, quitclaim deeds, affidavits, and satisfaction of mechanic's lien claims. The *purchaser* pays for recording charges incidental to the actual transfer of title. Usually such items include recording the deed that conveys title to the purchaser and a mortgage or deed of trust executed by the purchaser.

Transfer tax.   Most states require some form of transfer tax, conveyance fee, or tax stamps on real estate conveyances. This expense is most often borne by the seller, although customs vary.

Title expenses.   The responsibility for title expenses varies according to local custom. In most areas the seller is required to furnish evidence of good title and pay for the title search. If the buyer's attorney inspects the evidence or if the buyer purchases title insurance policies, the buyer is charged for these expenses.

Loan fees.   When the purchaser is securing a new loan to finance the purchase, the lender will ordinarily charge a loan origination fee of 1 percent of the loan. The fee is usually paid by the purchaser at the time the transaction is closed. If the buyer is assuming the seller's existing financing, there may be an assumption fee.

The seller also may be charged fees by a lender if provided for in the contract. If the buyer finances the purchase with a VA loan, the seller may be required to pay discount points. Also, under the terms of some loans the seller may be required to pay a prepayment charge or penalty for paying off the existing loan in advance of its due date.

Tax reserves and insurance reserves (escrows or impound accounts).   A *reserve* is a sum of money set aside to be used later for a particular purpose. The mortgage lender usually requires the borrower to establish and maintain a reserve so that the borrower will have sufficient funds to pay real estate taxes and renew hazard insurance policies when these items become due. To set up the reserve the borrower is required to make a lump-sum payment to the lender when the mortgage money is paid out (usually at the time of closing). Thereafter the borrower is required to pay into the reserve an amount equal to one month's portion of the *estimated* tax and insurance premium as part of the monthly payment made to the mortgage company (a PITI payment).

Appraisal fees.   Either the seller or the purchaser pays the appraisal fees, depending on who orders the appraisal. When the buyer obtains a mortgage, it is customary for the lender to require an appraisal, which the buyer pays for.

Survey fees.   The purchaser who obtains new mortgage financing customarily pays the survey fees. In some cases the sales contract may require the seller to furnish a survey.

Additional fees.   An FHA borrower owes a lump sum for partial payment of the mortgage insurance premium (MIP). A VA mortgagor pays the VA funding fee directly to the VA at closing. If a conventional loan carries private mortgage insurance, the buyer prepays one year's insurance premium at closing.

Prorations

Most closings involve the division of financial responsibility between the buyer and seller for such items as loan interest, taxes, rents, and fuel and utility bills. These allowances are called **prorations.** Prorations are necessary to ensure that expenses are divided fairly between the seller and the buyer. For example, the seller may owe current taxes that have not been billed; the buyer would want this settled at the closing. In states where taxes must be paid in advance the seller would be entitled to a rebate at the closing. If the buyer assumes the seller's existing mortgage or deed of trust, the seller usually owes the buyer an allowance for accrued interest through the date of closing.

Accrued items are items to be prorated (such as water bills and interest on an assumed mortgage) that are owed by the seller but eventually will be paid by the buyer. The seller therefore gives the buyer credit for these items at closing.

Prepaid items are items to be prorated—such as fuel oil in a tank—that have been prepaid by the seller but not fully earned (not fully used up). They are therefore credits to the seller.

General rules for prorating.   The rules or customs governing the computation of prorations for the closing of a real estate sale vary widely from state to state. In many states the real estate boards and the bar association have established closing rules and procedures. In some cases these rules and procedures control closings for the entire state; in others they merely affect closings within a given city, town, or county.

Here are some general rules to guide you in studying the closing procedure and preparing the closing statement:

1. In most states the seller owns the property on the day of closing, and prorations or apportionments are usually made *to and including the day of closing.* In a few states, however, it is provided specifically that the buyer owns the property on the closing date and that adjustments shall be made as of the day preceding the day on which title is closed.

2. Mortgage interest, real estate taxes, insurance premiums, and similar expenses are usually computed by using *360 days in a year and 30 days in a month.* However, the rules in some areas provide for computing prorations on the basis of the actual number of days in the calendar month and year of closing. (The methods for calculating prorations are explained in full later in the chapter.)

3. Accrued *real estate* taxes that are not yet due are usually prorated at the closing (see the following section). When the amount of the current real estate tax cannot be determined definitely, the proration is usually based on the last obtainable tax bill. *Special assessments* for such municipal improvements as sewers, water mains, or street paving are usually paid in annual installments over several years. As a general rule the municipality charges the property owner annual interest on the outstanding balance of future installments. In a sales transaction the seller pays the current installment and the buyer assumes all future installments. *The special assessment installment is generally not prorated at the closing;* some buyers, however, insist that the seller allow them a credit for the seller's share of the interest to the closing date.

4. *Rents* are usually adjusted on the basis of the *actual* number of days in the month of closing. It is customary for the seller to

receive the rents for the day of closing and to pay all expenses for that day. If any rents for the current month are uncollected when the sale is closed, the buyer will often agree by a separate letter to collect the rents if possible and remit the pro-rata share to the seller.

5. *Security deposits* made by tenants to cover the last month's rent of the lease or to cover the cost of repairing damage caused by the tenant are generally transferred intact by the seller to the buyer. Some leases may require the tenant's consent to such a transfer of the deposit.

Real estate taxes.   Proration of real estate taxes will vary widely, depending on how the taxes are paid in the area where the real estate is located. In some states real estate taxes are paid *in advance:* if the tax year runs from January 1 to December 31, taxes for the coming year are due on January 1. In that case the seller, who has prepaid a year's taxes, should be reimbursed for the portion of the year remaining after the buyer takes ownership of the tax-paid-up property. In other areas taxes are paid *in arrears,* on December 31 for the year just ended. In that case the buyer should be credited by the seller for the time the seller was occupying the property. Sometimes taxes are due during the tax year, partly in arrears and partly in advance; sometimes they are payable in installments. To compound the confusion city, state, school, and other property taxes may start their tax years in different months. Whatever the case may be in a particular transaction, the licensee should understand how the taxes are to be prorated.

Mortgage loan interest.   On almost every mortgage loan the interest is paid in *arrears,* so buyers and sellers must understand that the mortgage payment due on June 1, for example, includes interest due for the month of May. Thus the buyer who assumes a mortgage on May 31 and makes the June payment will be paying for the time the seller occupied the property and should be credited with a month's interest. On the other hand, the buyer who places a new mortgage loan on May 31 may be pleasantly surprised to hear that he or she will not need to make a mortgage payment until a month later.

Accounting for Credits and Charges

The items that must be accounted for in the closing statement fall into two general categories: prorations or other amounts due to either the buyer or seller (credit to) and paid for by the other party (debit to) and expenses or items paid by the seller or buyer (debit only). In the lists below the items marked by an asterisk (*) are not prorated; they are entered in full as listed.

Items credited to the buyer and debited to the seller.   These items include:

1. the buyer's earnest money*;
2. the unpaid principal balance of an outstanding mortgage loan being assumed by the buyer*;
3. interest on an existing assumed mortgage not yet paid (accrued);
4. the unearned portion of current rent collected in advance;
5. an earned janitor's salary (and sometimes vacation allowance);
6. tenants' security deposits*;
7. a purchase-money mortgage; and
8. unpaid water and other utility bills.

The *buyer's earnest money,* while credited to the buyer, *is not usually debited to the seller.* The buyer receives a credit because he or she has already paid that amount toward the purchase price. Under the usual sales contract the money is held by the broker or attorney until the settlement, when it will be included as part of the total amount due the seller. If the seller is paying off an existing loan and the buyer is obtaining a new one, these two items are accounted for with a debit only to the seller for the amount of the payoff and a credit only to the buyer for the amount of the new loan.

Items credited to the seller and debited to the buyer.   These items include:

1. the sales price*;
2. any fuel oil on hand, usually figured at current market price (prepaid);
3. an insurance and tax reserve (if any) when an outstanding mortgage loan is being assumed by buyer (prepaid);
4. a refund to the seller of prepaid water charge and similar expenses; and
5. any portion of general real estate tax paid in advance.

Accounting for expenses.   Expenses paid out of the closing proceeds are debited only to the party making the payment. Occasionally an expense item—such as an escrow fee, a settlement fee, or a transfer tax—may be shared by the buyer and the seller, and each party will be debited for one-half the expense.

THE ARITHMETIC OF PRORATING

Accurate prorating involves four considerations: what the item being prorated is; whether it is an **accrued item** that requires the determination of an earned amount; whether it is a **prepaid item** that requires the unearned amount—a refund to the seller—to be determined; and what arithmetic processes must be used. The information contained in the previous sections will assist in answering the first three questions.

The computation of a proration involves identifying a yearly charge for the item to be prorated, then dividing by 12 to determine a monthly charge for the item. It is usually also necessary to identify a daily charge for the item by dividing the monthly charge by the number of days in the month. These smaller portions are then multiplied by the number of months and/or days in the prorated time period to determine the accrued or unearned amount that will be figured in the settlement.

Using this general principle, there are two methods of calculating prorations:

1. The *yearly charge is divided by a 360-day year* (commonly called a banking year), or 12 months of 30 days each.

2. The *yearly charge is divided by 365* (366 in a leap year) to determine the daily charge. Then the actual number of days in the proration period is determined, and this number is multiplied by the daily charge.

The final proration figure will vary slightly, depending on which computation method is used. The final figure will also vary according to the number of decimal places to which the division is carried. *All of the computations in this chapter are computed by carrying the division to three decimal places.* The third decimal place is rounded off to cents only after the final proration figure is determined.

Accrued Items

When the real estate tax is levied for the calendar year and is payable during that year or in the following year, the accrued portion is for the period from January 1 to the date of closing (or to the day before the closing in states where the sale date is excluded). If the current tax bill has not yet been issued, the parties must agree on an estimated amount based on the previous year's bill and any known changes in assessment or tax levy for the current year.

For example, assume a sale is to be closed on September 17, current real estate taxes of $1,200 are to be prorated accordingly, and a 360-day year is being used. The accrued period, then, is eight months and 17 days. First determine the prorated cost of the real estate tax per month and day:

$$\frac{\$100 \text{ per month}}{12 \,) \, \$1,200} \qquad \frac{3.333 \text{ per day}}{30 \,) \, \$100.000}$$
months   days

Next multiply these figures by the accrued period and add the totals to determine the prorated real estate tax:

$$\begin{array}{ccc} \$100 & \$\ 3.333 & \$800.000 \\ \underline{\times\ 8}\text{ months} & \underline{\times\ 17}\text{ days} & \underline{+\ 56.661} \\ \$800 & \$56.661 & \$856.661 \end{array}$$

Thus the accrued real estate tax for eight months and 17 days is $856.66 (rounded off to two decimal places after the final computation). This amount represents the seller's accrued *earned* tax; it will be a *credit to the buyer* and a *debit to the seller* on the closing statement.

To compute this proration using the actual number of days in the accrued period, the following method would be used: The accrued period from January 1 to September 17 runs 260 days (January's 31 days plus February's 28 days, and so on). A tax bill of $1,200 ÷ 365 days = $3.288 per day; $3.288 × 260 days = $854.880, or $854.88.

Prepaid Items

Assume that the water is billed in advance by the city without using a meter. The six months' billing is $8 for the period ending October 31. The sale is to be closed on August 3. Because the water is paid to October 31, the prepaid time must be computed. Using a 30-day basis, the time period is the 27 days left in August plus two full months: $8 ÷ 6 =

$1.333 per month. For one day, divide $1.333 by 30, which equals $0.044 per day. The prepaid period is two months and 27 days, so:

$$
\begin{aligned}
27 \text{ days} \times \$0.044 &= \$1.188 \\
2 \text{ months} \times \$1.333 &= \$2.666 \\
&= \overline{\$3.854}, \text{ or } \$3.85
\end{aligned}
$$

This is a prepaid item and is *credited to the seller* and *debited to the buyer* on the closing statement.

To figure this on the basis of the actual days in the *month* of closing, the following process would be used:

$$
\begin{aligned}
\$1.333 \text{ per month} \div 31 \text{ days in August} &= \$0.043 \text{ per day} \\
\text{August 4 through August 31} &= 28 \text{ days} \\
28 \text{ days} \times \$0.043 &= \$1.204 \\
2 \text{ months} \times \$1.333 &= \$2.666 \\
\$1.204 + \$2.666 &= \$3.870, \text{ or } \$3.87
\end{aligned}
$$

SAMPLE CLOSING STATEMENTS

As stated previously, there are many possible formats for settlement computations. The remaining portion of this chapter illustrates two sample transactions, one using the HUD Uniform Settlement Statement in Figure 15.1 and the other using separate buyer's and seller's closing statements.

Uniform Settlement Statement

Basic information of offer and sale.   John and Joanne Iuro listed their home at 3045 North Racine Avenue in Riverdale, Illinois, with the Open Door Real Estate Company. The listing price was $118,500, and possession could be given within two weeks after all parties had signed the contract. Under the terms of the listing agreement the sellers agreed to pay the broker a commission of 6 percent of the sales price.

On May 18, the Open Door Real Estate Company submitted a contract offer to the Iuros from Brook Redemann, a bachelor, presently residing at 22 King Court, Riverdale. Redemann offered $115,000, with earnest money/down payment of $23,000 and the remaining $92,000 of the purchase price to be obtained through a new conventional loan. No private mortgage insurance will be necessary as the loan-to-value ratio will not exceed 80 percent. The Iuros signed the contract on May 29. Closing was set for June 15 at the office of the Open Door Real Estate Company, 720 Main Street, Riverdale.

The unpaid balance of the Iuros' mortgage as of June 1, 19___, will be $57,700. Payments are $680 per month with interest at 11 percent per annum on the unpaid balance.

The sellers submitted evidence of title in the form of a title insurance binder at a cost of $10. The title insurance policy paid by the sellers at the time of closing cost an additional $540, including $395 for lender's coverage and $145 for homeowner's coverage. Recording charges of $20 were paid for the recording of two instruments to clear defects in the sellers' title, and state transfer tax in the amount of $115 ($0.50 per $500 of sale price or fraction thereof) were affixed to the deed. In addition, the sellers must pay an attorney's fee of $400 for preparation of the deed and for legal representation; this amount will be paid from the closing proceeds.

The buyer must pay an attorney's fee of $300 for examination of the title evidence and legal representation, as well as $10 to record the deed. These amounts will also be paid from the closing proceeds.

Real estate taxes in Riverdale are paid in arrears. Taxes for this year, estimated at last year's figure of $1,725, have not been paid. According to the contract, prorations are to be made on the basis of 30 days in a month.

Computing the prorations and charges. Following are illustrations of the various steps in computing the prorations and other amounts to be included in the settlement thus far.

1. *Closing date:* June 15

2. *Commission:* 6% × $115,000 (sales price) = $6,900

3. *Sellers' mortgage interest:*
   11% × $57,700 (principal due after June 1 payment) = $6,347 interest per year
   $6,347 ÷ 360 days = $17.631 interest per day
   15 days of accrued interest to be paid by the sellers
   15 × $17.631 = $264.465, or $264.47 interest owed by the sellers
   $57,700 + $264.465 = $57,964.47 payoff of sellers' mortgage

4. *Real estate taxes* (estimated at $1,725):
   $1,725.00 ÷ 12 months = $143.75 per month
   $143.75 ÷ 30 days = $4.792 per day

Figure 15.1   RESPA Uniform Settlement Statement

A. **SETTLEMENT STATEMENT** U.S. DEPARTMENT OF HOUSING AND URBAN DEVELOPMENT		
HUD-1 Rev. 3/86		OMB NO. 2502-0265 (Exp. 12-31-86)

B. TYPE OF LOAN

1. ☐ FHA	2. ☐ FmHA	3. ☒ CONV. UNINS.	6. File Number	7. Loan Number	8.Mortgage Insurance Claim Case Number
4. ☐ VA	5. ☐ CONV. INS.				

C. NOTE: *This form is furnished to give you a statement of actual settlement costs. Amounts paid to and by the settlement agent are shown. Items marked "(p.o.c.)" were paid outside the closing; they are shown here for informational purposes and are not included in the totals.*

D. NAME AND ADDRESS OF BORROWER:	E. NAME AND ADDRESS OF SELLER:	F. NAME AND ADDRESS OF LENDER:
Brook Redemann 22 King Court Riverdale, Illinois	John and Joanne Iuro 3045 North Racine Avenue Riverdale, Illinois	Thrift Federal Savings 1100 Fountain Plaza Riverdale, Illinois

G. PROPERTY LOCATION: 3045 North Racine Avenue Riverdale, Illinois	H. SETTLEMENT AGENT: Open Door Real Estate Company PLACE OF SETTLEMENT: Open Door Real Estate Company 720 Main Street, Riverdale, Illinois	I. SETTLEMENT DATE: June 15, 1988

J. SUMMARY OF BORROWER'S TRANSACTION		K. SUMMARY OF SELLER'S TRANSACTION	
100. GROSS AMOUNT DUE FROM BORROWER:		**400. GROSS AMOUNT DUE TO SELLER:**	
101. Contract sales price	$115,000.00	401. Contract sales price	$115,000.00
102. Personal property		402. Personal property	
103. Settlement charges to borrower (line 1400)	5,075.84	403.	
104.		404.	
105.		405.	
Adjustments for items paid by seller in advance		*Adjustments for items paid by seller in advance*	
106. City/town taxes to		406. City/town taxes to	
107. County taxes to		407. County taxes to	
108. Assessments to		408. Assessments to	
109.		409.	
110.		410.	
111.		411.	
112.		412.	
120. GROSS AMOUNT DUE FROM BORROWER	$120,075.84	**420. GROSS AMOUNT DUE TO SELLER**	$115,000.00
200. AMOUNTS PAID BY OR IN BEHALF OF BORROWER:		**500. REDUCTIONS IN AMOUNT DUE TO SELLER:**	
201. Deposit or earnest money	23,000.00	501. Excess deposit (see instructions)	
202. Principal amount of new loan(s)	92,000.00	502. Settlement charges to seller (line 1400)	8,080.00
203. Existing loan(s) taken subject to		503. Existing loan(s) taken subject to	
204.		504. Payoff of first mortgage loan	57,964.47
205.		505. Payoff of second mortgage loan	
206.		506.	
207.		507.	
208.		508.	
209.		509.	
Adjustments for items unpaid by seller		*Adjustments for items unpaid by seller*	
210. City/town taxes to		510. City/town taxes to	
211. County taxes 1/1/88 to 6/15/88	790.63	511. County taxes 1/1/88 to 6/15/88	790.63
212. Assessments to		512. Assessments to	
213.		513.	
214.		514.	
215.		515.	
216.		516.	
217.		517.	
218.		518.	
219.		519.	
220. TOTAL PAID BY/FOR BORROWER	$115,790.63	**520. TOTAL REDUCTION AMOUNT DUE SELLER**	$ 66,835.10
300. CASH AT SETTLEMENT FROM/TO BORROWER		**600. CASH AT SETTLEMENT TO/FROM SELLER**	
301. Gross amount due from borrower (line 120)	120,075.84	601. Gross amount due to seller (line 420)	115,000.00
302. Less amounts paid by/for borrower (line 220)	(115,790.63)	602. Less reductions in amount due seller (line 520)	(66,835.10)
303. CASH (☐ FROM) (☐ TO) BORROWER	$ 4,285.21	**603. CASH (☐ TO) (☐ FROM) SELLER**	$ 48,164.90

I have carefully reviewed the HUD-1 Settlement Statement and to the best of my knowledge and belief, it is a true and accurate statement of all receipts and disbursements made on my account or by me in this transaction. I further certify that I have received a copy of the HUD-1 Settlement Statement.

_____   _____
Borrower   Seller

_____   _____
Borrower   Seller

The HUD-1 Settlement Statement which I have prepared is a true and accurate account of this transaction. I have caused or will cause the funds to be disbursed in accordance with this statement.

_____   _____
Settlement Agent   Date

Warning: It is a crime to knowingly make false statements to the United States on this or any other similar form. Penalties upon conviction can include a fine and imprisonment. For details see: Title 18 U.S. Code Section 1001 and Section 1010.

2128 (6-86) 41b

Figure 15.1   (continued)

– 2 –

L. SETTLEMENT CHARGES		PAID FROM BORROWER'S FUNDS AT SETTLEMENT	PAID FROM SELLER'S FUNDS AT SETTLEMENT
700. TOTAL SALES/BROKER'S COMMISSION based on price $ 115,000 @ 6 % =$6,900.00			
Division of Commission (line 700) as follows:			
701. $ to			
702. $ to			
703. Commission paid at Settlement			$6,900.00
704.			
800. ITEMS PAYABLE IN CONNECTION WITH LOAN			
801. Loan Origination Fee %		$ 920.00	
802. Loan Discount 2 %		$1,840.00	
803. Appraisal Fee $125.00 to Swift Appraisal		POC	
804. Credit Report $ 60.00 to ACME Credit Bureau		POC	
805. Lender's Inspection Fee			
806. Mortgage Insurance Application Fee to			
807. Assumption Fee			
808. Application Fee			
809. Wholesale Interest Differential Fee			
810. Underwriting Fee			
811. Buydown Fee			
812. Commitment Fee			
813.			
814. Messenger Service			
815. Shortfall			
816.			
817.			
818.			
819.			
900. ITEMS REQUIRED BY LENDER TO BE PAID IN ADVANCE			
901. Interest from 6/16/88 to 6/30/88 @ $ 25.556 /day		383.34	
902. Mortgage Insurance Premium for months to			
903. Hazard Insurance Premium for 1 years to Hite Insurance Co.		345.00	
904. One-Time FHA Insurance Premium			
905. VA Funding Fee			
906.			
907.			
1000. RESERVES DEPOSITED WITH LENDER			
1001. Hazard insurance 3 months @ $ 28.75 per month		86.25	
1002. Mortgage insurance months @ $ per month			
1003. City property taxes months @ $ per month			
1004. County property taxes 7 months @ $ 143.75 per month		1,006.25	
1005. Annual assessments months @ $ per month			
1006. months @ $ per month			
1007. months @ $ per month			
1008. months @ $ per month			
1100. TITLE CHARGES			
1101. Settlement or closing fee to			
1102. Abstract or title search to			
1103. Title examination to			
1104. Title insurance binder to			10.00
1105. Document preparation to			
1106. Notary fees to			
1107. Attorney's fees to		300.00	400.00
(includes above items numbers:)			
1108. Title insurance to			540.00
(includes above items numbers:)			
1109. Lender's coverage $ 395.00			
1110. Owner's coverage $ 145.00			
1111. Tax Service Contract Fee to			
1112. Amortization Schedule to			
1113.			
1114.			
1115.			
1116.			
1200. GOVERNMENT RECORDING AND TRANSFER CHARGES			
1201. Recording Fees: Deed $ 10.00 ; Mortgage $ 10.00 ; Releases $ 10.00		20.00	10.00
1202. City/county tax/stamps: Deed $; Mortgage $			115.00
1203. State tax/Stamps: Deed $ 115.00 ; Mortgage $			20.00
1204. Record two documents to clear title			
1205.			
1300. ADDITIONAL SETTLEMENT CHARGES			
1301. Survey to		175.00	
1302. Pest Inspection to			85.00
1303.			
1304.			
1305.			
1400. TOTAL SETTLEMENT CHARGES (enter on lines 103, Section J and 502, Section K)		$5,075.84	$8,080.00

HUD-1 Rev. 5/76

The earned period is from January 1 to and including June 15, and equals 5 months, 15 days:

$143.75 × 5 months = $718.750
$4.792 × 15 days   = $ 71.880
                       $790.630, or $790.63 seller owes buyer

5. *Transfer tax* ($0.50 per $500 of consideration or fraction thereof):
$115,000 ÷ $500 = $230
$230 × $0.50 = $115.00 transfer tax owed by sellers

The Iuros' loan payoff is $57,964.47, and they must pay an additional $10 to record the mortgage release as well as $85 for a pest inspection. Buyer Redemann's new loan is from Thrift Federal Savings, 1100 Fountain Plaza, Riverdale, in the amount of $92,000 at 10 percent interest. In connection with this loan he will be charged $125 to have the property appraised by Swift Appraisal and $60 for a credit report from the Acme Credit Bureau. (Because appraisal and credit reports are performed prior to loan approval, they are paid at the time of loan application, regardless of whether or not the transaction eventually closes. These items will be noted as POC—paid outside closing—on the settlement statement.) In addition, Redemann will pay for interest on his loan for the remainder of the month of closing—15 days at $25.556 per day, or $383.34. His first full payment (including July's interest) will be due August 1. He must deposit $1,006.25, or $7/12$ of the anticipated county real estate tax (of $1,725) into a tax reserve account. A one-year hazard insurance premium at $3 per $1,000 of appraised value ($115,000 ÷ $1,000 × 3 = $345) is paid in advance to Hite Insurance Company. An insurance reserve to cover the premium for three months is deposited with the lender. Redemann will have to pay an additional $10 to record the mortgage and $175 for a survey. He will also pay a loan origination fee of $920 and two discount points.

The Uniform Settlement Statement is divided into 12 sections. The most important information is included in Sections J, K, and L. The borrower's and seller's summaries (J and K) are very similar to one another and are used as are the other formats of closing statements illustrated in this chapter. For example, in Section J, the summary of the borrower's transaction, the buyer/borrower's debits are listed in lines 100 through 112 and totaled on line 120 (gross amount due from borrower). The total of the settlement costs itemized in Section L of the statement is entered on line 103 as one of the buyer's charges. The buyer's credits are listed on lines 201 through 219 and totaled on line 220 (total paid by/for borrower). Then the buyer's credits are subtracted from the charges to arrive at the cash due from the borrower to close (line 303).

In Section K, the summary of the seller's transaction, the seller's credits are entered on lines 400 through 412 and totaled on line 420 (gross amount due to seller). The seller's debits are entered on lines 501 through 519 and totaled on line 520 (total reduction amount due seller). The total of the seller's settlement charges is on line 502. Then the debits are subtracted from the credits to arrive at the cash due to the sellers in order to close (line 603).

Section L is a summary of all the settlement charges for the transaction; the buyer's expenses are listed in one column and the seller's expenses in the other. If an attorney's fee is listed as a lump sum in line 1107, the settlement should list by line number the services that were included in that total fee.

Buyer's and Seller's Closing Statements

Figure 15.2 details a buyer's closing statement and Figure 15.3 a seller's closing statement for the same transaction. The property is being purchased for $89,500, with $49,500 down and the seller taking back a mortgage for $40,000. Closing takes place on August 12.

Prorations.   Taxes in this area are paid in advance. The buyer is taking over a house on which taxes have been paid, in one case until the end of the year. The buyer will therefore reimburse the seller for the time the buyer will be living in a tax-paid house. Specifically, the seller paid city and school taxes of $1,176.35 for the tax year that started July 1 and will receive a large portion of that back as a credit from the buyer. County taxes of $309.06 were paid January I for the year ahead, so the buyer will also credit the seller for the four months and 18 days remaining in the year, an adjustment of $118.52.

The buyer owes the seller ("total seller's credits") the purchase price plus unearned taxes, for a total of $90,657.68. Toward this sum the buyer receives credit for an earnest money deposit of $500 in a broker's escrow account. (The seller's attorney and the broker will later take this sum into consideration when the commission is paid.) The buyer also receives credit for the $40,000 bond and mortgage given to the seller at closing. The buyer therefore gives the seller cash (or a certified check) for the remaining sum, $50,157.68.

Figure 15.2   Buyer's Closing Statement, Closing on August 12

SELLER'S CREDITS

Sale Price _____ $ 89,500.00

ADJUSTMENT OF TAXES

School Tax 7/1/   to 6/30/   Amount $ 1176.35   Adj. 10 mos. 18 days $ 1,039.16

City, School Tax 7/1/   to 6/30/   Amount $_____ Adj. _____ mos. _____ days $_____

County Tax 19____   Amount $ 309.06   Adj. 4 mos. 18 days $ 118.52

Village Tax 6/1/   to 5/31/   Amount $_____ Adj. _____ mos. _____ days $_____

City Tax Embellishments   Amount $_____ Adj. _____ mos. _____ days $_____

Total Seller's Credits $ 90,657.68

PURCHASER'S CREDITS

Deposit with Nothnagle _____ $ 500.00

(Assumed) (New) Mortgage with Seller $480.07 p/m $ 40,000.00

beg. 9-12-   , 12% int., 15 yrs. $_____

$_____

$_____

$_____

$_____

$_____

$_____

Total Purchaser's Credits $ 40,500.00

Cash (Rec'd) (Paid) at Closing $ 50,157.68

EXPENSES OF PURCHASER		EXPENSES OF SELLER	
Mortgage Tax	$ 275.00	Title Search Fee	$_____
Recording Mortgage	$ 11.00	Transfer Tax on Deed	$_____
Recording Deed	$ 12.00	Filing of Gains Tax Affidavit	$_____
		Discharge Recording Fee	$_____
		Mortgage Tax	$_____
		Surveyor's Fees	$_____
		Points	$_____
		Mortgage Payoff	$_____
		Real Estate Commission	$_____
		Water Escrow	$_____
Bank Attorney Fee	$_____		$_____
Points	$_____		$_____
Title Insurance	$_____		$_____
Interest	$_____		$_____
....	$_____	Legal Fee	$_____
....	$_____	Total	$_____
....	$_____		
Legal Fee	$ 500.00	Cash Received:	$
Total	$ 798.00	Less Seller's Expenses:	$_____
		Net Proceeds:	$

Cash paid to Seller: $ 50,157.68

Plus Purchaser's Expenses: $ 798.00

Total Disbursed: $ 50,955.68

Figure 15.3 Seller's Closing Statement, Closing on August 12

SELLER'S CREDITS

Sale Price _____ $ 89,500.00

ADJUSTMENT OF TAXES

School Tax 7/1/ to 6/30/	Amount $ 1176.35	Adj. 10 mos. 18 days	$ 1,039.16
City/School Tax 7/1/ to 6/30/	Amount $_____	Adj. ____ mos. ____ days	$_____
County Tax 19____	Amount $ 309.06	Adj. 4 mos. 18 days	$ 118.52
Village Tax 6/1/ to 5/31/	Amount $_____	Adj. ____ mos. ____ days	$_____
City Tax Embellishments	Amount $_____	Adj. ____ mos. ____ days	$_____

Total Seller's Credits $ 90,657.68

PURCHASER'S CREDITS

Deposit with ___Nothnagle_____ $ 500.00

(Assumed) (New) Mortgage with __seller__ $ 40,000.00

12% interest, 15 years, payments $_____

$ 480.07, beginning 9/12/ $_____

$_____

$_____

$_____

$_____

$_____

$_____

Total Purchaser's Credits $ 40,500.00

Cash (Rec'd) (Paid) at Closing $ 50,157.68

EXPENSES OF PURCHASER		EXPENSES OF SELLER	
Mortgage Tax .... $_____		Title Search Fee .... $ 220.00	
Recording Mortgage............... $_____		Transfer Tax on Deed .... $ 358.00	
Recording Deed................... $_____		Filing of Gains Tax Affidavit .. $ 1.00	
		Discharge Recording Fee ...... $_____	
ESCROWS:		Mortgage Tax .... $ 100.00	
____ mos. insurance $ _____		Surveyor's Fees .... $_____	
____ mos. school tax $ _____		Points .... $_____	
____ mos. county tax $ _____		Mortgage Payoff .... $_____	
____ mos. village tax $ _____		Real Estate Commission ...... $ 4870.00	
PMI FHA Insurance $ _____		Water Escrow .... $_____	
Total: $_____		19 - school tax ...... $ 1,182.14	
Bank Attorney Fee................. $_____		Federal express .... $ 14.00	
Points........................... $_____		.... $_____	
Title Insurance................... $_____		.... $_____	
Interest.......................... $_____		Legal Fee.................. $ 550.00	
.... $_____		Total..................... $ 7,295.14	
.... $_____			
.... $_____		Cash Received: $ 50,157.68	
Legal Fee........................ $_____		Less Seller's Expenses: $ 7,295.14	
Total............................ $_____		Net Proceeds: $ 42,862.54	
Cash paid to Seller: $			
Plus Purchaser's Expenses: $			
Total Disbursed: $			

The upper half of the closing statement accounts for the transaction between buyer and seller; the lower part details each one's individual expenses. The buyer pays to record the deed and mortgage and pays the mortgage tax. The buyer also pays his or her attorney.

The seller's expenses involve last-minute payment of the school tax (plus a small late-payment penalty) for which the seller is largely reimbursed, the required lender's share of the mortgage tax (seller/lender is a corporation), the remaining real estate commission, legal costs of proving title, transfer tax, and incidental out-of-pocket expenses incurred by seller's attorney, who also deducts his or her own fee and turns the net proceeds over to the seller.

SUMMARY

Closing a real estate sale involves both title procedures and financial matters. The broker, as agent of the seller, is often present at the closing to see that the sale is actually concluded and to account for the earnest money deposit.

Closings must be reported to the IRS on Form 1099.

The federal Real Estate Settlement Procedures Act (RESPA) requires disclosure of all settlement costs when a residential real estate purchase is financed by a federally related mortgage loan. RESPA requires lenders to use a Uniform Settlement Statement to detail the financial particulars of a transaction.

The actual amount to be paid by the buyer at the closing is computed by preparation of a *closing,* or settlement, *statement.* This lists the sales price, earnest money deposit and all adjustments and *prorations* due between buyer and seller. The purpose of this statement is to determine the net amount due the seller at closing. The buyer reimburses the seller for *prepaid items* like unused taxes or fuel oil. The seller credits the buyer for bills the seller owes that will be paid by the buyer (*accrued items*), such as unpaid water bills.

QUESTIONS

Please complete all of the questions before turning to the Answer Key.

1. When an item to be prorated is owed by the seller and has not yet been paid for, the amount owed is figured as

   a. a credit to the seller only.
   b. a debit to the buyer only.
   c. a credit to the seller and a debit to the buyer.
   d. a debit to the seller and a credit to the buyer.

2. Certain items in a closing statement are prorated, whereas other items are listed for their full amount. Which of the following items is always prorated?

   a. State transfer tax
   b. Earnest money
   c. The unpaid principal balance of the seller's mortgage loan that is assumed by the buyer
   d. The accrued interest on the seller's mortgage loan that is assumed by the buyer

3. The sales price of a property is

   a. a credit to the seller only.
   b. a debit to the buyer only.
   c. a credit to the buyer and a debit to the seller.
   d. a debit to the buyer and a credit to the seller.

4. The Uniform Settlement Statement (HUD Form 1) must be used to illustrate all settlement charges for

   a. all real estate transactions.
   b. transactions financed with FHA and VA loans only.
   c. residential transactions financed with federally related mortgage loans.
   d. all transactions in which mortgage financing is involved.

5.   Unpaid real estate taxes, water service, janitorial services, and so forth, are

   a.   a credit to the seller only.
   b.   a debit to the buyer only.
   c.   a credit to the seller and a debit to the buyer.
   d.   a debit to the seller and a credit to the buyer.

6.   Legal title always passes from the seller to the buyer

   a.   on the date of execution of the deed.
   b.   when the deed is delivered.
   c.   when the closing statement has been signed.
   d.   when the deed is placed in escrow.

7.   All of the following items are generally prorated between the seller and the buyer EXCEPT

   a.   recording charges.   c.   collected rents.
   b.   real estate taxes.   d.   mortgage interest.

8.   If a buyer's broker as well as a seller's broker is involved in the transaction, how would the commissions show on the closing statement?

   a.   Debit to the seller; credit to the buyer
   b.   Debit to the buyer; credit to the seller
   c.   Debit to both the seller and the buyer
   d.   Credit to both the seller and the buyer

9.   The earnest money given to the broker by the buyer is a

   a.   credit to the buyer only.
   b.   debit to the seller only.
   c.   a credit to the seller and a debit to the buyer.
   d.   a credit to the buyer and a debit to the seller.

10.   All of the following statements regarding a closing statement are true EXCEPT that it

   a.   determines the percentage of the broker's commission.
   b.   discloses the amount of money the seller will receive.
   c.   specifies the amount of cash the buyer must bring to the closing.
   d.   discloses the dollar amount of the down payment and closing costs.

11. The principal amount of the buyer's new mortgage loan is a

   a. credit to the seller.   c. debit to the seller.
   b. debit to the buyer.   d. credit to the buyer.

12. Which of the following statements is true of real estate closings in most states?

   a. Closings are generally conducted by real estate licensees.
   b. The buyer usually receives the collected rents for the day of closing.
   c. The buyer must reimburse the seller for any title evidence provided by the seller.
   d. The seller usually pays the property's expenses for the day of closing.

13. All of the following statements identify a benefit of closing a real estate transaction through escrow EXCEPT that

   a. the seller is assured that he or she will receive the buyer's payment for the property.
   b. the buyer is assured that he or she will not become the owner unless good title to the property is received.
   c. there are no closing costs to be paid.
   d. neither party needs to be present at the closing.

14. All encumbrances and liens shown on the title report, other than those waived or agreed to by the buyer and listed in the contract, must be removed so that the title can be delivered free and clear. The removal of such encumbrances is the obligation of the

   a. buyer.   c. broker.
   b. seller.   d. title company.

15. Which of the following would a lender generally require to be produced at the closing?

   a. Title insurance policy   c. Buyer's application form
   b. Market value appraisal   d. Buyer's credit report

16. When a transaction is to be closed in escrow, the seller generally deposits all of the following items with the escrow agent before the closing date EXCEPT the

   a. deed to the property.
   b. title evidence.
   c. reduction certificate.
   d. cash to complete the purchase.

17. Security deposits should be listed in a closing statement as a debit to the

   a. buyer.   c. tenants.
   b. seller.   d. escrow agent.

18. The Real Estate Settlement Procedures Act (RESPA) applies to the activities of

   a. brokers selling commercial and office buildings.
   b. securities salespeople selling limited partnership interests.
   c. Fannie Mae and Freddie Mac when purchasing packages of mortgages.
   d. lenders financing the purchase of borrowers' residences.

19. At the closing, the seller's attorney gave credit to the buyer for certain accrued items. These items were

   a. bills relating to the property that have already been paid by the seller.
   b. bills relating to the property that will have to be paid by the buyer.
   c. all of the seller's real estate bills.
   d. all of the buyer's real estate bills.

20. The purpose of RESPA is to

   a. make sure that buyers do not borrow more money than they can repay.
   b. make real estate licensees more responsive to buyers' needs.
   c. help buyers know how much money is required for their purchase.
   d. see that buyers and sellers know all of the settlement costs.

21. The annual real estate taxes are $1,800 and have been paid in advance for the calendar year. If the closing is scheduled for June 15, which of the following is true?

    a.   Credit the seller $825; debit the buyer $975
    b.   Credit the seller $975; debit the buyer $825
    c.   Credit the seller $975; debit the buyer $975
    d.   Credit the buyer $825; debit the seller $825

22. The seller collected the monthly rent of $550 from the tenant on August 1. At the August 15 closing, the

    a.   seller owes the buyer $550.
    b.   seller owes the buyer $275.
    c.   buyer owes the seller $275.
    d.   tenant owes the buyer $275.

23. At the closing, the broker's commission will usually be shown as a

    a.   credit to the seller.   c.   debit to the seller.
    b.   credit to the buyer.   d.   debit to the buyer.

24. The buyer of an $80,000 house has paid $5,000 as earnest money and has a loan commitment for 70 percent of the purchase price. How much more cash does the buyer need to complete the transaction?

    a. $5,000   c. $24,000
    b. $19,000   d. $29,000

25. A building was bought for $200,000 with 10 percent down and a loan for the balance. If the lender charged the buyer three discount points, how much cash did the buyer need to complete the transaction?

    a. $5,400   c. $20,000
    b. $14,600   d. $25,400

16: Real Estate Mathematics

KEY TERMS

area   rate
percentage   volume

Mathematics plays an important role in the real estate business. Math is involved in nearly every aspect of a typical transaction, from the moment a listing agreement is filled out until the final monies are paid at the closing. Reflecting this, state licensing examinations contain a substantial number of questions that involve math.

This chapter is designed to explain some of the math formulas used most frequently in the computations required on licensing examinations. These computations are also important in day-to-day transactions.

PERCENTAGES

Many real estate computations are based on the calculation of percentages. A **percentage** expresses a portion of a whole (percent means "per hundred"). For example, 50 percent means 50 parts of the possible 100 parts that comprise the whole. Percentages greater than 100 percent contain more than one whole unit. Thus, 163 percent is one whole and 63 parts of another whole. A whole is always expressed as 100 percent.

In problems involving percentages, *the percentages must be converted to either decimals or fractions.* To convert a percentage to a decimal, move the decimal two places to the left and drop the percent sign. Thus,

$$60\% = 0.6 \quad 7\% = 0.07 \quad 175\% = 1.75$$

To change a percentage to a fraction, place the percentage over 100. For example:

$$50\% = \frac{50}{100} \quad 115\% = \frac{115}{100}$$

These fractions may then be *reduced* to make it easier to work the problem. To reduce a fraction, determine the lowest number by which both numerator (top number) and denominator (bottom number) can be evenly divided, and divide each of them by that number. For example:

$^{25}/_{100} = \frac{1}{4}$ (both number divided by 25)
$^{49}/_{63} = \frac{7}{9}$ (both number divided by 7)

Percentage problems contain three elements: *percent, total,* and *part.* To determine a specific percentage of a whole, multiply the total by the percent. This is illustrated by the following formula:

$$\text{total} \times \text{percent} = \text{part}$$
$$200 \times 5\% = 10$$

This formula is used in calculating mortgage loan interests, brokers' commissions, loan origination fees, discount points, earnest money deposits, and income on capital investments.

For example: A broker is to receive a 7 percent commission on the sale of a $90,000 house. What will the broker's commission be?

$$0.07 \times \$90,000 = \textit{\$6,300 broker's commission}$$

A variation, or inversion, of the percentage formula is used to find the total amount when the part and percent are known:

$$\text{total} = \frac{\text{part}}{\text{percent}}$$

For example, the Masterson Realty Company received a $4,500 commission for the sale of a house. The broker's commission was 6 percent of the sales price. What was the sales price of this house?

$$\frac{\$4,500}{0.06} = \textit{\$75,000 sales price}$$

This formula is used to calculate the total sales price when the amount and percentage of commission or earnest money deposit are known. It also is used in computing the total mortgage loan principal still due if the monthly payment and interest rate are known, rent due if the monthly payment and interest rate are known, and market value of property if the assessed value and the ratio (percentage) of assessed value to market value are known.

To determine the percent when the amounts of the part and the total are known:

$$percent = \frac{part}{total}$$

This formula may be used to determine the tax rate when the taxes and assessed value are known, or the commission rate if the sales price and commission amount are known.

This formula works as effectively when the part is larger than 100 percent. To illustrate, the Hendersons recently sold their home for $215,892. If their appreciation was 8 percent, what was the original purchase price?

$$\frac{\$215,892}{1.08} = \$199,900$$

The answer may be checked by determining the dollar amount of appreciation at that sales price.

$$
\begin{array}{ll}
\$199,900 & \text{purchase price} \\
\underline{\times\,0.08} & \text{appreciation} \\
\$\ 15,992 & \text{gain}
\end{array}
$$

Then the purchase price is added back in: $199,900 plus a gain of $15,992 equals the $215,892 appreciated value at which it was sold.

The following diagram may be used as an aid in remembering the three formulas just discussed:

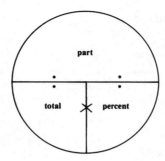

RATES

Property taxes, transfer taxes, and insurance premiums are usually expressed as rates. A **rate** is the cost expressed as the amount of cost per unit. For example, tax might be computed at the rate of $5 per $100 of assessed value in a certain county. The formula for computing rates is:

$$\text{value} \times \text{rate} = \text{total}$$

For example: A house has been assessed at $90,000 and is taxed at an annual rate of $2.50 per $100 assessed valuation. What is the yearly tax?

$$\$90{,}000 \times \frac{\$2.50}{\$100} = \text{total annual tax}$$

$$\frac{900}{\cancel{90{,}000}} \times \frac{\$2.50}{\cancel{100}} = \text{total annual tax}$$
$$1$$

$$900 \times \$2.50 = \$2{,}250 \; \textit{total annual tax}$$

See Chapter 9 for a further discussion of tax computations.

AREAS AND VOLUMES

People in the real estate profession must know how to compute the **area** of a parcel of land or figure the amount of living area in a house. To compute the area of a square or rectangular parcel, use the formula:

$$\text{length} \times \text{width} = \text{area}$$

Table 16.1   Units of Measurement

1 foot.	12 inches
1 yard	3 feet or 36 inches
1 rod	16.5 feet
1 chain	66 feet

1 square foot.	144 square inches
1 square yard	9 square feet
1 acre	43,560 square feet

1 cubic foot.	1,728 cubic inches
1 cubic yard	27 cubic feet

Thus, the area of a rectangular lot measuring 200 feet long by 100 feet is:

$$200' \times 100' = 20,000 \text{ square feet}$$

Area is always expressed in square units. Table 16.1 shows the relationships of different units of measurements.

To compute the amount of surface in a triangular-shaped area, use the formula:

$$\text{area} = \tfrac{1}{2} (\text{base} \times \text{height})$$

The base of a triangle is the bottom, the side on which the triangle rests. The height is an imaginary straight line extending from the point of the uppermost angle straight down to the base:

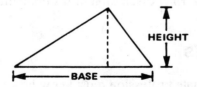

For example: A triangle has a base of 50 feet and a height of 30 feet. What is its area?

$$\tfrac{1}{2} (50' \times 30') = \text{area in square feet}$$
$$\tfrac{1}{2} (1500) = 750 \text{ square feet}$$

To compute the area of an irregular room or parcel of land, divide the shape into regular rectangles, squares, or triangles. Next, compute the area of each regular figure and add the areas together to obtain total area.

Example: Compute the area of a hallway.

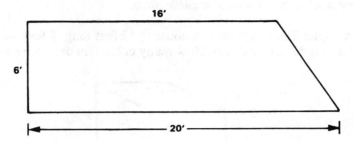

First, make a rectangle and a triangle by drawing a single straight line through the figure, as shown:

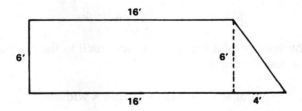

Compute the area of the rectangle:

$$\text{area} = \text{length} \times \text{width} \quad 16' \times 6' = 96 \text{ square feet}$$

Compute the area of the triangle:

$$\text{area} = \tfrac{1}{2}(\text{base} \times \text{height})$$
$$\tfrac{1}{2}(4' \times 6') = \tfrac{1}{2}(24) = 12 \text{ square feet}$$

Total the two areas:

$$96 + 12 = \textit{108 square feet in total area}$$

The cubic capacity of an enclosed space is expressed as **volume.** Volume is used to describe the amount of space in any three-dimensional area. It would be used, for example, in measuring the interior airspace of a room to determine what capacity heating unit is required. The formula for computing cubic or rectangular volume is:

$$\text{volume} = \text{length} \times \text{width} \times \text{height}$$

Volume is always expressed in cubic units.

For example: The bedroom of a house is 12 feet long, 8 feet wide, and has a ceiling height of 8 feet. How many cubic feet does the room enclose?

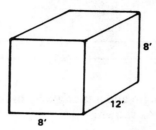

$$8' \times 12' \times 8' = 768 \text{ cubic feet}$$

To compute the volume of a triangular space, such as the airspace in an A-frame house, use the formula:

$$\text{volume} = \tfrac{1}{2} (\text{base} \times \text{height} \times \text{width})$$

For example: What is the volume of airspace in the house shown below?

First, divide the house into two shapes, rectangular and triangular, as shown:

Find the volume of T:

$$\text{volume} = \tfrac{1}{2} (\text{base} \times \text{height} \times \text{width})$$
$$\tfrac{1}{2} (25' \times 10' \times 40') = \tfrac{1}{2} (10{,}000 \text{ cubic feet}) = 5{,}000 \text{ cubic feet}$$

Find the volume of R:

$$25' \times 40' \times 12' = 12{,}000 \text{ cubic feet}$$

Add volumes T and R:

$$5{,}000 + 12{,}000 = \textit{17,000 cubic feet of airspace in the house}$$

Cubic measurements of volume are also used to compute the construction costs per cubic foot of a building and the amount of airspace being sold in a condominium unit.

Remember that when either area or volume is computed, *all dimensions used must be given in the same unit of measure.* For example, you may not multiply 2 feet by 6 inches to get the area; you have to multiply 2 feet by ½ foot or 24 inches by 6 inches.

PRORATIONS

As discussed in Chapter 15, the proration of taxes, insurance premiums, and other items is customary when a real estate transaction is closed. Questions concerning closing statements generally appear in real estate brokers' examinations. They appear less often in salespersons' exams. Knowledge of the arithmetic of prorations is valuable to all real estate licensees in the course of their business.

When an item is to be prorated, the charge must first be broken down into yearly, monthly, and daily amounts, depending on the type of charge. These smaller amounts are then multiplied by the number of years, months, and days in the prorated time period to determine the accrued or unearned amount to be credited or debited at the closing. Depending on local custom, prorations may be made on the basis of a standard 30-day month, 365-day year, or actual number of days in the month of closing.

For example, consider a one-year prepaid insurance policy with a premium of $450. The policy became effective on March 1, 1993; the date of the closing is August 9, 1993. The initial step in determining the unearned amount of the premium that will be credited to the seller at the closing is to figure out the time not yet used as of August 9, 1993, as follows:

	Years	Months	Days
		14	
	3	2	32
Expiration Date	1993	3	1
Closing Date	1993	8	9
		6	23 or 6 months and 23 days unearned

Then the monthly and daily breakdowns of the premium amount are determined. (Remember to carry all computations to three decimal places until a final figure is reached, then round off to the nearest penny.)

First, divide the yearly charge by 12 to determine the monthly premium:

$$\frac{\$\ 37.500}{12\ )\ \$450.000}\ \text{monthly premium}$$

Assuming your area computes such charges on the basis of a 30-day month, divide the monthly charge by 30 to arrive at the daily premium:

$$\frac{\$1.250}{30\ )\ \$37.500}\ \text{daily premium}$$

Finally, you must multiply the proper premium amounts by the appropriate number of months and days to determine the unearned amount to be prorated:

$$\begin{array}{r} \$\ 37.500 \\ \times\ \ \ \ \ \ 6 \\ \hline \$225.000 \ \text{for 6 months} \end{array}$$

$ 1.250
×   23
$28.750 for 23 days

$225.000
  28.750
$253.750, or *$253.75 unearned insurance premium*
               (a credit to the seller and a debit to the buyer)

Similar computations are used to prorate other items, such as real estate taxes and mortgage interest. For a more detailed discussion of closing statement computations, refer to Chapter 15.

SUMMARY

Mathematical computations are used in nearly every aspect of the real estate business, and are included in many states' real estate license examinations.

Problems that contain *percentages* involve three elements: percent, total, and part. To find a specific part of a whole, multiply the percentage by the whole.

A *rate* is the cost of an item, expressed as a particular cost per unit. Property taxes, transfer taxes and insurance premiums are usually expressed as rates.

To determine the *area* of a parcel of land or living area in a house, multiply the property's length by its width. To determine a specific *volume,* multiply the space's length by its width; then multiply this figure by the space's height.

To determine a proration for a prepaid or accrued item, the charge must be broken down into yearly, monthly, and/or daily amounts, then multiplied by the appropriate number of years, months, and/or days to be prorated.

QUESTIONS

Please complete all of the questions before turning to the Answer Key.

1. Broker *S* of Happy Valley Realty recently sold *H*'s home for $79,500. *S* charged *H* a 6½ percent commission and will pay 30 percent of that amount to the listing salesperson and 25 percent to the selling salesperson. What amount of commission will the listing salesperson receive from the *H* sale?

    a. $5,167.50   c. $3,617.25
    b. $1,550.25   d. $1,291.87

2. *L* signed an agreement to purchase a condominium apartment from *P.* The contract stipulated that *P* replace the damaged bedroom carpet. The carpet *L* has chosen costs $16.95 per square yard plus $2.50 per square yard for installation. If the bedroom dimensions are as illustrated, how much will *P* have to pay for the job?

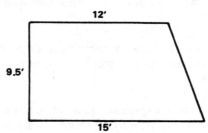

    a. $241.54   c. $277.16
    b. $189.20   d. $2,494.46

3. *H, O, R,* and *M* decided to pool their savings and purchase a small apartment building for $125,000. If *H* invested $30,000 and *O* and *R* each contributed $35,000, what percentage of ownership was left for *M?*

    a. 20 percent   c. 28 percent
    b. 24 percent   d. 30 percent

4. *D* is curious to know how much money his son and daughter-in-law still owe on their mortgage loan. *D* knows that the interest portion of their last monthly payment was $391.42. If they are paying interest at the rate of 11½ percent, what was the outstanding balance of their loan before that last payment was made?

   a. $43,713.00   c. $36,427.50
   b. $40,843.83   d. $34,284.70

5. The *N*s bought their home a year ago for $98,500. Property in their neighborhood is said to be increasing in value at a rate of 5 percent annually. If this is true, what is the current market value of the *N*s' real estate?

   a. $103,425   c. $104,410
   b. $93,575   d. $93,809

6. The *D*s' home is valued at $95,000. Property in their area is assessed at 60 percent of its value, and the local tax is $2.85 per $100. What is the amount of the *D*s' annual taxes?

   a. $2,451   c. $135.38
   b. $1,470.60   d. $1,624.50

7. The *F*s are planning to construct a patio in their backyard. An illustration of the surface area to be paved appears here. If the cement is to be poured as a six-inch slab, how many cubic feet of cement will be poured into this patio?

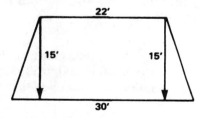

   a. 660 cubic feet   c. 330 cubic feet
   b. 450 cubic feet   d. 195 cubic feet

8. *M* receives a monthly salary of $1,000 plus 3 percent commission on all of his listings that sell and 2½ percent on all of his sales. None of the listings that *M* took sold last month, but he received $4,175 in salary and commission. What was the value of the property *M* sold?

   a. $147,000   c. $122,500
   b. $127,000   d. $105,833

9. The *Ps'* residence has proved difficult to sell. Salesperson *K* suggests it might sell faster if they enclosed a portion of the backyard with a privacy fence. If the area to be enclosed is as illustrated, how much would the fence cost at $6.95 per linear foot?

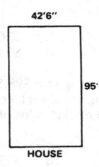

42'6"

95'

HOUSE

a.	$1,911.25	c.	$1,615.88
b.	$1,654.10	d.	$955.63

10. *T* leases the 12 apartments in the Overton Arms for a total monthly rental of $4,500. If this figure represents an 8 percent annual return on *T*'s investment, what was the original cost of the property?

a.	$675,000	c.	$54,000
b.	$450,000	d.	$56,250

For the following questions regarding closing statement prorations, base your calculations on a 30-day month. Carry all computations to three decimal places until the final solution.

11. A sale is to be closed on March 15. Real estate taxes for the current year have not been paid; taxes for last year amounted to $1,340. What is the amount of the real estate tax proration to be credited to the buyer?

a.	$1,060.85	c.	$223.33
b.	$279.15	d.	$1,116.60

12. The buyers are assuming an outstanding mortgage, which had an unpaid balance of $58,200 after the last payment on August 1. Interest at 12 percent per annum is paid in arrears each month; the sale is to be closed on August 11. What is the amount of mortgage interest proration to be debited to the seller at the closing?

a.	$698.40	c.	$368.60
b.	$582.00	d.	$213.40

13. In a sale of residential property real estate taxes for the current year amounted to $975 and have already been paid by the seller. The sale is to be closed on October 26; what is the amount of real estate tax proration to be credited the seller?

    a. $173.31   c. $798.96
    b. $162.51   d. $83.86

14. The buyer is assuming the seller's mortgage. The unpaid balance after the most recent payment (September 1) was $61,550. Interest is paid in arrears each month at 13 percent per annum. The sale is to be closed on September 22. What is the amount of mortgage interest proration to be credited to the buyer at the closing?

    a. $666.97   c. $177.82
    b. $488.97   d. $689.01

15. A 100-acre farm is divided into house lots. The streets require one-eighth of the whole farm, and there are 140 lots. How many square feet are there in each lot?

    a. 35,004   c. 27,225
    b. 31,114   d. 43,560

16. *R*'s commission on a sale was $14,100, which was 6 percent of the sales price. What was the sales price?

    a. $235,000   c. $705,000
    b. $470,000   d. $940,000

17. A triangular-shaped parcel of land has a base of 80 feet and a height of 50 feet. How many square yards are contained in this parcel?

    a. 222.22   c. 2,000
    b. 444.44   d. 4,000

18. How many acres are contained in a parcel of land that is one-eighth of a mile square?

    a. 10   c. 40
    b. 20   d. 80

19. In the computation of ad valorem taxes, how is one mill expressed in dollars?

    a. $.0001
    b. $.0010

    c. $.0100
    d. $.1000

20. Seller *W* agrees to pay a commission of 7 percent to broker *Q*. The property is appraised for $91,500 and is listed by *Q* for $90,500. If an offer is accepted by *W* for $89,500, the commission payable to *Q* would be

    a. $6,195.
    b. $6,265.

    c. $6,335.
    d. $6,305.

21. Buyer *E* finances the purchase of a residence with a 9 percent $75,000 loan. The monthly payment is $591.42. Approximately what portion of the first month's payment would be principal?

    a. $17
    b. $29

    c. $39
    d. $41

22. A two-story warehouse measures 20 feet by 60 feet. The first story is 12 feet high, and the second story is 10 feet high. If the cost of construction is $2.50 per cubic foot for the first floor and $2.30 per cubic foot for the second floor, what is the replacement cost of the structure?

    a. $60,720
    b. $63,120

    c. $63,600
    d. $66,000

23. Seller *J* sold a residence and received a check at the closing for $55,000 after paying $1,000 of closing costs and a 7 percent commission. What was the approximate sales price of the residence?

    a. $59,850.00
    b. $59,920.00

    c. $60,139.78
    d. $60,215.05

24. A real estate licensee negotiates the purchase of two parcels of land for one buyer at $2,100 per acre. One parcel is five acres and the other is one mile square. How much will both parcels cost?

    a. $346,500
    b. $682,500

    c. $1,270,500
    d. $1,354,500

25. Buyer *G* borrowed $12,000 on a straight note at 7 percent interest. Monthly payments are made for the full term of the loan. If the total interest paid was $2,100, for how many months was the loan written?

    a. 27
    b. 30

    c. 33
    d. 36

26. *K* owns a rectangular parcel of property. It contains 3.2 acres and has a depth of 381 feet. If a special assessment was levied in the amount of $1.85 per front foot, how much would *K* be taxed?

    a. $67.68
    b. $628.65

    c. $642.33
    d. $676.84

27. A lender loaned the owner of a parcel of land 70 percent of its appraised value. The interest rate on the loan was 9 percent, and the first month's interest payment was $420. What is the appraised value of the property?

    a. $45,360
    b. $56,000

    c. $60,480
    d. $80,000

28. The owner of an apartment building suffers a loss of $600 net income per month because a freeway was built near his building. If the property is valued using a 10 percent capitalization rate, what is the loss in value to the property?

    a. $6,000
    b. $7,200

    c. $60,000
    d. $72,000

29. A property has an effective gross income of $16,500 per month. The annual operating expenses are 37 percent of the effective gross income. What is the annual net operating income?

    a. $6,105
    b. $10,395

    c. $73,260
    d. $124,740

30. Buyer *F* purchased an income-producing property for $2,500,000 with a 5 percent down payment and financed the balance of the purchase price. One year later, the property was sold for $3,000,000. Leverage enabled *F* to make what percent profit on the down payment?

    a. 5 percent
    b. 25 percent

    c. 100 percent
    d. 400 percent

Please complete all of the questions before turning to the Answer Key.

1. A seller wants to net $65,000 from the sale of her house after paying a 6 percent commission. Her sales price will have to be

    a. $61,100.   c. $68,900.
    b. $61,321.   d. $69,149.

2. Under joint tenancy

    a.   a maximum of two people can own a property.
    b.   the fractional interests can be different amounts.
    c.   additional owners can be added later.
    d.   there is a right of survivorship.

3. According to the statute of frauds, an oral three-year lease is

    a.   illegal.   c.   renewable.
    b.   unenforceable.   d.   a long-term lease.

4. A qualified veteran offers to purchase a home for $67,000 using a VA-guaranteed loan. After the offer was accepted, a certificate of reasonable value (CRV) was issued on the property for $64,500. In this situation, the veteran may

    a.   purchase the property with a $2,500 down payment.
    b.   withdraw from the sale after paying a 1 percent penalty.
    c.   withdraw from the sale after paying a 2 percent penalty.
    d.   not withdraw from the sale.

5. A cloud on the title to a property may be cured by

    a. bringing an action to repudiate the title.
    b. paying cash for the property at the settlement.
    c. obtaining quitclaim deeds from all interested parties.
    d. bringing an action to register the title.

6. How many acres are there in the S ½ of the SE ¼ and the NE ¼ of the SE ¼ of a section?

    a. 20 acres   c. 80 acres
    b. 40 acres   d. 120 acres

7. Which of the following items is usually not prorated between the seller and the buyer at the closing?

    a. Recording charges   c. Prepaid rents
    b. Real estate taxes   d. Utility bills

8. For a deed to be valid, it must be signed by the

    a. grantor.   c. grantor and the grantee.
    b. grantee.   d. grantee and two witnesses.

9. *L,* who wants to sell his house, enters into a listing agreement with Broker *T.* Broker *F* obtains a buyer for the property, and *T* does not receive a commission. The listing agreement between *L* and *T* was probably a(n)

    a. exclusive-right-to-sell listing.
    b. exclusive-agency listing.
    c. open listing.
    d. multiple listing.

10. On behalf of seller *K,* Broker *Q* has been offering *K*'s house for sale at the price of $98,750. *J,* a minority group member, saw the house and was interested in it. When *J* asked the price of the house, *K* told him $110,000. According to the Federal Fair Housing Act of 1968, such a statement is

    a. illegal because the difference in the offering price and the quoted price was greater than 10 percent.
    b. illegal because the terms of the potential sale were changed for *J.*
    c. legal because all that is important is that *J* be given the opportunity to buy the house.
    d. legal because the representation was made by the broker and not directly by the owner.

11. A real estate loan that uses both personal property and real property as collateral is called a

    a. package loan.   c. growing-equity loan.
    b. blanket loan.   d. shared-appreciation loan.

12. An FHA-insured loan in the amount of $57,500 at 11½ percent interest for 30 years was closed on March 17. The first monthly payment is not due until May 1. If the interest is paid monthly in arrears, what was the amount of the interest adjustment that the buyer had to make at the settlement?

    a. $257.15   c. $551.20
    b. $312.29   d. $6,612.50

13. Broker *V* receives an earnest money deposit with a written offer that indicates the offeror will leave the offer open for the seller's acceptance for ten days. On the sixth day, and prior to the seller's acceptance, the offeror notifies *V* that he is withdrawing the offer and demanding the return of his earnest money. In this situation,

    a. the offeror cannot withdraw the offer—it must be held open for the full ten-day period.
    b. the offeror has the right to withdraw the offer and secure the return of the earnest money at any time before he is notified of the seller's acceptance.
    c. the offeror can withdraw the offer, and the seller and the broker will each retain one-half of the earnest money as liquidated damages.
    d. the offeror can withdraw the offer, and the broker will declare the earnest money forfeited and retain all of it in lieu of a commission.

14. A property manager leased a store for three years. The first year, the store's rent was $1,000 per month, and the rent was to increase 10 percent per year thereafter. The broker received a 7 percent commission for the first year, a 5 percent commission for the second year, and 3 percent for the balance of the lease. The total commission earned by the property manager was

    a. $840.
    b. $1,613.
    c. $1,932.
    d. $2,785.

15. *P,* age 59, just sold the home he had purchased three years before and moved in with his daughter and son-in-law. He had originally purchased the property for $77,800 and sold it for $106,100. In computing his income tax, *P* would pay taxes on

    a. $11,320.
    b. $16,980.
    c. $28,300.
    d. nothing.

16. Which of the following items is a lien on real estate?

    a. A recorded easement
    b. A recorded mortgage
    c. An encroachment
    d. A deed restriction

17. A residence with outdated plumbing is suffering from

    a. functional obsolescence.
    b. external obsolescence.
    c. curable physical deterioration.
    d. incurable physical deterioration.

18. The current value of a property is $40,000. For real estate tax purposes, the property is assessed at 40 percent of its current value, with an equalization factor of 1.5 applied to the assessed value. If the tax rate is $4 per $100 of assessed valuation, what is the amount of tax due on the property?

    a. $640
    b. $960
    c. $1,600
    d. $2,400

19. A contract signed under duress is

    a. discharged.
    b. void.
    c. breached.
    d. voidable.

20. A structure was built that had five stories. Several years after its completion, a city ordinance was passed prohibiting any structure taller than three stories. In this situation, the structure

    a.   would be a nonconforming use.
    b.   would have to be demolished.
    c.   would require a variance.
    d.   would require a conditional-use permit.

21. An agreement that ends all future lessor-lessee obligations under a lease is known as a(n)

    a.   assumption.   c.   novation.
    b.   surrender.   d.   breach.

22. A property has a net income of $30,000. An appraiser decides to use a 12 percent rather than a 10 percent capitalization rate on this property. The use of the higher rate results in

    a.   a 2 percent increase in the appraised value.
    b.   a $50,000 increase in the appraised value.
    c.   a $50,000 decrease in the appraised value.
    d.   no change in the appraised value.

23. An insurance company agreed to provide a developer with financing for a shopping center at a below-market interest rate in exchange for an equity position in the property. This type of arrangement is called a(n)

    a.   package loan.   c.   open-end loan.
    b.   blanket loan.   d.   participation loan.

24. A real estate transaction had a closing date of November 15. The seller, who was responsible for the costs up to and including the date of the settlement, had paid the property taxes of $1,116 for the calendar year. On the closing statement, the buyer would be

    a.   debited for $139.50.   c.   credited for $139.50.
    b.   debited for $976.50.   d.   credited for $976.50.

25. Assume a market interest rate of 8½ percent, discount points are at six, and the mortgage lender must obtain a yield of 9¼ percent. If the points drop to four, the interest rate will

   a. decrease by ½ percent.   c. decrease by ¼ percent.
   b. increase by ¼ percent.   d. increase by ½ percent.

26. If a storage tank that measures 8 feet by 9 feet by 12 feet was designed to store natural gas, and the cost of the gas is $1.82 per cubic foot, what does it cost to fill the tank to one-half its capacity?

   a. $685   c. $864
   b. $786   d. $1,572

27. On Monday, *P* offers to sell his residence to *J* for $52,000. On Tuesday, *J* counteroffers to buy the property for $50,500. On Friday, *J* withdraws his counteroffer and accepts *P*'s original price of $52,000. Under these circumstances

   a. there is a valid agreement, because *J* accepted *P*'s offer exactly as it was made, regardless that it was not accepted immediately.
   b. there is a valid agreement, because *J* accepted before *P* advised him that the offer was withdrawn.
   c. there is no valid agreement, because *P*'s offer was not accepted within 72 hours of its having been made.
   d. there is no valid agreement, because *J*'s counteroffer was a rejection of *P*'s offer, and once rejected, it cannot be accepted later.

28. The law that requires lenders to inform both sellers and buyers of all fees and charges is the

   a. Equal Credit Opportunity Act.
   b. Real Estate Settlement Procedures Act.
   c. Truth-in-Lending Act (Regulation Z).
   d. Real Estate Investment Trust Act.

29. A mortgage loan that requires monthly payments of $639.05 for 20 years and a final payment of $49,386.63 is called a(n)

   a. wraparound loan.   c. balloon loan.
   b. accelerated loan.   d. adjustable-rate loan.

30. A real estate salesperson may

    a. write checks from his or her trust account.
    b. advertise the property in his or her own name.
    c. collect a commission directly from the principal.
    d. act under the supervision of the employing broker.

31. After a snowstorm, a property owner offers to pay $10 to anyone who will shovel his driveway. This is an example of a(n)

    a. unilateral contract.   c. implied contract.
    b. executed contract.   d. void contract.

32. *L* is purchasing a home under the terms of a land contract. Until the contract is completed, *L* has

    a. legal title to the premises.
    b. no interest in the property.
    c. a legal life estate to the premises.
    d. equitable title in the property.

33. The Equal Credit Opportunity Act makes it illegal for lenders to refuse credit or otherwise discriminate because an applicant is

    a. unemployed.
    b. a single person.
    c. a new home buyer who does not have adequate credit history.
    d. a single parent who receives public assistance and cannot afford the payments.

34. A church has just purchased a large ranch that it intends to use for religious activities, including retreats and religious education. Which of the following outcomes can the owners of neighboring properties expect?

    a. An increase in value
    b. An increase in county services
    c. An increase in property taxes
    d. An increase in zoning enforcement

35. On a residential lot 70 feet square, the side-yard building setbacks are 10 feet, the front-yard setback is 25 feet, and the rear-yard setback is 20 feet. The maximum possible size for a one-story structure would be

     a.   1,000 square feet.   c.   1,250 square feet.
     b.   1,200 square feet.   d.   4,900 square feet.

36. The landlord of tenant *V* has sold his building to the state so that a freeway can be built. *V*'s lease has expired, but the landlord is letting him remain until such time as the building will be torn down. *V* continues to pay the same rent as indicated in his original lease. What type of tenancy does *V* have?

     a.   Holdover tenancy   c.   Tenancy at sufferance
     b.   Month-to-month tenancy   d.   Tenancy at will

37. By paying her debt after a foreclosure sale, the defaulted party has the right to regain her property under which of the following concepts?

     a.   Acceleration   c.   Reversion
     b.   Redemption   d.   Recovery

38. All of the following situations are in violation of the Federal Fair Housing Act of 1968 EXCEPT

     a.   the refusal of a property manager to rent an apartment to a Mormon couple who are otherwise qualified.
     b.   the general policy of a loan company to avoid granting home improvement loans to individuals living in transitional neighborhoods.
     c.   the intentional neglect of a broker to show an Asian family any property listings of homes in all-white neighborhoods.
     d.   the insistence of a widowed woman on renting her spare bedroom only to another widowed woman.

39. Broker *U* represented the seller in a transaction. Her client informed her that he did not want the deed to reflect the actual consideration that was paid for the property. In this situation, Broker *U*

a. may show only nominal consideration on the deed to the property.
b. should inform the seller that either the full price should be stated in the deed or all references to consideration should be removed.
c. must inform her client that only the actual price of the real estate can appear in the deed.
d. may show a price in the deed other than the actual price, provided that the variance is not greater than 10 percent of the purchase price.

40. When the title to real estate passes to a third party upon the death of a life tenant, what is the third party's interest in the property?

a. Remainder interest   c. Pur autre vie interest
b. Reversionary interest   d. Preemptory interest

41. An apartment building has an annual gross income of $87,500. Annual expenses are depreciation, $8,500; debt service, $34,000, including principal of $7,200; real estate taxes, $5,100; other operating costs, $14,100. The annual net operating income is

a. $25,800.   c. $41,500.
b. $34,300.   d. $68,300.

42. At the settlement, the lender asks for $345, which will be kept in a trust account. This money is most likely

a. a security deposit.
b. for taxes and insurance.
c. to ensure against borrower default.
d. to cover the expense of discount points.

43. A mortgage loan could be amortized with monthly payments of $1,200.22 for 15 years or monthly payments of $1,028.63 for 30 years. The 30-year loan results in total payments of what percent of the 15-year total payments?

a. 146%   c. 171%
b. 158%   d. 228%

44. In a sale-and-leaseback arrangement

   a. the buyer becomes the lessor of the property.
   b. the seller retains title to the real estate.
   c. the buyer gets possession of the property.
   d. the seller obtains a mortgage interest deduction.

45. *E* and *O,* co-owners of a corner parcel of vacant commercial property, have executed three open listings with three different brokers around town. All three brokers would like to place "for sale" signs on the sellers' property. Under these circumstances,

   a. only one "for sale" sign may be placed on the property at one time.
   b. upon obtaining the sellers' written consent, all brokers can place their "for sale" signs on the property.
   c. the broker who obtained the first open listing must consent to all signs being placed on the property.
   d. a broker does not have to obtain the seller's permission before placing a sign on the property.

46. In one commercial building, the tenant intends to start a health food store using her life savings. In an identical adjacent building is a catalog store leased to a major national retailing chain. Both tenants have long-term leases with identical rents. Which of the following statements is correct?

   a. An appraiser would most likely use a higher capitalization rate for the store leased to the national retailing chain.
   b. If the values of the buildings were the same before the leases, their values will be the same after they are leased.
   c. The building with the health food store will appraise for less than the other building.
   d. The most accurate appraisal method to be used would be the sales comparison analysis approach to value.

47. A conventional loan was closed on July 1 for $57,200 at 13½ percent interest amortized over 25 years at $666.75 per month. On August 1, what would the principal balance be after the first monthly payment was made?

   a. $56,533.25   c. $57,065.35
   b. $56,566.50   d. $57,176.75

48. What type of lease establishes a set rental payment and requires the lessor to pay for the taxes, insurance, and maintenance on the property?

    a.   A percentage lease   c.   A graduated lease
    b.   A net lease   d.   A gross lease

49. A parcel of ground over which an easement runs is called the

    a.   dominant tenement.   c.   prescriptive tenement.
    b.   servient tenement.   d.   eminent tenement.

50. *M* defaulted on his home mortgage loan payments, and the lender obtained a court order to foreclose on the property. At the foreclosure sale, however, *M*'s property sold for only $64,000 while the unpaid balance of the loan at the time of the foreclosure was $68,000. What must the lender do in an attempt to recover the $4,000 that *M* still owes?

    a.   Sue for specific performance
    b.   Sue for damages
    c.   Seek a judgment by default
    d.   Seek a deficiency judgment

51. What is the difference between a general lien and a specific lien?

    a.   A general lien cannot be enforced in court, while a specific lien can.
    b.   A specific lien is held by only one person, while a general lien is held by two or more.
    c.   A general lien is a lien against personal property, while a specific lien is a lien against real estate.
    d.   A specific lien is a lien against a certain parcel of real estate, while a general lien covers all of the debtor's property.

52. In an option to purchase real estate, the optionee

    a.   must purchase the property but may do so at any time within the option period.
    b.   is limited to a refund of the option consideration if the option is exercised.
    c.   has no obligation to purchase the property during the option period.
    d.   cannot obtain third-party financing on the property until after the option has expired.

53. The *K*s enter into a purchase contract with the *F*s to buy the *F*s' house for $84,500. The buyers pay $2,000 as earnest money and obtain a new mortgage for $67,600. The purchase contract provides for a March 15 settlement. The buyers and sellers prorate the previous year's real estate taxes of $1,880, which have been prepaid. The buyers have additional closing costs of $1,250, and the sellers have other closing costs of $850. How much cash must the buyers bring to the settlement?

    a. $19,638   c. $17,238
    b. $17,638   d. $16,388

54. Broker *M* took a listing and later discovered that her client had previously been declared incompetent by the court. The listing is now

    a.   unaffected, as *M* was acting in good faith as the owner's agent.
    b.   of no value to *M* because the contract is void.
    c.   the basis for recovery of a commission if *M* produces a buyer.
    d.   renegotiable between *M* and her client.

55. A broker receives a check for earnest money from a buyer and deposits it in an escrow or trust account to protect herself from the charge of

    a.   commingling.   c.   conversion.
    b.   novation.   d.   embezzlement.

56. Steering is

    a.   leading prospective homeowners to or away from certain areas.
    b.   refusing to make loans to persons residing in certain areas.
    c.   a requirement to join a multiple-listing service.
    d.   the practice of illegally setting commission rates.

57. What is a tenancy for years?

    a.   A tenancy with the consent of the landlord
    b.   A tenancy that expires on a specific date
    c.   A tenancy created by the death of the owner
    d.   A tenancy created by a testator

58. If a house was sold for $40,000 and the buyer obtained an FHA-insured mortgage loan for $38,500, how much money would be paid in discount points if the lender charged four points?

a. $1,600
b. $1,540
c. $1,500
d. $385

59. The Civil Rights Act of 1866 prohibits in all cases discrimination based upon a person's

a. sex.
b. race.
c. religion.
d. familial status.

60. A building was sold for $60,000 with the buyer making a 10 percent down payment and financing the balance. The lender charged a 1 percent loan origination fee. What was the total cash used for the purchase?

a. $540
b. $6,000
c. $6,450
d. $6,500

61. An individual seeking to be excused from the dictates of a zoning ordinance should request a

a. building permit.
b. certificate of alternate usage.
c. variance.
d. certificate of nonconforming use.

62. *J*'s real estate loan documents indicate that if she sells her property, she must immediately pay her lender in full. This clause is known as a(n)

a. acceleration clause.
b. alienation clause.
c. subordination clause.
d. habendum clause.

63. If the mortgage on a house is 80 percent of the appraised value and the mortgage interest rate of 8 percent amounts to $460 per month, what is the appraised value of the property?

a. $92,875
b. $86,250
c. $71,875
d. $69,000

64. *G* sold his property to *U*. In the deed of conveyance, *G*'s only guarantee was that the property was not encumbered during the time he owned it except as noted in the deed. The type of deed used in this transaction was a

a. general warranty deed.
b. special warranty deed.
c. bargain and sale deed.
d. quitclaim deed.

65. In the appraisal of a building constructed in the 1930s, the cost approach to value would be the least accurate method because of difficulties in

a. estimating changes in material costs.
b. obtaining 1930s building codes.
c. estimating changes in labor costs.
d. estimating accrued depreciation.

66. All of the following occurrences are violations of the Real Estate Settlement Procedures Act (RESPA) EXCEPT

a. directing the buyer to a particular lender.
b. accepting a kickback on a loan subject to RESPA requirements.
c. requiring the use of a particular title insurance company.
d. accepting a fee or charging for services that were not performed.

67. A man willed his estate as follows: 54 percent to his wife, 18 percent to his daughter, 16 percent to his son, and the remainder to his church. If the church received $79,000, how much did the daughter receive?

a. $105,333
b. $118,500
c. $355,500
d. $658,333

68. An example of external obsolescence would be

a. numerous pillars supporting the ceiling in a store.
b. roof leaks making premises unusable and therefore unrentable.
c. an older structure with massive cornices.
d. vacant and abandoned buildings in the area.

69. The type of loan that features increasing payments with the increases being applied directly to the debt reduction is a(n)

a. growing-equity mortgage.
b. shared-appreciation mortgage.
c. adjustable-rate mortgage.
d. graduated-payment mortgage.

70. When the buyer signs a purchase offer and the seller accepts it, the buyer acquires an immediate interest in the property, known as

    a. legal title.
    b. statutory title.
    c. defeasible title.
    d. equitable title.

71. Assuming that the listing broker and the seller broker in a transaction split their commission equally, what was the sales price of the property if the commission rate was 6½ percent and the listing broker received $2,593.50?

    a. $39,900
    b. $56,200
    c. $79,800
    d. $88,400

72. Q, no longer needing her large home, decides to sell it and move into a cooperative apartment building. Under the cooperative form of owner-ship, Q will

    a. become a stockholder in the corporation.
    b. not lose her apartment if she pays her share of the expenses.
    c. receive a fixed-term lease for her unit.
    d. have to take out a new mortgage loan on her unit.

73. The monthly rent on a warehouse was set at $1 per cubic yard. If the warehouse is 36 feet by 200 feet by 12 feet high, what would the annual rent be?

    a. $3,200
    b. $9,600
    c. $38,400
    d. $115,200

74. A broker would have to prove that he or she was the procuring cause un-der all of the following types of listing agreements EXCEPT a(n)

    a. net listing.
    b. open listing.
    c. exclusive-agency listing.
    d. exclusive-right-to-sell listing.

75. A man moved into an abandoned home, making extensive repairs and installing cabinets in the kitchen for his convenience. When the owner discovered the occupancy, he had the man ejected. What is the status of the cabinets?

    a. The man cannot get the cabinets back.
    b. The cabinets remain because they are trade fixtures.
    c. While the cabinets stay, the man is entitled to the value of the improvements.
    d. The man can recover the cabinets if they can be removed without damaging the real estate.

76. When placed in a printed advertisement, which of the following phrases would comply with the requirements of the Truth-in-Lending Act (Regulation Z)?

    a. "10 percent interest"
    b. "10 percent annual percent"
    c. "10 percent annual interest"
    d. "10 percent annual percentage rate"

77. On the settlement statement, the cost of the lender's title insurance policy that would be required for a new mortgage loan would usually be shown as a

    a. credit to the seller.   c. debit to the seller.
    b. credit to the buyer.   d. debit to the buyer.

78. If a home that originally cost $42,500 three years ago is now valued at 127 percent of its original cost, what is its current value?

    a. $33,465   c. $58,219
    b. $53,975   d. $65,354

79. Broker *E* listed widow *K*'s property at an 8 percent commission. After the property was sold and the settlement had occurred, *K* discovered that *E* had been listing similar properties in the area at a 6 percent commission rate. Based on this information,

    a. broker *E* has done nothing wrong.
    b. broker *E* can lose his license.
    c. widow *K* can cancel the transaction.
    d. widow *K* is entitled to a refund.

80. A farmer owns the W ½ of the NW ¼ of the NW ¼ of a section. The adjoining property can all be purchased for $300 per acre. Owning all of the NW ¼ of the section would cost the farmer

    a. $6,000.
    b. $12,000.
    c. $42,000.
    d. $48,000.

81. A borrower calculated the interest he was charged for the previous month on his $60,000 loan balance at $412.50. What is his interest rate?

    a. 7.5 percent
    b. 7.75 percent
    c. 8.25 percent
    d. 8.5 percent

82. A property manager would be LEAST likely to

    a. handle new leases.
    b. arrange for repairs and improvements.
    c. resolve tenant disputes as to property use.
    d. prepare depreciation schedules for tax purposes.

83. A veteran wants to refinance his home mortgage loan with a new VA-guaranteed loan. The lender is willing, but insists on 3.5 discount points. In this situation, the veteran

    a. can refinance with a VA-guaranteed loan, provided that there are no discount points.
    b. can refinance with a VA-guaranteed loan, provided that the discount points do not exceed two.
    c. can be required to pay a maximum of 1 percent of the loan as an origination fee.
    d. can proceed with the refinance loan and pay the discount points.

84. The requirements of the Real Estate Settlement Procedures Act (RESPA) apply to any residential real estate transactions that take place

    a. involving a federally related mortgage loan.
    b. in a state that has adopted RESPA.
    c. involving any mortgage financing less than $100,000.
    d. involving any purchase price less than $100,000.

85. When searching the public record, which of the following documents would ALWAYS be discovered?

    a. Encroachments
    b. Rights of parties in possession
    c. Inaccurate surveys
    d. Mechanics' liens

86. Capitalization rates are

    a. determined by the gross rent multipliers.
    b. the rates of return that a property will produce.
    c. mathematical values determined by the sales prices.
    d. determined by the amount of depreciation in properties.

87. A rectangular lot has an apartment structure on it worth $193,600. This value is the equivalent of $4.40 per square foot. If one lot dimension is 200 feet, what is the other dimension?

    a. 110 feet   c. 400 feet
    b. 220 feet   d. 880 feet

88. All of the following events will terminate an offer EXCEPT

    a. revocation of the offer before its acceptance.
    b. the death of the offeror before its acceptance.
    c. a counteroffer by the offeree.
    d. an offer from a third party.

89. *J* has just made the final payment on his mortgage loan to the bank. Regardless of this fact, the lender will still hold a lien on *J*'s mortgaged property until which of the following documents is recorded?

    a. A satisfaction   c. A novation
    b. A reconveyance   d. An estoppel

90. Discount points on a real estate loan are a potential cost to both the seller and the buyer. Such points are

    a. set by the FHA and the VA for their loan programs.
    b. charged only on conventional loans.
    c. limited by government regulations.
    d. determined by the market for money.

91.   What is the cost of constructing a fence 6 feet 6 inches high around a lot measuring 90 feet by 175 feet, if the cost of erecting the fence is $1.25 per linear foot and the cost of materials is $0.825 per square foot of fence?

    a. $1,752   c. $2,084
    b. $2,054   d. $3,505

92.   All of the following situations are exemptions to the Federal Fair Housing Act of 1968 EXCEPT

    a.   the listing of a single-family residence where the listing broker does not advertise the property.
    b.   the restriction of noncommercial lodgings by a private club to members of the club.
    c.   the rental of a unit in an owner-occupied three-family dwelling.
    d.   the restriction of residency in a monastery.

93.   All of the following statements are true regarding adverse possession EXCEPT

    a.   the person taking possession of the property must do so without the consent of the owner of the property.
    b.   occupancy of the property by the person taking possession must be continuous over a specified period of time.
    c.   the person taking possession of the property must compensate the owner at the end of the adverse possession period.
    d.   the person taking possession of the property could ultimately end up owning the property.

94.   What would it cost to put new carpeting in a den measuring 15 feet by 20 feet if the cost of the carpeting is $6.95 per square yard and the cost of laying it is an additional $250?

    a. $232   c. $610
    b. $482   d. $2,335

95.   If the landlord of an apartment building breaches his lease with one of his tenants and her unit becomes uninhabitable, which of the following events would be the most likely result?

    a.   Suit for possession   c.   Constructive eviction
    b.   Tenancy at sufferance   d.   Covenant of quiet enjoyment

96. The rescission provisions of the Truth-in-Lending Act (Regulation Z) apply to

   a.   business financing.   c.   consumer credit.
   b.   construction lending.   d.   real estate loans.

97. A house is sold for $84,500 and the commission rate is 7 percent. If the commission is split 60/40 between the selling broker and the listing broker, respectively, and each broker splits his share of the commission evenly with his salesperson, how much will the listing salesperson receive from this sale?

   a. $1,183   c. $2,366
   b. $1,775   d. $3,549

98. Failing to assert a right within a reasonable or statutory period of time might lead a court to determine that the right to assert it is now lost because of

   a.   laches.   c.   rescission.
   b.   novation.   d.   revocation.

99. Fannie Mae and Ginnie Mae are both

   a.   involved as primary market lenders.
   b.   involved in the secondary market.
   c.   federal agencies.
   d.   privately owned entities.

100. For a deed to be valid, all of the following must be included EXCEPT

   a.   a legal description of the property being conveyed.
   b.   the signature of the grantee.
   c.   a grantor having the legal capacity to execute the deed.
   d.   some form of consideration.

Glossary

abstract of title The condensed history of a title to a particular parcel of real estate, consisting of a summary of the original grant and all subsequent conveyances and encumbrances affecting the property and a certification by the abstractor that the history is complete and accurate.

acceleration clause The clause in a mortgage or deed of trust that can be enforced to make the entire debt due immediately if the borrower defaults on an installment payment or other covenant.

accession Acquiring title to additions or improvements to real property as a result of the annexation of fixtures or the accretion of alluvial deposits along the banks of streams.

accretion The increase or addition of land by the deposit of sand or soil washed up naturally from a river, lake or sea.

accrued items On a closing statement, items of expense incurred but not yet payable, such as interest on a mortgage loan or taxes on real property.

acknowledgment A formal declaration made before a duly authorized officer, usually a notary public, by a person who has signed a document.

actual eviction The legal process that results in the tenant's being physically removed from the leased premises.

actual notice Express information or fact; that which is known; direct knowledge.

adjustable-rate mortgage (ARM) A loan characterized by a fluctuating interest rate, usually one tied to a bank or savings and loan association cost-of-funds index.

adjusted basis *See* basis.

ad valorem tax A tax levied according to value, generally used to refer to real estate tax. Also called the *general tax.*

adverse possession The actual, open, notorious, hostile and continuous possession of another's land under a claim of title. Possession for a statutory period may be a means of acquiring title.

affidavit of title A written statement, made under oath by a seller or grantor of real property and acknowledged by a notary public, in which the grantor (1) identifies himself or herself and indicates marital status, (2) certifies that since the examination of the title on the date of the contracts no defects have occurred in the title and (3) certifies that he or she is in possession of the property (if applicable).

agency The relationship between a principal and an agent, usually a property owner and a real estate broker.

agency coupled with an interest An agency relationship in which the agent is given an estate or interest in the subject of the agency (the property).

agent One who acts or has the power to act for another. A fiduciary relationship is created under the *law of agency* when a property owner, as the principal, executes a listing agreement or management contract authorizing a real estate broker to be his or her agent.

air lot A designated airspace over a piece of land. An air lot, like surface property, may be transferred.

air rights The right to use the open space above a property, usually allowing the surface to be used for another purpose.

alienation The act of transferring property to another. Alienation may be voluntary, such as by gift or sale, or involuntary, as through eminent domain or adverse possession.

alienation clause The clause in a mortgage or deed of trust that states that the balance of the secured debt becomes immediately due and payable at the lender's option if the property is sold by the borrower. In effect this clause prevents the borrower from assigning the debt without the lender's approval.

allodial system A system of land ownership in which land is held free and clear of any rent or service due to the government; commonly contrasted to the feudal system. Land is held under the allodial system in the United States.

American Land Title Association (ALTA) policy A title insurance policy that protects the interest in a collateral property of a mortgage lender who originates a new real estate loan.

amortized loan A loan in which the principal as well as the interest is payable in monthly or other periodic installments over the term of the loan.

anticipation The appraisal principle that holds that value can increase or decrease based on the expectation of some future benefit or detriment produced by the property.

antitrust laws Laws designed to preserve the free enterprise of the open marketplace by making illegal certain private conspiracies and combinations formed to minimize competition. Most violations of antitrust laws in the real estate business involve either *price-fixing* (brokers conspiring to set fixed compensation rates) or *allocation of customers or markets* (brokers agreeing to limit their areas of trade or dealing to certain areas or properties).

appraisal An estimate of the quantity, quality or value of something. The process through which conclusions of property value are obtained; also refers to the report that sets forth the process of estimation and conclusion of value.

appreciation An increase in the worth or value of a property due to economic or related causes, which may prove to be either temporary or permanent; opposite of depreciation.

appropriation An action taken by a taxing body that authorizes the expenditure of funds and provides for the sources of money. Appropriation generally involves the adoption of an ordinance or the passage of a law setting forth the specifics of the proposed taxation.

area The space inside a two-dimensional shape. Area equals length times width.

assemblage The combining of two or more adjoining lots into one larger tract to increase their total value.

assignment The transfer in writing of interest in a bond, mortgage, lease or other instrument.

assumption of mortgage Acquiring title to property on which there is an existing mortgage and agreeing to be personally liable for the terms and conditions of the mortgage, including payments.

attachment The act of taking a person's property into legal custody by writ or other judicial order to hold it available for application to that person's debt to a creditor.

attorney-in-fact A person who performs one or more acts for another person according to the authority granted to them in a document known as a *power of attorney*.

attorney's opinion of title An abstract of title that an attorney has examined and has certified to be, in his or her opinion, an accurate statement of the facts concerning the property ownership.

automatic extension A clause in a listing agreement that states that the agreement will continue automatically for a certain period of time after its expiration date. In many states, use of this clause is discouraged or prohibited.

avulsion The sudden tearing away of land, as by earthquake, flood, volcanic action or the sudden change in the course of a stream.

balance The appraisal principle that states that the greatest value in a property will occur when the type and size of the improvements are proportional to each other as well as the land.

balloon payment A final payment of a mortgage loan that is considerably larger than the required periodic payments because the loan amount was not fully amortized.

bargain and sale deed A deed that carries with it no warranties against liens or other encumbrances but that does imply that the grantor has the right to convey title. The grantor may add warranties to the deed at his or her discretion.

base line The main imaginary line running east and west and crossing a principal meridian at a definite point, used by surveyors for reference in locating and describing land under the rectangular (government) survey system of legal description.

basis The financial interest that the Internal Revenue Service attributes to an owner of an investment property for the purpose of determining annual depreciation and gain or loss on the sale of the asset. If a property was acquired by purchase, the owner's basis is the cost of the property plus the value of any capital expenditures for improvements to the property, minus any depreciation allowable or actually taken. This new basis is called the *adjusted basis*.

benchmark A permanent reference mark or point established for use by surveyors in measuring differences in elevation.

beneficiary (1) The person for whom a trust operates or in whose behalf the income from a trust estate is drawn. (2) A lender in a deed of trust loan transaction.

bilateral contract *See* contract.

blanket loan A mortgage covering more than one parcel of real estate, providing for each parcel's partial release from the mortgage lien upon repayment of a definite portion of the debt.

blockbusting The illegal practice of inducing homeowners to sell their properties by making representations regarding the entry or prospective entry of persons of a particular race or national origin into the neighborhood.

blue-sky laws Common name for those state and federal laws that regulate the registration and sale of investment securities.

boot Money or property given to make up any difference in value or equity between two properties in an *exchange*.

branch office A secondary place of business apart from the principal or main office from which real estate business is conducted. A branch office usually must be run by a licensed real estate broker working on behalf of the broker who operates the principal office.

breach of contract Violation of any terms or conditions in a contract without legal excuse; for example, failure to make a payment when it is due.

broker One who acts as an intermediary on behalf of others for a fee or commission.

brokerage The bringing together of parties interested in making a real estate transaction.

buffer zone A strip of land, usually used as a park or designated for a similar use, separating land dedicated to one use from land dedicated to another use (e.g., residential from commercial).

building code An ordinance that specifies minimum standards of construction for buildings to protect public safety and health.

building permit Written governmental permission for the construction, alteration or demolition of an improvement, showing compliance with building codes and zoning ordinances.

bulk transfer *See* Uniform Commercial Code.

bundle of legal rights The concept of land ownership that includes ownership *of all legal rights to the land*—for example, possession, control within the law and enjoyment.

buydown A financing technique used to reduce the monthly payments for the first few years of a loan. Funds in the form of discount points are given to the lender by the builder or seller to buy down or lower the effective interest rate paid by the buyer, thus reducing the monthly payments for a set time.

capital gain The taxable profit derived from the sale of a capital asset. It is the difference between the sales price and the basis of the property after making adjustments for closing costs, capital improvements and allowable depreciation.

capitalization A mathematical process for estimating the value of a property using a proper rate of return on the investment and the annual net income expected to be produced by the property. The formula is expressed:

$$\frac{\text{Income}}{\text{Rate}} = \text{Value}$$

capitalization rate The rate of return a property will produce on the owner's investment.

cash flow The net spendable income from an investment, determined by deducting all operating and fixed expenses from the gross income. If expenses exceed income, a *negative cash flow* is the result.

cash rent In an agricultural lease, the amount of money given as rent to the landowner at the outset of the lease, as opposed to sharecropping.

caveat emptor A Latin phrase meaning "Let the buyer beware."

certificate of sale The document generally given to the purchaser at a tax foreclosure sale. A certificate of sale does not convey title; normally it is an instrument certifying that the holder received title to the property after the redemption period passed and that the holder paid the property taxes for that interim period.

certificate of title A statement of opinion on the status of the title to a parcel of real property based on an examination of specified public records.

chain of title The succession of conveyances, from some accepted starting point, whereby the present holder of real property derives title.

change The appraisal principle that holds that no physical or economic condition remains constant.

chattel *See* personal property.

Civil Rights Act of 1866 The first civil rights act passed in the United States, this law prohibits any type of discrimination based on race. "All citizens of the United States shall have the same right in every state and territory as is enjoyed by white citizens thereof to inherit, purchase, lease, sell, hold, and convey real and personal property." The constitutionality of this law was upheld by the Supreme Court in 1968 when it rendered its decision in the case of *Jones v. Mayer Company*. This decision, based on the 13th Amendment to the U.S. Constitution, has served as a basis for all subsequent civil rights legislation.

closing statement A detailed cash accounting of a real estate transaction showing all cash received, all charges and credits made and all cash paid out in the transaction.

cloud on title Any document, claim, unreleased lien or encumbrance that may impair the title to real property or make the title doubtful; usually revealed by a title search and removed by either a quitclaim deed or suit to quiet title.

clustering The grouping of homesites within a subdivision on smaller lots than normal, with the remaining land used as common areas.

codicil A supplement or an addition to a will, executed with the same formalities as a will, that normally does not revoke the entire will.

coinsurance clause A clause in insurance policies covering real property that requires the policyholder to maintain fire insurance coverage generally equal to at least 80 percent of the property's actual replacement cost.

commercial banks Institutional lenders with the following lending characteristics: small loans for short terms, such as construction, home improvement and mobile-home loans; relatively low loan-to-value ratio; regulated by the Federal Reserve Banking System; and deposits insured by the FDIC (Federal Deposit Insurance Corporation).

commingling The illegal act by a real estate broker of placing client or customer funds with personal funds. By law brokers are required to maintain a separate *trust account* for other parties' funds held temporarily by the broker.

commission Payment to a broker for services rendered, such as in the sale or purchase of real property; usually a percentage of the selling price of the property.

common elements Parts of a property that are necessary or convenient to the existence, maintenance and safety of a condominium or are normally in common use by all of the condominium residents. Each condominium owner has an undivided ownership interest in the common elements.

common law The body of law based on custom, usage and court decisions.

community property A system of property ownership based on the theory that each spouse has an equal interest in the property acquired by the efforts of either spouse during marriage. A holdover of Spanish law, found predominantly in western states; the system was unknown under English common law.

comparables Properties used in an appraisal report that are substantially equivalent to the subject property.

competition The appraisal principle that states that excess profits generate competition.

competitive market analysis (CMA) A comparison of the prices of recently sold homes that are similar to a listing seller's home in terms of location, style and amenities.

condemnation A judicial or administrative proceeding to exercise the power of eminent domain, through which a government agency takes private property for public use and compensates the owner.

conditional-use permit Written governmental permission allowing a use inconsistent with zoning but necessary for the common good, such as locating an emergency medical facility in a predominantly residential area.

condominium The absolute ownership of a unit in a multiunit building based on a legal description of the airspace the unit actually occupies, plus an undivided interest in the ownership of the common elements, which are owned jointly with the other condominium unit owners.

conformity The appraisal principle that holds that the greater the similarity among properties in an area, the better they will hold their value.

consideration (1) That received by the grantor in exchange for his or her deed. (2) Something of value that induces a person to enter into a contract.

construction loan A short-term loan usually made during the construction phase of a building project.

constructive eviction Actions of a landlord that so materially disturb or impair a tenant's enjoyment of the leased premises that the tenant is effectively forced to move out and terminate the lease without liability for any further rent.

constructive notice Notice given to the world by recorded documents. All people are charged with knowledge of such documents and their contents, whether or not they have actually examined them. Possession of property is also considered constructive notice that the person in possession has an interest in the property.

contingency A provision in a contract that requires a certain act to be done or a certain event to occur before the contract becomes binding.

contract A legally enforceable promise or set of promises that must be performed and for which, if a breach of the promise occurs, the law provides a remedy. A contract may be either *unilateral,* by which only one party is bound to act, or *bilateral,* by which all parties to the instrument are legally bound to act as prescribed.

contract rent The amount of rent the tenant must pay the landlord for the use of the leased premises as specified in the lease contract.

contribution The appraisal principle that states that the value of any component of a property is what it gives to the value of the whole or what its absence detracts from that value.

conventional loan A loan that is not insured or guaranteed by a government source.

cooperating broker *See* listing broker.

cooperative A residential multiunit building whose title is held by a trust or corporation that is owned by and operated for the benefit of persons living within the building, who are the beneficial owners of the trust or stockholders of the corporation, each possessing a proprietary lease.

co-ownership When title to one parcel of real estate is owned by two or more persons or organizations, such persons or organizations are said to be co-owners, or concurrent owners, of the property.

corporation An entity or organization, created by operation of law, whose rights of doing business are essentially the same as those of an individual. The entity has continuous existence until it is dissolved according to legal procedures.

correction lines Provisions in the rectangular survey (government survey) system made to compensate for the curvature of the earth's surface. Every fourth township line (at 24-mile intervals) is used as a correction line on which the intervals between the north and south range lines are remeasured and corrected to a full six miles.

cost approach The process of estimating the value of a property by adding to the estimated land value the appraiser's estimate of the reproduction or replacement cost of the building, less depreciation.

cost recovery An Internal Revenue Service term for *depreciation.*

counteroffer A new offer made as a reply to an offer received. It has the effect of rejecting the original offer, which cannot be accepted thereafter unless revived by the offeror.

covenant A written agreement between two or more parties in which a party or parties pledge to perform or not perform specified acts with regard to property; usually found in such real estate documents as deeds, mortgages, leases and contracts for deed.

covenant of quiet enjoyment The covenant implied by law by which a landlord guarantees that a tenant may take possession of leased premises and that the landlord will not interfere in the tenant's possession or use of the property.

credit On a closing statement, an amount entered in a person's favor—either an amount the party has paid or an amount for which the party must be reimbursed.

curtesy A life estate, usually a fractional interest, given by some states to the surviving husband in real estate owned by his deceased wife.

datum A horizontal plane from which heights and depths are measured.

debit On a closing statement, an amount charged; that is, an amount that the debited party must pay.

decedent A person who has died.

dedication The voluntary transfer of private property by its owner to the public for some public use, such as for streets or schools.

deed A written instrument that, when executed and delivered, conveys title to or an interest in real estate.

deed in trust An instrument that grants a trustee under a land trust full power to sell, mortgage and subdivide a parcel of real estate. The beneficiary controls the trustee's use of these powers under the provisions of the trust agreement.

deed of trust *See* trust deed.

deed of trust lien *See* trust deed lien.

deed restrictions Clauses in a deed limiting the future uses of the property. Deed restrictions may impose a vast variety of limitations and conditions—for example, they may limit the density of buildings, dictate the types of structures that can be erected or prevent buildings from being used for specific purposes or even from being used at all.

default The nonperformance of a duty, whether arising under a contract or otherwise; failure to meet an obligation when due.

defeasance clause A clause used in leases and mortgages that cancels a specified right upon the occurrence of a certain condition, such as cancellation of a mortgage upon repayment of the mortgage loan.

defeasible fee estate An estate in which the holder has a fee simple title that may be divested upon the occurrence or nonoccurrence of a specified event. There are two categories of defeasible fee estates: fee simple on condition precedent (fee simple determinable) and fee simple on condition subsequent.

deficiency judgment A personal judgment levied against the borrower when a foreclosure sale does not produce sufficient funds to pay the mortgage debt in full.

demand The amount of goods people are willing and able to buy at a given price; often coupled with *supply*.

denial, suspension or revocation of license The potential penalties for licensees who violate real estate statutes or rules and regulations.

density zoning Zoning ordinances that restrict the maximum average number of houses per acre that may be built within a particular area, generally a subdivision.

Department of Housing and Urban Development The federal agency charged wth responsibility of enforcing the Federal Fair Housing Act, specifically, the *Office of Equal Opportunity* (OEO).

depreciation (1) In appraisal, a loss of value in property due to any cause, including physical deterioration, *functional obsolescence* and *external obsolescence*. (2) In real estate investment, an expense deduction for tax purposes taken over the period of ownership of income property.

descent Acquisition of an estate by inheritance in which an heir succeeds to the property by operation of law.

developer One who attempts to put land to its most profitable use through the construction of improvements.

devise A gift of real property by will. The donor is the devisor, and the recipient is the devisee.

disclosed dual agent An agent who has received the informed, written consent of a buyer and seller to represent both parties to a transaction.

discount point A unit of measurement used for various loan charges; one point equals one percent of the amount of the loan.

dominant tenement A property that includes in its ownership the appurtenant right to use an easement over another person's property for a specific purpose.

dower The legal right or interest, recognized in some states, that a wife acquires in the property her husband held or acquired during their marriage. During the husband's lifetime the right is only a possibility of an interest; upon his death it can become an interest in land.

dual agency Representing both parties to a transaction. This is unethical unless both parties agree to it, and it is illegal in many states. *See* disclosed dual agent.

duress Unlawful constraint or action exercised upon a person whereby the person is forced to perform an act against his or her will. A contract entered into under duress is voidable.

earnest money Money deposited by a buyer under the terms of a contract, to be forfeited if the buyer defaults but applied to the purchase price if the sale is closed.

easement A right to use the land of another for a specific purpose, such as for a right-of-way or utilities; an incorporeal interest in land.

easement by necessity An easement allowed by law as necessary for the full enjoyment of a parcel of real estate; for example, a right of ingress and egress over a grantor's land.

easement by prescription An easement acquired by continuous, open and hostile use of the property for the period of time prescribed by state law.

easement in gross An easement that is not created for the benefit of any *land* owned by the owner of the easement but that attaches *personally to the easement owner.* For example, a right granted by Eleanor Franks to Joe Fish to use a portion of her property for the rest of his life would be an easement in gross.

economic life The number of years during which an improvement will add value to the land.

economic rent The amount of rent the property would command in a fully informed competitive marketplace. The *going* market rate for rental space.

emblements Growing crops, such as grapes and corn, that are produced annually through labor and industry; also called *fructus industriales.*

eminent domain The right of a government or municipal quasi-public body to acquire property for public use through a court action called *condemnation,* in which the court decides that the use is a public use and determines the compensation to be paid to the owner.

employee Someone who works as a direct employee of an employer and has employee status. The employer is obligated to withhold income taxes and social security taxes from the compensation of employees. *See also* independent contractor.

employment contract A document evidencing formal employment between employer and employee or between principal and agent. In the real estate business this generally takes the form of a listing agreement or management agreement.

enabling acts State legislation that confers zoning powers on municipal governments.

encroachment A building or some portion of it—a wall or fence for instance— that extends beyond the land of the owner and illegally intrudes on some land of an adjoining owner or a street or alley.

encumbrance Anything—such as a mortgage, tax, or judgment lien, an easement, a restriction on the use of the land or an outstanding dower right—that may diminish the value of a property.

Equal Credit Opportunity Act (ECOA) The federal law that prohibits discrimination in the extension of credit because of race, color, religion, national origin, sex, age or marital status.

equalization The raising or lowering of assessed values for tax purposes in a particular county or taxing district to make them equal to assessments in other counties or districts.

equalization factor A factor (number) by which the assessed value of a property is multiplied to arrive at a value for the property that is in line with statewide tax assessments. The *ad valorem tax* would be based on this adjusted value.

equitable lien *See* statutory lien.

equitable right of redemption The right of a defaulted property owner to recover the property prior to its sale by paying the appropriate fees and charges.

equitable title The interest held by a vendee under a contract for deed or an installment contract; the equitable right to obtain absolute ownership to property when legal title is held in another's name.

equity The interest or value that an owner has in property over and above any mortgage indebtedness.

erosion The gradual wearing away of land by water, wind and general weather conditions; the diminishing of property by the elements.

escheat The reversion of property to the state or county, as provided by state law, in cases where a decedent dies intestate without heirs capable of inheriting, or when the property is abandoned.

escrow The closing of a transaction through a third party called an *escrow agent* or *escrowee*, who receives certain funds and documents to be delivered upon the performance of certain conditions outlined in the escrow instructions.

escrow instructions A document that sets forth the duties of the escrow agent, as well as the requirements and obligations of the parties, when a transaction is closed through an escrow.

estate at sufferance The tenancy of a lessee who lawfully comes into possession of a landlord's real estate but who continues to occupy the premises improperly after his or her lease rights have expired.

estate at will An estate that gives the lessee the right to possession until the estate is terminated by either party; the term of this estate is indefinite.

estate for years An interest for a certain, exact period of time in property leased for a specified consideration.

estate from period to period An interest in leased property that continues from period to period—week to week, month to month or year to year.

estate in land The degree, quantity, nature and extent of interest a person has in real property.

estate taxes Federal taxes on a decedent's real and personal property.

estoppel Method of creating an agency relationship in which someone states incorrectly that another person is his or her agent, and a third person relies on that representation.

estoppel certificate A document in which a borrower certifies the amount owed on a mortgage loan and the rate of interest.

eviction A legal process to oust a person from possession of real estate.

evidence of title Proof of ownership of property; commonly a certificate of title, an abstract of title with lawyer's opinion or a Torrens registration certificate.

exchange A transaction in which all or part of the consideration is the transfer of *like-kind* property (such as real estate for real estate).

exclusive-agency listing A listing contract under which the owner appoints a real estate broker as his or her exclusive agent for a designated period of time to sell the property, on the owner's stated terms, for a commission. The owner reserves the right to sell without paying anyone a commission if he or she sells to a prospect who has not been introduced or claimed by the broker.

exclusive-right-to-sell listing A listing contract under which the owner appoints a real estate broker as his or her exclusive agent for a designated period of time to sell the property, on the owner's stated terms, and agrees to pay the broker a commission when the property is sold, whether by the broker, the owner or another broker.

executed contract A contract in which all parties have fulfilled their promises and thus performed the contract.

execution The signing and delivery of an instrument. Also, a legal order directing an official to enforce a judgment against the property of a debtor.

executor An individual named in a will to oversee the administration and distribution of the estate of a person dying testate.

executory contract A contract under which something remains to be done by one or more of the parties.

express agreement An oral or written contract in which the parties state the contract's terms and express their intentions in words.

express contract *See* express agreement.

external obsolescence Reduction in a property's value caused by outside factors (those that are off the property).

Farmers Home Administration (FmHA) An agency of the federal government that provides credit assistance to farmers and other individuals who live in rural areas.

Federal Fair Housing Act of 1968 Provides that it is unlawful to discriminate on the basis of race, color, religion, sex, or national origin when selling or leasing residential property.

Federal Home Loan Mortgage Corporation (FHLMC, Freddie Mac) A corporation established to purchase primarily conventional mortgage loans on the secondary mortgage market.

Federal National Mortgage Association (FNMA, Fannie Mae) A quasi-government agency established to purchase any kind of mortgage loan in the secondary mortgage market from the primary lenders.

Federal Reserve System The central banking system of the United States which is responsible for the nation's monetary policy by regulating the supply of money and interest rates.

fee simple absolute The maximum possible estate or right of ownership of real property, continuing forever.

fee simple defeasible *See* defeasible fee estate.

fee tail An estate in land in which the right of inheritance is limited to the fee tail tenant's blood descendants, referred to as heirs or issue "of the body."

feudal system A system of ownership usually associated with precolonial England, in which the king or other sovereign is the source of all rights. The right to possess real property was granted by the sovereign to an individual as a life estate only. Upon the death of the individual title passed back to the sovereign, not to the decedent's heirs.

FHA loan A loan insured by the Federal Housing Administration and made by an approved lender in accordance with the FHA's regulations.

fiduciary One in whom trust and confidence is placed; usually a reference to a broker employed under the terms of a listing contract.

fiduciary relationship A relationship of trust and confidence, as between trustee and beneficiary, attorney and client or principal and agent.

financing statement *See* Uniform Commercial Code.

fixture An item of personal property that has been converted to real property by being permanently affixed to the realty.

foreclosure A legal procedure whereby property used as security for a debt is sold to satisfy the debt in the event of default in payment of the mortgage note or default of other terms in the mortgage document. The foreclosure procedure brings the rights of all parties to a conclusion and passes the title in the mortgaged property to either the holder of the mortgage or a third party who may purchase the realty at the foreclosure sale, free of all encumbrances affecting the property subsequent to the mortgage.

fractional section A parcel of land less than 160 acres, usually found at the edge of a rectangular survey.

franchise A private contractual agreement to run a business using a designated trade name and operating procedures.

fraud Deception intended to cause a person to give up property or a lawful right.

freehold estate An estate in land in which ownership is for an indeterminate length of time, in contrast to a *leasehold estate*.

functional obsolescence A loss of value to an improvement to real estate arising from functional problems, often caused by age or poor design.

future interest A person's present right to an interest in real property that will not result in possession or enjoyment until some time in the future, such as a reversion or right of reentry.

gap A defect in the chain of title of a particular parcel of real estate; a missing document or conveyance that raises doubt as to the present ownership of the land.

general agent One who is authorized by a principal to represent the principal in a specific range of matters.

general lien The right of a creditor to have all of a debtor's property—both real and personal—sold to satisfy a debt.

general partnership *See* partnership.

general warranty deed A deed in which the grantor fully warrants good clear title to the premises. Used in most real estate

deed transfers, a general warranty deed offers the greatest protection of any deed.

government check The 24-mile-square parcels composed of 16 townships in the rectangular (government) survey system of legal description.

government lot Fractional sections in the rectangular (government) survey system that are less than one quarter-section in area.

government survey system *See* rectangular (government) survey system.

graduated lease A lease that allows for increases or decreases in the amount of rent being paid during the lease term, or any renewal of that term. Graduated leases are normally either step-up leases, allowing for previously agreed-upon increases in the amount of rent being paid, for example, increases of ten percent annually, or index leases, which allow rent increases or decreases periodically based on changes in some designated index, for example, the cost-of-living or consumer price index. Both provide the landlord with a hedge against inflation, but the index lease with its *floating* provision is considered to provide the best hedge against increasing costs for the landlord.

graduated-payment mortgage (GPM) A loan in which the monthly principal and interest payments increase by a certain percentage each year for a certain number of years and then level off for the remaining loan term.

grant deed Deed of conveyance used primarily in western states. They contain no expressed warranties, but the grantors are obligated by implied warranties established by state law.

grantee A person who receives a conveyance of real property from a grantor.

granting clause Words in a deed of conveyance that state the grantor's intention to convey the property at the present time. This clause is generally worded as "convey and warrant," "grant," "grant, bargain and sell" or the like.

grantor The person transferring title to or an interest in real property to a grantee.

gross income multiplier A figure used as a multiplier of the gross annual income of a property to produce an estimate of the property's value.

gross lease A lease of property according to which a landlord pays all property charges regularly incurred through ownership, such as repairs, taxes, insurance and operating expenses. Most residential leases are gross leases.

gross rent multiplier (GRM) The figure used as a multiplier of the gross monthly income of a property to produce an estimate of the property's value.

ground lease A lease of land only, on which the tenant usually owns a building or is required to build as specified in the lease. Such leases are usually long-term net leases; the tenant's rights and obligations continue until the lease expires or is terminated through default.

growing-equity mortgage (GEM) A loan in which the monthly payments increase annually, with the increased amount being used to reduce directly the principal balance outstanding and thus shorten the overall term of the loan.

habendum clause That part of a deed beginning with the words, "to have and to hold," following the granting clause and defining the extent of ownership the grantor is conveying.

heir One who might inherit or succeed to an interest in land under the state law of descent when the owner dies without leaving a valid will.

highest and best use The possible use of a property that would produce the greatest net income and thereby develop the highest value.

holdover tenancy A tenancy whereby a lessee retains possession of leased property after the lease has expired and the landlord, by continuing to accept rent, agrees to the tenant's continued occupancy as defined by state law.

holographic will A will that is written, dated and signed in the testator's handwriting.

home equity loan A loan (sometimes called a *line of credit*) under which a property owner uses his or her residence as collateral and can then draw funds up to a prearranged amount against the property.

homeowner's insurance policy A standardized package insurance policy that covers a residential real estate owner against financial loss from fire, theft, public liability and other common risks.

homestead Land that is owned and occupied as the family home. In many states a portion of the area or value of this land is protected or exempt from judgments for debts.

hypothecation The pledge of property as security for a loan.

implied agreement A contract under which the agreement of the parties is demonstrated by their acts and conduct.

implied contract *See* implied agreement.

improvement (1) Any structure, usually privately owned, erected on a site to enhance the value of the property—for example, building a fence or a driveway. (2) A publicly owned structure added to or benefiting land, such as a curb, sidewalk, street or sewer.

income approach The process of estimating the value of an income-producing property by capitalization of the annual net income expected to be produced by the property during its remaining useful life.

income capitalization approach The process of estimating the value of an income-producing property through capitalization of the annual net income expected to be produced by the property during its remaining useful life.

incorporeal right A nonpossessory right in real estate; for example, an easement or a right-of-way.

independent contractor Someone who is retained to perform a certain act but who is subject to the control and direction of another only as to the end result and not as to the way in which the act is performed. Unlike an employee, an independent contractor pays for all expenses and social security and income taxes and receives no employee benefits. Most real estate salespeople are independent contractors.

index lease A lease that provides for adjustments for rent according to changes in a price index, such as the consumer price index. The index used in establishing the escalation must be reliable and bear a closer relationship to the nature of tenant's business. The most frequently used indexes are the consumer price index (cost-of-living index) and the wholesale price index.

index method The appraisal method of estimating building costs by multiplying the original cost of the property by a percentage factor to adjust for current construction costs.

inflation The gradual reduction of the purchasing power of the dollar, usually related directly to the increases in the money supply by the federal government.

inheritance taxes State-imposed taxes on a decedent's real and personal property.

installment contract A contract for the sale of real estate whereby the purchase price is paid in periodic installments by the purchaser, who is in possession of the property even though title is retained by the seller until a future date, which may be not until final payment. Also called a *contract for deed* or *articles of agreement for warranty deed.*

installment sale A transaction in which the sales price is paid in two or more installments over two or more years. If the sale meets certain requirements, a taxpayer can postpone reporting such income until future years by paying tax each year only on the proceeds received that year.

instrument A formal, written legal document such as a contract, deed or lease.

interest A charge made by a lender for the use of money.

interim financing A short-term loan usually made during the construction phase of a building project (in this case often referred to as a *construction loan*).

Interstate Land Sales Full Disclosure Act A consumer protection act that requires those engaged in the interstate sale or leasing of 50 or more unimproved lots to register the details of the land with the U.S. Department of Housing and Urban Development (HUD). The seller is also required to furnish prospective buyers a property report containing all essential information about the property.

intestate The condition of a property owner who dies without leaving a valid will. Title to the property will pass to the decedent's heirs as provided in the state law of descent.

intrinsic value An appraisal term referring to the value created by a person's personal preferences for a particular type of property.

investment Money directed toward the purchase, improvement and development of an asset in expectation of income or profits.

involuntary alienation *See* alienation.

involuntary lien A lien placed on property without the consent of the property owner.

joint tenancy Ownership of real estate between two or more parties who have been named in one conveyance as joint tenants. Upon the death of a joint tenant, the decedent's interest passes to the surviving joint tenant or tenants by the *right of survivorship*.

joint venture The joining of two or more people to conduct a specific business enterprise. A joint venture is similar to a partnership in that it must be created by agreement between the parties to share in the losses and profits of the venture. It is unlike a partnership in that the venture is for one specific project only, rather than for a continuing business relationship.

judgment The formal decision of a court upon the respective rights and claims of the parties to an action or suit. After a judgment has been entered and recorded with the county recorder, it usually becomes a general lien on the property of the defendant.

junior lien An obligation, such as a second mortgage, that is subordinate in right or lien priority to an existing lien on the same realty.

laches An equitable doctrine used by courts to bar a legal claim or prevent the assertion of a right because of undue delay or failure to assert the claim or right.

land The earth's surface, extending downward to the center of the earth and upward infinitely into space, including things permanently attached by nature, such as trees and water.

land contract *See* installment contract.

law of agency *See* agency.

lease A written or oral contract between a landlord (the lessor) and a tenant (the lessee) that transfers the right to exclusive possession and use of the landlord's real property to the lessee for a specified period of time and for a stated consideration (rent). By state law leases for longer than a certain period of time (generally one year) must be in writing to be enforceable.

leasehold estate A tenant's right to occupy real estate during the term of a lease, generally considered to be a personal property interest.

lease option A lease under which the tenant has the right to purchase the property either during the lease term or at its end.

lease purchase The purchase of real property, the consummation of which is preceded by a lease, usually long-term. Typically done for tax or financing purposes.

legacy A disposition of money or personal property by will.

legal description A description of a specific parcel of real estate complete enough for an independent surveyor to locate and identify it.

legally competent parties People who are recognized by law as being able to contract with others; those of legal age and sound mind.

lessee *See* lease.

lessor *See* lease.

leverage The use of borrowed money to finance the bulk of an investment.

levy To assess; to seize or collect. To levy a tax is to assess a property and set the rate of taxation. To levy an execution is to officially seize the property of a person in order to satisfy an obligation.

license (1) A privilege or right granted to a person by a state to operate as a real estate broker or salesperson. (2) The revocable permission for a temporary use of land—a personal right that cannot be sold.

lien A right given by law to certain creditors to have their debts paid out of the property of a defaulting debtor, usually by means of a court sale.

lien theory Some states interpret a mortgage as being purely a lien on real property. The mortgagee thus has no right of possession but must foreclose the lien and sell the property if the mortgagor defaults.

life cycle costing In property management, comparing one type of equipment to another based on both purchase cost and operating cost over its expected useful lifetime.

life estate An interest in real or personal property that is limited in duration to the lifetime of its owner or some other designated person or persons.

life tenant A person in possession of a life estate.

limited liability company A relatively new business entity that combines the liability benefits of corporations with the tax benefits of partnerships, while retaining flexible management. LLCs are governed by state law.

limited partnership *See* partnership.

liquidated damages An amount predetermined by the parties to a contract as the total compensation to an injured party should the other party breach the contract.

liquidity The ability to sell an asset and convert it into cash, at a price close to its true value, in a short period of time.

lis pendens A recorded legal document giving constructive notice that an action affecting a particular property has been filed in either a state or a federal court.

listing agreement A contract between an owner (as principal) and a real estate broker (as agent) by which the broker is employed as agent to find a buyer for the owner's real estate on the owner's terms, for which service the owner agrees to pay a commission.

listing broker The broker in a multiple-listing situation from whose office a listing agreement is initiated, as opposed to the *cooperating broker,* from whose office negotiations leading up to a sale are initiated. The listing broker and the cooperating broker may be the same person.

littoral rights (1) A landowner's claim to use water in large navigable lakes and oceans adjacent to his or her property. (2) The ownership rights to land bordering these bodies of water up to the high-water mark.

lot-and-block (recorded plat) system A method of describing real property that identifies a parcel of land by reference to lot and block numbers within a subdivision, as specified on a recorded subdivision plat.

management agreement A contract between the owner of income property and a management firm or individual property manager that outlines the scope of the manager's authority.

market A place where goods can be bought and sold and a price established.

marketable title Good or clear title, reasonably free from the risk of litigation over possible defects.

market value The most probable price property would bring in an arm's-length transaction under normal conditions on the open market.

master plan A comprehensive plan to guide the long-term physical development of a particular area.

mechanic's lien A statutory lien created in favor of contractors, laborers and materialmen who have performed work or furnished materials in the erection or repair of a building.

meridian One of a set of imaginary lines running north and south and crossing a base line at a definite point, used in the rectangular (government) survey system of property description.

metes-and-bounds description A legal description of a parcel of land that begins at a well-marked point and follows the boundaries, using directions and distances around the tract, back to the place of beginning.

mill One-tenth of one cent. Some states use a mill rate to compute real estate taxes; for example, a rate of 52 mills would be $0.052 tax for each dollar of assessed valuation of a property.

minor Someone who has not reached the age of majority and therefore does not have legal capacity to transfer title to real property.

month-to-month tenancy A periodic tenancy under which the tenant rents for one month at a time. In the absence of a rental agreement (oral or written) a tenancy is generally considered to be month to month.

monument A fixed natural or artificial object used to establish real estate boundaries for a metes-and-bounds description.

mortgage A conditional transfer or pledge of real estate as security for the payment of a debt. Also, the document creating a mortgage lien.

mortgage banking companies These institutions operate primarily as loan correspondents. They originate mortgage loans with money belonging to other institutions, such as insurance companies and pension funds, or to individuals; and they act as the liaison between borrower and lender. Mortgage banking companies are involved in all types of real estate loan activities.

mortgage broker An agent of a lender who brings the lender and borrower together. The broker receives a fee for this service.

mortgagee A lender in a mortgage loan transaction.

mortgage lien A lien or charge on the property of a mortgagor that secures the underlying debt obligations.

mortgagor A borrower in a mortgage loan transaction.

multiperil policies Insurance policies that offer protection from a range of potential perils, such as those of a fire, hazard, public liability, and casualty.

multiple listing An exclusive listing (generally, an exclusive-right-to-sell) with the additional authority and obligation on the part of the listing broker to distribute the listing to other brokers in the multiple-listing organization.

multiple-listing clause A provision in an exclusive listing for the additional authority and obligation on the part of the listing broker to distribute the listing to other brokers in the multiple-listing organization.

multiple-listing service (MLS) A marketing organization composed of member brokers who agree to share their listing agreements with one another in the hope of procuring ready, willing and able buyers for their properties more quickly than they could on their own. Most multiple-listing services accept only exclusive-right-to-sell listings from their member brokers, although any broker can sell a property listed in an MLS.

mutual savings banks Institutions primarily in the northeastern section of the country that operate similarly to savings and loan associations. They are primarily savings institutions and are highly active in the mortgage market, investing in loans secured by income property as well as residential real estate.

negotiable instrument A written promise or order to pay a specific sum of money that may be transferred by endorsement or delivery. The transferee then has the original payee's right to payment.

net lease A lease requiring the tenant to pay not only rent but also costs incurred in maintaining the property, including taxes, insurance, utilities and repairs.

net listing A listing based on the net price the seller will receive if the property is sold. Under a net listing the broker can offer the property for sale at the highest price obtainable to increase the commission. This type of listing is illegal in many states.

nonconforming use A use of property that is permitted to continue after a zoning ordinance prohibiting it has been established for the area.

nonhomogeneity A lack of uniformity; dissimilarity. Because no two parcels of land are exactly alike, real estate is said to be nonhomogeneous.

note *See* promissory note.

novation Substituting a new obligation for an old one or substituting new parties to an existing obligation.

nuncupative will An oral will declared by the testator in his or her final illness, made before witnesses and afterward reduced to writing.

offer and acceptance Two essential components of a valid contract; a "meeting of the minds."

open-end loan A mortgage loan that is expandable by increments up to a maximum dollar amount, the full loan being secured by the same original mortgage.

open listing A listing contract under which the broker's commission is contingent on the broker's producing a ready, willing and able buyer before the property is sold by the seller or another broker.

option An agreement to keep open for a set period an offer to sell or purchase property.

option listing Listing with a provision that gives the listing broker the right to purchase the listed property.

ostensible agency A form of implied agency relationship created by the actions of the parties involved rather than by written agreement or document.

package loan A real estate loan used to finance the purchase of both real property and personal property, such as in the purchase of a new home that includes carpeting, window coverings and major appliances.

parol evidence rule A rule of evidence providing that a written agreement is the final expression of the agreement of the parties, not to be varied or contradicted by prior or contemporaneous oral or written negotiations.

partition The division of co-tenants' interests in real property when the parties do not all voluntarily agree to terminate the co-ownership; takes place through court procedures.

partnership An association of two or more individuals who carry on a continuing business for profit as co-owners. Under the law a partnership is regarded as a group of individuals rather than as a single entity. A *general partnership* is a typical form of joint venture in which each general partner shares in the administration, profits and losses of the operation. A *limited partnership* is a business arrangement whereby the operation is administered by one or more general partners and funded, by and large, by limited or silent partners, who are by law responsible for losses only to the extent of their investments.

party wall A wall that is located on or at a boundary line between two adjoining parcels of land and is used or is intended to be used by the owners of both properties.

patent A grant or franchise of land from the United States government.

payoff statement *See* reduction certificate.

percentage Less than 100 percent is a part or fraction of a whole unit; more than 100 percent is more than a whole unit. General formula for solving percentage problems is Percent × Total = Part.

percentage lease A lease, commonly used for commercial property, whose rental is based on the tenant's gross sales at the premises; it usually stipulates a base monthly rental plus a percentage of any gross sales above a certain amount.

periodic estate *See* estate from period to period.

personal property Items, called *chattels,* that do not fit into the definition of real property; movable objects.

physical deterioration A reduction in a property's value resulting from a decline in physical condition; can be caused by action of the elements or by ordinary wear and tear.

planned unit development (PUD) A planned combination of diverse land uses, such as housing, recreation and shopping, in one contained development or subdivision.

plat map A map of a town, section or subdivision indicating the location and boundaries of individual properties.

plottage The increase in value or utility resulting from the consolidation (*assemblage*) of two or more adjacent lots into one larger lot.

point of beginning (POB) In a metes-and-bounds legal description, the starting point of the survey, situated in one corner of the parcel; all metes-and-bounds descriptions must follow the boundaries of the parcel back to the point of beginning.

police power The government's right to impose laws, statutes and ordinances, including zoning ordinances and building codes, to protect the public health, safety and welfare.

power of attorney A written instrument authorizing a person, the *attorney-in-fact,* to act as agent for another person to the extent indicated in the instrument.

power-of-sale clause A clause in a mortgage authorizing the holder of the borrower's default. The proceeds from the public sale are used to pay off the mortgage debt first, and any surplus is paid to the mortgagor.

prepaid items On a closing statement, items that have been paid in advance by the seller, such as insurance premiums and some real estate taxes, for which he or she must be reimbursed by the buyer.

prepayment penalty A charge imposed on a borrower who pays off the loan principal early. This penalty compensates the lender for interest and other charges that would otherwise be lost.

price-fixing *See* antitrust laws.

primary market *See* secondary mortgage market.

principal (1) A sum loaned or employed as a fund or an investment, as distinguished from its income or profits. (2) The original amount (as in a loan) of the total due and payable at a certain date. (3) A main party to a transaction—the person for whom the agent works.

principal meridian The main imaginary line running north and south and crossing a base line at a definite point, used by surveyors for reference in locating and describing land under the rectangular (government) survey system of legal description.

prior appropriation A concept of water ownership in which the landowner's right to use available water is based on a government-administered permit system.

priority The order of position or time. The priority of liens is generally determined by the chronological order in which the lien documents are recorded; tax liens, however, have priority even over previously recorded liens.

private mortgage insurance (PMI) Insurance provided by any private carrier that protects a lender against a loss in the event of a foreclosure and deficiency.

probate A legal process by which a court determines who will inherit a decedent's property and what the estate's assets are.

procuring cause The effort that brings about the desired result. Under an open listing the broker who is the procuring cause of the sale receives the commission.

progression An appraisal principle that states that, between dissimilar properties, the value of the lesser-quality property is favorably affected by the presence of the better-quality property.

promissory note A financing instrument that states the terms of the underlying obligation, is signed by its maker and is negotiable (transferable to a third party).

property manager Someone who manages real estate for another person for compensation. Duties include collecting rents, maintaining the property and keeping up all accounting.

property reports The mandatory federal and state documents compiled by subdividers and developers to provide potential purchasers with facts about a property prior to their purchase.

prorations Expenses, either prepaid or paid in arrears, that are divided or distributed between buyer and seller at the closing.

protected class Any group of people designated as such by the Department of Housing and Urban Development (HUD) in consideration of federal and state civil rights legislation. Currently includes ethnic minorities, women, religious groups, the handicapped and others.

puffing Exaggerated or superlative comments or opinions.

pur autre vie For the life of another. A life estate pur autre vie is a life estate that is measured by the life of a person other than the grantee.

purchase-money loan A note secured by a mortgage or deed of trust given by a buyer, as borrower, to a seller, as lender, as part of the purchase price of the real estate.

pyramiding The process of acquiring additional properties by refinancing properties already owned and investing the loan proceeds in additional properties.

quantity survey method The appraisal method of estimating building costs by calculating the cost of all of the physical components in the improvements, adding the cost to assemble them and then including the indirect costs associated with such construction.

quitclaim deed A conveyance by which the grantor transfers whatever interest he or she has in the real estate, without warranties or obligations.

range A strip of land six miles wide, extending north and south and numbered east and west according to its distance from the principal meridian in the rectangular (government) survey system of legal description.

rate The percent of interest agreed upon. For computing interest, the formula is Principal × Rate × Time = Interest.

ratification Method of creating an agency relationship in which the principal accepts the conduct of someone who acted without prior authorization as the principal's agent.

ready, willing and able buyer One who is prepared to buy property on the seller's terms and is ready to take positive steps to consummate the transaction.

real estate Land; a portion of the earth's surface extending downward to the center of the earth and upward infinitely into space, including all things permanently attached to it, whether naturally or artificially.

real estate investment syndicate *See* syndicate.

real estate investment trust (REIT) Trust ownership of real estate by a group of individuals who purchase certificates of ownership in the trust, which in turn invests the money in real property and distributes the profits back to the investors free of corporate income tax.

real estate license law State law enacted to protect the public from fraud, dishonesty and incompetence in the purchase and sale of real estate.

real estate mortgage investment conduit (REMIC) A tax entity that issues multiple classes of investor interests (securities) backed by a pool of mortgages.

real estate recovery fund A fund established in some states from real estate license revenues to cover claims of aggrieved parties who have suffered monetary damage through the actions of a real estate licensee.

Real Estate Settlement Procedures Act (RESPA) Federal consumer law under the control of the Department of Housing and Urban Development (HUD). The law was created to ensure that the buyer and seller in a residential real estate transaction have knowledge of all settlement (closing) costs. RESPA applies only to transactions involving new first mortgage loans that are federally related. Requirements include: (1) delivery to the borrower of the HUD booklet, *Settlement Costs and You;* (2) a good faith estimate of settlement costs; (3) use of the Uniform Settlement Statement; and (4) a prohibition against illegal rebates and kickbacks by providers of settlement services.

real property The interests, benefits and rights inherent in real estate ownership.

REALTOR® A registered trademark term reserved for the sole use of active members of local REALTOR® boards affiliated with the National Association of REALTORS®.

reconciliation The final step in the appraisal process, in which the appraiser combines the estimates of value received from the sales comparison, cost and income approaches to arrive at a final estimate of market value for the subject property.

reconveyance deed A deed used by a trustee under a deed of trust to return title to the trustor.

recording The act of entering or recording documents affecting or conveying interests in real estate in the recorder's office established in each county. Until it is recorded, a deed or mortgage ordinarily is not effective against subsequent purchasers or mortgagees.

rectangular (government) survey system A system established in 1785 by the federal government, providing for surveying and describing land by reference to principal meridians and base lines.

redemption The right of a defaulted property owner to recover his or her property by curing the default.

redemption period A period of time established by state law during which a property owner has the right to redeem his or her real estate from a foreclosure or tax sale by paying the sales price, interest and costs. Many states do not have mortgage redemption laws.

redlining The illegal practice of a lending institution denying loans or restricting their number for certain areas of a community.

reduction certificate (payoff statement) The document signed by a lender indicating the amount required to pay a loan balance in full and satisfy the debt; used in the settlement process to protect both the seller's and the buyer's interests.

regression An appraisal principle that states that, between dissimilar properties, the value of the better-quality property is affected adversely by the presence of the lesser-quality property.

Regulation Z Implements the Truth-in-Lending Act requiring credit institutions to inform borrowers of the true cost of obtaining credit.

release deed A document, also known as a *deed of reconveyance,* that transfers all rights given a trustee under a deed of trust loan back to the grantor after the loan has been fully repaid.

remainder interest The remnant of an estate that has been conveyed to take effect and be enjoyed after the termination of a prior estate, such as when an owner conveys a life estate to one party and the remainder to another.

rent A fixed, periodic payment made by a tenant of a property to the owner for possession and use, usually by prior agreement of the parties.

rent schedule A statement of proposed rental rates, determined by the owner or the property manager or both, based on a building's estimated expenses, market supply and demand and the owner's long-range goals for the property.

replacement cost The construction cost at current prices of a property that is not necessarily an exact duplicate of the subject property but serves the same purpose or function as the original.

reproduction cost The construction cost at current prices of an exact duplicate of the subject property.

reverse-annuity mortgage (RAM) A loan under which the homeowner receives monthly payments based on his or her accumulated equity rather than a lump sum. The loan must be repaid at a prearranged date or upon the death of the owner or the sale of the property.

reversionary interest The remnant of an estate that the grantor holds after granting a life estate to another person.

reversionary right The return of the rights of possession and quiet enjoyment to the lessor at the expiration of a lease.

right of survivorship *See* joint tenancy.

riparian rights An owner's rights in land that borders on or includes a stream, river or lake. These rights include access to and use of the water.

risk management Evaluation and selection of appropriate property and other insurance.

rules and regulations Real estate licensing authority orders that govern licensees' activities; they usually have the same force and effect as statutory law.

sale and leaseback A transaction in which an owner sells his or her improved property and, as part of the same transaction, signs a long-term lease to remain in possession of the premises.

sales comparison approach The process of estimating the value of a property by examining and comparing actual sales of comparable properties.

salesperson A person who performs real estate activities while employed by or associated with a licensed real estate broker.

sandwich lease Created when a *sublease* is negotiated by a tenant under a lease. When the original tenant disposes of the leased premises through a sublease, he or she remains primarily liable for the payment of rent to the landlord. In essence, he or she is *sandwiched* between the owner (landlord) of the property and the end-user (subtenant) of the leased property.

satisfaction A document acknowledging the payment of a debt.

satisfaction of mortgage A document acknowledging the payment of a mortgage debt.

savings and loan associations The most active participants in the home loan mortgage market. They make short-term, medium-term and long-term conventional loans and, coupled with private mortgage insurance, they will lend up to 95 percent of a home's appraised value.

secondary mortgage market A market for the purchase and sale of existing mortgages, designed to provide greater liquidity for mortgages; also called the *secondary money market.* Mortgages are first originated in the *primary mortgage market.*

section A portion of township under the rectangular (government) survey system. A township is divided into 36 sections, numbered one through 36. A section is a square with mile-long sides and an area of one square mile, or 640 acres.

security agreement *See* Uniform Commercial Code.

security deposit A payment by a tenant, held by the landlord during the lease term and kept (wholly or partially) on default or destruction of the premises by the tenant.

separate property Under community property law, property owned solely by either spouse before the marriage, acquired by gift or inheritance after the marriage or purchased with separate funds after the marriage.

servient tenement Land on which an easement exists in favor of an adjacent property (called a *dominant estate*); also called a *servient estate.*

setback The amount of space local zoning regulations require between a lot line and a building line.

severalty Ownership of real property by one person only, also called *sole ownership.*

severance Changing an item of real estate to personal property by detaching it from the land; for example, cutting down a tree.

sharecropping In an agricultural lease, the agreement between the landowner and the tenant farmer to split the crop or the profit from its sale, actually sharing the crop.

shared-appreciation mortgage (SAM) A mortgage loan in which the lender, in exchange for a loan with a favorable interest rate, participates in the profits (if any) the borrower receives when the property is eventually sold.

situs The personal preference of people for one area over another, not necessarily based on objective facts and knowledge.

special agent One who is authorized by a principal to perform a single act or transaction; a real estate broker is usually a special agent authorized to find a ready, willing and able buyer for a particular property.

special assessment A tax or levy customarily imposed against only those specific parcels of real estate that will benefit from a proposed public improvement like a street or sewer.

special warranty deed A deed in which the grantor warrants, or guarantees, the title only against defects arising during the period of his or her tenure and ownership of the property and not against defects existing before that time, generally using the language, "by, through or under the grantor but not otherwise."

specific lien A lien affecting or attaching only to a certain, specific parcel of land or piece of property.

specific performance A legal action to compel a party to carry out the terms of a contract.

square foot method The appraisal method of estimating building costs by multiplying the number of square feet in the improvements being appraised by the cost per square foot for recently constructed similar improvements.

statute of frauds That part of a state law that requires certain instruments, such as deeds, real estate sales contracts and certain leases, to be in writing to be legally enforceable.

statute of limitations That law pertaining to the period of time within which certain actions must be brought to court.

statutory lien A lien imposed on property by statute—a tax lien, for example—in contrast to an *equitable lien,* which arises out of common law.

statutory redemption The right of a defaulted property owner to recover the prop-

erty after its sale by paying the appropriate fees and charges.

steering The illegal practice of channeling home seekers to particular areas, either to maintain the homogeneity of an area or to change the character of an area to create a speculative situation.

straight-line method A method of calculating depreciation for tax purposes, computed by dividing the adjusted basis of a property by the estimated number of years of remaining useful life.

straight loan A loan in which only interest is paid during the term of the loan, with the entire principal amount due with the final interest payment.

subagent One who is employed by a person already acting as an agent. Typically a reference to a salesperson licensed under a broker (agent) who is employed under the terms of a listing agreement.

subdivider One who buys undeveloped land, divides it into smaller, usable lots and sells the lots to potential users.

subdivision A tract of land divided by the owner, known as the *subdivider,* into blocks, building lots and streets according to a recorded subdivision plat, which must comply with local ordinances and regulations.

sublease *See* subletting.

subletting The leasing of premises by a lessee to a third party for part of the lessee's remaining term. *See also* assignment.

subordination Relegation to a lesser position, usually in respect to a right or security.

subordination agreement A written agreement between holders of liens on a property that changes the priority of mortgage, judgment and other liens under certain circumstances.

subrogation The substitution of one creditor for another, with the substituted person succeeding to the legal rights and claims of the original claimant. Subrogation is used by title insurers to acquire from the injured party rights to sue in order to recover any claims they have paid.

substitution An appraisal principle that states that the maximum value of a property tends to be set by the cost of purchasing an equally desirable and valuable substitute property, assuming that no costly delay is encountered in making the substitution.

subsurface rights Ownership rights in a parcel of real estate to the water, minerals, gas, oil and so forth that lie beneath the surface of the property.

suit for possession A court suit initiated by a landlord to evict a tenant from leased premises after the tenant has breached one of the terms of the lease or has held possession of the property after the lease's expiration.

suit to quiet title A court action intended to establish or settle the title to a particular property, especially when there is a cloud on the title.

supply The amount of goods available in the market to be sold at a given price. The term is often coupled with *demand*.

supply and demand The appraisal principle that follows the interrelationship of the supply of and demand for real estate. As appraising is based on economic concepts, this principle recognizes that real property is subject to the influences of the marketplace just as is any other commodity.

surety bond An agreement by an insurance or bonding company to be responsible for certain possible defaults, debts or obligations contracted for by an insured party; in essence, a policy insuring one's personal and/or financial integrity. In the real estate business a surety bond is generally used to ensure that a particular project will be completed at a certain date or that a contract will be performed as stated.

surface rights Ownership rights in a parcel of real estate that are limited to the surface of the property and do not include the air above it (*air rights*) or the minerals below the surface (*subsurface rights*).

survey The process by which boundaries are measured and land areas are determined; the on-site measurement of lot lines, dimensions and position of a house on a lot, including the determination of any existing encroachments or easements.

syndicate A combination of people or firms formed to accomplish a business venture of mutual interest by pooling resources. In a *real estate investment syndicate* the parties own and/or develop property, with the main profit generally arising from the sale of the property.

tacking Adding or combining successive periods of continuous occupation of real property by adverse possessors. This concept enables someone who has not been in possession for the entire statutory period to establish a claim of adverse possession.

taxation The process by which a government or municipal quasi-public body raises monies to fund its operation.

tax credit An amount by which tax owed is reduced directly.

tax deed An instrument, similar to a certificate of sale, given to a purchaser at a tax sale. *See also* certificate of sale.

tax lien A charge against property, created by operation of law. Tax liens and assessments take priority over all other liens.

tax sale A court-ordered sale of real property to raise money to cover delinquent taxes.

tenancy by the entirety The joint ownership, recognized in some states, of property acquired by husband and wife during marriage. Upon the death of one spouse the survivor becomes the owner of the property.

tenancy in common A form of co-ownership by which each owner holds an undivided interest in real property as if he or she were sole owner. Each individual owner has the right to partition. Unlike joint tenants, tenants in common have right of inheritance.

tenant One who holds or possesses lands or tenements by any kind of right or title.

tenant improvements Alterations to the interior of a building to meet the functional demands of the tenant.

testate Having made and left a valid will.

testator A person who has made a valid will. A woman often is referred to as a testatrix, although testator can be used for either gender.

tier (township strip) A strip of land six miles wide, extending east and west and numbered north and south according to its distance from the base line in the rectangular (government) survey system of legal description.

time is of the essence A phrase in a contract that requires the performance of a certain act within a stated period of time.

time-sharing A form of ownership interest that may include an estate interest in property and which allows use of the property for a fixed or variable time period.

title (1) The right to or ownership of land. (2) The evidence of ownership of land.

title insurance A policy insuring the owner or mortgagee against loss by reason of defects in the title to a parcel of real estate, other than encumbrances, defects and matters specifically excluded by the policy.

title theory Some states interpret a mortgage to mean that the lender is the owner of mortgaged land. Upon full payment of the mortgage debt the borrower becomes the landowner.

Torrens system A method of evidencing title by registration with the proper public authority, generally called the *registrar,* named for its founder, Sir Robert Torrens.

township The principal unit of the rectangular (government) survey system. A township is a square with six-mile sides and an area of 36 square miles.

township strips *See* tier.

trade fixture An article installed by a tenant under the terms of a lease and removable by the tenant before the lease expires.

transactional broker A broker whose practice is limited to neutrally facilitating a real estate transaction between a buyer and a seller, but who represents neither party's interest.

transfer tax Tax stamps required to be affixed to a deed by state and/or local law.

trust A fiduciary arrangement whereby property is conveyed to a person or institution, called a *trustee,* to be held and administered on behalf of another person, called a *beneficiary.* The one who conveys the trust is called the *trustor.*

trust deed An instrument used to create a mortgage lien by which the borrower conveys title to a trustee, who holds it as security for the benefit of the note holder (the lender); also called a *deed of trust.*

trust deed lien A lien on the property of a trustor that secures a deed of trust loan.

trustee The holder of bare legal title in a deed of trust loan transaction.

trustee's deed A deed executed by a trustee conveying land held in a trust.

trustor A borrower in a deed of trust loan transaction.

undivided interest *See* tenancy in common.

unenforceable contract A contract that has all the elements of a valid contract, yet neither party can sue the other to force performance of it. For example, an unsigned contract is generally unenforceable.

Uniform Commercial Code A codification of commercial law, adopted in most states, that attempts to make uniform all laws relating to commercial transactions, including chattel mortgages and bulk transfers. Security interests in chattels are created by an instrument known as a *security agreement*. To give notice of the security interest, a *financing statement* must be recorded. Article 6 of the code regulates *bulk transfers*—the sale of a business as a whole, including all fixtures, chattels and merchandise.

Uniform Settlement Statement (HUD-I) The standard HUD Form 1 required to be given to the borrower, lender and the seller at or prior to settlement by the settlement agent in a transaction covered under the Real Estate Settlement Procedures Act. The lender must retain its copy for at least two years.

unilateral contract A one-sided contract wherein one party makes a promise so as to induce a second party to do something. The second party is not legally bound to perform; however, if the second party does comply, the first party is obligated to keep the promise.

unit-in-place method The appraisal method of estimating building costs by calculating the costs of all of the physical components in the structure, with the cost of each item including its proper installation, connection, etc.; also called the *segregated cost method*.

unity of ownership The four unities that are traditionally needed to create a joint tenancy—unity of title, time, interest and possession.

usury Charging interest at a higher rate than the maximum rate established by state law.

valid contract A contract that complies with all the essentials of a contract and is binding and enforceable on all parties to it.

VA loan A mortgage loan on approved property made to a qualified veteran by an authorized lender and guaranteed by the Department of Veteran Affairs in order to limit the lender's possible loss.

value The power of a good or service to command other goods in exchange for the present worth of future rights to its income or amenities.

variance Permission obtained from zoning authorities to build a structure or conduct a use that is expressly prohibited by the current zoning laws; an exception from the zoning ordinances.

vendee A buyer, usually under the terms of a land contract.

vendor A seller, usually under the terms of a land contract.

voidable contract A contract that seems to be valid on the surface but may be rejected or disaffirmed by one or both of the parties.

void contract A contract that has no legal force or effect because it does not meet the essential elements of a contract.

volume The space that a space contains. Volume = length × width × height.

voluntary alienation *See* alienation.

voluntary lien A lien placed on property with the knowledge and consent of the property owner.

warranty deed A deed in which the grantor fully warrants good clear title to the premises. Used in most real estate deed transfers, a warranty deed offers the greatest protection of any deed.

waste An improper use or an abuse of a property by a possessor who holds less than fee ownership, such as a tenant, life tenant, mortgagor or vendee. Such waste ordinarily impairs the value of the land or the interest of the person holding the title or the reversionary rights.

will A written document, properly witnessed, providing for the transfer of title to property owned by the deceased, called the *testator.*

workers' compensation acts Laws that require an employer to obtain insurance coverage to protect his or her employees who are injured in the course of their employment.

wraparound loan A method of refinancing in which the new mortgage is placed in a secondary, or subordinate, position; the new mortgage includes both the unpaid principal balance of the first mortgage and whatever additional sums are advanced by the lender. In essence it is an additional mortgage in which another lender refinances a borrower by lending an amount over the existing first mortgage amount without disturbing the existence of the first mortgage.

zoning ordinance An exercise of police power by a municipality to regulate and control the character and use of property.

Answer Key

Chapter 1	Chapter 2	Chapter 3	Chapter 4	Chapter 5
1. d	1. c	1. d	1. b	1. b
2. c	2. a	2. a	2. a	2. b
3. b	3. d	3. a	3. d	3. c
4. b	4. b	4. b	4. a	4. d
5. a	5. b	5. d	5. a	5. a
6. c	6. d	6. d	6. d	6. c
7. b	7. c	7. c	7. c	7. d
8. a	8. a	8. d	8. c	8. a
9. b	9. b	9. b	9. a	9. d
10. c	10. d	10. c	10. d	10. a
11. d	11. b	11. d	11. a	
12. a	12. d	12. b	12. d	
13. d	13. c	13. c	13. d	
14. b	14. b	14. b	14. c	
15. c	15. d		15. b	
	16. b		16. b	
	17. d		17. b	
	18. a		18. c	
	19. b		19. b	
	20. d		20. c	

Radisson®
HERITAGE HOTEL CHELMSFORD

10 Independence Drive
Chelmsford, Massachusetts 01824
Telephone: (508) 256-0800

$$x - 0.07x = 5,500$$

$$x - 0.07x - 1,000 = 5,500$$

$24,543.46$

128.25

$14.25 \quad 277.16$

$1,000$
$55,000$
1.58
12.66

$19.45 \, 58/44$

$1550.25 \quad 79,520$

$4,000,000$
$2,000$
$2,000$

When your meeting breaks, we've got what it takes...

Independence Pub: Snack Food, TV Entertainment, Pool Table, Darts
Open Daily from 11:30 a.m. – Midnight

Julie's Ristorante Italiano, Full Service Restaurant
Open 6:30 a.m. – 10:00 p.m.

$$135,000.$$
$$.027$$
$$135,000$$
$$135$$
$$81$$
$$27$$
$$\overline{3.645.000}$$

INCOME

TOTAL × CAP Rate

$$120,000$$
$$\$18,000$$
$$? \times .15$$

$$109,000$$
$$.085$$

$$545000$$
$$872000$$
$$12\overline{)9265.000}$$
$$772.50$$
$$84$$
$$8625$$

$$180\overline{)18.0}.10$$

$$350$$
$$.15$$
$$\overline{52500} = 4383.$$
$$12$$

$$144\overline{)52,500}4$$
$$576$$

Chapter 6	Chapter 7	Chapter 8	Chapter 9	Chapter 10
1. a	1. a	1. b	1. b	1. b
2. b	2. a	2. b	2. c	2. d
3. c	3. c	3. b	3. a	3. c
4. b	4. d	4. c	4. a	4. b
5. c	5. b	5. d	5. c	5. c
6. a	6. d	6. a	6. b	6. c
7. b	7. a	7. c	7. c	7. a
8. c	8. b	8. d	8. c	8. b
9. d	9. c	9. a	9. d	9. a
10. c	10. b	10. c	10. b	10. a
11. d	11. c	11. c	11. a	11. a
12. a	12. a	12. b	12. b	12. c
13. b	13. d	13. d	13. a	13. d
14. d	14. d	14. c	14. c	14. d
15. a	15. d	15. c	15. b	15. c
16. c	16. c	16. b	16. d	16. b
17. b	17. d	17. d	17. c	17. c
18. c	18. b	18. b		18. b
19. a		19. c		19. d
20. d		20. a		20. b
21. b		21. c		
22. b		22. a		
23. c		23. b		
24. c		24. c		
25. a		25. a		
26. b		26. d		
27. c		27. d		
28. d		28. c		
29. a				
30. d				

Chapter 11	Chapter 12	Chapter 13	Chapter 14	Chapter 15
1. c	1. c	1. a	1. c	1. d
2. d	2. b	2. b	2. c	2. d
3. a	3. a	3. d	3. b	3. d
4. d	4. b	4. b	4. d	4. c
5. b	5. b	5. d	5. a	5. d
6. a	6. d	6. a	6. c	6. b
7. d	7. a	7. d	7. d	7. a
8. b	8. d	8. c	8. a	8. c
9. d	9. a	9. d	9. a	9. a
10. d	10. b	10. a	10. b	10. a
11. b	11. a	11. c	11. b	11. d
12. a	12. c	12. c	12. c	12. d
13. d	13. a	13. b	13. a	13. c
14. b	14. d	14. b	14. b	14. b
15. c	15. a	15. d	15. a	15. a
16. d	16. c	16. c	16. c	16. d
17. d	17. b	17. a	17. d	17. b
18. d	18. c	18. d	18. b	18. d
19. b	19. d	19. c	19. c	19. b
20. b	20. b	20. d	20. b	20. d
21. b	21. b		21. d	21. c
22. a	22. d		22. d	22. b
23. b	23. c		23. b	23. c
24. c	24. d		24. b	24. b
25. a	25. a		25. c	25. d
26. a	26. a			
27. b	27. a			
28. d	28. d			
29. b	29. c			
	30. a			

SOLUTIONS FOR CHAPTER 16 QUESTIONS

1. Answer: b
   Solution: $79,500 sales price × 0.065 rate = $5,167.50 gross commission
   $5,167.50 × 0.30 rate for the listing salesperson = $1,550.25 commission for the listing salesperson

2. Answer: c
   Solution: (9.5 feet × 12 feet) + ½(9.5 feet × 3 feet) = 128.25 square feet
   128.25/9 = 14.25 square yards
   14.25 × (16.95 carpet + $2.50 installation) = $277.16 cost

3. Answer: a
   Solution: $30,000 (H) + $35,000 (Q) + $35,000 (R) = $100,000
   $125,000 − $100,000 = $25,000 (R)
   $25,000/$125,000 = 20% (R)

4. Answer: b
   Solution: $391.42 × 12 months = $4,697.04 annual interest
   $4,697.04/0.115 rate = $40,843.83 principal balance

5. Answer: a
   Solution: $98,500 sales price × (1.00 base rate + 0.05 appreciation) = $103,425 appreciated value

6. Answer: d
   Solution: $95,000 value × 0.60 assessment rate = $57,000
   $57,000 × ($2.85/$100 tax rate) = $1,624.50 annual tax

7. Answer: d
   Solution: (22 feet × 15 feet) + ½(4 feet × 15 feet)
   + ½(4 feet × 15 feet) = 390 square feet
   390 × 0.5 feet = 195 cubic feet

8. Answer: b
   Solution: $4,175 salary and commission − $1,000 salary = $3,175 commission
   $3,175/0.025 rate = $127,000 sales volume

9. Answer: c
   Solution: 95 feet + 42.5 feet + 95 feet = 232.5 feet
   232.5 × $6.95 linear foot = $1,615.88 cost

10. Answer: d
    Solution: $4,500 = 0.08 annual return on investment
    $4,500 × 12 = $54,000 ÷ .08 = $675,000

11. Answer: b
    Solution: $1,340 tax/360 days = $3.722 per day
    $3.722 × 75 days = $279.15 credit to the buyer

12. Answer: d
    Solution: $58,200 loan balance × 0.12 rate/360 days = $19.40 per day
    $19.40 × 11 = $213.40 debit to the seller

13. Answer: a
    Solution: $975 tax/360 days = $2.708 per day $2.708 × 64 days =
    $173.31 credit to the seller

14. Answer: b
    Solution: $61,550 loan balance × 0.13 rate/360 days = $22.226 per day
    $22.226 × 22 days = $488.97 credit to the buyer

15. Answer: c
    Solution: 100 acres × 43,560 square feet = 4,356,000 square feet
    4,356,000 × 1/8 = 544,500 square feet 4,356,000 −
    544,500/140 lots = 27,225 square feet per lot

16. Answer: a
    Solution: $14,100 commission/0.06 rate = $235,000 sales price

17. Answer: a
    Solution: ½(80 feet × 50 feet)/9 = 222.22 square yards

18. Answer: a
    Solution: 1/8 mile × 1/8 mile = 1/64 square mile
    1/64 × 640 acres = 10 acres

19. Answer: b
    Solution: Definition = 1 mill equals 1/10 of $0.01, or $0.001

20. Answer: b
    Solution: $89,500 sales price × 0.07 rate = $6,265.00

21. Answer: b
    Solution: $75,000 loan amount × 0.09 rate/12 = $562.50 interest
    $591.42 payment − $562.50 = $28.92

22. Answer: c
    Solution: 20 feet × 60 feet × 12 feet × $2.50 = $36,000 (first floor)
    20 feet × 60 feet × 10 feet × $2.30 = $27,600 (second floor)
    $36,000 + 27,600 = $63,600 cost

23. Answer: d
    Solution: ($55,000 net + $1,000 costs)/(1.00 − 0.07) = $60,215.05 price

24. Answer: d
    Solution: (5 acres + 640 acres) × $2,100 per acre = $1,354,500

25. Answer: b
    Solution: $12,000 loan amount × 0.07 rate/12 = $70 interest per month
    $2,100/70 = 30 months

26. Answer: d
    Solution: 3.2 acres × 43,560 square feet = 139,392 square feet
    139,392/381 feet deep = 365.858 feet frontage
    365.858 × $1.85 = $676.84 tax

27. Answer: d
    Solution: $420 × 12/0.09 = $56,000 loan
    $56,000/0.70 loan-to-value = $80,000

28. Answer: d
    Solution: $600 per month × 12 = $7,200 lost income per year
    $7,200/0.10 capitalization rate = $72,00 lost value

29. Answer: d
    Solution: $16,500 × 12 = $198,000 annual effective gross income
    $198,000 × 0.37 expense rate = $73,260
    $198,000 – $73,260 = $124,740 net operating income

30. Answer: d
    Solution: $2,500,000 × 0.05 = $125,000 down payment
    $3,000,000 sales price – $2,500,000 cost = $500,000 profit
    $500,000/$125,000 = 400%

SAMPLE EXAMINATION

1. d	14. c	27. d	40. a	53. b
2. d	15. c	28. b	41. d	54. b
3. b	16. b	29. c	42. b	55. a
4. a	17. a	30. d	43. c	56. a
5. c	18. b	31. a	44. a	57. b
6. d	19. d	32. d	45. b	58. b
7. a	20. a	33. b	46. c	59. b
8. a	21. b	34. c	47. d	60. c
9. c	22. c	35. c	48. d	61. c
10. b	23. d	36. d	49. b	62. b
11. a	24. a	37. b	50. d	63. b
12. a	25. b	38. d	51. d	64. b
13. b	26. b	39. a	52. c	65. d

66. a	74. d	82. d	90. d	98. a
67. b	75. a	83. d	91. d	99. b
68. d	76. d	84. a	92. a	100. b
69. a	77. d	85. d	93. c	
70. d	78. b	86. b	94. b	
71. c	79. a	87. b	95. c	
72. a	80. c	88. d	96. c	
73. c	81. c	89. a	97. a	

Index